MW01253651

PSYCHOLOGY OF GENDER DIFFERENCES

PSYCHOLOGY RESEARCH PROGRESS

Additional books in this series can be found on Nova's website
under the Series tab.

Additional e-books in this series can be found on Nova's website
under the e-book tab.

PSYCHOLOGY OF GENDER DIFFERENCES

SARAH P. MCGEOWN
EDITOR

Nova Science Publishers, Inc.
New York

Library of Congress Cataloging-in-Publication Data

Psychology of gender differences / editor, Sarah McGeown.
p. cm.
Includes bibliographical references and index.
ISBN 978-1-62081-391-1 (hardcover)
1. Sex differences (Psychology) I. McGeown, Sarah.
BF692.2.P7643 2011
155.3'3--dc23
2012009334

Published by Nova Science Publishers, Inc. † New York

CONTENTS

PREFACE

An interest in gender differences is common to researchers and the general public alike. Gender refers not only to biological differences between males and females (of which the term 'sex' is often used), but also to the context in which males and females develop. Within this book, each chapter presents scientific research and up-to-date reviews of relevant literature, providing a diverse account of the range of areas in which males and females differ. Collectively, the chapters offer insight into our current understanding of differences between males and females. Below is a brief summary of each of the chapters; these chapters are presented in a developmental sequence, from studies with infants and children, to those with adolescents, adults and lastly animals.

INFANCY

Anme, Shinohara, Sugisawa, Watanabe, Tong, Tanaka, Tomisaki, Mochizuki, Tokutake and the Japan Children's Study Group use a longitudinal research design to explore sex differences and age related changes in children's social competence (using the Interaction Rating Scale) following children from eighteen months to seven years.

Lindsey examines sex differences in pre-school children's play activities, focusing on differences in play type (e.g., exercise play, rough and tumble, fantasy play, socio-dramatic play) and choice of play companions (whether same or different sex). Sex differences are analysed using natural observations in the pre-school environment.

CHILDHOOD

Yeung, Craven and Kaur argue that gender differences in achievement motivation among school aged children may be influenced or mediated by cultural factors. The study highlights the importance of considering grade, and in particular, culture when examining gender differences in achievement motivation.

Ferrie, Lamswood and McGeown examine differences between boys and girls in the primary school classroom in terms of preference to engage in group work activities. Their results are discussed in relation to the benefits and difficulties in implementing group work activities within the classroom.

Van de Sompel, Vermeir and Pandelaere examine sex differences in children's playing behaviour, levels of creativity and the relationship between these factors. The authors discuss the results in relation to gender prejudices, stereotypical perceptions and the influence of parents on children's playing choices and behaviours.

Mullola, Jokela, Hintsanen, Alatupa, Rvaja and Keltikangas-Järvinen examine how teachers perceive boys' and girls' temperament, examining the differences between male and female teachers, and the interaction between pupils and teachers of the same or different gender. Implications for teacher training are discussed.

ADOLESCENCE

Bugler, St.Clair-Thompson and McGeown differentiate between sex (i.e., being male or female) and gender identity (i.e., identification with masculine and feminine traits) to examine the academic motivation and classroom behaviours of adolescents. The authors argue that the distinction between sex and gender identity is important and may help to elucidate differences commonly found among adolescents.

ADULTHOOD

Ziegler-Hill and Myers provide an in-depth review of sex differences in self-esteem, focusing on levels of self-esteem, age related changes and domain specific findings with regard to self-esteem.

Hang Yue and Ming Shuange examine sex differences in psychological capital (self-efficacy, hope, resilience and optimism) among adults. The authors highlight the importance considering sex, gender orientation and gender identity to better understand individual differences in psychological capital.

Nori, Piccardi, Palermo, Guariglia and Giusberti review the literature examining visuo-spatial imagery and examine visuo-spatial working memory (VSWM) load as a possible explanation for sex differences in imagery tasks.

Voyer and Doyle examine sex differences on the mental rotations task, and carry out an in-depth analysis of this task (using an item by item approach) to identify the magnitude of sex differences across items. The authors also examine differences in the guessing behaviour of men and women.

Rau provides an in-depth review of the literature examining sex differences in trust and reciprocity by reviewing the results from numerous trust and gift exchange games. The author argues that the results of this research may be useful to understand differences in behaviour between men and women within business.

Mwachofi and Broyles study the influence of household gender-structure on reported physical health, comparing female-headed households with male-headed households. Implications of the results for the provision of resources to improve physical health are discussed.

Mwachofi and Broyles also examine differences between female-headed households and male headed-households in terms of mental health (focusing on depression and anxiety). These results are discussed in relation to budget and policy considerations in mental health.

ANIMAL RESEARCH

Chamizo reviews sex differences in spatial learning, focusing primarily on rat studies but with the inclusion of studies with human participants. The implications of these studies are discussed, with particular reference to the impact of these results on the treatment or rehabilitation of people suffering from disorientation difficulties.

Sarah P. McGeown
Psychology Department, University of Hull, Hull, UK

In: Psychology of Gender Differences
Editor: Sarah P. McGeown

ISBN: 978-1-62081-391-1
© 2012 Nova Science Publishers, Inc.

Chapter 1

GENDER DIFFERENCES IN CHILDREN'S SOCIAL COMPETENCE DEVELOPMENT FROM EIGHTEEN MONTHS TO SEVEN YEARS OLD USING THE INTERACTION RATING SCALE (IRS)

T. Anme, R. Shinohara, Y. Sugisawa,*
T. Watanabe, L. Tong, E. Tanaka, E. Tomisaki,
H. Mochizuki, K. Tokutake
and Japan Children's Study Group
Graduate School of Comprehensive Human Sciences,
University of Tsukuba, Japan

ABSTRACT

The purpose of this paper is to describe the gender differences of social competence development using the Interaction Rating Scale (IRS) from eighteen months to seven year old. The participants in our study, which was conducted as part of a Japan Science and Technology Agency (JST) cohort study project, were 370 dyads of children with their caregivers who were followed up and surveyed at eighteen and thirty months and 82 dyads at seven years old. The participants completed the five minute interaction session and were observed using the IRS.

The results indicated the gender differences of IRS scores. Girls achieved a higher score at all ages. Girls were more likely to demonstrate empathy at eighteen months, emotional regulation at eighteen months and thirty months, motor regulation at thirty months and seven years old, compared to boys.

Along with the patterns of difference between boys and girls, the IRS is effective in describing features of social competence development.

* E-mail address: tokieanme@gmail.com.

INTRODUCTION

Increasing numbers of impulsive behavior and maladjustment to society in school-aged children and adolescents requires society to prepare appropriate education and environments for those children [1]. Children's social development is determined by the complex interaction between the child themselves, their home environment, peer relationships, and the larger sociocultural environment [2]. Researchers, caregivers, and practitioners have been attracted to the study of children's social development for decades. Social competence is defined as the ability to understand others in the context of social interaction and to engage in smooth communication with them. Accordingly, children's social skills should be evaluated by the interaction between the child and social environment [3]. However, the methodology that considers children in conjunction with their social environment across developmental stages has not yet been well developed.

Many researchers are focused on measuring the quality of children's rearing environment and parenting, based on the theory that early rearing environment is significantly related to child development. Two instruments, namely, the Home Observation for Measurement of the Environment (HOME) [4] and the Index of Child Care Environment (ICCE) [5] are often used in research related to child development

The HOME and the ICCE evaluate the children's rearing environment within natural settings, which reflects the caregivers' emotional and verbal responsiveness to the child, and the caregivers' acceptance of the child's behavior. The HOME has been adopted by studies conducted at the National Institute of Child Health and Human Development (NICHD) in the United States [6], and is also widely used in more than one hundred countries. The ICCE has been used to investigate the effect of child care on children's development in Japan [7]-[9]. In addition, the Mediated Learning Experience Rating Scale (MLERS) has been used to assess the sensitivity and teaching of adults (caregivers and teachers) toward children through observation of the adult-child interaction [10].

The tool that is currently used to assess social competence is the Social Skills Rating System (SSRS) [11], which was used in the study conducted at the NICHD. The SSRS evaluates children's social competence on the basis of information provided by parents and teachers; however, this method of evaluating social competence suffers from the inevitable drawbacks of the possibility of parents and teachers missing out on or distorting information. The Nursing Child Assessment Satellite Training (NCAST), which emphasizes the role of the caregiver in the development of social competence, was developed in the United States. The validity of NCAST had been confirmed for evaluating the communication and interactional patterns between caregiver and child [12]. It is useful to evaluate the quality of child-rearing objectively, but it was much concentrated on caregiver's teaching skills, so cannot be used directly for assessing children's social skills development.

The Interaction Rating Scale (IRS) can evaluate the child-caregiver interactions in a short period of time in daily situations. The inter-observer reliability of the IRS was found to be 90% [13]. The purpose of this paper is to describe the features of Interaction Rating Scale (IRS) as an evidence-based practical index of children's social skills and parenting.

METHODS

Participants

The participants in our study, which was conducted as part of a Japan Science and Technology Agency (JST) cohort study project, were 370 dyads of children with their caregivers who were followed up and surveyed at aged eighteen months, thirty months and 82 dyads at seven years old.

In order to comply with the ethical standards laid down by the JST, before conducting the research, the families of all the participants signed informed consent forms and were made aware that they had the right to withdraw from the experiment at any time. As the infants were too young to provide informed consent, we carefully explained the purpose, content, and methods of the study to the caregivers and obtained their consent. To maintain confidentiality of the personal information of the participants, their personal information was collected anonymously, and a personal ID system was used to protect personal information. Further, all the image data were stored on a disk, which was password protected; only the researchers who were granted permission from the chairman, were given access to the data. This study was approved by the ethics committee of the JST.

Measures

The IRS is used to measure the child's social competence and the caregiver's child rearing competence through five minute observations of caregiver-child interactions. It is appropriate for the assessment of interactions between caregivers and children from infant to eight-year-old. It includes 70 items for a behavioral score and 11 items for an impression score, grouped into ten subscales. Five subscales focus on children's social competences: 1) Autonomy, 2) Responsiveness, 3) Empathy, 4) Motor regulation, and 5) Emotional regulation. Another five items assess the caregiver's parenting skills: 6) Respect for autonomy development, 7) Respect for responsiveness development, 8) Respect for empathy development, 9) Respect for cognitive development, and 10) Respect for social-emotional development. And one item assesses an overall impression of synchronous relationships.

The total of 81 items was composed from several sources: original items by the study authors, several overlapping items from the HOME (Home Observation for Measurement of the Environment) [4], the SSRS (Social Skills Rating Systems) [11], and the NCAST (Nursing Child Assessment Satellite Training) [12] teaching scales (36 items). A training manual for the IRS has been developed for practitioners and researchers [14]. Two different sets of variable are scored: behavior items and impression items for each subscale. Each subscale assesses the presence of behavior (1=Yes, 0=No), and the sum of all items in the subscale provides the overall behavior score. Scores on the impression items and the overall impression item are on a five-point scale, where 1=not evident at all, 2=not evident, 3=neutral, 4=evident, 5=evident at high level.

The evaluator completes the checklist composed of 25 items focusing on children's behavior toward caregivers (e.g., Child looks at caregiver's face as social referencing) and 45 items focusing on the caregiver behavior.

The observer then provides an impression on a 5-point scale of the level of development for each subscale and for an overall impression. Internal consistency in each categories, as measured by Cronbach's alpha, ranged from .43 to .88, and the total internal consistency was excellent (.85 - .91).

Procedure

In this study, the IRS was evaluated as follows: a five minute video recording of the setting of the child-caregiver interaction (the child and caregiver playing with blocks and putting them in a box) was conducted. The caregiver-child interactions were videotaped in a controlled laboratory environment. The recording was carried out in a room with five video cameras; one camera was placed at each of the four corners and one was placed in the central ceiling position.

The dyads of children were escorted into a room (with dimensions of 4 X 4 meters) furnished with a small table and a small-sized chair meant for a child. The caregiver introduced herself to the child and interacted with the child in a natural manner, just as she would on a regular day.

To score the behavior, two members of the research teamed coded the behaviors observed. A third child professional, who had no contact with the participants, also scored the behavior. The behavior of the children and caregiver during the caregiver-child interaction was coded as follows. If the child displayed the behavior described in the item, a score of 1 was given; conversely, if the child failed to display the behavior described in the item, a score of 0 was given. A child's total score was the sum of the score that he/she received on all the subscales.

A higher score indicated a higher level of development. The same method of coding was used to evaluate the caregivers' behavior. The total IRS score was the total score of the child plus the total score of the caregiver. Overall, 231 (eighteen months), 344 (thirty months), and 82 (seven years) data were used without missing value data.

RESULTS

Figure 1 shows the scores on the Interaction Rating Scale for eighteen-month, thirty-month, and seven-year-old children.

Significant age differences were found on the subscales of autonomy, and emotional regulation. Autonomy at thirty months and emotional regulation at seven years old was significantly higher than those at eighteen months. Gender differences were clear in all age. Girls got higher score at eighteen months, thirty months and seven years old.

There were also gender differences among specific subscales, revealing important differences, for example, in types of interactions.

Girls were more likely to demonstrate empathy at eighteen months, emotional regulation at eighteen months and thirty months, motor regulation at thirty months and seven years old, compared to boys.

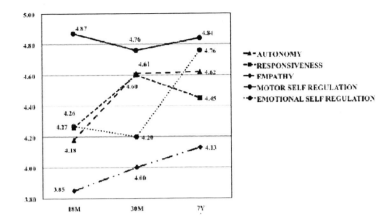

Figure1. Trajectory of social competence development.

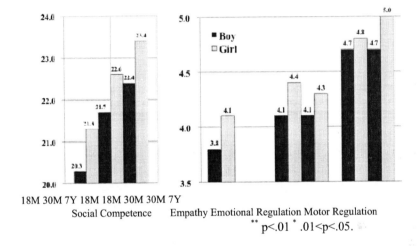

18M 30M 7Y 18M 18M 30M 30M 7Y
Social Competence   Empathy Emotional Regulation Motor Regulation
** p<.01 * .01<p<.05.

Figure 2. Gender differences of social competence development.

DISCUSSION

This study clarified the gender differences by the IRS score. IRS is a reliable, valid, feasible and practical tool for the studies of caregiver-child interaction over time [15].

First of all, using IRS for the gender differences of social competence was valid, because IRS has high adaptability for cohort studies, which can be used with the same subscales framework across ages from infants to 8 years old.

Secondly, the IRS can be used in international comparative studies, because it is based on the most common frameworks used all over the world. The child subscales are based on various categories which are widely used in the research of social skills indicators.

Third, the IRS has high correlations with the SDQ (Strength and Difficulties Questionnaire), and high reliability [16]. There were significant correlations between the "empathy", "motor regulation," "emotional regulation" in the IRS and the "hyperactivity-inattention domain" in the SDQ.

Also, "autonomy", "responsiveness," "empathy" in the IRS and less "peer problems domain" in the SDQ, "responsiveness," "empathy," "motor regulation" in the IRS and "prosocial behavior domain" in the SDQ. The results of gender differences in this study may relate to these features of IRS.

While the IRS provides valuable insights, it is also important to acknowledge its limitations. First, the IRS subscales might not cover all dimensions of social skills, although we used the most common frameworks of social skills. Second, while the IRS expects to use the same scoring standard from birth to eight years old as a standardized tool in cohort studies, different developmental features of items across developmental stages might be better to take into consideration. Despite these limitations, the IRS can be considered an established, valid screening instrument reflecting child-related attributes of the caregiver-child interaction. Further research has the potential to reveal the features of the gender differences of caregiver-child interaction development, and enhance knowledge of implications for caregivers and child-care professionals.

APPENDIX

Japan Children's Study Group:

Chairman: Zentaro Yamagata (Department of Health Sciences, School of Medicine, University of Yamanashi), Hideaki Koizumi (Advanced Research Laboratory, Hitachi, Ltd.)

Participating Researchers: Kevin K. F. Wong, Yoko Anji, Hiraku Ishida, Mizue Iwasaki, Aya Kutsuki, Misa Kuroki, Haruka Koike, Daisuke N Saito, Akiko Sawada, Yuka Shiotani, Daisuke Tanaka, Shunyue Cheng, Hiroshi Toyoda, Kumiko Namba, Tamami Fukushi, Tomoyo Morita, Hisakazu Yanaka (Research Institute of Science and Technology for Society, Japan Science and Technology Agency), Yoichi Sakakihara (Department of Child Care and Education, Ochanomizu University), Kanehisa Morimoto (Graduate School of Medicine, Osaka University), Kayako Nakagawa (Graduate School of Engineering, Osaka University), Shoji Itakura (Graduate School of Letters, Kyoto University), Kiyotaka Tomiwa (Graduate School of Medicine, Kyoto University), Shunya Sogon (The Graduate Divisiton of the faculty of Human Relations, Kyoto Koka Women's University), Toyojiro Matsuishi (Department of Pediatrics and Child Health, Kurume University), Tamiko Ogura (Graduate School of Humanities, Kobe University), Masako Okada (Koka City Educational Research Center), Hiroko Ikeda (National Epilepsy Center Shizuoka Institute of Epilepsy and Neurological Disorder), Norihiro Sadato (National Institute for Physiological Sciences, National Institutes of Natural Sciences), Mariko Y. Momoi, Hirosato Shiokawa, Takanori Yamagata (Department of Pediatrics., Jichi Medical University), Tadahiko Maeda, Tohru Ozaki (The Institute of Statistical Mathematics, Research Organization of Information and Systems), Tokie Anme (Graduate School of Comprehensive Human Sciences, University of Tsukuba), Takahiro Hoshino (Graduate School of Arts and Sciences, The University of Tokyo), Osamu Sakura (Interfaculty Initiative in Information Studies, The University of Tokyo), Yukuo Konishi (Department of Infants' Brain and Cognitive Development, Tokyo Women's Medical University), Katsutoshi Kobayashi (Center for Education and Society, Tottori University), Tatsuya Koeda, Toshitaka Tamaru, Shinako Terakawa, Ayumi Seki, Ariko Takeuchi (Faculty of Regional Sciences, Tottori University), Hideo Kawaguchi

(Advanced Research Laboratory, Hitachi, Ltd.), Sonoko Egami (Hokkaido University of Education), Yoshihiro Komada (Department of Pediatric and Developmental Science, Mie University Graduate School of Medicine Institute of Molecular and Experimental Medicine), Hatsumi Yamamoto, Motoki Bonno, Noriko Yamakawa (Clinical Research Institute, Mie-chuo Medical Center, National Hospital Organization), Masatoshi Kawai (Institute for Education, Mukogawa Women's University), Yuko Yato (College of Letters, Ritsumeikan University), Koichi Negayama (Graduate School of Human Sciences, Waseda University)

ACKNOWLEDGMENTS

This research was supported by the RandD Area "Brain-Science and Society" of JST RISTEX, and as a part of "Exploring the effect factors on the child's cognitive and behavior development in Japan", and Grants-in-Aid for Scientific Research (23330174).

REFERENCES

[1] Gary, W. L. The role of gender, Emotion, and culture in children's social competence and peer relations. In: Gary, W. L., editors. Children's Peer Relations and social competence. London: Yale University Press; 2005. P286-320.

[2] Lidz, C. S. Practitioner's guide to dynamic assessment. New York: Guilford Press; 1991.

[3] Feuerstein, R. R. and Y., Hoffman, M. B. The dynamic assessment of retarded performers: The Learning Potential Assessment Device: Theory, instruments and techniques. Baltimore: University Park Press; 1979.

[4] Caldwell, B. M., Bradley, R. H. Home Observation for Measurement of the Environment. Little Rock: Center for Research on Teaching and Learning, University of Arkansas, 1974

[5] Anme, T., Segal, U. Center-based evening child care: Implications for young children's development. *Early Childhood Education Journal*. 2003; 30(3): 137-143.

[6] NICHD Early Child Care Research Network. Relations between family predictors and child outcomes: Are they weaker for children in child care? *Developmental Psychology*. 1998; 34(5): 1119-1128.

[7] Anme, T. Evidence based Child Care: Enhance Quality of Care and Environment. Tokyo: Keiso Shobo; 2004.

[8] Anme, T., Segal, U. Implications for the development of children placed in 11+ hours of center-based care. *Child: care, health and development*. 2004; 30(4): 345-352.

[9] Anme, T., Tanaka, H., Sakai, H., Shoji, T., Miyazaki, K. Maruyama A, Fuchita E. Quality of Environment and child development: Five-year follow up study. *Child Youth and Environmental Studies*. 2005; 1(1): 1-6.

[10] Burchnal, M. R., Campbell, F. A., Bryant, D. M., Warsik, B. H., Ramey, C. T. Early Intervention and Mediating Process in Cognitive Performance of Children of Low-Income African American Families. *Child Development*; 1997; 68(5): 935-954.

[11] Gresham, F. M., Elliot, S. N. Social Skills Rating System - Secondary. Circle Pines, MN: American Guidance Service. 1990.

[12] Barnard, K. *Nursing Child Assessment Satellite Training Manual*. 1994.

[13] Anme, T., Yato, Y., Shinohara, R., Sugisawa, Y. The reliability and validity of the assessment method for children's social competence: Parent-child Interaction Rating Scale. *Japanese Journal of Health Care and Welfare*, 2007; 14: 23-31.

[14] Anme, T. Manual of Interaction Rating Scale. Tokyo: Japan Pediatric Press. 2009.

[15] Anme, T., Shinohara, R., Sugisawa, Y., et.al. Gender differences of children's social skills and parenting using Interaction Rating Scale (IRS), *Procedia Social and Behavioral Sciences*, 2010; 2: 260-268.

[16] Sugisawa, Y., Shinohara, R., Tong, L., Tanaka, E., Anme, T. The relationship between Interaction Rating Scale and Strength and Difficulties Questionnaire. *68th Conference of Japanese Public Health*. 2008.

In: Psychology of Gender Differences
Editor: Sarah P. McGeown

ISBN: 978-1-62081-391-1
© 2012 Nova Science Publishers, Inc.

Chapter 2

GIRL'S AND BOY'S PLAY FORM PREFERENCES AND GENDER SEGREGATION IN EARLY CHILDHOOD

Eric W. Lindsey[*]
Penn State Berks, Pennsylvania, US

ABSTRACT

This chapter describes a study designed to examine associations between preschool children's pretend and physical play with same-sex, other-sex, and mixed sex peers. One-hundred-sixty-seven predominately middle-class preschool children (89 boys and 78 girls, M age in months = 57.61) were observed on the playground at their school over a period of 4 months. Children's same-sex, other-sex, and mixed-sex peer play was recorded. Analyses revealed that both boys and girls spend the majority of their time playing with same-sex peers. Girl's same-sex peer play was characterized predominately by fantasy and sociodramatic play, whereas boy's same-sex peer play was made up of exercise play, fantasy play, and rough-and-tumble play. Boys engaged in more rough-and-tumble play with same-sex peers than girls, whereas girls engaged in more sociodramatic play with same-sex peers than boys. There was no difference in the amount of time that boys and girls spent in other-sex and mixed-sex peer play. When both boys and girls engaged in play with other-sex peers it was most frequently exercise play. When girls and boys engaged in play in mixed-sex peer groups it was most frequently sociodramatic play and exercise play. The results suggest that play form is an important element in children's tendency to play with same-sex, other-sex, and mixed-sex peer groups.

INTRODUCTION

Segregation by sex is a pervasive characteristic of preschool children's interactions with peers. It has been well documented that during early childhood children spend the majority of their time in same-sex peer play (Harper and Huie, 1978; Maccoby, 1998; Maccoby and

---

[*] E-mail: EWL10@psu.edu.

Jacklin, 1987). Beginning around the age of 3 children in both nonindustrial (Whiting and Edwards, 1973) and industrialized societies (LaFreniere, Strayer, and Gauthier, 1984) have been observed to show a preference for playing with same-sex age mates. Preschool children do play in other-sex and mixed-sex peer groups, although these interactions tend to be of limited duration and of lower sophistication than same-sex peer interactions (Fabes, Martin, and Hanish, 2003; Martin and Fabes, 2001). Factors that account for individual differences in children's propensity to play with same- or other-sex peers remain poorly understood.

Based on principles of sexual selection theory whereby gender differentiated behavior is posited to stem from differences in adult's reproductive roles, it has been suggested that males preference for physical activity may be the primary driving force in patterns of gender segregation among children (Archer, 1996; Pellegrini, 2004). Specifically, because males on average are larger in size than females among the human species they also are typically primed to be more physically active from a very early age (Blackenhorn, 2005; Byers, 1998). Male's developing muscular, skeletal, and brain systems contribute to a propensity toward, and attraction to, higher levels of physical activity than females. This biologically driven pattern of disparity between males and females engagement in physical activity is considered to contribute to a proclivity toward behavioral compatibility in young children's play. Thus, boys show a tendency to interact with each other because their relatively active behavior is incompatible with girl's behavior, and girl's generally avoid boys because they find highly active behavior unpleasant (Maccoby, 1998). This behavioral compatibility hypothesis for explaining children's gender segregated pattern of peer interaction is supported by evidence that physical activity play is more characteristic of boys' peer interactions than girls' peer interactions (DiPietro, 1981; Lindsey and Mize, 2001; Pellegrini, 1989; Whiting and Edwards, 1988). Furthermore, Bukowski, Gauze, Hoza, and Newcomb (1993) found that boys who liked activities that required gross motor skills, such as physical activity play, showed a stronger same-sex playmate preference than did boys less interested in these activities.

Physical activity play is defined as: moderate to vigorous physical activity that takes place in a playful context and includes such forms of play as run, chase, flee, and wrestle (Pellegrini and Smith, 1998). This definition suggests that physical activity play is a complex phenomenon that includes several distinct sub-types of play (Boulton, 1996; Fry, 1990). Pellegrini and Smith (1998) distinguish between 2 forms of physical play: exercise play and Rough-and-Tumble (R&T) play. Exercise play is defined as "gross locomotor movement in the context of play" that "...may or may not be social" (Pellegrini and Smith, 1998, p. 578). Exercise play appears during infancy, increases from the toddler to the preschool period, and tends to peak around the age of 4–5 years (Field, 1994; Smith, 2010). The second sub-type R&T play emerges as early as the age of 2, and by preschool makes up approximately 5% of children's play time with peers (Humphreys and Smith, 1987). To date, most researchers have focused on only one particular sub-type of physical activity play, either R&T or exercise play, or have combined the two types in their observational codes, so that it remains unclear to what extent the two types of play, and their separate dimensions, manifest themselves in children's naturally occurring play with same- and other-sex peers.

As previously mentioned, physical activity play serves as the foundation for the behavioral compatibility hypothesis explaining young children's gender segregation. Evidence consistently indicates that boys engage in more physical activity play than girls, both R&T play and exercise play (Brown et al., 2009). However, some studies suggest that gender differences may be more pronounced for certain subtypes of physical activity play than others. For example, Boulton (1996) found that boys engaged in more R&T play fighting than girls, but observed no gender difference in physical activity play chasing. Likewise, researchers have found that apart from play fighting, boys and girls engage in similar levels of R&T play (Aldis, 1975; Fry, 1990; Jarvis, 2007). In a similar vein, Brown et al. (2009) found that boys engaged in more exercise play than girls when in contexts where no toys were present, but observed no gender difference in children's exercise play that included toys or playground equipment. These findings raise the possibility that gender segregated patterns of peer play may be more prevalent in certain types of physical activity play than others. Additional studies that assess unique types of physical activity play are needed to better understand the role of physical activity play in children's gender segregation. It also remains an open empirical question as to whether other forms of play may be related to children's gender segregation.

One alternative form of play in early childhood that has received considerable theoretical attention is pretend, or pretense, play defined as "a symbolic behavior in which one thing is playfully treated as if it were something else" (Fein, 1989, p. 282). From a very early age children use pretend play to initiate and sustain social relationships with peers (Connolly and Doyle, 1984; Doyle, Ceschin, Tessier, and Doehring, 1991). As children grow older the nature and function of pretense changes, advancing from rudimentary imitation of particular pretense acts by a peer partner, to a more sophisticated sharing of nonliteral meanings in the context of joint activity (Howes and Matheson, 1992).

By the preschool age (i.e., 31 to 36 months) children have been observed to engage in two related, but distinct type of pretend play: fantasy play and socio-dramatic play. Fantasy play is characterized by an "'as if' orientation to the world and involves actions, use of objects, and verbalizations" (Pelligrini and Smith, 1998, p. 52). Fantasy begins during the second year of life, peaks during the late preschool years, accounting for 10% to 17% of preschoolers' play behaviors, and then declines (Fein, 1989). Sociodramatic play, on the other hand, has been described as extended social role playing that involves the acting-out of complex narrative sequences (Smilansky, 1968).

The more sophisticated role-playing of sociodramatic play typically does not emerge until the age of 3, and is accompanied by meta-communication about play with peers (e.g., proposing a play script, prompting the other child) (Howes, Unger, and Matheson, 1991). There is reason to hypothesize that pretend play may have a role in young children's gender segregated play preferences. Some studies indicate that girls engage in more pretend play with peers than boys do (Jones and Glenn, 1991; Lindsey and Mize, 2001; Wall, Pickert, and Gibson 1990; Weinberger and Starkey, 1994; Werebe and Baudonniere, 1991), whereas other studies indicate that boys engage in more pretend play with peers than girls do (Doyle, Ceschin, Tessier, and Doehring, 1991; Rubin, Maioni, and Hornung, 1976; Rubin, Watson, and Jambor, 1978; Singer, 1973). However, the majority of researchers report no differences in the amount of pretend play girls and boys engage in with peers (e.g., Connolly and Doyle, 1984; Farver and Shin, 1997; Howes, Unger, Seidner, 1989; Pellegrini and Perlmutter, 1989; Rubin and Maioni, 1975).

As suggested by Goncu, Patt, and Kouba (2002), differences in methodologies or observational settings across studies may account for these discrepancies. According to these authors (Goncu et al., 2002) more naturalistic studies of children's pretend play, in contexts where children have a wide range of choices, and chose what type of play to engage in without intervention or manipulation, will help to elucidate whether there are gender differences in children's participation in pretend play.

A clear understanding of possible gender differences in the occurrence of pretend play will, in turn, assist in formulating hypotheses concerning how pretend play is linked to patterns of gender segregation in early childhood. When considering different forms of play, it is important to note that children often combine multiple play forms. For example, R&T play often contains elements of pretend or fantasy play (Flannery and Watson, 1993; Pellegrini and Perlmutter, 1988; Smith and Connolly, 1980). Because most researchers focus on either pretend or physical play, instances in which these forms co-occur are usually combined into a larger category.

As pointed out by Pellegrini (2002), because most research has been focused on pretend play, the prevalence of physical activity play during the preschool period may be under reported. It may also be that connections between particular play forms and children's functioning have been obscured due to the failure to delineate clearly between pretend and physical activity play. For this reason, research designed to investigate fantasy play, sociodramatic play, exercise play, and R&T play is needed in order to identify possible gender differences in the prevalence of different play forms, as well as to specify possible connections between play and children's gender segregation tendency.

There were two goals in conducting the study described in this chapter. First, we wanted to obtain descriptive data concerning naturally occurring peer play among preschoolers. Specifically, we wanted to assess the amount of exercise play, R&T play, fantasy play, and sociodramatic play in which preschoolers engage, and we wanted to avoid confounding the different forms of play.

Second, we also wanted to identify the extent to which children engaged in these forms of play with same-sex and other-sex children. Based on previous evidence it was predicted that boys would engage in more exercise and more R&T play than girls. Given the discrepancies across studies concerning gender differences in pretend play, no specific hypotheses were formed concerning gender differences in pretend play, or differences in pretend play with same- and other-sex peers.

METHOD

Participants

Data for this study come from 167 children (89 boys and 78 girls, M age in months = 57.61 at year of first recruitment) who attended a University laboratory child care center in a Midwest town from fall 2001 to spring 2005. There were 54 children with data from 2001 to 2003, 53 children with data from 2002 to 2004, and 60 children with data from 2003 to 2005. Most of the children 121 (73%) were European-American, 22 (13%) were Mexican-American, 12 (7%) were African-American, and 12 (7%) were of other ethnic origin. Children came from predominately middle- and upper-middle class families, with 86% of fathers employed in professional occupations (based on Entwisle and Astone, 1994, Total-based Socioeconomic Index). ANOVA comparisons revealed no significant differences between children based on years of participation on demographic characteristics or any measure used in the study. The institutional review board (IRB) of the University where the data was collected approved the procedures associated with this study. As a condition of children attending the University child care center, parents and guardians consented to have their children involved in approved research, but were allowed to opt out of any study or study component. In addition, children were able to refuse to take part in any research activity. For this study, parents of 32 children did not give consent, and 16 additional children did not want to be interviewed. Thus, the sample for this study represents 78% of all eligible children who attended the center during the 4 years of data collection.

Procedure

In each year, data were collected from September to May. At the beginning of the school year each child's mother, or primary caregiver was asked to give consent for their child to participate by signing a consent form and completing a demographic survey. Beginning in November and continuing through April of each year trained research assistants videotaped children's behavior in the child care setting. Researchers spent 1 week in the classrooms pretending to videotape children without turning the camera on in order to acclimate children to their presence and reduce reactivity. Following a predetermined, random list of names, researchers followed a target child with the videocamera for 5 minutes. After recording one child's behavior, the researcher moved to observe the next child on the list, until each child in the classroom had been observed once. Then the researcher started over by choosing a child's name from the list, at random, and proceeding through the list again in consecutive order. In this way, the order of observation was changed with each pass to control for order effects. This procedure was repeated on each visit, with each researcher averaging 3 visits to a classroom per week over the four month period.

In year 1, a total of 3048 5-minute scans were collected over the 6 month period, for an average of 24 scans (120 minutes) per child, and a range of 20 to 27 scans (100 to 135 minutes). The average number of scans for boys was 25.81 (129.05 minutes), with a range of 21 to 27 (105 to 135 minutes), and the average number of scans for girls was 23.18 (115.90 minutes), with a range of 20 to 25 (100 to 125 minutes). In year 2, a total of 3048 5-minute scans were collected over the 6 month period, for an average of 24 scans (120 minutes) per child, and a range of 20 to 27 scans (100 to 135 minutes). The average number of scans for boys was 25.81 (129.05 minutes), with a range of 21 to 27 (105 to 135 minutes), and the average number of scans for girls was 23.18 (115.90 minutes), with a range of 20 to 25 (100 to 125 minutes). Differences in the observation time across children were the result of absences and limited availability of children.

Measures

Coding Naturalistic Observations of Children's Behavior

Using observational schemes similar to those employed in previous research with young children in school settings (see Fabes et al., 2003; Ladd, Birch, and Buhs, 1999; Mize and Ladd, 1988), 10 trained research assistants who were unaware of the hypothesis guiding the study coded the videotapes of children's behavior in the preschool setting. Researchers received 30 hours of training before coding data to be used in analyses that included: reviewing the coding manual, reviewing practice tapes with the primary investigator who identified exemplars of behaviors from each scale, and independently coding practice tapes until they achieved 80% agreement with the primary investigator. Once reliability was achieved, coders were randomly assigned video tapes to code. To assess reliability during ongoing coding, approximately 20% of the tapes ($N = 50$) were assigned randomly to a primary coder (whose ratings were used in the analysis) and a reliability coder. The coders independently rated their assigned tapes and were blind as to which tapes had been assigned for reliability purposes. Each tape contained approximately 25 5-minute scans. Reliability between the primary and reliability coders was calculated using Kappa coefficients.

Peer play. Because we were interested in assessing children's naturally occurring play behavior with peers, video records were coded using a micro-analytic coding scheme. The focus of this coding scheme was children's peer play behavior, thus only those segments of videotape that were made during two 40-min free-play periods that took place at the child-care setting each day; one in the morning and one in the afternoon, were coded. For this coding scheme, 10 trained research assistants who were unaware of the hypothesis guiding the study coded each 30-s segment of video. For each observation, researchers coded the target child's behavior on a variety of dimensions. First, the coder identified the child's *social involvement*, by noting whether the child was engaged in solitary activity, interacting with one or more adults, interacting with one or more peers, or interacting with both an adult and one or more peers. Reliability between observers for child's social involvement was $\alpha = .90$. Second, if the child was identified as interacting with peers, coders noted if the child was interacting exclusively with same-sex peers, exclusively with other-sex peers, or with both same- and other-sex peers. Reliability between observers for child's social involvement was $\alpha = .96$. Third, coders identified the type of activity the child was engaged in based on the following categories: (1) Play: the child is engaged in some form of play activity which appears to have no other purpose than enjoyment, (2) Instructional activity: the child is engaged in some form of activity designed to promote learning or improvement of skills (e.g., labeling objects, outdoor art activity, gardening activity, reading a book), (3) Eating: the child is eating snack, (4) Conversation: the child is engaged in communication with someone, (5) Other behavior: the child is engaged in an activity that does not fall into the activity categories of 1-6 and is not engaged in onlooking behavior or no activity, (6) Onlooking behavior: the child is watching the activity of another child or adult without interacting with them, (7) No activity: the child is unoccupied or is not engaged in any clearly discernable behavior; the child is sitting quietly with no clear focus of attention. Activity could be double coded, so that within a given 30-s segment coders recorded every activity that the child is engaged in by identifying multiple categories as necessary. Reliability for type of activity was $\alpha = .83$. If children's activity was identified as play, coders next recorded the *form of play* in which the child was engaged. The five play categories used in this study were: (1) exercise play: gross locomotor movements that occur in the context of play and are characterized by physical vigor, but which may or may not be social (e.g., running, jumping, climbing, swinging, and tumbling) and may or may not involve objects, such as balls, bats, tricycles, monkey bars etc..., (2) R&T play: any playful contact or agonistic behavior that is performed in a playful mode and that is social in nature (e.g., tickling, wrestling, boxing, play fighting, kicking, hit and run, and chasing), characterized by positive emotion, (3) fantasy play: using play objects to represent other objects, including verbal relabeling of objects, (4) socio-dramatic play: assuming play roles, including role transformations, and (5) other play: any play activity not fitting into one of the above categories (i.e., functional, construction, singing, drawing). Again, any given segment could be double coded for multiple types of play. Reliability for play type was $\alpha = .86$.

Based on the observational codes, three sets of scores were created to reflect the proportion of intervals in which children were coded as being engaged with same-sex peers, the proportion of intervals children were coded as being engaged with other-sex peer/s, and the proportion of intervals children were coded as being engaged with mixed-sex peer/s, in exercise play, R&T play, pretend play, socio-dramatic play, or other play. Specifically, the summed total of the number of intervals for each category of partner-play type combination was divided by the total number of 30-s intervals in which the child was coded as interacting with peers in play. Thus, each child received five scores for peer play type: (a) *exercise play*, (b) *R&T play*, (c) *fantasy play*, (d) *socio-dramatic play*, and (e) *other play*, for each of the three social participation categories: (a) same-sex play, (b) other-sex play, and (c) mixed-sex play, for a total of 15 proportion scores. In order to comprehensively capture children's engagement in particular play forms, intervals that were double coded were allowed to count for each play category. Thus, for example, an interval that was coded as both fantasy play and R&T play for a particular child was included in the sum for fantasy play and the sum for R&T play for that child. The average number of double-coded intervals was relatively small ($n = 220$). Thus, scores represent the proportion of peer-play interactions that children spent in each form of play. These variables were transformed (i.e., arcsine) to reduce the skew of the data and to better approximate a normal distribution (Cohen and Cohen, 1975).

Table 1. Descriptive Statistics for Girls' and Boys' Peer Play Behavior

	Girls (n = 78)			Boys (n = 89)		
	M	*SD*	Range	*M*	*SD*	Range
Other-sex peer play	.18	.08	.00 - .11	.23	.09	.00 - .11
Fantasy play	.03	.10	.00 - .11	.05	.08	.00 - .10
Sociodramatic play	.05	.05	.00 - .08	.04	.07	.00 - .09
Exercise play	.06	.12	.00 - .17	.07	.14	.00 - .18
R&T play	.02	.08	.00 - .10	.04	.07	.00 - .08
Other play	.02	.05	.00 - .08	.03	.07	.00 - .10
Same-sex peer play	.53	.12	.00 - .19	.54	.15	.00 - .22
Fantasy play	.17	.14	.00 - .31	.15	.14	.00 - .28
Sociodramatic play	.13	.13	.00 - .22	.09	.12	.00 - .17
Exercise play	.12	.14	.00 - .20	.15	.21	.00 - .28
R&T play	.04	.08	.00 - .11	.11	.18	.00 - .24
Other play	.06	.11	.00 - .11	.04	.10	.00 - .11
Mixed-sex peer play	.29	.11	.00 - .11	.23	.10	.00 - .12
Fantasy play	.06	.11	.00 - .18	.04	.10	.00 - .11
Sociodramatic play	.09	.16	.00 - .16	.07	.13	.00 - .16
Exercise play	.07	.13	.00 - .18	.08	.15	.00 - .18
R&T play	.04	.08	.00 - .10	.02	.06	.00 - .07
Other play	.03	.07	.00 - .09	.02	.06	.00 - .08

RESULTS

Table 1. displays the mean (and standard deviation) scores for all variables separately for girls and boys. In descriptive analyses, the correlations (Pearson's r) of major variables with age were computed, and MANOVAs with child sex were calculated.

Then, correlational analyses were employed to investigate the relations among and between play form variables with other, same-, and mixed-sex peers.

In order to illuminate possible sex differences in patterns of association, separate coefficients were calculated for girls and boys (see Table 2).

Descriptive Analyses

Correlation analyses were conducted to examine relations between child age and the major study variables. Results revealed that older children engaged in more socio-dramatic play ($r = .30$, $p < .01$) and more R&T play ($r = .27$, $p < .05$), whereas younger children engaged in more exercise play ($r = -.24$, $p < .05$). No other significant associations with child age were found.

Sex of Child and Social Interaction Effects on Children's Play Form

In order to examine child sex and sex of peer partner effects on the amount of time children spent in different play types, arc-sine scores of child-peer interaction were subjected to a 2 x 3 x 6 (sex of child x partner identity x play type) repeated measures multivariate analysis of variance (MANOVA).

Play type (fantasy play, sociodramatic play, exercise play, R&T play, and other play) and sex of peer (same-sex, mixed-sex, other-sex) were within subjects variables, whereas child sex was a between subjects variable. Based on Wilks's criterion, the MANOVA revealed a significant main effect for partner identity, $F (2, 165) = 30.16$, $p < .001$, $n^2 = .33$, which was qualified by a significant sex of child x partner identity interaction, $F (6, 161) = 8.73$, $p < .05$, $n^2 = .14$.

This main effect was accounted for by the fact that children spent more time playing with same-sex peers ($M = .53$, $SD = .12$, and $M = .54$, $SD = .15$, for girls and boys, respectively) than with other-sex peers ($M = .18$, $SD = .08$, and $M = .23$, $SD = .09$, for girls and boys, respectively) or with mixed-sex peers ($M = .29$, $SD = .11$, and $M = .23$, $SD = .10$, for girls and boys, respectively). There also was a significant main effect for play type, $F (5, 42) = 21.83$, $p < .001$, $n^2 = .24$, which was qualified by a significant sex of child x play type interaction, $F (7, 160) = 13.25$, $p < .05$, $n^2 = .17$.

The play type main effect was accounted for by the fact that children spent more time engaged in exercise play than in any other play form. Children also spent significantly more time engaged in fantasy play and sociodramatic play, than in R&T play and other play.[1]

---

[1] The three play types included in "other" category were:
   (1) functional play: intentional manipulation of objects to elicit their properties (e.g., shaking, rolling),
   (2) instructive play: naming or requesting naming of objects, colors, or numbers, and
   (3) construction: building, stacking, arranging of objects, or arranging objects within or on a construction made of blocks.

Table 2. Correlations Among Play Variables

	1	2	3	4	5	6	7	8	9	10	11	12	13	14	15
Other-sex peers															
1. Fantasy play		.36**	-.10	-.27*	.02	-.24*	-.32*	-.02	-.12	-.08	.37***	.22*	-.28*	-.08	.08
2. Sociodramatic	.33*		-.07	-.38*	.08	-.21*	-.28*	-.17	-.08	-.13	.24*	.32*	-.21*	-.11	.11
3. Exercise play	.18	.28*		.24*	.10	-.36*	-.20*	.24*	.10	-.28*	.10	-.15	.35*	.25*	.05
4. R&T play	.45**	.05	-.34*		.14	-.32*	-.14	.16	.34*	-.21*	.14	-.17	.22*	.20*	.02
5. Other play	-.31*	.11	.15	-.46**		.22*	.07	-.32*	.03	.23*	.03	.12*	-.32*	.03	-.12
Same-sex peers															
6. Fantasy play	-.39**	-.27*	.11	-.08	.32*		.58**	.07	-.32*	.23*	.22*	.30*	-.14	-.11	.21*
7. Sociodramatic	-.28*	-.24*	.03	-.14	.28*	.56***		.04	-.28*	.28*	.28*	.34*	-.05	-.05	.25*
8. Exercise play	.05	.12	.14	.13	-.10	.12	.14		.30*	-.31*	-.10	-.23*	.30*	.20*	.10
9. R&T play	.11	.15	.15	.11	-.23*	.30*	.23*	.42**		-.22*	-.14	-.37**	.23*	.32*	.02
10. Other play	.27*	.24*	.08	-.11	.22*	-.28*	-.22*	.18	-.38**		.03	.08	.06	-.25*	.36**
Mixed-sex peers															
11. Fantasy play	.25*	.20*	.11	.07	.12	.24*	.20*	.14	.12	.17		.26*	.10	.03	.10
12. Sociodramatic	.22*	.32*	.14	.12	.12	.23*	.14	.03	.14	.06	.32*		.12	-.20*	.27*
13. Exercise play	-.16	-.13	.28*	.07	-.13	-.02	.03	.32*	.03	-.12	.12	.15		.23*	-.03
14. R&T play	-.33*	-.22*	.18*	.11	-.19*	-.08	-.32*	.20*	-.32*	-.09	-.08	-.12	.22*		-.12*
15. Other play	.26*	.21*	-.10	-.14	.22*	.18*	.28*	.07	-.23*	.20*	.10	.20*	.13	-.20*	

Note: Correlations for boys are presented below the diagonal line.

* = $p < .05$; ** = $p < .01$.

Follow up, one-way ANOVAs were used to interpret the interaction between child sex and play partner identity, and child sex and play form. These analyses revealed that boys engaged in significantly more other-sex peer play, F (2, 165) = 15.57, $p < .05$, $n^2 = .12$, than girls did, whereas girls engaged in significantly more mixed-sex peer play, F (2, 165) = 18.34, $p < .01$, $n^2 = .14$, than boys did. As for the child sex by play form interaction, girls engaged in significantly more sociodramatic play, F (2, 165) = 17.10, $p < .05$, $n^2 = .16$, than boys did, whereas boys engaged in significantly more R&T play, F (2, 165) = 28.34, $p < .001$, $n^2 = .30$, than girls did.

Associations among Play Forms

Correlations among children's play form variables are presented in Table 2. Given the fact that gender differences were observed in the amount of children's play, correlations were conducted separately for boys and girls. Because of the possibility that child age was confounded with the play form variables, partial correlations that control for age were computed.

Although there were no specific hypotheses concerning these associations, as might be expected based on coding categories, within each category of sex of peer partner, high levels of fantasy play were associated with high levels of socio-dramatic play, and high levels of exercise play were associated with high levels of R&T play, for both boys and girls. This lends support to the validity of the coding scheme having captured unique, but related forms of pretend and physical activity play. As for correlations across categories of sex of peer partner, it is interesting to note that for both girls and boys high levels of fantasy and socio-dramatic play with same sex-peers was significantly, negatively, associated with fantasy play and socio-dramatic play with other-sex peers. In contrast, for girls, but not boys, high levels of exercise and R&T play with same-sex peers were significantly, positively associated with high levels of exercise and R&T play with other-sex peers.

For both girls and boys high levels of fantasy play with same-sex peers was positively associated with high levels of fantasy play with mixed-sex peers. Likewise, high levels of exercise play with same-sex peers was positively associated with high levels of exercise play with mixed-sex peers for both girls and boys. For girls only, high levels of socio-dramatic play with same-sex peers was positively, associated with high levels of socio-dramatic play with mixed-sex peers, and high levels of R&T play with same-sex peers was positively associated with high levels of R&T play with mixed-sex peers. In contrast, for boys, R&T play with same-sex peers was significantly negatively associated with R&T play with mixed-sex peers.

For girls and boys, high levels of fantasy play with mixed-sex peers was positively associated with high levels of fantasy play with other-sex peers, high levels of socio-dramatic play with mixed-sex peers was associated with high levels of socio-dramatic play with other-sex peers, and high levels of exercise play with mixed-sex peers was associated with high levels of exercise play with other-sex peers. For girls, but not boys, high levels of R&T play with mixed-sex peers was positively associated with high levels of R&T play with other-sex peers.

CONCLUSION

A major goal for the study reported in this chapter was to address the question of how individual differences in children's engagement in play are linked to their peer relationships. Of particular interest was the identification of the particular dimensions of play that may be associated with spending more time with same-sex or other-sex peers. To accomplish this goal we assessed both structural aspects of play and social interactive characteristics of play. The results from the study described in this chapter both replicate and extend the body of empirical evidence concerning the role of children's play form preferences on the prevalence of gender segregation in early childhood (Fisher, 1997).

Specifically, the data point to a link between boy's and girl's preference for particular types of play and their tendencies to spend time in same-sex, other-sex, and mixed-sex peers groups. A noteworthy contribution of this study is the assessment of children's engagement in multiple forms of both pretend play and physical activity play. To the best of our knowledge, this study is the first in which multiple forms of physical play, namely exercise play and R&T play, and multiple forms of pretend play, namely fantasy play and sociodramatic play were examined.

Moreover, our results join with other empirical evidence that points to the importance of considering the role of both child sex and sex of playmate in examining rates of children's involvement in different forms of play (Coplan, Gavinski-Molina, Lagace-Seguin, and Wichmann, 2001). It is important to note, however, that our findings do not address the question of direction of effect. It is equally possible that children who prefer to play with same-sex or other-sex peers engage in particular forms of play as it is that play contributes to children playing with same-sex or other-sex peers. Questions concerning the direction of effect between play and children's gender segregation await future longitudinal research.

One of the goals of the present study was to extend information concerning descriptive accounts of preschool children's engagement in physical activity play. In this regard, our data replicate previous evidence of gender differences in the frequency of children's R&T play (DiPietro, 1981; Pellegrini, 1989) in that boys were observed to spend 17% of their time in R&T play with peers, whereas girls spent 10% of their time engaged in R&T play. Contrary to previous evidence (Eaton and Enns, 1986; Colwell and Lindsey, 2005), no gender differences were found for exercise play, in that boys were observed to spend 30% of their time in exercise play, and girls spent 26% of their time in exercise play. The results obtained from the more nuanced approach of assessing physical activity play in the present study supports arguments made by Pellegrini and Smith (1998) that observed gender differences in children's play may be conflated by combining exercise and R&T play. A better understanding of the similarities and differences in physical activity play among preschool boys and girls may lead to greater insights into gendered patterns of peer interaction. Thus, future researchers who focus on the forms of play in which children engage should make distinctions between different types of physical play in order to capture an accurate picture of the complexity of children's play.

The pattern of gender differences in particular forms of physical activity play lend further support to the hypothesis that boy's proclivity to engage in R&T play may play a major role in patterns of gender segregated play during early childhood. More importantly, the findings suggest that it is specifically R&T play, rather than other forms of physical activity play, which may account for gender segregation, as no gender differences were observed in children's exercise play. At the same time, however, the results suggest it is wise to urge caution in attributing gender segregation patterns to a single form of play by one gender, given that the overall rates of R&T play were quiet low compared to other forms of play. To attribute the ubiquitous propensity of preschool children to spend most of their time playing with same-sex peers to a particular form of play that is relatively infrequent seems to be an overly simplistic explanation for a complex phenomenon.

Consistent with the literature on children's development of pretend play (Goncu et al., 2002), the preschool children in this sample spent from 42% to 55% of their time in pretend play, which was the predominate form of peer play. The data also extend existing evidence by indicating that the majority of children's pretend play, 23% to 29%, was made up of fantasy play, rather than socio-dramatic play, which made up 19% to 26% of pretend play. Furthermore, the findings offer some possible clarification for discrepancies in past literature concerning gender differences in children's pretend play. Specifically, girls were observed to engage in more socio-dramatic play than boys, whereas no difference was observed between boys and girls engagement in fantasy play.

The majority of past studies on preschool children's pretend play have found no gender differences (e.g., Connolly and Doyle, 1984; Farver and Shin, 1997; Howes et al., 1989; Pellegrini and Perlmutter, 1989; Rubin and Maioni, 1975), whereas others have (e.g., Lindsey and Mize, 2001; Rubin et al., 1978; Weinberger and Starkey, 1994). The present study suggests that this discrepancy may be attributable to the measures of pretend used across studies. Specifically, operational definitions of pretend play that fail to differentiate between fantasy play and socio-dramatic play, or that focus on only one form of play, may account for the differences across studies. Although in need of replication before definitive conclusions can be drawn, the present study suggests that unique forms of pretend play may be linked to differences in the play patterns of boys and girls.

Although a significant advancement of the current study was the focus on different forms of both physical activity play, and pretend play, it is important to note that there may be additional forms of play not examined in the current study with relevance to children's gender segregation. For example, Smith and his colleagues have categorized R&T play into 13 distinct forms (Boulton and Smith, 1989; Smith et al., 1992). Even play fighting itself may be broken down into different categories (Boulton, 1996). Our findings suggest that it will be worthwhile for future research to examine more types of physical activity play in relation to children's play with same-sex and other-sex children.

In addition, research clearly indicates that contextual features such as the amount of space that children have, the number of toys available, as well as the number of teachers present influence children's physical activity play (Brown et al., 2009). Consequently, characteristics of the present sample and child care setting may limit the generalizability of the findings. Future research should include comparisons of children's behavior from different child care settings, as well as indoor and outdoor play. In addition to the limitation in our ability to offer a directional or causal explanation for the associations between children's play forms and their preference for playing with peers of same or other sex, it is important to note that the magnitude of effects for our findings are relatively low, clearly a function of sample size, and should be understood as such. Additional research with larger and more heterogeneous sample would help expand the generalizability of these findings.

With these limitations in mind, the results of the current study point to the need for further empirical investigation of the complexity of children's play and provides a guide for future study of the connections between distinct forms of physical activity play and children's gender segregation. The results from the present study both replicate and extend empirical evidence concerning the importance of physical activity play for children's tendency to engage in play with same-sex peers (see Pellegrini, 2002, for review). A noteworthy contribution of this study to existing research was the assessment of children's engagement in two forms of physical play, namely exercise play and R&T play. The study also joins with other empirical evidence pointing to the importance of considering the role of both child gender and gender of playmate (Colwell and Lindsey, 2005; Coplan et al., 2001), in examining gender segregated patterns of peer interaction in early childhood.

ACKNOWLEDGMENTS

This investigation was supported by faculty development grants from the College of Human Sciences at Texas Tech University. The author would like to thank Laura Villa, Malathi Apparala, Jennifer Chapman, Erin Oats, Ginny Fowler, and Jennifer Meschi for their help in various phases of data collection and coding. Appreciate is also expressed to the children and teachers of the Texas Tech Child Development Research Center for their time and participation.

REFERENCES

Aldis, O. (1975). *Play fighting*. New York: Academic Press.
Archer, J. (1996). Sex differences in social behavior: Are social role and evolutionary explanations compatible? *American Psychologist, 51,* 909–917. doi:10.1037/0003-066X.51.9.909.
Blanckenhorn, W. U. (2005). Behavioral causes and consequences of sexual size dimorphism. *Ethology, 111,* 977–1016. doi:10.1111/j.1439–0310.2005.01147.x.
Boulton, M. J. (1991). Partner preferences in middle school children's play fighting and chasing. *Ethology and Sociobiology, 12,* 177–193.
Boulton, M. J. (1996). A comparison of 8- and 11- year old girls' and boys' participation in specific types of rough-and-tumble play and aggressive fighting: Implications for functional hypotheses. *Aggressive Behavior, 22,* 271-287.
Brown, W. H., Pfeiffer, K. A., McIver, K. L., Dowda, M., Addy, C. I., and Pate, R. R. (2009). Social and environmental factors associated with preschoolers' nonsedentary physical activity. *Child Development, 80,* 45-58.
Byers, J. A. (1998). Biological effects of locomotor play: Getting into shape or something more specific? In M. Bekoff and J. A. Byers (Eds.), *Animal play: Evolutionary, comparative, and ecological perspectives* (pp. 205–220). Cambridge, England: Cambridge University Press.
Connolly, J. A., and Doyle, A. (1984). Relation of social fantasy play to social competence in preschoolers. *Developmental Psychology, 20,* 797-806.

Coplan, R. J., Gavinski-Molina, M., Lagace-Seguin, D. G., and Wichmann, C. (2001). When girls versus boys play alone: Nosocial play and adjustment in kindergarten. *Developmental Psychology, 37*, 464-474.

DiPietro, J. A. (1981). Rough and tumble play: A function of gender. *Developmental Psychology, 17*, 50-58.

Doyle, A., Ceschin, F., Tessier, O., and Doehring, P. (1991). The relation of age and social class factors in children's social pretend play in cognitive and symbolic ability. *International Journal of Behavioral Development, 14*, 395-410.

Doyle, A., and Connolly, J. (1989). Negotiation and enactment in social pretend play: Relations to social acceptance and social cognition. *Early Childhood Research Quarterly, 4*, 289-302.

Eaton, W. C., and Enns, L. R. (1986). Sex differences in human motor activity level. *Psychological Bulletin, 100*, 19-28.

Entwisle, D. R., and Astone, N. M. (1994). Some practical guidelines for measuring youth's race/ethnicity and socioeconomic status. *Child Development, 65*, 1521-1540.

Fabes, R. A., Martin, C. L., and Hanish, L. D. (2003). Young children's play qualities in same-, other-, and mixed-sex peer groups. *Child Development, 74*, 921-932.

Farver, J. A. M., and Shin, L. (1997). Social pretend play in Korean- and Anglo-American preschoolers. *Child Development, 68*, 544-556.

Fein, G. (1981). Pretend play: An integrative review. *Child Development, 52*, 1095-1118.

Field, T. M. (1994). Infant day care facilitates later social behavior and school performance. In E. V. Jacobs and H. Goelman (Eds.), *Children's play in child care settings* (pp. 69-84). Albany: State University of New York Press.

Fisher, E. P. (1997). The impact of play on development: A meta-analysis. *Play and Culture, 5*, 159-181.

Flannery, K. A., and Watson, M. W. (1993). Are individual differences in fantasy play related to peer acceptance levels? *Journal of Genetic Psychology, 154*, 407-416.

Fry, D. (1987). Differences between play fighting and serious fighting among Zapotec children, *Ethology and Sociobiology, 8*, 285–306.

Goncu, A., Patt, M. B., and Kouba, E. (2002). Understanding young children's pretend play in context. In P. K. Smith and C. H. Hart (Eds.), *Blackwell handbook of childhood social development* (pp. 418-437.) Oxford: Blackwell.

Harper, L. V., and Huie, K. (1978). The development of sex differences in human behavior: Cultural impositions, or a convergence of evolved responses tendencies and cultural adaptations? In G. M. Burghardt and M. Bekoff (Eds.), *The development of behavior* (pp. 297–318). New York: Garland Publishing.

Howes, C. and Matheson, C. C. (1992). Sequences in the development of competent play with peers: Social and social pretend play. *Developmental Psychology, 28*, 961-974.

Howes, C., Unger, O. A., and Matheson, C. C. (1991). *The social construction of pretend.* Albany; State University of New York Press.

Howes, C., Unger, O. A., and Seidner, L. B. (1989). Social pretend play in toddlers: Parallels with social play and with solitary pretend. *Child Development, 60*, 77-84.

Humphreys, A. P., and Smith, P. K. (1987). Rough-and-tumble play, friendship, and dominance in school children: Evidence for continuity and change with age. *Child Development, 58*, 201-212.

Jarvis, P. (2007). Monsters, magic and Mr. Psycho: A biocultural approach to rough and tumble play in the early years of primary school. *Early Years, 27,* 171-188.

Jones, A., and Glenn, S. M. (1991). Gender differences in pretend play in a primary school group. *Early Child Development and Care, 77,* 127-135.

Ladd, G. W. (1983). Social networks of popular, average, and rejected children in school settings. *Merrill-Palmer Quarterly, 29,* 283-307.

Ladd, G. W., Birch, S. H., and Buhs, E. S. (1999). Children social and scholastic lives in kindergarten: Related spheres of influence? *Child Development, 70,* 1373-1400.

LaFreniere, P., Strayer, F. F., and Gauthier, R. (1984). The emergence of same-sex affiliative preferences among preschool peers: A developmental/ethological perspective. *Child Development, 55,* 1958–1965. doi: 10.2307/1129942

Lindsey, E. W., and Mize, J. (2001). Contextual differences in parent-child play: Implications for children's gender role development. *Sex Roles, 44,* 155-176.

Maccoby, E. E. (1998). *The two sexes.* Cambridge, MA: Harvard University Press.

Maccoby, E. E., and Jacklin, C. N. (1987). Gender segregation in children. In H. W. Reece (Ed.), *Advances in child development and behavior.* (pp. 239-287). New York: Academic Press.

Martin, C. L. (1994). Cognitive influences on the development and maintenance of gender segregation. In C. Leaper (Ed.), *Childhood gender segregation: Causes and consequences.* (pp. 57-66). San Francisco: Jossey-Bass.

Martin, C. L., and Fabes, R. A. (2001). The stability and consequences of young children's same-sex peer interaction. *Developmental Psychology, 37,* 431-446.

Martin, C. L., Fabes, R. A., Evans, S. M., and Wyman, H. (1999). Social cognition on the playground: Children's beliefs about playing with girls versus boys and their relation to sex segregated play. *Journal of Social and Personal Relationships, 16,* 751-772.

Mize, J., and Ladd, G. W. (1988). Predicting preschoolers' peer behavior and status from their interpersonal strategies: A comparison of verbal and enactive responses to hypothetical social dilemmas. *Developmental Psychology, 24,* 782-788.

Pellegrini, A. D. (1993). Boys' rough-and-tumble play, social competence, and group composition. *British Journal of Developmental Psychology, 11,* 227-248.

Pellegrini, A. D. (2002). Rough-and-tumble play from childhood through adolescence: Development and possible functions. In P. K. Smith and C. H. Hart (Eds.), *Blackwell handbook of childhood social development* (pp. 438-454.) Oxford: Blackwell.

Pellegrini, A. D. (2004). Sexual segregation in childhood: A review of evidence for two hypotheses. *Animal Behaviour, 68,* 435–443. doi: 10.1016/j.anbehav.2003.07.023.

Pellegrini, A. D., and Perlmutter, J. (1988). Rough and tumble play in the elementary school playground. *Young Children, 42,* 14-17.

Pellegrini, A. D., and Smith, P. K. (1998). Physical play activity: The nature and function of a neglected aspect of play. *Child Development, 69,* 577-874.

Rubin, K. H., and Coplan, R. J. (1998). Social and nonsocial play in childhood: An individual difference perspective. In O. N. Saracho and B. Spodek (Eds.), *Multiple perspectives on play in early childhood education.* (pp. 144-170.) Albany, NY: State University of New York Press.

Rubin, K. H., and Maioni, T. L. (1975). Play preference and its relationship to egocentrism, popularity, and classification skills in preschoolers. *Merrill-Palmer Quarterly, 21,* 171-179.

Rubin, K. H., Maioni, T. L., and Hornung, M. (1976). Free play behaviors in middle-class and lower-class preschoolers: Parten and Piaget revisited. *Child Development, 47*, 414-419.

Rubin, K. H., Watson, K. S., and Jambor, T. W. (1978). Free-play behaviors in preschool and kindergarten children. *Child Development, 49*, 534-536.

Singer, J. L. (1973). *The child's world of make-believe: Experimental studies of imaginative play*. New York: Academic Press.

Smilansky, S. (1968). *The effects of sociodramatic play on disadvantaged children: Preschool children*. New York: Wiley.

Smith, P. K. (2010). *Children and Play*. New York, NY: J. Wiley.

Smith, P. K., and Connolly, K. (1990). *The ecology of preschool behavior*. Cambridge, England: Cambridge University Press.

Sroufe, L. A., Bennett, C., Englund, M., Urban, J., and Shulman, S. (1993). The significance of gender boundaries in preadolescence: Contemporary correlates and antecedents of boundary violation and maintenance. *Child Development, 64*, 455-466.

Wall, S. M., Pickert, S. M., and Gibson, W. B. (1990). Fantasy play in 5- and 6-year-old children. *Journal of Psychology, 123*, 245-256.

Weinberger, L. A., and Starkey, P. (1994). Pretend play by African-American children in Head Start. *Early Childhood Research Quarterly, 9*, 327-343.

Werebe, M. J. G., and Baudonniere, P. M. (1991). Social pretend play among friends and familiar preschoolers. *International Journal of Behavioral Development, 14*, 411-428.

Whiting, B., and Edwards, C. P. (1973). A cross-cultural analysis of sex differences in the behavior of children aged three through 11. *Journal of Social Psychology, 91*, 171–188.

Whiting, B. B., and Edwards, C. P. (1988). *Children of different worlds: The formation of social behavior*. Cambridge, MA: Harvard University Press.

In: Psychology of Gender Differences
Editor: Sarah P. McGeown

ISBN: 978-1-62081-391-1
© 2012 Nova Science Publishers, Inc.

Chapter 3

GENDER DIFFERENCES IN ACHIEVEMENT MOTIVATION: GRADE AND CULTURAL CONSIDERATIONS

Alexander Seeshing Yeung, *Rhonda G. Craven*
and Gurvinder Kaur
University of Western Sydney, Australia

ABSTRACT

Research on gender issues in achievement motivation has often yielded conflicting results. Whereas boys seem to have a higher sense of competence and girls seem to have higher interest in school work, gender differences tend to be small and inconsistent across curriculum areas. Gender patterns also vary from culture to culture and in different grade levels.

Using a sample of Australian students from six primary schools, the study reported here examined gender differences in four motivation constructs (mastery goal, value of schooling, sense of competence, and affect to learning). Analysis of variance was conducted to test gender and grade differences for Anglo and Asian Australians' construct scores.

More culture differences than gender differences were found with this sample. For Anglo-Australians, girls were found to display higher scores compared to boys in all four constructs irrespective of grade. For Asian-Australians, boys were higher in all four construct scores compared to girls in third grade but the disadvantage of boys disappeared thereafter.

The inconsistent gender patterns found in different grade levels and different cultures call for the consideration of background variables such as culture, grade level, school setting, and curriculum focus when examining students' gender differences in achievement motivation.

Keywords: Motivation; self-concept; primary; culture; gender; grade

---

*Phone: +61 (2) 9772 6264, Fax: +61 (2) 9772 6432, e-mail: a.yeung@uws.edu.au.

INTRODUCTION

Gender research has always attracted a lot of attention and has found some interesting results. However a lot of inconsistencies have been found in gender research. These inconsistencies may be due to the effect of culture and level of maturity. The present chapter attempts to study gender differences in students' motivation in school and examine whether patterns of gender differences and similarities can be generalized across cultures and grade levels in primary education. The sample was primary school students from six schools in Western Sydney, Australia. The multicultural school environment of Australian schools provides an interesting context to study these issues. The issue of potential culture x gender x grade interaction effects on student motivation is worth exploring as it has not been fully elucidated in the literature, and may help to explain the inconsistencies found in contemporary gender research.

Academic Motivation Constructs

The critical variables we examined in the research were academic motivation constructs. It is important for researchers and practitioners to understand these constructs because research has shown that students' academic behavior and achievement are related to their academic motivation (e.g., McInerney and Ali, 2006; Smith, Duda, Allen, and Hall, 2002). Students' mastery goal orientation, for example, is important for engaging students in learning activities so as to achieve (Dweck and Leggett, 1988; Elliot, 2005). Perceived value of schooling has been shown to have significant influence on performance and other educational outcomes (Wigfield and Eccles, 2000). Furthermore, students' self-beliefs tend to have significant influence on essential academic outcomes including achievement (e.g., McInerney, Yeung, and McInerney, 2001; Smith et al., 2002). They may also impact on both short-term outcomes such as ongoing participation, and long-term outcomes such as academic aspirations and future educational plans (Yeung, 2005). However, although the existent literature has provided knowledge about the significant roles the various motivational constructs may play, there has been no rigorous study on how culture and grade influence gender effects on these constructs. Our purpose of the investigation reported here is to study culture, gender, and grade effects and their interactions on four well documented academic motivation factors (mastery, value, competence, and affect).

Mastery. Mastery goal orientation is an important construct of goal theory and is one of the most researched constructs in motivation studies (Dweck and Leggett, 1988; Elliot, 2005; Nicholls, 1989; Pintrich and Schunk, 2002). A student with a mastery goal orientation is one who is interested in acquiring new skills and improving competence even in the face of obstacles. Students having a strong mastery goal orientation tend to assess their achievement in terms of self-referenced standards rather than in comparison with others. As such, they emphasize active participation in learning and understanding, which may involve the use of deep cognitive processing (Ames and Archer, 1988; Meece, Blumenfeld, and Hoyle, 1988). Mastery orientation has been found to have positive effects on learning (Midgley et al., 2000; Yeung and McInerney, 2005), as students strong in mastery goal orientation are likely to have better perseverance with difficult tasks (Ryan and Pintrich, 1998), and are able to maintain effort and interest in learning (Robins and Pals, 2002). More importantly, mastery goals are found to be positively and significantly related to student achievement (Wentzel, 1993), and have therefore gained the attention of many researchers in education.

Value of schooling. Value of schooling is the extent students believe what they learn at school is useful, important, and relevant (Martin, 2007; Pintrich, Smith, Garcia, and McKeachie, 1991). How much students find school as beneficial to them is important in facilitating or inhibiting their motivation to achieve. This is also consistent with the utility value of the expectancy-value theory (Eccles, 1983; Wigfield, 1994; see also Wigfield, Eccles, and Rodriguez, 1998) stating that perceived value is an important construct of motivation. Perceived value of schooling is known to be positively related to academic achievement (McInerney, Dowson, and Yeung, 2005). Students who value school find interest in and enjoy school and learning (Martin, 2003a). Student values relate positively to their use of cognitive strategies as well as their self-regulation (Pintrich and DeGroot, 1990). Therefore, students' valuing of a learning task contributes significantly to their motivation and active engagement in the learning task (Wigfield and Eccles, 2000). In essence, values predict current and future activity choices (Eccles and Wigfield, 1995; Wigfield, 1994). Hence researchers have emphasized the importance of students' value of schooling for both short-term and long-term gains.

Competence. Student's beliefs about their own abilities or competence have received considerable attention in research (Blumenfeld, Pintrich, Meece, and Wessels, 1982; Nicholls, 1984). Marsh and colleagues have demonstrated the causal relations between competence (the cognitive component of academic self-concept) and achievement outcomes (e.g., Marsh and Craven, 2006). Other researchers have also emphasized that self-competence beliefs are related to, and can effectively predict, achievement (Eccles, Wigfield, Harold, and Blumenfeld, 1993; Meece, Parsons, Kaczala, Goff, and Futterman, 1982; Wigfield, Eccles, Mac Iver, Reuman, and Midgley, 1991). Interestingly, students' sense of competence in academic work is often found to be even a stronger predictor than students' actual ability in the specific task (Pajares and Schunk, 2002). Hence researchers have emphasized the enhancement of students' sense of competence as vital in all educational settings (see Marsh and Craven, 2006; Craven Marsh, and Burnett, 2003). It has also been demonstrated that a high self-perception of competence promotes goals, coping mechanisms, and behaviors that facilitate performance and work experiences in the long-term (e.g., Sommer and Baumeister, 2002).

Affect. From a twofold multidimensional perspective (Arens, Yeung, Craven, and Hasselhorn, 2011), affect can be conceptualized as the affective component of self-concept (Marsh, Craven, and Debus, 1999). For example, in relation to school self-concept the affective component is the extent to which a student likes school work. The affective component to learning is an important construct in educational settings because students learn only when they find themselves interested (Ryan and Deci, 2000). The relation between affect and achievement has been observed by some researchers. In simple terms, students who like a particular curriculum area do better than those who dislike it (Johnson, Crosnoe, and Elder 2001; Singh, Granville, and Dika, 2002). Because of its influence on learning and personal goals, Bjornebekk (2008) has emphasized including affect as an important construct for analyzing any learning process. Desirable learning processes and outcomes identified by researchers as attributable to positive affect include intention stability, a mechanism by which intentions are translated into action (Armitage, 2008), attention, positive attitudes, engagement in academic work, and persistence in learning (Linnenbrink-Garcia, Durik, Conley, Barron, Tauer, Karabenick, and Harackiewicz, 2010; Trautwein and Lüdtke, 2009; Van Damme, De Fraine, Van Landeghem, Opdenakker, and Onghena, 2010), as well as better performance, higher motivation, and greater persistence (Erez and Isen, 2002). Yeung (2005) argues that the extent to which students like school and enjoy engaging in school work and learning activities has important long-term benefits to learners of all ages, although immediate benefits may not always be apparent.

Gender Issues

Research on motivation has indicated that there may be gender differences on some motivational constructs. Girls have been found to have a higher level of mastery goal orientation than boys (Midgley, Kaplan, and Middleton, 2001). Although boys and girls may start with similar levels of motivation, the gap emerges at early developmental stages and continues to widen from primary through secondary school (Usher and Pajares, 2008). Researchers have often attributed gender differences to gender stereotypes which lead to boys' and girls' differential perceptions of activities and behaviors in their social context. Consistent with gender stereotypes, boys and girls tend to be motivated to master skills and knowledge relevant to their gender role. For example, differentiating boys' and girls' homework compliance, Trautwein and Lüdtke (2009) found that boys appeared to be more motivated and were more compliant in curriculum areas such as math and physics that are thought to be 'masculine'. In contrast, girls showed less compliance and displayed more tendency of avoidance or withdrawal. Furthermore, gender differences are also evident in value beliefs. Gender norms and stereotypes have again been used to explain such differences. For example, boys have been found to place higher value on sports activities and girls have been found to place higher values on musical and reading activities (Eccles et al., 1993). However, when school motivation in general is concerned, gender differences tend to be small. For example, Graham, Tisher, Ainley, and Kennedy (2008) found no significant gender differences on a composite approach motivation factor that included task goals and ability-approach goals. In fact, even though there has been evidence of gender differences in school motivation constructs, the differences are often small (Crain, 1996; Kelly and Decker, 2009; Marsh, Tracey, and Craven, 2006; Mucherah and Yoder, 2008; Yeung, 2011; Yeung, Lau, and Nie, 2011). For ability beliefs, boys have been reported to hold higher competence beliefs in math and sports whereas girls have higher competence beliefs in verbal and social domains (Eccles, Wigfield, Flanagan, Miller, Reuman, and Yee 1989; Eccles et al., 1993; Marsh, 1989; Wigfield et al., 1991). Such differences between boys' and girls' motivation-related beliefs and behaviors are often influenced by gender role stereotypes (Meece, Glienke, and Burg, 2006). Nevertheless, even though boys generally have a higher sense of competence (Midgley et al., 2001), their actual achievement scores may not be really higher than girls' (Klapp Lekholm and Cliffordson, 2009; Marsh and Yeung, 1998). In other words, boys tend to overestimate their abilities whereas girls often underestimate their abilities (Metallidou and Vlachou, 2007). For students' affect to learning, there seems to be a general phenomenon that girls are more positive and show better interest in learning activities (Mucherah and Yoder, 2008), although this tendency may be stronger in some particular curriculum areas. Based on research findings showing the positive effects of affect on learning outcomes (Armitage, 2008; Erez and Isen, 2002; Linnenbrink-Garcia et al., 2010; Trautwein and Lüdtke, 2009; Van Damme et al., 2010), we might speculate that girls, being more positive toward learning, would do better than boys academically. This may partly explain the findings of some researchers showing girls performing better than boys throughout primary and middle school education (e.g., Lai, 2010).

Grade Issues

In considering developmental trends, researchers have suggested a downward developmental trend in motivation in most cases (Lau, 2009; Meece and Miller, 2001, Yeung, 2011; Yeung et al., 2011). It seems that the decline in motivation constructs and competence beliefs occurs in both boys and girls (Meece and Miller, 2001). Lau (2009) further suggests that motivational decline may be a common phenomenon for both Asian and Western students. In science, for example, students' motivation seems to decrease as they progress to higher grade levels, such that 7th graders are more motivated than 8th and 9th graders (Gungoren and Sungur, 2009). Research has shown that intrinsic motivation for learning and competence beliefs decline from elementary school age through adolescence (e.g., Bouffard, Marcoux, Vezeau, and Bordeleau, 2003; Gottfried, Fleming, and Gottfried, 2001). For example, Yeung and McInerney (2005) reported declines in various motivational constructs through high school years. Similarly, Lepper, Corpus, and Iyengar (2005) reported significant linear decrease in students' intrinsic motivation. However, they also found very little change in extrinsic motivation from 3rd grade through 8th grade. This implies that it is mainly intrinsic motivation, such as mastery goal orientation, that suffers most. The researchers attributed the decrease in intrinsic motivation to decontextualization of education, which makes students feel that what they learn in the classroom is not relevant to their daily lives. They also suggested that the increased control over students' learning and decreased opportunity for students to make choices and feel autonomous in schooling environments may be a cause for reduced student motivation over time. Increasing difficulty, tougher expectations, and higher demands in higher grades may also act upon students' motivation and competence beliefs. As such, Eccles et al. (1993) found a decline in the students' competence beliefs and perceptions about the usefulness and importance of learning tasks over time among elementary and middle school students. Competence beliefs start to emerge in early elementary school (Eccles et al., 1993), and such beliefs are built upon performance and feedback. As expectations get higher and competition gets increasingly vigorous, competence beliefs may suffer. Consistent with this conjecture, Wigfield and Eccles (1994) reported that students' competence beliefs in all domains tend to decline over time. Similarly, Metallidou and Vlachou (2007) found, with a sample of 5th and 6th graders in Greece, younger students' perceptions of competence and motivation in language and math tended to be higher than the perceptions of older students. Fortunately, the decline may not continue forever. For example, Jacobs, Lanza, Osgood, Eccles, and Wigfield (2002) reported that in language arts, competence beliefs declined rapidly during the elementary school years, but then leveled off. Yeung (2011) also reported that the decline of Australian students' affect and effort goal orientation (an intrinsic motivation factor) tended to slow down after 9th grade. Nevertheless, the rate of decline and leveling trends seems to be different for different motivation constructs (Watt, 2008; Yeung, 2011). Watt (2008) reported that even though the decline for intrinsic value was found to be fairly consistent between boys and girls, girls' perceptions seemed to decline faster at an earlier stage, after which boys' decline became faster in the secondary school. However the rate of decline for other motivational constructs may be different for boys and girls. For example, Jacobs et al. (2002) found that boys' sense of competence tended to drop faster than girls' sense of competence. In contrast, Yeung (2011) found that the decline between primary and secondary schooling seemed faster for girls than for boys. As such, there obviously exist discrepancies in research findings regarding gender and grade differences in motivation and competence beliefs.

Cultural Issues

The inconsistent findings regarding gender and grade differences in motivational constructs may be due to cultural characteristics. Considering Eastern and Western cultures and student performance in these cultures, we may find a contrasting pattern showing boys having higher self-concept and performing better than girls in Western cultures (e.g., Nagy, Watt, and Eccles, Trautwein, Lüdtke, and Baumert, 2010), but girls performing better than boys in Eastern cultures (e.g., Lai, 2010). For academic motivation, culture and cultural context play an important role in shaping students' achievement goals (Markus and Kitayama, 1991).

Because their achievement goals are rooted in cultural and societal values (Dekker and Fischer, 2008), students' understanding of learning and its relevance to themselves may differ according to cultural values and priorities. Hence even though motivation may be universal to all individuals and cultures, the ways in which it is constructed and perceived depend upon the specific cultural values and characteristics. Li (2002), for example, proposes a model of "heart and mind for wanting to learn" that is typical of some non-Western cultures. The model emphasizes that knowledge seeking is a long-term goal in certain non-Western cultures. In particular, she found that Chinese students reported more positive beliefs and benefits of learning than their American peers, and such beliefs seemed to start emerging in early years. She further claims that students from Chinese culture view learning as a process that gives meaning to life and they seek learning to acquire self-perfection.

In contrast, the American culture emphasizes thinking processes and the learner's psychological characteristics such as learning style and intelligence. Summarizing the findings from recent cross-cultural studies, it seems that individual inborn characteristics (such as ability) are valued more in Western cultures whereas nurtured characteristics (such as effort) are valued more in Asian cultures (Hau and Salili, 1991; Stevenson and Stigler, 1992; Yeung, 2005). Interestingly studies have revealed that cultural values tend to influence the links between gender and motivation. For example, in more masculine countries (where there are more rigidly-defined gender roles favoring males), girls have been found to display lower reading achievement compared to girls in other countries (Chiu and Chow, 2010).

Comparing Asian students with Western students, we may expect higher intrinsic motivation (such as mastery goal orientation) for Asian students because it is related to more remote outcomes and less immediate tangible rewards (Grant and Dweck, 2001). Nevertheless, despite the Asian culture emphasizing long-term benefits of education (Li, 2002; Shecter, Durik, Miyamoto, and Harackiewicz, 2011) and undermining immediate performance outcomes, Asian students (e.g., Filipino and Indonesians) have been found to be performing significantly better than Western students (e.g., Australians) (Liem, Martin, Nair, Bernado, and Prasetya, 2009).

It is unclear whether the advantage of these Asian students was due to their cultural ideology of collectivism as opposed to Western individualism (Hofstede, 1980; Triandis, 1994). Nevertheless, when student motivation is considered, because Asian students are more motivated by distal utility value, whereas Westerners are more motivated by proximal utility value (Shecter et al., 2011), we may expect higher mastery goal orientation observed in Asian students but higher competence beliefs in Western students (such as Australians).

Because cultural systems are open systems that evolve with time and are constantly influencing learning orientations (Kitayama, 2002), cultural influences may be even stronger than gender stereotype influences. Therefore it is possible that inconsistencies found in previous gender research on student motivation have been masked by cultural influences that have not been seriously considered.

The Present Investigation

For the present study, a diverse sample of primary school students in Australia ($N = 730$) participated and their self-beliefs and perceived value of schooling were examined. The student population in Western Sydney, being multicultural, provided an interesting context for the study of cultural, gender, and grade similarities and differences in the motivation constructs of mastery goal, value of schooling, sense of competence, and affect to learning.

Based on previous research revealing certain differences between Asian and Western students' pattern of motivation and self-perception development, we may expect some interesting differences between Asian and Western students, all living in Australia, a Western country. Findings for any potential culture x gender x grade interaction effects, which few researchers have explored, would have important implications for educational researchers and teachers.

METHOD

Participants

Australian students from six schools in Western Sydney ($N = 730$) participated in this study. Students in the primary schools came from grades 3, 4, 5, and 6 (353 boys, 377 girls). Typical of students in public schools of the Western Sydney Region, they were multicultural and were mostly from families of relatively lower socio-economic status compared to other regions in Sydney. In this sample, about 88 different languages were reported, and most families spoke a variety of languages, with less than 35% of the students from monolingual English-speaking families. The present study focused on Anglo-Australian students ($n = 446$: 221 boys and 225 girls) and Asian-Australian students ($n = 284$: 132 boys and 152 girls), categorized on the basis of the ethnic background of the students' father. 'Asian' ethnicities in the sample refer to students whose father was born in Cambodia, Indonesia, Malaysia, Indian,

Sri Lanka, Bangladesh, Korea, Japan, Lebanon, Iraq, Vietnam, China, and other Asian and middle-east countries.

Materials

In a survey, the students were asked to rate themselves on four factors (mastery, value, competence, and affect). Background variables included age, gender, ethnicity, and language background. For the four factors, there were a total of 18 items with four to six items in each factor (see Appendix). They were:

Mastery The scale had six items adapted from Marsh, Craven, Hinkley and Debus's (2003) mastery goal scale. An example is: "I feel most successful in school when I reach personal goals".

Value of schooling. Perceived value of schooling was adapted from Martin's (2003b) Student Motivation and Engagement Scale. An example is: "What I learn at school will be useful one day".

Competence. This is the cognitive component of self-concept adapted from Marsh (1993) Academic Self-Description Questionnaire II (SDQII). An example is: "I am good at all school subjects".

Affect. This is the affective component of self-concept which was also adapted from Marsh's (1993) SDQII (also see Yeung et al., 2004). An example is: "I am interested in all school subjects".

Procedure

The schools were randomly selected and the principals of the schools were invited to participate. Data collection was conducted in the second half of the school year. Due to the large sample size, the whole data collection process took about 2 months.

Procedures of the research followed university guidelines to ensure confidentiality and approval was obtained from the university's ethics committee. Informed consent was obtained from the school and the parents of the students before data collection.

The survey was piloted at the beginning of the year and the scales and items were refined after preliminary analysis. The survey was administered in groups by a research assistant, and in some schools the class teacher also assisted to ensure students who needed help would be supported. The students responded to the survey items in a random order on a 5-point scale (1 = false to 5 = true).

Statistical Analysis

The students' responses to the survey items were coded such that higher scores reflected more favorable responses. In preliminary analysis, we examined the Cronbach's alpha estimate of internal consistency of each *a priori* scale. Then we conducted confirmatory factor analysis (CFA) with the statistical package of Mplus, Version 6.0 (Muthén and

Muthén, 1998-2010). Although the amount of missing was very small (about 1%), we used the full information maximum likelihood (FIML) estimator for imputation of missing values.

The procedures for conducting CFA have been described elsewhere (e.g., Byrne, 1998; Jöreskog and Sörbom, 2005; Pedhazur and Schmelkin, 1991) and are not further detailed here. The goodness of fit of the CFA models was evaluated based on suggestions of Marsh, Balla, and McDonald (1988) and Marsh, Balla, and Hau (1996), with an emphasis on the Tucker-Lewis index (TLI, also known as the non-normed fit index) as the primary goodness-of-fit index.

However, the chi-square test statistic and root mean square error of approximation (RMSEA) and the comparative fit index (CFI), are also reported. In general, for an acceptable model fit, the values of TLI and CFI should be equal to or greater than .90 for an acceptable fit and .95 for an excellent fit to the data. For RMSEA, according to Browne and Cudeck (1993), a value of .05 indicates a close fit, values near .08 indicate a fair fit, and values above .10 indicate a poor fit.

Specifically, based on commonly accepted criteria (see Browne and Cudeck, 1993; Jöreskog and Sörbom, 2005; Marsh, et.al., 1996; Marsh, et.al., 1988), support for an acceptable model requires: (a) acceptable reliability for each scale (i.e., alpha = .70 or above), (b) an acceptable model fit (i.e., TLI and RNI = .90 or above and RMSEA < .08), (c) acceptable factor loadings for the items loading on the respective factors (> .30), and (d) acceptable correlations among the latent factors such that they would be distinguishable from each other ($r < .90$).

The purpose of the CFA was to establish the measurement of the four critical motivation factors (mastery, value, competence, and affect). Then based on the established factors, we examined grade, gender, and cultural differences. A 2 (culture: Anglo vs. Asian) x 2 (gender: boys vs. girls) x 4 (grade: 3, 4, 5, 6) multivariate analysis of variance (MANOVA) was conducted with mastery, value, competence, and affect as dependent variables. We hypothesized that: (1) gender differences would be small, (2) motivational constructs would be weaker in higher grades, and (3) differences between Asian-Australians and Anglo-Australian would be significant whereby Asian-Australians would display significantly higher scores for all four constructs measured.

RESULTS

CFA

The alpha reliability of each scale was acceptable ($\alpha > .70$), providing preliminary support for the *a priori* factors. The lowest alpha value was .75 for Value and the highest alpha was .91 for Affect (Appendix). The CFA model resulted in a proper solution.

The model (TLI = .97, CFI = .97, RMSEA = .05), provided a good fit to the data (Table 1). Table 1 also presents the standardized solution of the model. The factor loadings were acceptable (all > .5). The factor correlations ranged from .51 to .88, indicating that the factors can be clearly differentiated from one another.

Table 1. Solution of CFA Model

Variable	Mastery	Value	Competence	Affect	Uniqueness
Mean	4.45	4.50	3.67	3.66	
SD	0.74	0.69	0.86	1.14	
Factor Loadings					
mastery1	.71*	--	--	--	.50*
mastery2	.80*	--	--	--	.36*
mastery3	.78*	--	--	--	.40*
mastery4	.78*	--	--	--	.40*
mastery5	.77*	--	--	--	.41*
mastery6	.80*	--	--	--	.36*
value1	--	.66*	--	--	.57*
value2	--	.68*	--	--	.55*
value3	--	.58*	--	--	.66*
value4	--	.73*	--	--	.46*
compet1	--	--	.63*	--	.60*
compet2	--	--	.73*	--	.47*
compet3	--	--	.68*	--	.54*
compet4	--	--	.85*	--	.28*
affect1	--	--	--	.79*	.38*
affect2	--	--	--	.83*	.30*
affect3	--	--	--	.89*	.22*
affect4	--	--	--	.89*	.20*
Factor Correlations					
value	.88*	--			
competence	.59*	.51*	--		
affect	.61*	.62*	.78*	--	

Note: $N = 730$. Parameters estimates are completely standardized. * $p < .05$. Model fit: $\chi^2 = 373.61$ (129 *df*), TLI = .97, CFI = .97, RMSEA = .05.

Group Comparisons

The scores of items for each scale were averaged to obtain a scale score. The means and standard deviations for boys and girls in two cultural groups across four grades (Anglo-Australians and Asian-Australians) are presented in Table 3. The results showed that for each of the four motivation constructs, all the students tended to have a high mean score (all *Ms* > 2.5 on a 5-point scale). For the Anglo-Australian students, girls tended to score higher than boys in all four motivation constructs across all grades. For Asian-Australian students, gender differences are not so clear (Table 2). Furthermore, there is a general pattern showing that

Asian-Australians scored higher than Anglo-Australians for all factors. MANOVA was conducted using the four motivation factors as dependent variables (mastery, value, competence, and affect), and culture, gender, and grade as independent variables. The analysis found statistically significant effects of culture, but gender and grade differences seemed to be small for most of the variables.

Gender. Gender differences were not statistically significant for Mastery, Value, and Competence, Fs (1, 714) = 0.85, 3.54, and 0.50. For Affect, gender difference was statistically significant, $F(1, 714) = 4.89$, $p < .05$. However, the effect size was small ($\eta^2 = .01$), indicating that even though girls seemed to be higher in affect to school work, the difference may not be of practical significance in the school setting.

Grade. Grade differences were statistically significant for Value and Affect, Fs (3, 714) = 2.99 and 9.92 respectively, $p > .05$, but not for Mastery and Competence, Fs (3, 714) = 0.59 and 2.32 respectively, $p > .05$. However, despite statistical significance found in Value, the effect size was small ($\eta^2 = .01$), indicating that the difference may not be of practical significance in the school setting. In contrast, the effect size for Affect ($\eta^2 = .04$) may be worth attention. A follow-up oneway ANOVA with Scheffe range tests found that students in both 3rd and 4th grades had higher scores for Value than both 5th and 6th graders, F (3, 726) = 10.93, $p < .001$. This indicates that students' valuing of school may become weaker when they mature.

Culture. Cultural difference was statistically significant for Mastery, $F(1, 714) = 24.24$, $MSE = 0.52$, $p < .001$, $\eta^2 = .03$; Value, $F(1, 714) = 16.86$, $MSE = 0.45$, $p < .001$, $\eta^2 = .02$; Competence, $F(1, 714) = 33.34$, $MSE = 0.70$, $p < .001$, $\eta^2 = .04$; and Affect, $F(1, 714) = 118.24$, $MSE = 1.03$, $p < .001$, $\eta^2 = .14$. For all four variables, Asian-Australian students had higher scores than their Anglo-Australian peers. That is, the results showed that Asian-Australian students had higher mastery orientation, higher perceived value of schooling, higher sense of competence, and higher affect to schooling than their Anglo-Australian peers.

Gender x Grade interaction. The interaction between gender and grade was not statistically significant for any of the four variables, $F(3, 714) = 0.68, 1.51, 0.15$, and 0.72 for Mastery, Value, Competence, and Affect respectively, $p > .05$.

Gender x culture interaction. The interaction between gender and culture was found to be significant for all four variables, $Fs(1, 714) = 6.67, 7.96$, and 5.54, respectively for Mastery, Value, and Competence, $p < .05$, $\eta^2 = .01$; and $F(1, 714) = 12.89$ for Affect, $p < .001$, $\eta^2 = .02$. A comparison between boys and girls in the Anglo and Asian subsamples showed that for all four variables, Anglo girls scored higher than Anglo boys whereas Asian girls did not always score higher than Asian boys in these variables. That is, the advantage of girls found in the Anglo subsample did not exist in the Asian subsample.

Grade x culture interaction. The grade x culture interaction was found to be statistically significant for Competence, $F(3, 714) = 3.26$, $p < .001$, $\eta^2 = .01$. An inspection of the mean scores of Competence found that Anglo-Australian students tended to decline in their sense of competence to a greater extent than Asian-Australian students as they progressed to higher grade levels. The grade x culture interaction was also statistically significant for Affect, $F(3, 714) = 5.17$, $p < .001$, $\eta^2 = .02$. Again, decline in affect for the Anglo-Australian students seemed to be greater than for Asian-Australian students as they progressed to higher grade levels. The interaction effect was not significant for Mastery and Value, $Fs(3, 714) = 1.92$ and 0.46, respectively.

Table 2. Means and (Standard Deviations) by Group and ANOVA Results

Variable	Anglo-Australians (N = 446)								Asian-Australians (N = 284)							
	Year 3		Year 4		Year 5		Year 6		Year 3		Year 4		Year 5		Year 6	
	Boys	Girls	Boys	Girls	Boys	Girls	Boys	Girls	Boys	Girls	Boys	Girls	Boys	Girls	Boys	Girls
N	63	59	64	47	49	56	45	63	43	47	38	32	31	40	20	33
Mastery	4.23	4.57	4.24	4.43	4.29	4.37	4.26	4.43	4.64	4.31	4.68	4.74	4.81	4.62	4.57	4.66
	(0.79)	(0.70)	(1.01)	(0.79)	(0.82)	(0.77)	(0.77)	(0.73)	(0.48)	(0.74)	(0.61)	(0.47)	(0.31)	(0.58)	(0.74)	(0.38)
Value	4.15	4.49	4.29	4.61	4.30	4.57	4.48	4.52	4.71	4.30	4.66	4.33	4.67	4.69	4.62	4.64
	(0.84)	(0.71)	(1.02)	(0.52)	(0.82)	(0.58)	(0.67)	(0.47)	(0.54)	(0.78)	(0.52)	(0.29)	(0.69)	(0.43)	(0.52)	(0.46)
Competence	3.60	3.80	3.52	3.56	3.34	3.54	3.36	3.41	3.98	3.63	4.18	4.02	3.91	3.70	3.92	3.85
	(1.07)	(0.76)	(1.03)	(0.85)	(0.83)	(0.85)	(0.83)	(0.89)	(0.75)	(0.74)	(0.64)	(0.69)	(0.90)	(0.68)	(0.60)	(0.65)
Affect	3.30	4.16	3.42	3.56	2.65	3.32	2.98	3.12	4.21	3.96	4.49	4.54	4.19	4.06	4.00	3.91
	(1.18)	(0.94)	(1.31)	(1.14)	(1.09)	(1.09)	(1.17)	(0.94)	(0.91)	(0.96)	(0.65)	(0.59)	(0.97)	(0.84)	(0.86)	(0.89)

ANOVA Results	Gender		Grade		Culture		Ge x Gr		Ge x Cu		Gr x Cu		Ge x Gr x Cu		
	$F(1,714)$	η^2	$F(3,714)$	η^2	$F(1,714)$	η^2	$F(3,714)$	η^2	$F(1,714)$	η^2	$F(3,714)$	η^2	$F(3,714)$	η^2	MSE
Mastery	0.85	.00	0.59	.00	24.24**	.03	0.68	.00	6.67*	.01	1.92	.01	1.64	.01	0.52
Value	3.54	.01	2.99*	.01	16.86**	.02	1.51	.01	7.96*	.01	0.46	.00	2.62	.01	0.45
Competence	0.50	.00	2.32	.01	33.34**	.04	0.15	.00	5.54*	.01	3.26*	.01	0.39	.00	0.70
Affect	4.89*	.01	9.92**	.04	118.24**	.14	0.72	.00	12.89**	.02	5.71**	.02	2.49	.01	1.03

Note: *p<.05. **p<.001.

Gender x grade x culture interaction. The three-way interactions were not statistically significant for all four variables, $Fs(3, 714) = 1.64, 2.62, 0.39$, and $2.49, p > .05$. To sum up, more culture differences were found than gender differences with this sample. For Anglo-Australians, girls were found to score higher than boys in all four constructs in all grades. For Asian-Australians, boys scored higher in these constructs in 3rd grade but the advantage of boys disappeared after that.

DISCUSSION

In the present study, we sought to investigate the differences in motivation constructs between primary boys and girls of Australia. We also examined the interaction effects of gender, grade, and culture on the dependent variables. Before we examined these group differences on motivational constructs, we first established the validity of the measurement. It was found that the CFA model with four motivational constructs provided a reasonable fit to the data.

Gender Differences

For gender comparisons, hypothesis 1 seems to be supported. For the main effect of gender, no significant differences were found on three of the four motivational constructs (Mastery, Value, and Competence). The only variable that showed noteworthy gender differences was Affect, but even so, the effect size was small ($\eta^2 = .01$). This finding seems to be consistent with previous findings showing either no significant gender differences in motivation, or trivial gender differences that may not have significant practical implications (e.g., Crain, 1996; Graham et al., 2008; Kelly and Decker, 2009; Marsh et al., 2006; Mucherah and Yoder, 2008; Yeung, 2011; Yeung et. al., 2011).

Nevertheless, the consistent pattern of the gender x culture interaction effect on each of the four variables suggests that existing gender differences within the sample may have been masked by cultural characteristics. That is, gender differences may exist but have remained undetected because the gap favoring boys in one culture but favoring girls in another culture may have resulted in a seemingly equivalent average score overall. An inspection of the mean scores for Mastery (Table 2), for example, found that for Anglo-Australians, boys had consistently lower scores than girls (4.23 vs. 4.57 in 3rd grade, 4.24 vs. 4.43 in 4th grade, 4.29 vs. 4.37 in 5th grade, and 4.26 vs. 4.43 in Year 6). In contrast, the boys in the Asian-Australian group did not show a consistently lower score, and in fact boys were higher than girls in Mastery in 3rd grade (4.64 vs. 4.31) and in 5th grade (4.81 vs. 4.62). Hence, there was support for girls having a higher level of mastery goal orientation than boys (Midgley et al., 2001) but for the Anglo subsample only. For Value, the patterns were similar to Mastery. That is, girls in the Anglo group were consistently higher in their perceived value of schooling whereas the advantage of girls was not found in the Asian subsample.

For Competence, boys in the Asian subsample were found to have consistently higher scores than girls (3.98 vs. 3.63 in 3rd grade, 4.18 vs. 4.02 in 4th grade, 3.91 vs. 3.70 in 5th grade, and 3.92 vs. 3.85 in Year 6). This finding was consistent with previous research showing that boys had a higher sense of competence (Midgley et al., 2001). However, this pattern was not found in the Anglo subsample, in which the pattern of gender difference was not consistent at all.

In contrast, for students' affect to learning, there seems to be support for the phenomenon that girls are more positive than boys and show better interest in learning activities (Mucherah and Yoder, 2008). However, this supportive pattern is found only in the Anglo subsample and not in the Asian subsample.

Grade Differences

For grade differences, hypothesis 2 was supported only for the Affect variable ($\eta^2 = .04$). For the variable of Value, although the main effect of grade was statistically significant, the effect was too small to be of practical significance ($\eta^2 = .01$). For both Anglo and Asian subsamples, 3rd graders and 4th graders seemed to be a little higher in scores than 5th and 6th graders, but the differences were not great. Hence there was only weak support for a general decline in motivational constructs over time (e.g., Eccles et al. 1993; Wigfield and Eccles, 1994; Yeung and McInerney, 2005). Even for Affect in which a significant main effect of grade was found, an inspection of the means scores across grades found declines only after 4th grade.

Interestingly, the patterns across grades were quite consistent between boys and girls. This is reflected in the nonsignificant gender x grade interactions. Furthermore, the significant gender x culture interaction for Affect indicates that the decline tended to be faster for the Anglo subsample than the Asian subsample. A similar pattern was also observed for Competence, but the effect was small ($\eta^2 = .01$).

Cultural Differences

For cultural comparisons, hypothesis 3 was supported. For all four variables, Asian-Australian students reported significantly higher scores than their Anglo-Australian peers. That is, Asian-Australian students had higher mastery orientation, higher perceived value of schooling, higher sense of competence, and higher affect to schooling than their Anglo-Australian peers. The results are consistent with previous research suggesting that Asian students are more motivated to learn (e.g., Li, 2002).

Students tend to attach different meanings to education and learning depending on their cultural values and priorities. Asian students' perception of learning to acquire knowledge and to realize their long-term goals may have kept them motivated to learn. This attached relevance to learning for distal goals is often missing in non-Asian cultures (Shecter et al., 2011). It is important to note here that these Asian cultural characteristics seemed to exist despite the fact that these students were residing in Sydney, Australia, far from their Asian origins. This implies that the influence of cultural beliefs and values could have enduring effects on individuals starting from a very young age and are sustainable even after migrating to distant lands.

Implications

Asians live in a culture that highlights the social embeddedness of the individual. Conceptions of self are intertwined with concerns about others. This highlights the holistic manner with which Asians construe personal achievement. This could be why Asian-Australians in comparison to Anglo-Australians in this investigation are more motivated in relation to mastery, value, competence, and affect constructs. For educators and practitioners in a multilingual, multicultural society, it is important to understand these cultural characteristics. While most educators and researchers have focused on gender issues, cultural characteristics that frame gender stereotypes and beliefs are often neglected.

For grade differences, it was observed that not only did Anglo-Australians' sense of competence tend to decline faster with increasing grades than Asian-Australians, but their interest in school work also declined faster with increasing grades compared to Asians. As children mature, their self-perceptions may also change as they re-evaluate their competence. Students' perceptions of competence in school work tend to also become increasingly more domain specific (Marsh et al., 1999), and such perceptions tend to decline as they grow older. This may be due to the fact that children at a very young age may have unrealistic expectations which are higher than their actual ability and as children understand their performance outcomes more clearly, their beliefs about usefulness decrease and so does their interest (Wigfield and Eccles, 1992). Consequently in this investigation, motivation tends to decline with increasing age for both Anglo-Australians and Asian-Australians; however the decline in this investigation was greater for Anglo-Australian students.

One probable reason could be varying emphasis on the ability versus effort across cultures (Hau and Salili, 1991; Stevenson and Stigler, 1992; Yeung, 2005). Anglo students who tend to emphasize ability more may feel inadequate when they are unable to cope with more diversified curriculum and thus lose interest, whereas Asian-Australians who endorse effort continue to work hard and this keeps them motivated as compared to their Anglo peers.

This could be one reason for the comparatively faster decline in the constructs among Anglo-Australians than Asian-Australians. These results also imply that educators may need to devise ways to enhance the importance of effort to enhance Anglo students' motivation and persistence on tasks. As such, it seems useful for teachers and curriculum designers to effectively cater to the differential motivational needs of students from different cultures at different stages of schooling. In this sense, gender differences may become less prominent than cultural issues.

Nevertheless, considering gender differences for both cultures studied here, it was observed that Anglo-Australian girls were more motivated than Anglo-Australian boys whereas this advantage was not observed in the Asian subsample. Girls have been reported to be more motivated than boys in some previous studies (Mucherah and Yoder, 2008). The findings of our investigation are also partly consistent with the recent findings of Yeung et al. (2011) who reported that boys were lower in motivation and sense of competence than girls in primary schools.

However, this pattern favoring girls was found only in our Anglo-Australian subsample. That is, whereas Yeung et al. (2011) found that boys tended to be lower in motivation and competence beliefs in Singapore (an Asian context), the Asian boys in our Australian context did not seem to suffer from such lowered scores. Perhaps the Australian cultural context in having less rigidly defined masculine gender roles in comparison to Asian cultural contexts mitigates gender differences for Asian-Australians in particular. This explanation is consistent with the findings of Chiu and Chow (2010) who found that in more masculine countries (where there are more rigidly-defined gender roles favoring males), girls had lower reading achievement compared to girls in other countries. However, the lack of rigid gender role stereotypes among Anglo-Australians also does not inhibit the Anglo-Australian girls as they tend to be more motivated than Anglo-Australian boys. Hence differential cultural effects are apparent that are worthy of further research investigation.

Strengths and Limitations

This study adds to the literature an empirical examination of Anglo-Australian and Asian-Australian primary students' school motivation to explicate patterns of gender and age differences and similarities across cultures and grade levels in primary education. This study also has some limitations which need to be accounted for in interpreting the findings. Students sampled in this study were not fully representative of all cultural sub-groups in the Australian population. Hence it would be useful to examine additional cultural groups in the Australian population in future research to study gender and cultural differences in motivation across a variety of cultural groups.

Also, this study was based on cross-sectional data. Future studies would benefit from employing a longitudinal design to undertake a more nuanced analysis of developmental and cultural influences on motivation over time. Students' motivation patterns may also differ in different curriculum areas. Hence it would be useful to explore the influence of gender and age cross-culturally in relation to specific curriculum areas. There is also a need for research aiming to advance understandings of the complexities of personality and context in relation to motivation.

CONCLUSION

To conclude, the present study found that more cultural differences were found than gender differences. For Anglo-Australians, girls were found to display higher motivation scores than Anglo-Australian boys in all four motivation constructs measured in all grades considered. For Asian-Australians, boys displayed higher motivation scores compared to Asian-Australian girls in relation to all motivation constructs in third grade but thereafter the advantage of boys disappeared. The inconsistent gender patterns found in different grade levels and different cultures call for the consideration of background variables such as culture, grade level, and school setting when examining students' gender differences in achievement motivation. Since motivation has important influences on learning and is related to long-term goals, researchers and educators need to consider ways to optimize these constructs, particularly for Anglo-Australian boys in primary schools. Our findings have important implications for theory, research, and practice. Understanding and accounting for cultural influences on motivation would be useful when designing interventions to optimize the benefits of adaptive motivational orientations.

APPENDIX: VARIABLES USED IN THE STUDY

Factor/Example Items	Alpha
Mastery (6 items)	.90
I feel most successful in school when I really improve	
I feel most successful in school when I do my best work	
Value (4 items)	.75
What I learn at school will be useful one day	
Learning at school is important	
Competence (4 items)	.81
Work in all school subjects is easy for me	
I am good at all school subjects	
Affect (4 items)	.91
I enjoy doing work in all school subjects	
I look forward to all school subjects	

REFERENCES

Ames, C., and Archer, J. (1988). Achievement goals in the classroom: students' learning strategies and motivation processes. *Journal of Educational Psychology, 80,* 260–267.

Arens, A. K., Yeung, A. S., Craven, R. G., and Hasselhorn, M. (2011). The twofold multidimensionality of academic self-concept: Domain specificity and separation between competence and affect components. *Journal of Educational Psychology.* doi: 10.1037/a0025047.

Armitage, C. J. (2008). Cognitive and affective predictors of academic achievement in schoolchildren. *British Journal of Psychology, 99,* 57–74.

Bjornebekk, G. (2008). Positive affect and negative affect as modulators of cognition and motivation: The rediscovery of affect in achievement goal theory. *Scandinavian Journal of Educational Research, 52*, 153-170.

Blumenfeld, P., Pintrich, P., Meece, J., and Wessels, K. (1982). The formation and role of self perceptions of ability in elementary school classrooms. *Elementary School Journal, 82*, 401-420.

Bouffard, T., Marcoux, M. F., Vezeau, C., and Bordeleau, L. (2003). Changes in self perceptions of competence and intrinsic motivation among elementary school children. *British Journal of Educational Psychology, 73*, 171-186.

Browne, M. W., and Cudeck, R. (1993). Alternative ways of assessing model fit. In K. A. Bollen and J. S. Long (Eds.), *Testing structural equation models* (pp. 136-162). Newbury Park, CA: Sage.

Byrne, B. M. (1998). *Structural equation modeling with LISREL, PRELIS, and SIMPLIS: Basic concepts, applications, and programming.* Mahwah, NJ: Erlbaum.

Crain, R. (1996). The influence of age, race, and gender on child and adolescents' multidimensional self-concept. In B. Bracken (Ed.), *Handbook of self-concept: Developmental, social, and clinical considerations* (pp. 395–420). New York: Wiley.

Chiu, M. M., and Chow, B. W. Y. (2010). Culture, motivation and reading achievement, high school students in 41 countries. *Learning and Individual Differences, 20*, 579-592.

Craven, R. G., Marsh, H. W., and Burnett, P. C. (2003).Cracking the self-concept enhancement conundrum: A call and blueprint for the next generation of self-concept enhancement research. In H. W. Marsh, R. G. Craven and D. M. McInerney (Eds.), *International advances in self research: Speaking to the future* (pp.67-90). Greenwich, CT: Information Age.

Dekker, S., and Fischer, R. (2008). Cultural differences in academic motivation goals: A meta-analysis across 13 societies. *The Journal of Educational Research, 102*, 99-110.

Dweck, C. S., and Leggett, E. L. (1988). A social-cognitive approach to motivation and personality. *Psychological Review, 95*, 256–273.

Eccles, J. S. (1983). Attributional processes as mediators of sex differences in achievement. *Journal of Educational Equity and Leadership, 3*, 19-27.

Eccles, J. S., and Wigfield, A. (1995). In the mind of the achiever: The structure of adolescents' academic achievement related-beliefs and self-perceptions. *Personality and Social Psychology Bulletin, 21*, 215–225.

Eccles, J. S., Wigfield, A., Flanagan, C.A., Miller, C., Reuman, D. A., and Yee, D. (1989). Self-concepts, domain values, and self-esteem: Relations and changes at early adolescence. *Journal of Personality, 57*, 283-310.

Eccles, J. S., Wigfield, A., Harold, R., and Blumenfeld, P. (1993). Age and gender differences in children's achievement self-perceptions during the elementary school years. *Child Development, 64*, 830–847.

Elliot, A. J. (2005).A conceptual history of the achievement goal construct. In A. J. Elliot and C. S. Dweck (Eds.), *Handbook of competence and motivation* (pp. 5272). New York: Guilford.

Erez, A., and Isen, A. M. (2002). The influence of positive affect on the components of expectancy motivation. *Journal of Applied Psychology*, 87, 1055–1067.

Gottfried, A. E., Fleming, J. S., and Gottfried, A. W. (2001). Continuity of academic intrinsic motivation from childhood through late adolescence: A longitudinal study. *Journal of Educational Psychology, 93,* 3-13.

Graham, J., Tisher, R., Ainley, M., and Kennedy, G. (2008). Staying with the text: The contribution of gender, achievement orientations and interest to students' performance on a literacy task. *Educational Psychology, 28,* 757-776.

Grant, H., and Dweck, C.S. (2001). Cross-cultural response to failure: considering outcome attributions with different goals. In F. Salili, G. Ghiu, and Y. Hong (Eds.), *Student motivation: The culture and context of learning* (pp. 203–219). New York: Kluwer.

Gungoren, S., and Sungur, S. (2009). The effect of grade level on elementary school students' motivational beliefs in science. *The International Journal of Learning, 16,* 495-506.

Hau, K. T., and Salili, F. (1991). Structure and semantic differential placement of specific cases: Academic causal attributions by Chinese students in Hong Kong. *International Journal of Psychology, 26,* 175–193.

Hofstede, G. (1980). *Culture's consequences: International differences in work-related values.* Beverly Hills, CA: Sage.

Jacobs, J. E., Lanza, S., Osgood, D. W., Eccles, J. S., and Wigfield, A. (2002). Changes in children's self-competence and values: Gender and domain differences across grades one through twelve. *Child Development, 73,* 509–527.

Johnson, M., Crosnoe, R., and Elder, G. (2001) Student attachment and academic engagement: the role of ethnicity. *Sociology of Education, 74,* 318–340.

Kelly, M. J., and Decker, E. O. (2009). The current state of motivation to read among middle school students. *Reading Psychology, 30,* 466–485.

Kitayama, S. (2002). Culture and basic psychological processes—toward a system view of culture: comment on Oyserman et al. (2002). *Psychological Bulletin, 128,* 89–96.

Klapp Lekholm, A., and Cliffordson, C. (2009). Effects of student characteristics on grades in compulsory school. *Educational Research and Evaluation, 15,* 1–23.

Jöreskog, K. G., and Sörbom, D. (2005). *LISREL 8.72: Structural equation modeling with SIMPLIS command language.* Chicago, IL: Scientific Software International.

Lai, F. (2010). Are boys left behind? The evolution of the gender achievement gap in Beijing's middle schools. *Economics of Education Review, 29,* 383-399.

Lau, K. (2009). Grade differences in reading nnotivation among Hong Kong primary and secondary students. *British Journal of Educational Psychology, 79,* 713-733.

Li, J. (2002). Models of learning in different cultures. In J. Bempechat and J. G. Elliott (Eds.), *New directions in child and adolescent development, no.* 96: Achievement motivation in culture and context: Understanding children's learning experiences. San Francisco, CA: Jossey-Bass.

Lepper, M. R., Corpus J. H., and Iyengar, S. S. (2005). Intrinsic and extrinsic orientations in the classroom: Age differences and academic correlates. *Journal of Educational Psychology, 97,* 184–196.

Liem, G.A.D., Martin, A. J., Nair, E., Bernardo, A. B. I., and Prasetya, P. H. (2009). Cultural factors relevant to secondary school students in Australia, Singapore, the Philippines and Indonesia: Relative differences and congruencies. *Australian Journal of Guidance and Counselling ,19,* 161–178.

Linnenbrink-Garcia, L., Durik, A. M., Conley, A. M. M., Barron, K. E., Tauer, J. M., Karabenick, S. A., and Harackiewicz, J. M. (2010). Measuring situational interest in academic domains. *Educational and Psychological Measurement, 70*, 647-671.

Markus, H. R., and Kitayama, S. (1991). Culture and the self: Implications for cognition, emotion, and motivation. *Psychological Review, 98*, 224-253.

Marsh, H. W. (1989). Age and sex effects in multiple dimensions of self-concept: Preadolescence to early adulthood. *Journal of Educational Psychology, 81*, 417-430.

Marsh, H. W., Balla, J. R., and Hau, K. T. (1996). An evaluation of incremental fit indices: A clarification of mathematical and empirical processes. In G. A. Marcoulides, and R. E. Schumacker (Eds.), *Advanced structural equation modeling techniques* (pp. 315-353). Hillsdale, NJ: Erlbaum.

Marsh, H. W., Balla, J. R., and McDonald, R. P. (1988). Goodness-of-fit indices in confirmatory factor analyses: The effect of sample size. *Psychological Bulletin, 103*, 391-410.

Marsh, H. W., and Craven, R. G. (2006). Reciprocal effects of self-concept and performance from a multidimensional perspective: Beyond seductive pleasure and unidimensional perspectives. *Perspectives on Psychological Science, 1*, 133-163.

Marsh, H. W., Craven, R. G., and Debus, R. (1999). Separation of competency and affect components of multiple dimensions of academic self-concept: A developmental perspective. *Merrill-Palmer Quarterly, 45,* 567-601.

Marsh, H. W., Craven, R., Hinkley, J. W., and Debus, R. L. (2003). Evaluation of the big two factor theory of motivation orientation: An evaluation of jingle-jingle fallacies. *Multivariate Behavioral Research, 38*, 189-224.

Marsh, H. W., Tracey, D. K., and Craven, R. G. (2006). Multidimensional self-concept structure for preadolescents with mild intellectual disabilities: A hybrid multigroup-MIMIC approach to factorial invariance and latent mean differences. *Educational and Psychological Measurement, 66*, 795–818.

Marsh, H. W., and Yeung, A. S. (1998). Longitudinal structural equation models of academic self-concept and achievement: Gender differences in the development of math and English constructs. *American Educational Research Journal, 35*, 705-738.

Martin, A. J. (2003a). Boys and motivation. *Australian Educational Researcher, 30*, 43-65.

Martin, A. J. (2003b). The Student Motivation Scale: Further testing of an instrument that measures school students' motivation. *Australian Journal of Education, 47,* 88-106.

Martin, A. J. (2007). Examining a multidimensional model of student motivation and engagement using a construct validation approach. *British Journal of Educational Psychology, 77*, 413-440.

McInerney, D. M., and Ali, J. (2006) Multidimensional and hierarchical assessment of school motivation: Cross-cultural validation. *Educational Psychology, 26*, 717-734.

McInerney, D. M., Dowson, M., and Yeung, A. S. (2005). Facilitating conditions for school motivation: Construct validity and applicability. *Educational and Psychological Measurement, 65,* 1046.

McInerney, D. M., Yeung, A. S., and McInerney, V. (2001). Cross-cultural validation of the Inventory of School Motivation (ISM): Motivation orientations of Navajo and Anglo students. *Journal of Applied Measurement, 2,* 135-153.

Meece, J. L., Blumenfeld, P. C., and Hoyle, R. H. (1988). Students' goal orientations and cognitive engagement in classroom activities. *Journal of Educational Psychology, 80,* 514–523.

Meece, J. L., Glienke, B. B., and Burg, S. (2006). Gender and motivation. *Journal of School Psychology, 44,* 351-373.

Meece, J. L., and Miller, S. D. (2001). A longitudinal analysis of elementary school students' achievement goals in literacy activities. *Contemporary Educational Psychology, 26,* 454–480.

Meece, J. L., Parsons, J. E., Kaczala, C. M., Goff, S. B., and Futterman, R. (1982). Sex differences in math achievement: Toward a model of academic choice. *Psychological Bulletin, 91,* 324–348.

Metallidou, P., and Vlachou, A. (2007). Motivational beliefs, cognitive engagement, and achievement in language and mathematics in elementary school children. *International Journal of Psychology, 42,* 2-15.

Midgley, C., Kaplan, A., and Middleton, M. (2001). Performance-approach goals: Good for what, for whom, under what circumstances, and at what cost? *Journal of Educational Psychology, 93,* 77-86.

Midgley, C., Maehr, M. L., Hruda, L. Z., Anderman, E., Anderman, L., Freeman, K. E., Gheen, M., Kaplan, A., Kumar, R., Middleton, M. J., Nelson, J., Roeser, R., and Urdan, T. (2000). *Manual for the Patterns of Adaptive Learning Scales (PALS).* Ann Arbor, MI: University of Michigan.

Mucherah, W., and Yoder, A. (2008). Motivation for reading and middle school students' performance on standardized testing in reading. *Reading Psychology, 29,* 214–235.

Muthén, L. K., and Muthén, B. O. (1998 –2010). *Mplus user's guide* (5th ed.). Los Angeles, CA: Muthén and Muthén.

Nagy, G., Watt, H. M. G., Eccles, J. S., Trautwein, U., Lüdtke, O., and Baumert, J. (2010). The development of students' mathematics self-concept in relation to gender: Different countries, different trajectories? *Journal of Research on Adolescence, 20,* 482-506.

Nicholls, J. G. (1984). Achievement motivation: Conceptions of ability, subjective experience, task choice, and performance. *Psychological Review, 91,* 328-346.

Nicholls, J. G. (1989). *The competitive ethos and democratic education.* Cambridge, MA: Harvard.

Pajares, F., and Schunk, D.H. (2002). Self and self-belief in psychology and education: A historical perspective. In J. Aronson (Ed.), *Improving academic achievement: Impact of psychological factors on education* (pp. 3–21). San Diego, CA: Academic Press.

Pedhazur, E. J., and Schmelkin, L. P. (1991). *Measurement, design, and analysis: An integrated approach.* Hillsdale, NJ: Erlbaum.

Pintrich, P. R., and De Groot, E. (1990). Motivational and self-regulated components of classroom academic performance. *Journal of Educational Psychology, 82,* 33-40.

Pintrich, P. R., and Schunk, D. H. (2002). *Motivation in education: Theory, research, and applications.* Upper Saddle River, NJ: Merrill Prentice-Hall.

Pintrich, P R., Smith, D. A. E., Garcia, T., and McKeachie, W. J. (1991). *A manual for the use of the Motivated Strategies for Learning Questionnaire (MSLQ).* Ann Arbor, MI: National Center for Research to Improve Postsecondary Teaching and Learning.

Robins, R. W., and Pals, J. L. (2002). Implicit self-theories in the academic domain: Implications for goal orientation, attributions, affect, and self-esteem change. *Self and Identity, 1,* 313–336.

Ryan, R., and Deci, E. (2000). Self-determination theory and the facilitation of intrinsic motivation, social development, and well-being. *American Psychologist, 55,* 68-78.

Ryan, A. M., and Pintrich, P. R. (1998). Achievement and social motivational influences on help seeking in the classroom. In S. A. Karabenick (Ed.), *Strategic help seeking: Implications for learning and teaching* (pp. 117-139). Mahwah, NJ: Erlbaum.

Shechter, O. G., Durik, A. M., Miyamoto, Y., and Harackiewicz, J. M. (2011).The role of utility value in achievement behavior: The importance of culture. *Personality and Social Psychology Bulletin, 37,* 303–317.

Singh, K., Granville, M., and Dika, S. (2002) Mathematics and science achievement: effects of motivation, interest, and academic engagement, *The Journal of Educational Research, 95,* 323–332.

Smith, M., Duda, J., Allen, J., and Hall, H. (2002). Contemporary measures of approach and avoidance orientations: Similarities and differences. *British Journal of Educational Psychology, 72,* 155-190.

Sommer, K., and Baumeister, R. F. (2002). Self-evaluation, persistence, and performance following implicit rejection: The role of trait self-esteem. *Personality and Social Psychology Bulletin, 28,* 926–938.

Stevenson, H. W., and Stigler, J. W. (1992). *The learning gap: Why our schools are failing and what we can learn from Japanese and Chinese education.* New York: Simon andSchuster.

Trautwein, U., and Lüdtke, O. (2009). Predicting homework motivation and homework effort in six school subjects: The role of person and family characteristics, classroom factors, and school track. *Learning and Instruction, 19,* 243-258.

Triandis, H. C. (1994). *Culture and social behavior.* New York: McGraw-Hill.

Usher, E. L., and Pajares, F. (2008). Self-efficacy for self-regulated learning. A validation study. *Educational and Psychological Measurement, 68,* 443–463.

Van Damme, J., De Fraine, B., Van Landeghem, G., Opdenakker, M-C., and Onghena, P. (2010). A new study on educational effectiveness in secondary schools in Flanders: An introduction. *School Effectiveness and School Improvement, 13,* 383-397.

Watt, H. M. G. (2008). A latent growth curve modeling approach using an accelerated longitudinal design: The ontogeny of boys' and girls' talent perceptions and intrinsic values through adolescence. *Educational Research and Evaluation, 14,* 287–304.

Wentzel, K. R. (1993). Motivation and achievement in early adolescence : The role of multiple classroom goals. *Journal of Early Adolescence, 13,* 4-20.

Wigfield, A. (1994). Expectancy-value theory of achievement motivation: A developmental perspective. *Educational Psychological Review, 6,* 49–78.

Wigfield, A., and Eccles, J. S. (1994). Children's competence beliefs, achievement values, and general self esteem change across elementary and middle school. *Journal of Early Adolescence, 14,* 107–138.

Wigfield, A., and Eccles, J. S. (2000). Expectancy-value theory of motivation. *Contemporary Educational Psychology, 25,* 68-81.

Wigfield, A., Eccles, J. S., MacIver, D., Reuman, D. A., and Midgley, C. (1991). Transitions during early adolescence: Changes in children's domain specific self-perceptions and general self-esteem across the transition to junior high school. *Developmental Psychology, 27*, 552–565.

Wigfield, A., Eccles, J. S., and Rodriguez, D. (1998). The development of children's motivation in school contexts. *Review of Research in Education, 23*, 73-118.

Yeung, A. S. (2005). Reconsidering the measurement of student self-concept: Use and misuse in a Chinese context. In H. W. Marsh (Ed.), *The new frontiers of self research* (pp. 233–257). Sydney: Information Age.

Yeung, A. S. (2011). Student self-concept and effort: gender and grade differences. *Educational Psychology, 31*, 749-772.

Yeung, A. S., Chow, A. P. Y., Chow, P. C. W., Luk, F., and Wong, E. K. P. (2004). Academic self-concept of gifted students: When the big fish becomes small. *Gifted and Talented International, 19*, 91–97.

Yeung, A. S., Lau, S., and Nie, Y. (2011). Primary and secondary students' motivation in learning English: Grade and gender differences. *Contemporary Educational Psychology, 36*, 246-256.

Yeung, A. S., and McInerney, D. M. (2005). Students' school motivation and aspiration over high school years. *Educational Psychology, 25*, 537-554.

In: Psychology of Gender Differences
Editor: Sarah P. McGeown

ISBN: 978-1-62081-391-1
© 2012 Nova Science Publishers, Inc.

Chapter 4

Exploring Sex Differences in Primary School Children's Preference for Group Work

Paula Ferrie, Sarah Lamswood and Sarah P. McGeown*
Psychology Department, University of Hull, Hull, UK

Abstract

The present study investigated sex differences in children's preference for group work activities and also examined whether different characteristics in boys and girls make them more inclined to work in groups.

In total, three hundred and ninety eight children (aged 8 to 11) from four primary schools participated. The study focused on three different aspects of group work; children's enjoyment of group work, their level of participation in group work activities and their perceived benefits of group work.

Children also completed assessments of reading skill and personality. Whilst girls reported higher levels of participation in classroom group activities, there were no sex differences in enjoyment or benefits. However differences were found between boys and girls in terms of the characteristics associated with group work activities. Implications for the primary school classroom are discussed.

Introduction

Group Work

Group work activities within the classroom play an important part in the daily school life and learning of primary school pupils (Cohen, 1994). Research suggests that when pupils are given help and support to use group work effectively, this can lead to improved academic and social outcomes (Wang, Haertel, and Walberg, 1994). Engagement in group work activities

---

*E-mail: S.P.McGeown@hull.ac.uk.

starts from a very young age, and research suggests that from at least aged 6 to 7, children can begin to engage in and benefit from collaborative interaction. Whilst younger children do engage in social learning through co-ordination and cooperation they also learn via imitation and instructed learning (Baines, Blatchford and Kutnick, 2003). Group work is utilised in classrooms to help teach curriculum subjects and carry out project work. It teaches children not only how to communicate with their peers, but also gives them the skills they will need in the wider society once they have left the education system, such as active listening, turn taking and sharing ideas, amongst many more (Bains et al., 2003). In recent years, researchers have been interested in how group work influences the dynamics of the classroom, interaction between pupils, and the way in which teachers plan and deliver their lessons (Blatchford, Kutnick, Baines and Galton, 2003). Researchers have also started to investigate the benefits of group work on children's learning and how to maximise children's academic and social potential through the use of group work and cooperative learning (Blatchford et al., 2003). When children work cooperatively together, they learn to give and receive help, share ideas, listen to other students' perspectives and seek new ways to clarify differences and resolve problems. This process may result in students performing higher academically and being more motivated to achieve than if they worked alone (Johnson and Johnson, 1994). Although many studies have reported the benefits of using co-operative learning as a teaching strategy, few have reported on what actually happens in groups that facilitates learning; fewer still have reported on pupils' perceptions of their cooperative learning experiences. Understanding what happens as students work in small groups and how they perceive their small-group learning experiences is critical to understanding the processes involved in cooperative learning (Gillies, 2003). Research by Kutnick, Blatchford and Baines (2002) examined five core themes relating to grouping and pupil experiences in groups: group size, group composition (i.e., ability and sex), learning task, within group interaction and adult presence. The results suggested that teachers may not think strategically about the size and composition of groups in relation to the tasks assigned. In addition, it was suggested that teachers may not be comfortable or supportive of group work and that pupils may not be confident in their ability to interact with others. Other research suggests that although teachers often organise the classroom in a way that would be conducive to group work (i.e., pupils seated in a group work structure), many pupils are still instructed to work alone on individuated tasks (Bennett and Dunne, 1992). Webb and Palincsar (1996) argued that in many classroom settings, pupils are actively discouraged from interacting with their classmates because of talking when they should not be and generally being off task, and so they fail to develop skills that will help them behave in ways that are productive. Indeed, research suggests that teachers have doubts about group work in the classroom, that they find group work disruptive and not conducive to learning (Cohen and Intilli, 1981) and too time consuming to implement (Plummer and Dudley, 1993). Therefore whilst some argue that classroom group work is beneficial, groups need to be created and managed appropriately to be effective and conducive to children's learning and development.

Sex Differences

Sex differences within primary school education are of increasing concern, with boys, in general, underachieving compared to girls (Department for Education, 2011). This has led to growing concern regarding boys' underachievement and efforts made to raise boys' attainment (Department for Education and Skills, 2005). In addition to differences in attainment, sex differences in school motivation and attitudes to school are often found (Gentry, Gable and Rizza, 2002; Logan and Johnston, 2009), although sex differences in attitudes and motivation vary across different curriculum subjects. For example, whilst girls report higher value in reading and music, boys report higher value in sport (Eccles, Wigfield, Harold and Blumenfeld, 1993). In a large scale study of pupils in Grade 3 – Grade 8, Gentry, et al. (2002) investigated sex differences in levels of interest, challenge, choice and enjoyment in classroom activities. Gentry et al. (2002) found that girls, on average, rated their classroom activities as more enjoyable, but no sex differences were found in levels of challenge or choice; sex differences in levels of interest were small and less consistent than those found in enjoyment. Therefore in order to reduce sex differences in educational attainment and school enjoyment, it is important to identify the type of learning environment that both boys and girls enjoy, such as the use of group work activities within the classroom.

Previous research by Logan (2009) examined sex differences in children's preferred learning environment (whether working alone, in a group, or as a whole class), examining both school work activities and reading activities. Compared to boys, girls reported a greater preference to read alone and work alone in class. Boys, on the other hand, reported a preference to work in groups or as a whole class and to also carry out reading activities within groups or as a whole class. However, these differences were not significant, but rather represented trends in terms of preference.

In order for groups to work effectively together, the group composition (i.e., mix of pupils of different sexes, ability etc) needs to be considered. Webb (1984) found that both sex and ability differences within a group influences group interactions and learning. Webb (1984) found that in groups in which sex and ability were balanced, boys and girls had similar interaction patterns. However, in sex-imbalanced groups, girls' experiences were not particularly beneficial; they tended to be ignored in majority male groups. In addition, whilst boys received information from both boys and girls within their group, girls were less likely to receive explanations from boys. Indeed, overall girls were generally more responsive to requests for help than boys were. In addition, girls were more responsive to requests regardless of sex, whereas boys responded more to other boys rather than girls (particularly in sex-imbalanced groups with only one girl). Interestingly, despite boys and girls being of similar ability, in both majority-male and majority-female groups, boys obtained higher learning outcomes than girls. This suggests greater benefits to boys from working in groups. In a similar study investigating sex composition of groups, Underwood, McCaffrey and Underwood (1990) studied pairs of primary school aged pupils on a computer task, in which children received no instruction on how to work together. The results illustrated that same-sex pairs were more productive than mixed-sex pairs; same-sex pairs were found to work by discussion and agreement, with each member of the pair contributing, whilst mixed-sex pairs tended not to work by discussion, but rather divided the task between them. Kutnick and Kingston (2005) found that girls working in friendship pairs performed at a higher cognitive level than girls working in acquaintance pairs, whereas the reverse was true for boys; boys worked better when working with an acquaintance than with a friend.

More recently, Pryor (1995) investigated sex differences in group work with computers, as he suggested that boys are more likely to use and be confident in using computers. His study found that girls are more likely to ask boys for help when it comes to questions about computers. Interestingly, this study also demonstrated that personality characteristics and ability were important when working in groups. Girls who were equally assertive and had equal ability were able to work together whereas boys of equal ability and assertiveness were not. Finally, Hallam, Ireson and Davies (2004) found that teachers were more likely to create mixed sex groups to promote more conscientious work and keep boys on task; girls were regarded as a calming influence on boys that would ensure higher levels of group effectiveness.

Taken together, these studies illustrate differences in how boys and girls work in groups and the benefits they gain from group work. These differences may be due, in part, to differences between boys and girls in dominant personality characteristics. Whilst girls are more likely to identify with more feminine characteristics such as compassion or warmth, boys are more likely to identify with masculine traits such as competitiveness or dominance (Boldizar, 1991; McGeown, Goodwin, Henderson and Wright, 2011) which may influence the way in which they engage in groups.

Study Aims

The focus of the current study was to examine sex differences in children's engagement in group work activities in the primary school classroom. As group work forms a relatively large component of children's learning activities, it is important to identify whether there are sex differences in the extent to which boys and girls enjoy group work, the extent to which they participate in group work and also the benefits they perceive from working in groups within the classroom. In addition, the study also focused on the characteristics (i.e., age, ability and personality) of boys and girls that may make them more inclined to work in groups.

It was predicted that girls would report greater participation in group work activities but that boys would report greater benefits of group work; no sex differences were predicted with regard to enjoyment. Finally, it was predicted that the characteristics (i.e., ability, age and personality) associated with engagement in group work activities would be similar for boys and girls.

METHOD

Participants

In total, three hundred and ninety eight children; 191 male (48%) and 207 females (52%) with an average age of 9 years and 11 months (1.15 SD) took part in this study. Children were all primary school aged and were in Year 3 (83 pupils; Mage = 8 years 3 months, .31 SD), Year 4 (87 pupils; Mage = 9 years 3 months, .28 SD), Year 5 (104 pupils; Mage = 10 years 2 months, .30 SD) or Year 6 (124 pupils; Mage = 11 years 3 months, .30 SD). Age was requested at the time of testing to examine age related changes in boys' and girls' preference for group work. Children were from four primary schools in England.

Materials

Educational Attainment: Reading Assessment

A standardised assessment of reading skill (Group Reading Test II; Macmillan Test Unit, 2000) was used as a measure of educational attainment as the majority of curriculum subjects within primary schools rely, to a large extent, on reading skill. The Group Reading Test II (age 6 - 14) is a group-administered test measuring reading comprehension.

In accordance with manual guidelines, children in Year 3 and 4 completed Form A or B and children in Year 5 or 6 completed Form C or D. This assessment measures reading comprehension via sentence completion (e.g. "The ___ was filled with hay" Options: play, idea, barn, horse, table). To prevent copying, Forms A and B or C and D were alternately given based on where the children were seated. The examiner read through the practice items with the children beforehand to ensure they understood the test. Children then worked independently on the assessment, with no assistance from the teacher or examiner. No time limit was imposed for completion of the 45 item test. Standardised scores were used in the analysis.

Group Questionnaire

This was a 15 item test that examined how children felt about group work at school. Three different dimensions of group work were examined; enjoyment of group work (i.e., the extent to which children enjoy working in groups: Q1, 2, 8, 13 and 15), participation in group work (i.e., the extent to which children take part in group work activities: Q3, 9, 10, 11, 14) and benefits of group work (i.e., the benefits children feel they gain from working in groups: Q4, 5, 6, 7, 12).

See Appendix for this questionnaire. Cronbach's alpha was used to evaluate internal consistency which was relatively high within each dimension; enjoyment (α = .81), participation (α = .67) and benefits (α = .64). Children completed the questionnaire by agreeing or disagreeing with each of the statements (e.g., "I enjoy group work) using a 5 point Likert scale (1 = Not at all like me, 2 = Not like me, 3 = A bit like me, 4 = A lot like me, 5 = Very much like me). Raw scores were used in the analysis.

Personality Questionnaire

Five Factor Personality Inventory - Children (McGhee, Ehrler and Buckhalt, 2007)

The FFPI-C consists of five subscales that correspond to the Big 5 personality factors (agreeableness, extraversion, openness to experience, conscientiousness, neuroticism/ emotional regulation). In this study, only three of these sub-scales were used: agreeableness, openness to experience and conscientiousness.

Agreeableness includes traits such as trustworthiness, straightforwardness, altruism, compliance, modesty and tendermindedness. Openness to experience includes imagination, interest in aesthetics, intellectual curiosity, and openness to feelings, actions, and other values.

Finally, conscientiousness includes sensibleness, organisation, moral obligation, achievement striving, self-discipline and carefulness. These personality traits were believed to be most closely related to children's attainment and it was felt that a shortened version of the questionnaire would be more appropriate for the age group being studied; by removing two subscales the length of the questionnaire was reduced from 75 items to 45 items. Each item consisted of a target statement and two opposing anchor statements.

All items were read aloud by the experimenter and the children were required to choose the anchor statement that mostly closely represented their opinion. This questionnaire only has standardisation norms for children in Year 5 and over, therefore only children in Year 5 and 6 completed this questionnaire and were included in the analysis using personality characteristics. Standardised scores were used in the analysis.

Procedure

All assessments were carried out within the children's classroom with the teacher present. The testing session took approximately 40 minutes for children in Year 3 and 4 and 1 hour for children in Year 5 and 6 (as these children also completed the personality assessment). Children completed the assessments in the following order: group questionnaire, reading assessment, personality assessment.

RESULTS

Initially sex differences were examined in age, reading attainment, personality and group constructs. There were no sex differences in age; $F(1, 391) = .26, p > .05$, reading attainment; $F(1, 391) = 1.62, p > .05$, enjoyment of group work; $F(1, 391) = .26, p > .05$ or perceived benefits of group work; $F(1, 391) = .39, p > .05$. However girls reported significantly higher levels of participation in group work; $F(1, 391) = 4.71, p < .05$ ($\eta_p^2 = .01$), but this difference was very small. In addition, there were no sex differences in any personality traits; agreeableness; $F(1, 391) = 1.56, p > .05$; openness to experience; $F(1, 391) = .31, p > .05$ or consciousness; $F(1, 391) = 3.40, p > .05$. See Table 1 for means and standard deviations.

Table 1. Sex differences in age, attainment, group work and personality

	Male	Female
Age	9.92 (1.16)	9.94 (1.14)
Reading Attainment	94.08 (10.82)	95.48 (11.52)
Group (enjoy)	17.32 (5.42)	17.58 (4.84)
Group (participation)	18.78 (3.96)	19.62 (3.67)
Group (benefit)	17.05 (4.21)	17.32 (4.27)
Personality (agreeableness)	98.23 (14.45)	100.57 (12.80)
Personality (openness to experience)	99.45 (15.27)	100.52 (12.33)
Personality (conscientiousness)	101.12 (13.66)	104.22 (10.72)

Note: N = 393 for age, attainment and group, N = 210 for personality.

Correlations were carried out to examine the strength of association between age, ability, personality characteristics and each aspect of group work (enjoy, participate, benefit); separate analyses were carried out for boys and girls. See Table 2.

Whilst ability did not correlate with personality or group work characteristics in boys, among girls, ability was significantly correlated with the personality trait of conscientiousness and negatively correlated with enjoyment of group work and benefits of group work (those girls with higher ability were more likely to report enjoying group work less and perceived less benefits of group work). With regard to age, girls' age was also inversely associated with their enjoyment of work, whilst boys' age was unrelated to any group work aspects.

For both boys and girls, personality characteristics were only associated with group participation, not benefits or enjoyment. For boys, the following aspects of personality were associated with reported participation in group activities; openness to experience and conscientiousness. For girls, only agreeableness was associated with group participation.

Table 2. Correlations examining association between child characteristics and group work (split for males/females)

	1	2	3	4	5	6	7	8
1	---	-.01	-.15	-.01	-.05	-.14	-.08	-.14
2	-.03	---	-.27**	-.09	-.19	.04	-.01	.09
3	.03	-.15	---	.45**	.66**	.01	.15	.03
4	.01	-.25**	.29**	---	.59**	.04	.27**	.19
5	.30**	-.15	.33**	.44**	---	.08	.26*	.14
6	-.30**	-.23**	.14	.07	-.10	---	.66**	.68**
7	-.06	-.13	.23*	.12	.04	.56**	---	.68**
8	-.22**	-.10	.13	-.05	-.17	.65**	.62**	---

Note: 1 = Ability, 2 = Age, 3 = Personality (agreeableness), 4 = Personality (openness to experience), 5 = Personality (conscientiousness), 6 = Group (enjoyment), 7 = Group (participation), 8 = Group (benefits). Upper right quadrant represents scores for males and lower left quadrant represents, scores for females. N (boys) = 189, N (girls) = 207 for age, attainment and group, N (boys) = 106, N (girls) = 117 for personality. * $p < .01$, ** $p < .05$.

Following this, analysis was carried out with the older children to examine the extent to which age, attainment and personality traits predicted enjoyment of, participation in and perceived benefits of group work. Separate analyses were carried out for males and females.

There were similarities in the factors predicting children's enjoyment in, participation in and perceived benefits of group work. For both males and females, children's ability (i.e., reading skill) was the only significant predictor of the extent to which children enjoyed working in groups (age and personality predicted no variance).

For males and females, the lower the child's ability, the more they enjoyed working in groups. The same was also true of perceived benefits of group work; both boys and girls ability alone predicted variance in their perceived benefits; those with lower ability perceiving greater benefits of working in groups.

Finally, the groups differed slightly in the extent to which different factors predicted group participation; for boys, openness to experience predicted variation in boys' group participation, for girls, no personality traits were significant predictors.

Table 3. Regression analyses examining sex differences in the factors predicting group enjoyment, participation and benefits

	R^2	Final β		R^2	Final β
Male			*Female*		
Group enjoyment					
Age	.000	.028		.028	-.143
Ability	.028	-.177*		.096	-.258*
Agreeableness		-.036			.074
Openness to experience		.099			.105
Conscientiousness	.043	.055		.114	-.023
Group participation					
Age	.005	-.012		.007	-.043
Ability	.010	.059		.008	-.018
Agreeableness		.046			.167
Openness to experience		.200*			.166
Conscientiousness	.098	.102		.073	-.029
Group benefits					
Age	.003	-.040		.010	-.085
Ability	.039	-.198*		.051	-.175*
Agreeableness		-.021			.121
Openness to experience		.127			.079
Conscientiousness	.056	.018		.068	-.124

Note: N (boys) = 106, N (girls) = 117. ** $p < .05$.

DISCUSSION

Whilst girls reported greater participation in group work activities within the classroom, this difference was very small and no sex differences were found in enjoyment or benefits of group work activities. Whilst girls' ability was significantly related to their reported enjoyment and benefits of group work, boys' ability was unrelated to all aspects of group work. In addition, girls' age was negatively associated with their enjoyment of group work, whilst boys' age was unrelated to all group work aspects. Interestingly, personality characteristics were only associated with children's participation in group work activities; for boys, both openness to experience and conscientiousness were associated with participation in group activities, whereas for girls, agreeableness was associated. Finally, when examining the skills best predicting group work, ability emerged as the best predictor of both boys and girls enjoyment and benefits of group work (being negatively related), whereas personality characteristics were the strongest predictors of participation in group work (for boys, openness to experience was a significant predictor).

In the present study, no sex differences were found in the personality characteristics of conscientiousness, agreeableness or openness to experience. This is consistent, to some extent, with previous research examining sex differences in personality. For example, in a meta-analysis reviewing sex differences in personality, Feingold (1994) found that the presence of sex differences in personality among children differed across studies, therefore there is no strong evidence of consistent sex differences in personality. In addition, no sex differences in ability (reading skill) or age were found, therefore any differences between males and females in terms of group work could not be attributed to differences in ability or age.

In the current study, girls' ability was negatively associated with their enjoyment and perceived benefits of group work; boys showed no significant association between their ability and their preference for group work. It is important that teachers take into account the level of ability among group members so that groups can work effectively. This appears to be particular important for girls, as more able girls are less likely to enjoy working in groups and perceive less benefits of group work. Previous research has examined the influence of ability (mixed versus same ability) on group effectiveness (e.g., Ireson, Hallam and Plewis, 2001) but has not examined the role of sex.

In addition, whilst girls' enjoyment of group work significantly decreased with age, so did boys (although this trend was not significant). Teachers should take into account the fact that as children mature and progress through school, they may be less inclined to want to work in groups, but rather work independently and demonstrate their ability through their own work. Alternatively, given concern regarding the effectiveness of groups (Cohen and Intilli, 1981; Kutnick et al., 2002; Plummer and Dudley, 1993) it may be that older children have had more negative or ineffective experiences when working in groups and therefore rate their enjoyment of group work lower.

Interestingly, whilst ability predicted enjoyment and perceived benefits of group work for both boys and girls, personality characteristics were a better predictor of pupils' participation in groups. For boys, being open to experiences (i.e., imaginative, intellectually curious, open to feelings, actions and other values) was associated with greater reported participation in groups. For girls, whilst no personality characteristics were significant predictors, agreeableness and openness to experiences were the strongest predictors. This suggests some similarities between boys and girls in the traits that predict their reported levels of group participation.

The current study focused on the specific child characteristics that may make boys and girls more or less inclined to work in groups. However, the group task is also going to influence how effective a group is. For example, Gillies (2003) found that group activities are more effective when they are well planned and have a good structure, with clear learning objectives and outcomes; pupils in structured groups are more likely to be co-operative and are more likely to give verbal help and assistance to each other in the group. Therefore a consideration of how boys and girls perform in both structured and less structured groups would be of interest, considering that both likely feature within a typical primary school classroom.

Further Research

Future research examining boys' and girls' enjoyment, participation and perceived benefits of group work as they work in groups of different composition would be of interest. For example, Webb (1984) suggests that gender balance/imbalance within a group can influence boys' and girls' behaviour patterns. In the current study this was not assessed.

However, up to date research investigating this is necessary as this may influence children's reported levels of preference for group work.

Furthermore, it would be interesting to examine whether the pattern of results found in this study would be similar across a range of different academic subjects. In the current study, no subject was specified when pupils were asked about their enjoyment, participation or perceived benefits of group work, however it may be that boys' and girls' perceptions of group work changes based on the specific subject. There is strong evidence to suggest sex differences in boys' and girls' motivation and competency beliefs for specific academic subjects (e.g., Eccles et al., 1993). In addition, previous research has considered academic subject when considering optimal group composition with regard to sex (e.g., Scanlon, 2000). It may be that these differences are also found in the type of learning environment (i.e., group versus individual) that boys and girls would prefer to work in.

In the current study, only three of the Big 5 personality traits were included; those that were included were those that are most commonly associated with academic attainment (Poropat, 2009; Laidra et al., 2007). However, it is likely that neuroticism (also known as emotional regulation), which includes traits such as anxiety, angry-hostility, depression, self-consciousness, impulsiveness and vulnerability and also extraversion, which includes traits such as warmth, gregariousness, assertiveness, excitement-seeking, and positive emotions such as optimism, would also be associated with pupils' engagement in group work activities. Future research should take into account a wider range of personality characteristics.

ACKNOWLEDGMENTS

The authors would like to thank the children and teachers for participating in this project. The project was funded, in part, by a Nuffield Foundation Undergraduate Research Bursary awarded to Sarah P McGeown and Sarah Lamswood.

APPENDIX: GROUP WORK QUESTIONNAIRE

Enjoyment of group work:
Q1. I enjoy group work
Q2. I prefer working in a group than alone
Q8. I think working in a group is fun
Q13. I would like to spend more time doing group work in class
Q15. I like group work better than most other things we do in class.

Participation in group work:
Q3. I ask for help when I am stuck from others in my group
Q9. I work hard when I am working in a group
Q10. I share ideas when working in a group
Q11. I work well with others when doing group work
Q14. I help others in my group when they are stuck

Benefits of group work:

Q4. Working in groups improves my concentration

Q5. I learn more working in a group than alone

Q6. I feel I can ask others in my group things I would not ask the teacher

Q7. Group work has allowed me to make more friends.

Q12. Group work has improved my confidence in me and my work

REFERENCES

Baines, E., Blatchford, P. and Kutnick, P. (2003) Changes in grouping practice over primary and secondary school. *International Journal of Educational Research 39*, 9-34.

Bennett, N. and Dunne, E. (1992) *Managing Classroom Groups*. Hemel Hempstead: Simon and Schuster Education.

Blatchford, P., Kutnick, P., Baines, E., and Galton, M (2003). Toward a social pedagogy of classroom group work. *International Journal of Educational Research 39*, 153-72.

Boldizar, J.P. (1991). Assessing sex typing and androgyny in children: The children's sex role inventory. *Developmental Psychology, 27*(3), 505–515. doi:10.1037/0012-1649.27.3.505.

Cohen, E. (1994). Restructuring the Classroom: Conditions for productive small groups. *Review of Educational Research, 64*(1), 1-35.

Cohen, E.G. and Intilli, J.K. (1981). Interdependence and Management in Bilingual Classrooms. (Final Report No. NIE-G-80-0217). Stanford University, School of Education.

Department for Education and Skills (2005). Raising Boys' Achievement. Research Report No 636. ISBN 1 84478 458 4. Downloaded from: https://www.education.gov.uk /publications/eOrderingDownload/RR636.pdf on 7th November 2011

Department for Education (2011). DfE: Interim Results for Key Stage 2 and 3 National Curriculum Assessments in England, 2010/11/ Dowloaded from: http://www.education. gov.uk/rsgateway/DB/SFR/s001018/index. shtml on 7th November 2011.

Eccles, J., Wigfield, A., Harold, R. D., and Blumenfeld, P. (1993). Age and gender differences in children's self- and task perceptions during elementary school. *Child Development, 64*, 830-847.

Feingold, A. (1994). Gender differences in personality: A meta-analysis. *Psychological Bulletin, 116*(3), 429-456. doi: 10.1037/0033-2909.116.3.429.

Gentry, M., Gable, R. K., and Rizza, M. G. (2002) Students' perceptions of classroom activities: Are there grade-level and gender differences? *Journal of Educational Psychology, 94*(3), 539–544.

Gillies, R. (2003). Structuring cooperative group work in classrooms. *International Journal of Educational Research, 39*, 35-49.

Hallan, S., Ireson, J., and Davies, J. (2004). Primary pupils' experiences of different types of grouping in school. *British Educational Research Journal, 30*(4), 515-533.

Johnson, D.W. and Johnson, R.T. (1994). Collaborative learning and argumentation. In P. Kutnick and C. Rogers (Eds.) *Groups in Schools*. London: Cassell.

Kutnick, P., Blatchford, P. and Baines, E. (2002). Pupil groupings in primary school classrooms: sites for learning and social pedagogy. *British Educational Research Journal, 28*, 2, 189-208.

Kutnick, P. and Kington, A. (2005). Children's friendships and learning in school; cognitive enhancement through social interaction? *British Journal of Educational Psychology, 75*(4), 1-19.

Laidra, K.; Pullmann, H.; Allik, J. (2007). Personality and intelligence as predictors of academic achievement: A cross-sectional study from elementary to secondary school. *Personality and Individual Differences, 42*(3), 441-451.

Logan, S. (2009). Children's reading development. Examining the effects of reading instruction and gender differences on children's reading. VDM Verlag.

Logan, S., and Johnston, R. (2009). Gender differences in reading ability and attitudes: examining where these differences lie. *Journal of Research in Reading, 32*(2), 199-214.

Macmillan Test Unit. (2000). Group reading test II 6–14. Windsor: NFER-Nelson.

McGhee, R. L.; Ehrler, D. J.; Buckhalt, J. A. (2007). Five-Factor Personality Inventory-Children (FFPI-C). PRO-ED, Inc, Texas, U.S.

McGeown, S., Goodwin, H., Henderson, N., and Wright, P. (2011). Gender differences in reading motivation: does sex or gender identity provide a better account? *Journal of Research in Reading,* doi 10.1111/j.1467-9817.2010.01481.x.

Plummer, G. and Dudley P. (1993) *Assessing Children Learning Collaboratively.* Chelmsford: Essex Development Advisory Service.

Poropat, A. E. (2009). A meta-analysis of the five-factor model of personality and academic performance. *Psychological Bulletin, 135*(2), 322-338.

Pryor, J. (1995). Gender issues in groupwork – a case study involving with computers. *British Educational Research Journal, 21*(3), 277 – 288.

Scanlon, E. (2000). How gender influences learners working collaboratively with science stimulations. *Learning and Instruction, 10*(6), 463-481.

Underwood, G., McCaffrey, M., and Underwood, J. (1990). Gender differences in a co-operative computer based language task. *Educational Researcher, 32*(1),44–49.

Wang, M. C., Haertel, G. D., and Walberg, H. J. (1994). What helps students learn? *Educational Leadership, 51,* 74-79.

Webb, N. (1984). Sex differences in interaction and achievement in cooperative small groups. *Journal of Educational Psychology, 75,* 33–44.

Webb, N. M., and Palincsar, A. S. (1996). Group processes in the classroom. In D. C. Berliner, and R.C. Calfee (Eds.), *Handbook of Educational Psychology* (pp. 841–873). New York: Macmillan.

In: Psychology of Gender Differences
Editor: Sarah P. McGeown

ISBN: 978-1-62081-391-1
© 2012 Nova Science Publishers, Inc.

Chapter 5

GENDER DIFFERENCES IN CHILDREN'S CREATIVITY AND PLAY BEHAVIOR

Dieneke Van de Sompel[1], Iris Vermeir[1] and Mario Pandelaere[2]*

[1] University College Ghent / Ghent University, Ghent, Belgium
[2] Ghent University, Ghent, Belgium

ABSTRACT

Due to biological and sociological factors, men and woman are different and these differences show early in life. Examining children's behavior will provide a deeper understanding of the constitution of these gender differences. The current chapter focuses on children's creativity, play behavior and the possible relationship between both. In addition, we investigate parents' insights in gender differences in their children's level of creativity.

Although gender inequalities still exist when it comes to awarding creative abilities, we find that seven to nine year old girls outperform boys of the same age in two divergent creativity tasks, except for the elaboration measure of these tasks. We find no differences in convergent creativity. In addition, we find that mothers and fathers also evaluate girls as more creative than boys.

Because playing is an important aspect of children's developmental process, the chapter examines if there are differences between girls' and boys' play activities and examines whether parents notice these differences. Our chapter shows gender differences in attitude toward particular play activities. Boys (in comparison to girls) have a better aptitude for playing with Lego, cars, action figures etc. Girls (in comparison to boys) on the other hand have a better aptitude toward crafting, drawing, coloring, painting, making music etc. A follow-up study reveals that the toys and games girls evaluated positively are in fact found to be the most conducive to creative expression. We also show that children's toy and game attitudes are consistent with parents' measures of the actual play frequency of their children regarding these toys or games.

The implications of these findings are interesting in regard to the way gender prejudices might be shifting. Since parents are well aware of the fact that girls may be

*E-mail: dieneke.vandesompel@hogent.be.

more creative than boys and like other play activities, we believe girls nowadays might be stimulated more by their parents and environment to break through certain stereotypical influences. Perhaps they are - even in childhood - stimulated to try new things, which could mean that girls may be more likely to develop creative abilities.

INTRODUCTION

It seems that today, women represent the minority of the most creatively awarded people. Fast Company annually publishes a list with the 100 most creative people in business (Fast Company, 2011). In 2011, only two women were included in the top ten of the list (three in 2010 and two in 2009). Even historically, there seem to be more men than women who stood out for their creative capabilities (Stoltzfus et al., 2011; Abra and Valentine-French, 1991). When asked to think about history's most creative people, some would undoubtedly arise: Picasso, Gaudi, Shakespeare, Einstein, and Beethoven. Certainly there were some women in history who would be included on some shortlist of great creative minds, among which Marie Curie, Coco Chanel and Jane Austen.

However, we cannot fail to notice that despite being less represented, there are some differences in the specific domains in which women excelled with their creative capabilities. Women seemingly excelled in arts such as literature and fashion design, whereas men, for example, excelled in music composition, poetry and science (Abra and Valentine-French, 1991).

These gender differences in creativity might stem from genuine differences between men and women. Biological theories for gender differences draw on evolutionary thinking. Men and woman have different biological roles and responsibilities, most of them related to reproduction (Maccoby, 1988). Most importantly, in the past, women were typically the members of the family responsible for caretaking. This role was formed biologically, because only women are capable of being pregnant and giving childbirth, nurturance and lactation (Costa, Terracciano and McCrae, 2001). Another biological difference between men and women are their hormonal levels. These hormonal levels might cause women to react differently than men. Women are, for example, more emotional and less rational thinkers (Costa et al., 2001). These biological differences might explain why women historically focused on specific creative domains, such as literature, a particular art where emotions are easily expressed.

Sociological theories focus on the role of social structure and culture in the development of gender differences. Gender roles, for example, are implied by the society a person lives in (Maccoby, 1988). Social and cultural differences appear for instance in gender stereotypes (Albert and Porter, 1986) and gender differences in social status (Maccoby, 1988). According to the sociological view on gender differences, social influences on gender differences in emotional levels might arise because parents often teach their sons to control their emotions whereas they teach their daughters to express them (Leaper, 2002). As for gender differences in creativity, women were perhaps historically forced to canalize their creativity in certain domains as a result from the application of gender stereotypes. Costa et al. (2001) investigated gender differences in several personality characteristics across cultures. Overall, they compared 30 personality traits in men and women. They found that most differences were consistent with gender stereotypes and this was true over different cultures. They specifically found that women are thought to be more submissive, more concerned with feelings than with ideas, have a greater tendency for nurturance and score higher on negative affect. Women are also considered more passive and supportive instead of experimental, active and willing to engage in new activities than men are. As the traits typically ascribed to women are also indicative of low levels of creativity, such gender stereotypes imply that women are less creative than men are.

One could argue that due to biological and/or sociological influences, men are or have to be more creative than women. Contradictory to these commonly held thoughts, however, previous creativity research is rather inconclusive about gender differences in creativity. In their overview of gender differences in creativity levels, Baer and Kaufman (2008) argued that the majority of these studies found no gender differences. They also argue that literature shows a vast amount of different findings. Some recent studies show that men are more creative than woman (Stoltzfus et al., 2011). Other studies, in contrast, found that -in some instances- women are more creative than men (Cheung and Lau, 2010). Due to these inconsistent findings regarding the relationship between gender and creativity, more research is needed. In this chapter, we specifically focus on children's creativity and explore gender differences in both creativity and play behavior. Gender differences and gender stereotypes are found in very young children (Albert and Porter, 1986; Lever, 1976). Therefore, examining children's behavior will provide a deeper understanding of the constitution of these gender differences.

Defining Creativity

Ever since Guilford's seminal work on creativity to now, research on creativity has become more eminent over the years and has grown especially since the 1950s (Sternberg and Lubart, 1999). Despite a large number of varying definitions of creativity, there seems to be a general acceptance, that creativity can be described as "the ability to produce work that has an aspect of originality (or novelty) and work that is useful, valuable or appropriate" (Sternberg and Lubart, 1999; El-Murad and West, 2004). This definition implies that creativity does not exclusively arise in reputed artists or scientists, but that it can be found and studied in every individual (Sternberg and Lubart, 1999). Creativity should therefore not only be seen as an expression form exclusively preserved for arts and inventions, but can also be found in people's everyday lives (Runco, 2004).

Creative people are often characterized by a wide range of different personality traits (Sternberg and Lubart, 1999). One of the most extensively examined characteristics linked to creative behavior is the human intellect (Runco, 2004). Other than overall intelligence, some personality traits that are prevalent in creative people are being open to new experiences (McCrae, 1987), risk taking behavior (Friedman and Förster, 2001; Dewett, 2006), fear (El-Murad and West, 2004) and introversion (Feist, 1999). Creativity is also linked to self regulatory focus (Friedman and Förster, 2001; Friedman and Förster, 2002). Creativity should therefore not be seen as an exceptional personality trait, but as a unique and rare synchronized occurrence of less unique personality traits in one and the same person (Martindale, 1999). A creative person therefore often shows high levels of intelligence, combined with high scores on unconventionality measures etc. Literature takes on different points of view when talking about the creative potential of an individual and, consequently, conceptualizes creativity in many different ways. The most prominent distinction to be found in literature is the distinction between divergent and convergent creative thinking. Convergent creativity is mostly seen as the ability to solve a problem that only has one correct solution (Gilhooly et al., 2007; Plucker and Renzulli, 1999). An example of a convergent creative thinking test is Mednick's Remote Associations Test (1962), where three words are given and the respondent needs to find the one correct answer that matches the description. Divergent creativity on the other hand is seen as the ability to generate several different answers to solve a particular problem (Gilhooly et al., 2007; Plucker and Renzulli, 1999). Divergent creativity is related to the previously mentioned perception that creativity is in fact a bundling of many different aspects and special personality traits in one person. A person would need several abilities to solve divergent creativity problems. Therefore, divergent creativity tests usually rely on three different underlying concepts to determine how creative a particular answer is: fluency, flexibility and originality. Fluency refers to the number of different ideas someone can construct, flexibility refers to the diversity in the ideas and originality refers to how unusual or unique these ideas are (Runco, 2004). Sometimes an elaboration score is added to these three concepts to identify how detailed a person describes the given ideas.

Children's Creativity and Play Behavior

Creativity is a characteristic that supposedly develops early in life (Runco, 2006). Although creativity in children is different from creativity in adults, creative abilities are expressed in children's everyday behavior. Creative behavior can, for example, emerge in pretend play when children rely on their imagining capabilities to construct a play setting. Creativity can also be seen when children use certain toys in an unusual manner or when they use original methods to play. Merging creativity and play behavior in research is important, especially because they are both fundamental for children's maturation process. Playing is seen an essential element in the process of children's development, because it enables many learning opportunities (Messier, Ferland and Majnemer, 2007). Despite the importance of playing, little is known about the reason why children particularly like certain types of games and toys. Even in early childhood, children can choose from a wide variety of toys and games and can exhibit many different types of play behavior. Over the years, these differences were investigated and several authors found that gender might have an impact on the way children play. Children as young as four to six years old are starting to learn and use gender role differences (Albert and Porter, 1986). This means that they are becoming aware of their specific role as boy or girl and start to act according to that role. As mentioned in the introduction, gender differences are believed to be formed biologically or social/culturally. Both the biological and the sociological perspective argue that gender typed play behavior already arises at young ages (Green, Bigler and Catherwood, 2004). Relating to the biological perspective, research indicated that even children of six months old show gender differences in attention to gender-typed toys (such as dolls) (Alexander, Wilcox and Woods, 2009). The environmental influences on gender differences in play behavior are, for example, seen in the influence of parents on their children's play behavior. Parents and teachers are important role models for children's play activities. When children observe their parents and teachers and model their play behavior after them, they possibly assimilate general gender roles. Children, with female role models who are primarily responsible of caretaking in the household, might do this by playing house and taking care of dolls (Leaper, 2002). Parents can also actively transmit gender roles by playing with the child. They can reinforce gender-typical play behavior by selecting gender-typed toys for the children (Leaper, 2002). In 1976, Lever already argued that adult gender roles can be identified in children's play behavior and that different play activities may even cause the development of particular stereotypical social skills (such as conformity and nurturance for girls and competitiveness and performance for boys). Therefore, it is important to investigate if gender does influence the types of toys and games children prefer. If gender differences arise in elementary school children's play preferences, they have already encountered these (either biological or social/cultural) influences. The aforementioned gender differences might also have an impact on children's creativity levels and play behavior. In this chapter, we therefore want to address two basic research questions. First, we want to investigate if creativity levels are different for girls and boys who are still in elementary school. Second, we wonder if gender differences also appear in attitudes for toys or games and in play frequencies. Investigating the play interests across gender is an important issue, because it can provide insights in the development of children. If girls and boys have differential play interests, this might give us an indication of their development. Some toys and games are seemingly more creative (such as coloring, drawing etc.), so perhaps children who prefer these types of toys and games have the most creative potential.

Parental Evaluation of Children's Creativity and Play Behavior

Parents see how their children behave in their home environment. This behavior is often expressed in playing, since playing is important for children to express themselves (Landreth, 2001). When children are playing, they might for example show their creativity and express their personality. Playing might therefore give signals to parents that help them assess their children's personality and play behavior. Therefore, in this chapter, we will assess parent's identification of their children's play frequency and investigate if this correlates with children's actual attitude toward certain toys or games. We will also investigate if parents see gender differences in their children's level of creativity. If gender differences in play behavior or creativity appear and parents see these differences, this is important because the family of a child is an important stimulator of creative behavior (Csikszentmihalyi, 1999; Runco, 2006). Noticing differences might be a key to stimulation of creative behavior.

METHOD

Procedure

Our results are based on a paper-and-pencil study conducted during summer holidays. A total of 123 children aged seven to eleven years ($M = 8.8$; $SD = .78$; 59% girls) were recruited in a summer day camp. The experiment was deliberately not conducted at schools or at home, as this might have biased the results (for example by social pressure of parents, teachers or the school environment). These summer day camps were chosen because all children attending them spent at least one week of their summer holiday there and were therefore accustomed to the environment. This method also accounted for an appropriate and representative distribution in intelligence, giftedness and place of living, since the children attending these summer day camps go to diverse school types in the area (for example both town centers and rural places). On arrival at the summer day camp, children and parents were asked for their willingness and permission to participate in the experiment. During the day at the summer day camp, small groups of maximum four children were brought to an outdoor pavilion that was located outside the camp site, so they could not be disturbed by others while responding to the questionnaire. Although they were in small groups, they were unable to see the other children's answers, since they were placed at separate tables and out of sight of each other. We decided to put the children in small groups, because they would feel more at ease. Each child was presented with the questionnaire and all children were interviewed without the presence of parents, teachers or camp leaders. After a brief description of the study, children completed tests measuring their aptitude towards several toys and games and completed three creativity tasks. The children were then debriefed, asked not to talk about the study, and compensated with a small reward in return for their participation. The procedure took approximately 30 minutes to complete.

Additionally, all parents of participating children received a questionnaire to fill out at home. This questionnaire consisted of three parts. In the first part, either the mother or the father represented both parents and responded to questions about their child's play frequency with particular toys and games and additionally answered some questions about their child's play preferences. In the second part of the questionnaire, we asked mother and father to individually respond to a creativity question concerning their child. Parents were asked to complete the questionnaire within the same week and a total of 104 parents returned the questionnaire.

Measures

At the beginning of the experiment, children were explained how to answer all questions in the questionnaire. They received a test question and first filled out some demographic measures to get accustomed to the method (they were asked to indicate their gender, their birth year, how many brothers and sisters they had etc.).

Play Behavior

Prior to the study, the researchers selected a number of different toys and games based on existing toy websites and brochures. Based on these brochures and websites, different categories were selected, from which the twenty most common and appropriate toys and games were retained in the final list. In the experiment, all children first received an aptitude measure containing these twenty specific toys or games, among which 'playing with jigsaw puzzles', 'playing with dolls', 'painting', 'drawing' etc. This aptitude measure was presented to the children as a list where they were asked to indicate how much they liked each particular toy or game. To account for biases caused by reading abilities, the toys and games were read aloud by the interviewer. The children answered on a five-point Likert scale, for which each answer possibility had verbal and non-verbal anchor points. The verbal anchor points ranged from 'I really don't like this toy/game', 'I don't like this toy/game', 'I like this toy/game somewhat, but also dislike it somewhat', 'I like this toy/game' to 'I really like this toy/game'. The non-verbal anchor points were emoticons that indicated respectively two sad faces, one sad face, a neutral face, one happy face and two happy faces. An additional text box was added as a sixth option, allowing the children to indicate they did not know the toy or game, a question mark was added as the non-verbal anchor point.

Parents received the same toy and game list, but they were instead asked to indicate how often their child played with the particular toy or game on an average week. This question served as a play frequency measure for each toy or game. Parents could answer this question on a seven-point Likert scale, ranging from 'never' (1) to 'daily' (7).

Creativity Measures

Creativity was measured with three different creativity tasks in the child's questionnaire (two divergent thinking tasks and one convergent thinking task) and two different questions in the parental questionnaire.

The divergent tasks administered to the children were two items of the Torrance Test of Creative Thinking (TTCT, 1966) and belonged to the 'Thinking Creatively with Words' subset. The first creativity task was an unusual uses task in which children had to find creative ways to employ a typical everyday object, namely a cardboard box. Children were told they could play a game and received a piece of paper. They were asked to provide all responses they could think of to use a cardboard box, other than just throwing it away. The second divergent thinking task was a product improvement test, in which children were asked for ways to improve a stuffed toy. This specific toy was used, in order to match this question with the other ones. Children were asked to provide all responses they could think of that the makers of the displayed stuffed animal could change to improve the toy, so it would be more fun to play with for children. For both tasks, children were given four guidelines: they were asked to give answers that nobody else would think of (which relates to the originality measure of the task), to try and come up with as many answers as possible (which relates to the fluency measure of the tasks), to describe each answer as precisely as possible (which relates to the elaboration measure of the task) and to keep in mind that there were no right or wrong answers. Children were given a limited time span for each of the two tasks, and received filler questions in between both tasks. For both divergent thinking tasks, the number of relevant answers constituted the fluency measure. Responses were relevant when the idea fully responded to the question at hand. The originality score was calculated by determining which answers were the more original ones. Responses that were seen as the least original ones were not rewarded with an originality score (these responses were coded as '0'). Responses that were unusual and thus seen as very original answers received most credit (these responses were coded as '1'). For the unusual uses task, one of the less original answers given was 'crafting something with the box' (coded as '0'). Amongst the more original answers were for example 'make an ice cream cart of the box' and 'use the cover as a table tennis bat' (coded as '1'). For the product improvement task, a response that was coded as an unoriginal answer was for example 'changing the color' (coded as '0'). Examples of very original answers were: 'make its mouth turn into an oven' and 'give it whiskers and let them wag' (coded as '1'). Additionally, two independent judges rated the flexibility and elaboration level of each answer. The judges were blind to any information (such as gender) other than the answer itself. Elaboration was measured by counting the specific details that were added to the answer. For the flexibility dimension, the answers were ranged in different categories and each answer was related to one of these categories. One such category was "storage" for the unusual uses task and "changing color" for the product improvement task. Subsequently, for each task, we counted the number of categories for which the child had provided at least one response. For the unusual uses task, both reliabilities were adequate: correlations were r = .72 ($p < .01$) for the elaboration measure and r = .82 ($p < .01$) for the flexibility measure. For the product improvement test, inter-rater reliability was high for the flexibility measure ($r = .85$, $p < .01$), but lower for the elaboration measure ($r = .50$, $p < .01$). To improve our measures, rater disagreements were resolved through discussion.

A third creativity test for children was an adapted version of the Remote Associations Test of Mednick (1962). We adapted the test according to the studies of Bowden and Beeman (2003) and Shamas (1994). In this task, participants are presented with three seemingly unrelated words. Participants need to find the one word that fits before or after each of the given words to form an existing composition and thus associates with all three words. The underlying thought is that creative people are able to make associations between these words even when the problem at hand is seen as rare or unusual (Shamas, 1994). In our questionnaire, children were presented with seven of these triads and thus needed to find seven words. These seven triads were based on triads used in previous research (Shamas, 1994; Bowden and Beeman, 2003), but all of them were adapted for the specific target age and language group. Therefore, we created our own list of seven triads that were appropriate for this specific age group. One item consisted of the words "cream", "skate" and "water" and the solution was "ice". All correct answers were counted and this summated measure indicated the total convergent creativity score. The test was introduced as a game and one additional test-item was given to make sure that all participating children had understood the purpose of the task. Children were timed and received one minute for each triad, but were told that not finding a matching word was not an issue. Some of the triads were identified as more difficult than other triads, but all triads were solved at least one time by one of the respondents. In the parental questionnaire, we asked both mother and father of the child to indicate how creative they thought their child was. Answers were given on a seven-point Likert scale, ranging from 'absolutely not creative' (1) to 'absolutely creative' (7). Additionally one parent was asked to evaluate two aspects of the child's play behavior: 'My child often plays with a similar toy or game' and 'my child often asks for new toys or games'. They indicated if they agreed with these statements on a seven-point Likert scale, ranging from 'totally disagree' (1) to 'totally agree'(7).

RESULTS

Gender Differences in Children's Creative Abilities

To determine whether creative abilities differ across gender, several independent samples t-tests were conducted. Table 1 summarizes the analyses of all creativity measures used in this chapter.

First, the two divergent thinking tasks were analyzed. For the unusual uses task, the fluency measure, the flexibility measure and the originality measure were all significantly higher for girls than for boys. Only for the elaboration measure, no significant difference was found between boys and girls. Boys and girls were consequently providing equally detailed answers.

The second divergent thinking task was the product improvement task. For this task, significant differences were found for the fluency measure, the flexibility measure and the originality measure. Consistent with the results of the unusual uses task, girls scored on average significantly higher than boys on all these measures. Also consistent with the findings of the unusual uses task, the elaboration measure of the product improvement task showed no significant differences between boys and girls. These analyses reveal that except for the elaboration measure, girls outperform boys of the same age with respect to their divergent creative abilities.

For the convergent creativity measure (the Remote Associations Test), results are different. Boys and girls score equally well on this measure, so no significant differences arise ($t(122) = .82$; $p = .41$). This result is consistent with previous research of Harris (2004), who found no gender differences on RAT-scores. The absence of gender differences might be due to the correlation of the Remote Associations Test with overall intelligence. Harris (2004) found that the Remote Associations Test is related to verbal intelligence and argues that this can be explained by the nature of the test, which is finding associations between words. Having an extended vocabulary will facilitate this process and is in fact the basis of verbal intelligence.

In a next step, we investigated if parent's assessments of their children's creativity also showed these gender differences. We asked both father and mother to assess their child's creativity level. Parents responded to questions about their child, so gender can be compared and linked to parental measures. Parent's assessments correlated significantly with each other, indicating that mothers and fathers had similar judgments of their child's creative abilities ($r = .79$; $p < .01$). Mothers evaluate daughters as more creative than sons ($t(95) = -2.56$; $p < .05$). Fathers also evaluate their daughters as more creative than sons ($t(90) = -3.46$; $p < .01$). We can therefore conclude that both parents find girls to be more creative than boys. When correlation measures between each child's creativity test and parent's measures were compared, no significant correlation was detected, nor were there any specific differences in the correlation patterns when correlations were performed specifically for girls and boys. Previous research indicated several factors that dilute peers' and teachers' correct evaluation of children's creativity (Lau and Li, 1996), such as for example the popularity of a child in a class. This dilution is therefore also present in this specific study, indicating that parents are, at an individual level, no perfect assessors of their children's creativity. However, since we find that parents' gender related creativity scores are consistent with the divergent creativity measures of their children, we can assume that they are able to identify gender differences in creativity.

Gender Differences in Children's Play Behavior

In the second part of this chapter, we assess whether gender also accounts for children's play behavior. We identify if there are gender differences in preference for particular types of games and toys and examine gender differences in different aspects of play behavior (such as the frequency with which a child plays a game). Additionally, we assess whether parents also notice these differences. Therefore, we gave parents a list of games and made them indicate how often their children played the particular toys or game (play frequency). The children received the same list, but they were asked to indicate how much they liked each of the games/toys on the list (attitude toward the toy or game).

The results document gender differences in aptitude toward particular play activities. As shown in the second section of table 2, boys (in comparison to girls) have a more positive attitude for playing with *Lego* ($t(122) = 5.91$; $p < .001$), playing with *action figures* ($t(122) = 3.09$; $p < .01$), playing with *construction sets* ($t(116) = 5.16$; $p < .001$), playing *computer games* ($t(121) = 2.85$; $p < .01$) and playing with *cars* ($t(91) = 6.75$; $p < .001$).

Table 1. Gender differences in creativity measures: descriptive statistics

Creativity measure	N	Mean	SD	N	Mean	SD	t	Df	p
	Boys			Girls					
Unusual Uses test									
Elaboration	52	.52	.94	73	.88	1.38	-1.61	123	.11
Fluency	51	2.84	1.35	73	3.74	1.86	-2.95	122	<.01
Flexibility	52	2.17	1.00	73	2.85	1.18	-3.37	123	<.01
Originality	52	3.60	2.22	73	4.55	3.18	-1.86	123	.065
Total	51	9.25	4.05	73	12.01	5.61	-3.00	122	<.01
Product improvement test									
Elaboration	52	.54	.96	73	.68	1.01	-0.82	123	.42
Fluency	52	3.02	1.54	73	4.23	1.90	-3.80	123	<.01
Flexibility	52	1.98	1.04	73	2.56	1.30	-2.78	121	<.01
Originality	52	4.06	2.34	73	5.42	3.03	-2.73	123	<.01
Total	52	9.60	4.63	73	12.90	5.84	-3.40	123	<.01
Remote Associations Test	51	1.71	1.29	73	1.52	1.20	.82	122	.41
Parent measures									
Mother's evaluation	40	5.00	1.24	57	5.60	1.05	-2.56	95	<.05
Father's evaluation	38	4.87	1.26	54	5.69	1.00	-3.46	90	<.01

Girls (in comparison to boys) on the other hand have a more positive attitude toward *crafting* ($t(82) = -3.3$; $p < .01$), *drawing* ($t(120) = -3.07$; $p < .01$), *coloring* ($t(123) = -4.49$; $p < .001$), *painting* ($t(119) = -3.07$; $p < .01$), playing with *dolls* ($t(121) = -7.86$; $p < .001$), playing with *iron on beads* ($t(82) = -5.72$; $p < .001$), *dressing up* ($t(118) = -2.89$; $p < .01$) and *making music* ($t(119) = -2.22$; $p < .05$).

Only seven of the twenty games comprised in the list are equally favored by girls and boys. These games are playing with *Playmobil* ($t(122) = -1.02$; $p = .31$), *playing with jigsaw puzzles* ($t(119) = -1.31$; $p = .19$), playing *videogames* ($t(120) = 1.40$; $p = .16$), playing *hide-and-seek* ($t(120) = -.54$; $p = .59$), playing *board games* ($t(120) = -.82$; $p = .41$), *biking* ($t(121) = -1.70$ $p = .09$) and *pretend play* ($t(120) = -.50$; $p = .62$).

Because parents see their children when they are playing, playing might give them real assessable signals of the attitudes of their children. In order to be able to correctly identify the relationship between children's attitude toward the toys/games and their play frequency as it is perceived by parents, the intercorrelation between these variables was examined. Most of the attitude and frequency measures were significantly correlated, which is shown in the first section of table 2. Toys or games where attitude and play frequency was not correlated were: playing with action figures, playing hide-and-seek and playing board games. Interesting to notice is that for all of the toys or games that were preferred by girls, attitude and play frequency is highly correlated at the .01 level. This research setting does not allow for a full understanding of this phenomenon, but we could believe this might be due to the specific nature of these toys and games. Most of these games are to some extent visible games (coloring, drawing). They are also games that allow children to show their parents the end-result.

Interestingly, these attitude measures are consistent with parents' measures of the actual play frequency of their children for these play activities. As is shown in the third section of table 2, parents indicate that boys (in comparison to girls) play more frequently with *Lego* ($t(65) = 4.64$; $p < .001$), *action figures* ($t(69) = 2.97$; $p < .01$), *construction sets* ($t(62) = 4.94$; $p < .001$) and *cars* ($t(49) = 6.04$; $p < .001$).

A first difference between the attitude measures of the children and parental frequency measures can be found in computer games. Boys had a more positive attitude toward *computer games*, but parents do not indicate that boys play them more frequently than girls do ($t(100) = .94$; $p = .35$).

Parents also report higher playing frequency for girls for those play activities they prefer. These are *crafting* ($t(66) = -3.87$; $p < .01$), *drawing* ($t(60) = -5.08$; $p < .001$), *coloring* ($t(56) = -5.78$; $p < .001$), playing with *dolls* ($t(80) = -9.25$; $p < .001$), *iron on beads* ($t(101) = -3.90$; $p < .001$), *dressing up* ($t(101) = -3.24$; $p < .01$) and *painting* ($t(98) = -1.92$; $p = .06$).

A second difference when comparing the attitudinal and frequency results is that parents indicate that girls engage more frequently in *pretend play* ($t(101) = -1.97$; $p = .05$) than boys do, even though there were no attitudinal differences. Girls did have a more positive attitude toward *making music*, but parents do not indicate it as something girls do more frequently ($t(100) = -1.07$; $p = .29$).

Consistent results can also be found for some of the toys and games where children's attitude was not significantly different. Parents indicate no gender differences in frequency of playing with *Playmobil* ($t(100) = .42$; $p = .67$), *playing with jigsaw puzzles* ($t(101) = -1.36$; $p = .18$), playing *videogames* ($t(99) = 1.75$; $p = .08$), playing *hide-and-seek* ($t(100) = -1.64$; $p = .10$), playing *board games* ($t(101) = 0.51$; $p = .61$) and *biking* ($t(101) = .16$; $p = .88$).

These results highlight that parents are aware of their children's play preferences at this age, since they can identify their child's play frequency and this play frequency is consistent with children's attitude toward most of these toys or games.

Parental measures were also used to determine if children had particular playing habits. We find that parents indicate that girls ($M = 5.07$; $SD = 1.24$) prefer playing more different activities, whereas boys ($M = 5.51$; $SD = 1.05$) have one favorite activity they keep on playing ($t(100) - 1.90$; $p = .06$). This is consistent with the study of Lever (1976). She had children hold a diary in which they indicated their play activities during a half year. She found that the play activities of boys lasted longer than the play activities of girls. Despite their interest in one particular type of play activity, boys ($M = 4.56$; $SD = 1.21$) ask for new toys more frequently ($t(100) = 2.23$; $p < .05$) than girls do ($M = 3.93$; $SD = 1.63$). Perhaps asking for new toys or games relates to the types of games children play. Boys' most preferred games are Lego, construction sets, action figures etc. All of these examples are types of games that depend on collecting newer types of the toy or game or additions to the existing game. Probably these play activities are types of play activities where extension of the same game type is necessary. This means that boys can prefer playing the same type of game, but ask their parents for toys on a more regular basis. Contrastingly, the toys or games girls preferred are especially games where the utilities to perform the game are less often perceived as belonging to a game as such. Asking for new pencils for example, might not come across to many parents as asking for a new game.

Table 2. Gender differences in children's attitude for toys/games, parent's assessment of their child's play frequency and correlations between attitudes and play frequencies

	Correlations toy/game attitude and play frequency		Toy/game attitude children's measures				Play frequency parent's measure		
	N	r		N	Mean	SD	N°	Mean	SD
Toys or games for which boys have a more positive attitude									
Lego									
	102	.50**	Boys	52	4.13	.93	41	3.95	2.05
			Girls	72	2.99	1.16	61	2.25	1.41
Playing with action figures									
	102	.19	Boys	51	2.98	1.57	42	2.81	2.02
			Girls	73	2.14	1.45	61	1.74	1.44
Playing with construction sets									
	96	.30**	Boys	48	3.67	1.34	42	3.10	1.72
			Girls	70	2.36	1.36	61	1.62	1.05
Playing computer games									
	100	.21*	Boys	51	4.49	.86	42	4.48	1.85
			Girls	72	4.00	.99	60	4.17	1.48
Playing with cars									
	100	.51**	Boys	51	3.33	1.28	41	3.15	1.78
			Girls	72	1.89	1.00	61	1.38	.71
Toys or games for which girls have a more positive attitude									
Coloring									
	102	.38**	Boys	52	3.21	1.09	41	3.78	2.04
			Girls	73	4.04	.96	61	5.80	1.12
Crafting									
	98	.46**	Boys	48	3.79	1.17	42	4.14	1.66
			Girls	72	4.44	.89	61	5.28	1.11
Playing with dolls									
	101	.63**	Boys	51	1.39	.94	42	1.31	.68
			Girls	72	3.01	1.35	61	3.75	1.89
(Iron on) Beads									
	100	.42**	Boys	49	2.27	1.38	42	1.71	.92
			Girls	70	3.59	1.00	61	2.48	1.01
Drawing									
	100	.23**	Boys	51	3.75	1.11	42	4.45	1.84
			Girls	71	4.30	.87	61	6.05	1.06
Dressing up									
	99	.43**	Boys	49	2.71	1.44	42	2.48	1.19
			Girls	71	3.42	1.23	61	3.34	1.43
Painting									
	96	.29**	Boys	49	3.24	1.25	42	2.83	1.43

	Correlations toy/game attitude and play frequency		Toy/game attitude children's measures				Play frequency parent's measure		
	N	r		N	Mean	SD	N°	Mean	SD
Toys or games without attitude differences for boys and girls									
			Girls	72	3.92	1.14	58	3.34	1.22
Making music									
	98	.53**	Boys	49	3.18	1.47	41	2.41	1.73
			Girls	72	3.74	1.26	61	2.82	1.96
Playmobil									
	101	.68**	Boys	51	3.53	1.43	42	3.57	2.15
			Girls	73	3.78	1.28	60	3.40	1.92
Playing with jigsaw puzzles									
	100	.22*	Boys	50	2.92	1.12	42	2.21	1.28
			Girls	71	3.18	1.06	61	2.54	1.13
Playing videogames									
	98	.51**	Boys	49	4.18	1.48	42	4.10	2.26
			Girls	73	3.84	1.25	59	3.32	2.14
Playing hide-and-seek									
	99	.17	Boys	51	3.49	1.05	42	3.19	1.50
			Girls	71	3.59	1.02	60	3.67	1.40
Playing board games									
	101	.14	Boys	50	4.04	1.07	42	4.21	1.41
			Girls	72	4.19	.99	61	4.08	1.23
Biking									
	101	.32**	Boys	50	4.16	1.04	42	5.17	1.59
			Girls	73	4.44	.78	61	5.11	1.68
Pretend Play									
	100	.37**	Boys	51	3.14	1.56	42	3.26	1.98
			Girls	71	3.27	1.30	61	4.03	1.94

°N is the number of parents that responded to this question for their daughter or for their son.
*$p < .05$ ** $p < .01$.

An additional explanation for this effect might be a gender-typical difference in the ways to reduce elements of boredom in playing behavior. Since boys play with one type of toy or game for a longer period, they might experience a certain amount of boredom after a while. Since they prefer playing with the same toys and games over and over again, they might try to reduce boredom in these games by adding new elements in it, such as asking for new additions to the existing game. Girls on the other hand might reduce this boredom by simply playing something else. In this way, they also need fewer materials, as they can just return to the game when they want to resume their play.

Results Creativity, Gender and Play Preference

Although the play activities preferred by girls appear to be the most creative ones (such as coloring, drawing, painting etc.), creativity and attitude toward the particular toy and games are not always correlated. The results show some clear tendencies towards the belief that creativity levels are different for children who prefer other types of toys and games. The total creativity score of the product improvement test, for example, correlated negatively with the attitude toward four of the five toys or games that were preferred by boys, namely Lego (r = -.20, $p < .05$), playing with construction sets ($r = -.20$, $p < .05$), playing computer games $(r$ = -.25, $p < .01$) and playing with cars ($r = -.25$, $p < .01$).

The game 'playing with jigsaw puzzles' also correlated negatively with total creativity of the product improvement test ($r = -.20$, $p < .05$). No correlations with attitude toward any of the toys or games were found for the second divergent creativity test, the unusual uses test.

Follow-up Study

A follow-up study aimed to elucidate the relationship between girls' play behavior and their higher creativity than boys. We particularly examine if some of the games that were evaluated more positively by girls are in fact more creative. In the follow-up study, 50 children aged seven to ten years old ($M = 8$; $SD = .63$) were recruited in schools, where they conducted a paper-and-pencil test at the class room and were unable to see each other's answers. All children received a list with ten toys and games. These ten toys or games were selected from the list of toys and games used in the previous study. Three games were selected from the list in the previous study, because they were evaluated better by boys than by girls (playing with Lego, playing computer games and playing with cars). Four games were selected for which girls had more positive attitudes than boys (crafting, coloring, dressing up and making music). Finally, three games were selected for which we had not obtained attitude differences as a function of gender (playing board games, playing with jigsaw puzzles and playing hide-and-seek).

All children were asked to indicate how they normally play each of the games and were able to do so by choosing from three answer possibilities. The first possibility they received was to play the game according to the game rules or by following a certain manual and is thus seen as an uncreative way to play (assigned score 1). The second possibility was to play the game by sometimes following the game rules and sometimes using own imagination (assigned score 2). The third possibility was to play the game by using own imagination and fantasy, which was seen as the most creative way to play a game (assigned score 3). When a child is using their own imagination to play with a toy or game, this can be seen as a facet of divergent creativity, since it defies relying on standardized game rules (which would be uncreative).

The results indicate that all of the games preferred by girls appear in the top range of toys and games where children think they have to use their imagination. These games were dressing up ($M = 2.22$; $SD = .77$), coloring ($M = 2.16$; $SD = .77$), crafting ($M = 2.15$; $SD = .83$) and making music ($M = 2.08$; $SD = .85$). Playing with cars ($M = 2.19$; $SD = .84$) also engenders a high score and is the only game that shows an atypical result. The two games that are most appropriate to play with in an uncreative way are playing with Lego ($M = 1.64$; $SD = .70$) and playing computer games ($M = 1.73$; $SD = .82$). These were both games that boys preferred. The three toys or games where no attitude differences were found across gender appeared in the middle range of the creativity index. These games were playing hide-and-seek ($M = 1.98$; $SD = .89$), playing with jigsaw puzzles ($M = 1.86$; $SD = .81$) and playing board games ($M = 1.75$; $SD = .79$). We can thus conclude that the games girls preferred in the first study, are also the ones that are perceived as the toys or games where children should use their imagination, and are hence seen as creative games.

DISCUSSION

The purpose of this chapter is to get a better understanding of the influence gender has on children's creative abilities and play behavior. With this chapter, we also want to gain insights into the capacity of parents to correctly assess these aspects with their own children.

This chapter shows that girls outperform boys in overall divergent creativity abilities. Except for elaboration, all divergent creativity facets (flexibility, fluency and originality) were higher for girls than for boys. Additionally, we found that gender influences the play preferences of children. Boys have a more positive attitude toward particular toys or games (such as Lego, construction sets, cars etc.) and girls show a more positive attitude for other toys or games (such as drawing, coloring, playing with dolls, making music etc.). Some toys or games engendered an equally positive attitude of both boys and girls (such as playing with Playmobil, playing hide-and-seek, playing board games etc.).

This chapter assessed the relation between creativity and play behavior in two ways. First, one divergent creativity measure (the product improvement test) was correlated to children's toy or game attitude. Results indicated that some of the games preferred by boys (such as Lego) were indeed negatively correlated to creativity. Second, a follow-up study showed that the games coloring, crafting and making music are seen as the games where creative play is needed, whereas Lego and playing computer games are most appropriate for uncreative play behavior. These findings show that girls, who were found to be more creative, actually do prefer the most creative toys and games. Future research should examine whether playing certain games in fact enhances creativity or, in contrast, whether differences in game/play preference merely reflect existing differences in creativity.

Most of children's attitudes toward a toy or game and parent's reports of frequency of play for their children also correlated and the pattern obtained for children's attitude measures shows a strong similarity with the pattern in parents' measures of the actual play frequency of their children for these play activities. Interestingly, the attitude measures for the games preferred by girls correlated highly with parent's measures. Future research should investigate if this is due to the visibility of these types of games. Since parents see their children when they are playing, they are especially aware of both their creativity level and their play preference. Future research could investigate whether children's preferred play activities give parents direct cues to assess their children's creative skills. We found that parents indicate that girls prefer playing more different activities, whereas boys have one favorite activity they keep on playing. Despite their interest in one particular type of play activity, boys ask for new toys more frequently than girls do. These findings might be related to attitudinal differences for toys and games. Probably the play activities where boys showed a more positive attitude (which were, for example, construction sets, action figures and cars) are types of play activities where extension of the same game type is necessary. Boys might keep playing the same activity, but are in fact required to ask for new versions of the toys or additions to the toys more frequently than the games girls play with. These latter games were, after all, especially games where the utilities to perform the game are possibly less often perceived as belonging to a game as such. Asking for new pencils for example, might not come across to many parents as asking for a new game. An additional explanation for this effect might rely on the gender differences in the method to reduce boredom in games. Since we find that girls prefer a variety of play activities, they might be less inclined to need new toys. Variation in their play habits might be enough to keep them satisfied. Boys, on the other hand, might need new toys just because they keep on playing the same game. For them, new toys (or additions to the same toys) might be a way to stay interested.

Our findings suggest that gender prejudices regarding creativity might be shifting. Since parents are well aware of the fact that girls are more creative than boys and prefer other play activities, we believe girls nowadays might be stimulated more by their parents and environment to break trough certain stereotypical influences. Perhaps they are - even in childhood - stimulated to try new things, which could mean that girls are more likely to develop or hone creative abilities. This would indicate that their creativity level is enhanced by social/cultural influences. Further research should elaborate on these findings by, for example, investigating the biological or social causes of these differences. Do stereotypical environments or claims evoke these differences by reinforcing girls to stimulate some sort of coping behavior and cause them to behave extraordinary? Or are there biological facets that cause girls to score better on certain creativity tests? Creativity should also be evaluated as either a stable or a changing personality characteristic in people. Age should therefore be examined to get a deeper understanding of the true developmental facets underlying creative abilities. Longitudinal studies might therefore shed light on the ways in which age and developmental differences arise.

REFERENCES

Abra, J.C., and Valentine-French, S. (1991). Gender differences in creative achievement: A survey of explanations. *Genetic, Social and General Psychology Monographs, 117*(3), 233-284.

Albert, A. A., and Porter, J. R. (1986). Children's Gender Role Stereotypes: A Comparison of the United States and South Africa. *Journal of Cross-Cultural Psychology, 17*(1), 45-65.

Alexander, G.M., Wilcox, T., and Woods, R. (2009). Sex differences in infants' visual interest in toys. *Archives of Sexual Behavior, 38,* 427-433.

Baer, J., and Kaufman, J.C. (2008). Gender Differences in Creativity. *Journal of Creative Behavior, 42,* 75-106.

Bowden, E.M., and Beeman, M.J. (2003). Normative Data for 144 Compound Remote Associate Problems. *Behavior Research Methods, Instruments, and Computers, 35*(4), 634-639.

Cheung, P.C., and Lau, S. (2010). Gender Differences in the Creativity of Hong Kong School Children: Comparison by Using the New Electronic Wallach-Kogan Creativity Tests. *Creativity Research Journal, 22* (2), 194-199.

Costa, P.T. Jr., Terracciano, A., and McCrae R.R. (2001). Gender Differences in Personality Traits Across Cultures: Robust and Surprising Findings. *Journal of Personality and Social Psychology, 81*(2), 322-331.

Csikszentmihalyi, M. (1999). Implications of a Systems Perspective for the Study of Creativity. In R. J. Sternberg (Ed.), Handbook of Creativity (pp. 313-335). Cambridge, UK: Cambridge University Press.

Dewett, T. (2006). Exploring the Role of Risk in Employee Creativity. *Journal of Creative Behavior, 40*(1), 27-45.

El-Murad, J., and West, D. C. (2004). The Definition and Measurement of Creativity: What Do We Know? *Journal of Advertising Research, 44*(2), 188-201.

Fast Company (2011). Most creative people 2011. Retrieved from http://www.fastcompany.com/most-creative-people/2011

Feist, G.J. (1999). The Influence of Personality on Artistic and Scientific Creativity. In R. J. Sternberg (Ed.), Handbook of Creativity (pp. 273-296). Cambridge, UK: Cambridge University Press.

Friedman, R. S., and Förster, J. (2001). The Effects of Promotion and Prevention Cues on Creativity. *Journal of Personality and Social Psychology, 81*(6), 1001-1013.

Friedman, R. S., and Förster, J. (2002). The Influence of Approach and Avoidance Motor Actions on Creative Cognition. *Journal of Experimental Social Psychology, 38,* 41-55.

Gilhooly, K.J., Fioratou, E., Anthony, S.H., and Wynn, V. (2007). Divergent Thinking: Strategies and Executive Involvement in Generating Novel Uses for Familiar Objects. *British Journal of Psychology, 98,* 611-625.

Green, V.A., Bigler, R., and Catherwood, D. (2004). The Variability and Flexibility of Gender-Typed Toy-Play: A Close Look at Children's Behavioural Responses to Counterstereotypic Models. *Sex Roles, 51,* 371-386.

Harris, J.A. (2004). Measured Intelligence, Acievement, Openness to Experience, and Creativity. *Personality and Individual Differences, 36,* 913-929.

Landreth, G.L. (2001). Innovations in Play Therapy: Issues, Process, and Special Populations, 3th edition. Philadelphia: Brunner-Routledge.

Lau, S., and Li, WL. (1996). Peer Status and Perceived Creativity: Are Popular Children Viewed by Peers and Teachers as Creative? *Creativity Research Journal, 9* (4), 347-352.

Leaper, C. (2002). Parenting Girls and Boys. In M. H. Bornstein (Ed.), Handbook of Parenting, Volume 1: Children and parenting (pp. 189-225). Mahwah, NJ: Lawrence Erlbaum.

Lever, J. (1976). Sex Differences in the Games Children Play. *Social Problems, 23,* 478-487.

Maccoby, E.E. (1988). Gender as a Social Category. *Developmental Psychology, 24*(6), 755-765.

Martindale, C. (1999). Biological Bases of Creativity. In R. J. Sternberg (Ed.), Handbook of Creativity (pp. 137-152). Cambridge, UK: Cambridge University Press.

McCrae, R.R. (1987). Creativity, Divergent Thinking, and Openness to Experience. *Journal of Personality and Social Psychology, 52* (6), 1285-1265.

Mednick, S.A. (1962). The Associative Basis of the Creative Process. *Psychological Review, 69,* 220-232.

Messier, J., Ferland, F., and Majnemer, A. (2007). Play Behavior of School Age Children with Intellectual Disability: Their Capacities, Interests and Attitude. *Journal of Developmental and Physical Disabilities, 20,* 193-207.

Plucker, J.A., and Renzulli, J. S. (1999). Psychometric Approaches to the Study of Human Creativity. In R. J. Sternberg (Ed.), Handbook of Creativity (pp. 35-61). Cambridge, UK: Cambridge University Press.

Runco, M. (2004). Creativity. *Annual Review of Psychology, 55,* 657–687.

Runco, M. (2006). The Development of Children's Creativity. In M. A. Spodek, and O. Saracho (Eds.), Handbook of Research on the Education of Young Children, 2nd ed. (pp. 121-131). Mahwah, NJ: Erlbaum.

Shamas, V.A. (1994). Is There Such a Thing as Implicit Problem-solving? Unpublished doctoral dissertation, University of Arizona.

Sternberg, R. J., and Lubart, T. I. (1999). The concept of creativity: Prospects and paradigms. In R. J. Sternberg (Ed.), Handbook of Creativity (pp. 3-15). Cambridge, UK: Cambridge University Press.

Stoltzfus, G., Nibbelink, B. L., Vredenburg, D., and Thyrum, E. (2011). Gender, Gender Role, and Creativity. *Social Behavior and Personality, 39*(3), 425-432.

Torrance, E. P. (1966). Torrance Tests of Creative Thinking: Norms-technical Manual. Princeton, NY: Personnel Press.

In: Psychology of Gender Differences
Editor: Sarah P. McGeown

ISBN: 978-1-62081-391-1
© 2012 Nova Science Publishers, Inc.

Chapter 6

SAME TEMPERAMENT, DIFFERENT APPRECIATION: TEMPERAMENT'S INFLUENCE ON SCHOOL ACHIEVEMENT DEPENDS ON STUDENT'S AND TEACHER'S GENDER AND TEACHER'S AGE

Sari Mullola,[1] Markus Jokela,[2]
Mirka Hintsanen,[2,3] Saija Alatupa,[2] Niklas Ravaja[4,5]
and Liisa Keltikangas-Järvinen[2,]*

[1]Department of Teacher Education, University of Helsinki, Finland
[2]IBS, Unit of Personality, Work and Health Psychology,
University of Helsinki, Finland
[3]Helsinki Collegium for Advanced Studies, University of Helsinki, Finland
[4]Department of Social Research, University of Helsinki, Finland
[5]Center for Knowledge and Innovation Research (CKIR),
Aalto University, Finland

ABSTRACT

Evidence exists that different genders might be treated in different ways or even unequally in the school context. Boys have been found to be at greater risk to miss out on their teachers' educational attention and guidance. Boys are also more frequently sent for clinical consultations, and later on, they are more likely to drop out. This is apparent also in Finland, where the secondary school students have continuously achieved in the top of the international PISA results.

Most interestingly, boys are shown to receive approximately one grade lower grade point average in adolescence than girls. This book chapter, based on the series of studies to be carried out in the large nationally representative Finnish sample, presents the research evidence which emphasizes the significance of student's biologically based innate temperament in relation to individual gender differences in school context and in

---

[*]E-mail: Liisa.Keltikangas-Jarvinen@helsinki.fi.

academic outcomes. Male and female teachers seem to perceive different temperament traits as more supportive for different genders; the same temperament trait might be negative or positive depending whether it refers to a girl or boy student and whether teacher and student are of the same or different gender.

Research evidence showed that teachers perceived boys' temperament and educational competence (EC: i.e., cognitive ability, motivation and maturity) more negatively than girls'. However, the differences between genders were not as large when perceived by male teachers, as they were when perceived by females. Males perceived boys more positively and as more capable in EC and in 'teachability' than females. They were also stricter regarding their perceptions of girls' traits. Boys received lower mother language (ML) grades but higher Math grades than girls, independently of teacher-perceived temperament and EC, the gender differences being stronger for ML than for Math. Positive mood predicted ML grades more strongly in boys than in girls and teachers' age was more strongly associated with lower ML grades in boys compared to girls.

Inhibition and maturity were stronger predictors of boys' ML grades among older teachers compared to younger teachers. Gender differences in Math grades emerged only when EC, persistence and distractibility were adjusted for. In other words, boys' underlying advantage over girls in Math was suppressed by their less favorable teacher-perceived EC and temperament. On average, girls had higher ML grades than boys, and almost two-thirds (62%) of this difference was accounted for by gender differences in teacher-perceived temperament and EC. Findings and implications are discussed in terms of the need and significance of temperament-conscious teacher training.

INTRODUCTION

School achievement is a crucial factor for educational trails and for later life trajectories of success, as it influences a student's accomplishment or failure in his/her eligibility for further studies and opportunities for the choice of career profession. Insofar as school achievement is intended to refer to the learning potential and academic performance of the student, it is important to aspire at minimizing the "external" influences that might bias the assessment of school achievement, e.g., student and teacher gender, temperament, personality, and/or whether students act in all respects as their teacher would like them to act. However, the present school grades and grade point averages (GPAs) are mostly based on the teacher assigned ratings rather than objective standardized tests and are likely to be influenced by the subjective perceptions of the teachers and biased by teachers' personal expectations, opinions, values, and attitudes [1].

Above all, there is evidence that different genders might be treated in different ways or even unequally in the school context [2, 3, 4]. Boys have been found to have a stronger risk to the negative student-teacher relationship characterized with conflict and dependency [2], to miss out of their teachers' educational attention and task-specific guidance [3, 4] and to repeat a year or more of their schooling [5]. Boys are also more frequently sent to special education and clinical consultations [6], and later on, they are more likely to drop out [5]. This is apparent also in Finland, where the secondary school students have continuously achieved in the top of the international PISA (The OECD Programme for International Student Assessment) results [7, 8, 9, 10]. Most interestingly, boys are constantly shown to receive lower school grades and approximately one grade lower grade point averages (GPAs) in adolescence than girls [5].

Another, as important concern is that despite girls' underlying advantage in school grades, in GPAs and in general school success, girls do not seem to maintain this benefit unless they tend to underachieve in the later professional education and career in comparison with boys [5].

This chapter, based on the series of studies to be carried out in the large nationally representative Finnish sample, demonstrates that innate temperament and teachers' perception of "right", ideal and teachable "school temperament" (i.e., "teachability") may be biased by both student and teacher gender and teacher age, which is important to understand individual gender differences in school context. Male and female teachers perceive different temperament traits as more valued for different genders; the same temperament trait might be negative or positive depending on whether it refers to a girl or boy student and whether teacher and student are of the same or different gender [11, 12, 13]. Along with "teachability", it might be a question of teacher's latent and culturally slanted gender role perceptions and expectations [14, 15].

Research has shown that student's temperament and teachability plays a significant role in teachers' conceptions of student's ability [16, 17, 18, 19], affecting their student-teacher interactions [20, 21], teacher's attitudes and expectations [22, 23, 24] and even educational decisions toward a given student [23, 25, 26]. Consequently, student temperament and teachability has been demonstrated to be an influential factor in predicting school success and academic outcomes measured by both standardized achievement tests and teacher-rated school grades [22, 24, 27, 28, 124].

This phenomenon biased by gender may have far-reaching consequences because it may be associated with student's later school achievement, the choice of professional career and further possibility to either underachieve or even drop out. For the present, the association between temperament and early drop out, especially considering male students is still unexplored, at least in Finland.

TEMPERAMENT IN SCHOOL ENVIRONMENT

Temperament is an individual's innate and unique behavioral way of approaching, experiencing and reacting to the world [29, 30, 31, 32]. Temperament also forms an emotional basis and core for later personality development [33]. As it is biologically rooted, temperament has strong associations with brain functioning [29, 30].

Although temperament may affect a student's school achievement through his or her learning style [26, 34, 35], cognitive working strategies [36], interests and general enjoyment of school life [24, 37], as well as energy and willingness to approach certain learning tasks [18, 22, 35, 38, 39,], temperament is independent of student motivation and maturity [32]. Above all, temperament is not related to intelligence [18, 24, 35, 40] and is also largely independent of other cognitive functions [32, 41]. As a consequence, temperament should not be associated with student school achievement by associating it with cognitive abilities. However, teachers tend to perceive students with a certain combination of temperament as more intelligent and capable of cognitive ability, more mature and more motivated than students with the other sets of temperaments [16, 42, 43]. The difference is not real unless it is an interpretation, which reflects the values, attitudes and gender role expectations of the predominant society and culture [14, 15]. Teachers may view girls' quiet and persistent ways of working as more mature, motivated and "teachable" than those of energetic and active boys. They may also view the behaviour of inflexible boys as difficultness because boys may not easily adjust to the many changes in classroom demands [18, 25]. At least so far, there is, however, no research-based evidence of gender differences in adaptability [44], as it is defined by Thomas and Chess [32] as referring to a student's ability to adjust to those repeated changes in school.

Gender Differences in Temperament

Considering temperament traits relevant in school settings, researchers have found boys to be less persistent and flexible [45], and more active [46, 47, 48, 49] and distractible [50], than girls, who in turn have been found to be less hyperactive [51] and more sensitive [46] [45], and, as an indicator of positive affect [52], to smile more [46, 53, 54, 55]. Regarding the greater male activeness, the difference is found after the first year of life and increases with age [44, 48, 49]. Recently, teachers have rated girls higher on inhibitory control and attention focusing and lower on irritability than boys [55]. As well, the meta-analysis found a very large gender difference in effortful control (including attention span dimensions, inhibitory control, and perceptual sensitivity) favouring girls [44] which has been concluded to be associated with a previously found greater male incidence of attention deficit and/or hyperactivity problems [56], aggressive behaviour, and substance abuse [44, 57, 58, 59]. Furthermore, small to moderate gender differences in surgency (characterized by high activity, high impulsivity, and high-intensity pleasure) favouring boys and only negligible gender differences in negative affectivity were reported in the same meta-analytical study [44]. The results suggest that girls may have an overall better ability to regulate or allocate their attention, control inappropriate responses and behaviours, and perceive low-intensity environmental stimuli that may lead to better awareness of subtle environmental changes [44].

Gender-Related Link between Temperament and School Achievement

In addition to gender differences in temperament, the associations between temperament and school achievement are well-established [18, 35]. Earlier studies have reported moderate gender differences favoring girls in predicting pre-reading abilities by temperament, especially by persistence [60], and students' off-task behavior by temperamental task orientation [61]. Davis and Carr [36] looked for gender differences in Mathematics (Math) problem-solving and reported that boys' Math retrieval strategy use was related to their levels of temperamental impulsiveness, while that of girls was related to their levels of inhibition. In a sample of Korean students, boys with higher self-directedness had higher GPAs than boys with lower self-directedness, whereas girls with higher harm avoidance had higher GPAs than girls with lower harm avoidance [62]. Further, in the same study, both girl and boy students, who had higher GPAs, were differentiated as higher in persistence and lower in novelty seeking in comparison with students with lower GPAs [62]. However, several studies have observed no modifying role of student gender in the association between temperament and academic achievement [47, 61, 63]. Overall, the findings are not consistent on this issue and further investigation is needed.

Goodness or Poorness of Fit

Although temperament emerges in early childhood and is relatively stable over time, place and different situations [31, 32], changes in social environment may cause changes in the expression of emotional reactions aroused by temperament [26, 29, 32, 40, 64].

Therefore, a key position in understanding the role of temperament in school environment and in school achievement is the fit between temperament and school context, i.e., the compatibility (i.e., goodness of fit) or dissonance (i.e., poorness of fit) between learning circumstances offered by the school environment and the student's own behavioral characteristics, learning style and capacity [64]. This compatibility and "goodness of fit" in school environment [32, 64] should be equally possible and achievable for both genders and for all kinds of temperaments. Before anything, both genders should have equal rights to be as teachable students, who have the same possibilities of success according to their actual ability.

TEACHABILITY AND ITS GENDER-RELATED ASSOCIATIONS WITH SCHOOL ACHIEVEMENT

Barbara Keogh and her research group was the first one who established the concept of "student teachability" [17,18, 42]). It means the teacher's perceptions of the attributes of an ideal model student, who has compliant ability to receive teaching by reacting in the "right" way the teacher desires. Initially, the concept of "teachability" is more related to developmental psychology than to education. Thus it is also more psychological than the pedagogical term. The problem is that teacher's perception of student teachability is not absolutely based on student's actual ability, but also on student's innate, temperamental characteristics. Teachers' perception of students' teachability refers to affirmative "school temperament" [22] and is composed of three factors related to the student's temperamental characteristics: high task orientation, high personal-social flexibility, and low reactivity [42] [65].

Task Orientation

The first factor related to teachability, "task orientation", is further divided into temperamental activity, persistence and distractibility [17]. Activity refers to the frequency and intensity of motor activity, while persistence refers to attention span and the tendency to continue seeking a solution to difficult learning or performance problems [22, 66]. Distractibility reflects the ease with which student's attention can be interrupted by low-level environmental stimuli [22, 66]. These three traits have been associated to student's learning styles like attention focusing and how students approach a learning task [22, 39]. Students with low task orientation are perceived by their teachers as less teachable reflecting poor educational competence (EC; i.e., cognitive ability, motivation and maturity) [17, 18]. This means that compared with the results of standardized cognitive tests, teachers tend to underestimate their intelligence [27, 42], motivation, maturity and cognitive ability [16, 43] [67]. Consequently, low task orientation correlates with lower grade point averages (GPAs) [62] and teacher-rated school grades [22, 28]. Teachers are susceptible to perceive boys lower except in task orientation [16], also in general attention focusing [44, 55] in comparison with girls.

Personal-Social Flexibility

The second factor related to teachability, "personal-social flexibility", is comprised of high approach, positive mood and high adaptability [16]. Student's personal-social flexibility is essentially positive by nature and has an indirect association in his/her school achievement. Research has shown that students with a positive mood and high adaptability receive higher grades than might be expected on the basis of their standardized achievement tests [16, 43] [27]. In addition, students with better temperamental fit to teacher demands and expectations have received higher teacher ratings for academic ability and adjustment as well as higher GPAs than students with poorer temperamental fit [43]. In everyday school life, teachers mostly recognize student temperament through a "we know it when we see it" attitude [18]. However, research has shown that this practical and subjective perception by a teacher may lead in addition to self-fulfilling prophecies [1], also to a "halo effect" between temperament, EC, and school grades [28, 42]. The latter means, that a teacher may subconsciously transfer or mix his/her perceptions of a student's temperament and EC with school grades and may be inclined to give a particular student a high grade on the basis on his/her learning style (i.e., because she or he works hard, and is persistent and adaptable). The same teacher may thus not give adequate acknowledgement to a student perceived as less adaptable and less persistent and more susceptible to being interrupted [28, 42]. The behavior of students with low flexibility is usually seen as disobedience in school environment [18]. Teachers perceive them as intentionally stubborn in many transitional periods of the school day. However, these kinds of students work very cooperatively when the class rules and routines are stable, and when they are given enough time to prepare and adjust to the upcoming changes [18, 35]. Boys are perceived by their teachers as being higher in inhibition and lower in positive mood compared to girls [16]. Boys are also rated as less flexible and less adaptable [16, 45, 68] and have difficulties in showing appropriate school behavior and adjusting to the classroom demands [16, 25].

Reactivity

The third component of teachability, "reactivity" consists of negative mood, high intensity of response and high reactivity [16] and is essentially negative by nature. It contributes to teachers' opinions of students, such as how much the teacher likes the student and how rewarding he/she experiences the teaching of the given student [16]. The association between student reactivity and school achievement is indirect where the student-teacher interaction has an important intermediary role [18, 21]. When there is a good consensus and good fit between the teacher and the student, it arouses emotions in a teacher that he/she is a good and successful teacher. This further assists the positive interaction between a teacher and a student [21, 69]. In comparison, if the student's course of action does not meet teacher's demands and expectations, it may arouse a feeling of professional inferiority. This phenomenon may occur although the given student would have reached all required learning targets. The feeling that has been aroused in a teacher influences how he/she experiences and evaluates the student and which type of interaction is going to form between them. The experience of poor teaching may first develop into the negative attitude to the student. At the same time, the student-teacher interaction may diminish and the student can become distant to the teacher. Consequently, this may influence the teacher's teaching methods and pedagogical decisions, which may become careless, too strict or otherwise inconsistent toward the certain student. Thus, the concept of student's teachability is more related to the teacher's personality than his/her pedagogical teaching style. However, the teacher's pedagogical style may change considering the student, whose temperament and learning style does not meet teacher's demands and expectations. In addition that reactivity has found to be associated with the teacher's perception of the students social position in the class [70], teachers generally view highly reactive students as less able [43], irritable and "prickly", and difficult to teach [18]. Teachers have also been found to show trust less to the students they perceive as less teachable [71]. Consequently, children with poor student-teacher relationships, manifested by conflict and dependency, receive lower grades at school [2, 20]. For the most part, boys are perceived as being higher in reactivity [44] and lower in teachability [16, 71] than girls.

SOCIETAL AND CULTURAL GENDER-RELATED DIFFERENCES AND EXPECTATIONS

Research has shown that gender differences exist in the acceptability of different temperament traits; that is, in boys and girls, similar temperament may be viewed as more or less appropriate or desirable depending on cultural gender role norms and expectations [46] [14, 15, 72, 73, 74, 75], which in turn, and in all likelihood, may moderate teachers' perceptions of an ideal and "teachable" student [14, 15, 18]. The cultural and socio-economic context in which children develop shapes the development of temperamental characteristics [46, 55, 72, 76, 77, 78, 79] and especially the way different temperament traits are valued [14]. The extent to which a culture values or accepts certain behaviors may drive the reinforcement or punishment of these behaviors, resulting in different developmental outcomes (e.g., in social skills, peer relationships, and later adjustment) [15, 46, 55, 80, 81, 82], and long term consequences concerning temperament-related inter-personal processes (e.g., the age of marrying and having children) [44, 83]. This process becomes activated and visible especially in school environment, where the manners and customs of behavior are, in addition to culturally bounded, also slow to change. Previous research has shown that teachers with opposite gender have found to be more susceptible to perceive a student as inattentive, disruptive, or omit homework than a teacher with the same gender [84]. Teacher ratings have been found to be even more gender typed than parents' ratings because teachers frequently see students interacting in peer groups with the same gender, which has been seen to magnify gender role differences [44, 85].

Student and Teacher Gender and Teacher Age

Despite the repeated excellent PISA (The OECD Programme for International Student Assessment) results among secondary school students in Finland [7, 8, 9, 10], there has been a lively conversation among educators and educational policy and decision makers about the number and position of males in teacher training and as practitioners in education. Whether there are too few male teachers in the Finnish educational system, and whether students, especially boys, would increasingly need teaching and interaction with male teachers as role models has been discussed [86]. This conversation has also been topical in some other OECD countries, where female teachers have been found to account for the largest proportion of secondary school teachers [87, 88, 89, 90]. Previously, teachers' female gender has been suggested to have a positive impact on students' reading performance [91], language learning [92] and both genders' general achievement [93, 94]. There are also dissimilar and conflicting findings of a positive male teacher effect on students' Math learning [95], same-gender effect on students' achievement [96] or no gender effect on either Math [92] or any other subject outcomes [97]. It has been also argued whether the feminization of the teacher profession would be the explanation for boys' underachievement [98, 99] and whether boys would need male teachers in order to achieve better [89, 100] or to assume a positive male role model [88, 90]. Both Bettinger and Long [101] and Dee [100] found in their wide and longitudinal studies that same gender teachers increased student's interest and engagement in a teacher's subject. Among females, the influence was strong in several subjects, particularly in mathematics and statistics but among males only in education [101] revealing a positive role-model effect in such fields where that gender is underrepresented. There is also evidence from studies where same-gender matching did not have an effect on student's outcomes [97, 102] [86] or studies where boys' school attitudes were even more positive when taught by female teachers [103, 104]. On the other hand, based on teachers' practical perceptions and partly tacit assumptions, male teachers have been assumed to practice somewhat more relaxed pedagogy with their students compared to female teachers, or teach in ways that are more appealing to boys [90, 99, 105].

There are two extensive international studies where the effects of teachers' gender were studied in the context of teaching and teacher training. In these studies, female teachers perceived their students as less teachable and showed less trust to their students [71], and punished actions committed with recidivism more than male teachers [106], who in turn preferred girl students both in teachability and in trust [71] and punished actions perpetrated by an academically good student more often than female teachers [106].

Instead, older teachers have been found to show more trust in their students compared with younger teachers independent of teacher-perceived teachability [71]. Teachers' age has also found to be associated with the motivational factors of teacher professionalization [107], teachers' emotional responses to educational change [108] and teachers' severity of sanction in the classroom [106].

However, no previous study has taken student temperament into account in any of these contexts. In addition to incoherent or less research on the effect of teacher gender and age on students' outcomes, there is lack of knowledge on how being of the same or different gender as the student affects perceptions and outcomes. That is; does it matter, whether the teacher and the student are of the same or different gender?

SUBJECT-RELATED DIFFERENCES BETWEEN TEMPERAMENT AND SCHOOL ACHIEVEMENT

The role of temperament in school achievement may also be specific to school subjects and the task demands set by those different subjects, such as whether the subject requires the ability to concentrate as well as high task engagement (related to high task orientation) or, for instance articulacy, creativity with new problem-solving strategies and/or engagement in new situations (related to flexibility and reactivity) [17, 42, 109].

In Mother Language (ML) instruction, the Finnish curriculum involves various working methods in versatile domains, such as grammar, literature and reading, creative writing, and articulacy and drama [110]. These domains contain both fixed as well as free forms of study content, working styles and methods. By contrast, a Maths curriculum is more limited and focused in its approach, and the working methods may be more consistent and compact even though the content of the study programme is also as highly multifaceted and divergent with detailed skills as in ML [110]. Recent European research that considered gender differences in educational outcomes has indicated that boys achieve better outcomes in Mathematics but lower in ML and in literature in comparison with girls [5].

Considering the association between temperament and school subject, temperament has been previously found to be slightly more strongly related to Mother Language (ML) than to Math [22, 24, 27, 34, 40, 63], although contrary findings also exist [111], as well as findings where teacher-rated temperament has been congruently related to both subjects [40, 112]. Because of these inconsistent findings, future research is needed to investigate the possible differential association of temperament with Math and ML.

THE FINNISH EDUCATIONAL SCHOOL SYSTEM

The Finnish education system, which is illustrated in Figure 1 [110], consists of nine years of compulsory schooling between the age of 7 and 15 (six years at primary school and three years at lower secondary school). The whole age group can be studied because there are no private schools or parallel school systems. Teachers are similarly educated and all schools follow the same national curriculum. For the following reasons, the Finnish comprehensive school is the most appropriate "real-life laboratory". Approximately 97% of students in each age group goes through this public comprehensive school in regular classes (of which approximately 7% are under special, individual supervision, approximately 2% are in special, "tailored" classes, and less than 1% leave without completing this education). After comprehensive school almost all students continue on either to Senior High Schools (approximately 64%) or Vocational Institutions (approximately 30%), and less than nine percent drop out of this secondary education [123].

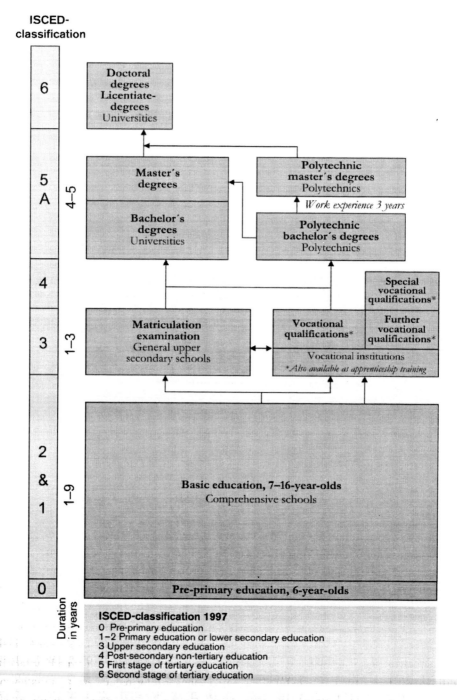

Reference: Ministery of Education and Culture: Formal Education in Finland:
http://www.minedu.fi/export/sites/default/OPM/Koulutus/koulutusjaerjestelmae/liitteet/finnish_educati
on.pdf.

Figure 1. The construction of the formal education system in Finland.

Evaluation Process

The Finnish National Board of Education (FNBE) has stated the principles and rules for pupils' assessment in the National Core Curriculum for Basic Education intended for pupils' in compulsory education [110]. Practically, the school grades and GPAs in the Finnish lower-secondary education system are based on a) examinations constructed and set by an individual teacher, b) model examinations offered by the authors of the textbooks and workbooks, c) teacher's subjective perceptions of students' participative activity, students' carefulness and conscientiousness with the given assignments during school lessons and working periods, and d) teacher's subjective perceptions of student's ability to perform the required teaching-learning-process in a teacher's planned and desired way. In the national evaluation guidelines [110], The Finnish National Board of Education has stated and briefed Finnish teachers to take student's lesson activity and learning process into account in school assessment so that they may increase or decrease student's final grade as one grade, if the teacher considers it necessary. Instead, the roles of national standardized tests are briefed to be mainly suggestive and to be used only once or at the most twice in a school year and only in some selected subjects, mostly in Mother Language, in Math and in foreign language.

Furthermore, the final grade point of the certain school subject generally contains teacher's subjective perceptions of student's excitement and motivation toward that subject. Practically, this means that student's interest toward the certain subject may increase the grade point although student's cognitive knowledge and skills would not correspondence with the required target level. Above all, the final grade is a combination of all these sectors mentioned above assigned by an individual teacher. That sector that is under the main focus on a teacher's assessment may vary under the different schools, classes and teachers.

However among Finnish teachers, student's progress in the certain learning process has an important place in teacher's assessment. In addition, particularly in elementary school, grades are supplemented with teacher assigned verbal assessments considering student's perceived abilities, working skills, adjustment to required learning process and general adjustment to school environment.

RESEARCH EVIDENCE

The following research evidence focuses on the series of three published studies [11, 12, 13] with three research problems considering *first;* the gender differences in teachers' perceptions of student temperament, EC, and teachability, *second;* the effect of teacher and student gender and teacher age on teacher-perceived temperament, EC, and teachability, and whether there is a significant same gender or different gender association between teachers and students in this relationship, and *third;* whether student and teacher gender and teacher age modify the association between teacher-perceived temperament and EC with school achievement. The characteristics of the data used in studies I – III [11, 12, 13] are given in Table 1. The participants included at the most 3212 ninth grade adolescents and their 221 teachers who took part in the cross-sectional Finnish Study of Temperament and School Achievement (FTSA) [113], a nationally representative sample of lower secondary schools compiled in winter 2005–2006. Temperament was assessed with scales from the TABC-R

[114] and DOTS-R [66] batteries, EC consists of cognitive ability, motivation, and maturity developed for the current study. School achievement was measured by the respective grades of Math and ML taken from the students' latest school reports (range = 4-10; 4 means fail, 5-6 poor, 7-8 good and 9-10 excellent).

Table 1. Characteristics of the Data Used in Studies I-III

Participants	Study I			Study II			Study III		
	Number	%	Age M (sd)	Number	%	Age M (sd)	Number	%	Age M (sd)
Students	3212		15.1 (0.37)	3212		15.1 (0.37)	1063		15.1 (0.33)
Girls	1619	50.4		1619	50.4		529	49.8	
Boys	1593	49.6		1593	49.6		534	50.2	
Teachers	221		46.1 (9.53)	221		46.1 (9.53)	72		
Women	162	73.3		166	75.1		55	76.4	47.0 (10.33)
Men	59	26.7		55	24.9		17	23.6	50.6 (7.88)

GENDER DIFFERENCES IN TEACHERS' PERCEPTIONS OF STUDENT TEMPERAMENT, EDUCATIONAL COMPETENCE, AND TEACHABILITY

Figure 2 shows the results of gender differences in teachers' perceptions of student temperament, EC, and teachability based on three phase series of published studies [11, 12] [13]. It was found that teachers perceive boys' activity, negative emotionality, inhibition, and distractibility as higher, but persistence, mood, and EC as lower than those of girls [11, 12, 13]. This is in line with previous studies [28, 42, 45, 50, 115] and confirms the lower level of teacher-perceived boys' 'task orientation' involving high activity, high distractibility, low persistence, and low mood, referring also to boys' lower teacher-perceived teachability [42] [65]. This temperament pattern is also consistent with a 'difficult' temperament as defined by Thomas and Chess [32]. Teachers usually perceive students with 'difficult' temperament, mostly boys, as irritable and annoying, because they may have problems in adapting to classroom routines and changes [18, 32]. This is seen as indicating problems in boys' compliance with teacher demands [116] and causing more conflictual relationships with their teachers [2, 21, 69]. Furthermore, this temperament pattern makes boys generally more vulnerable to a negative teacher–student relationship [21, 117], which in turn has been shown to lead to lower school grades [2, 20], especially if the teacher and the student have been of opposite gender [100]. The present results support the possibility of these unwanted consequences, although we did not investigate the association of teacher-perceived students' temperament on the teacher–student relationship.

Additionally, the results replicated the previous findings that teacher-perceived students' low task orientation is associated with teacher-perceived students' low EC, and teachability [16, 25]. Here, it was true especially for boys. The results might reveal a 'halo effect' where teachers tend to underestimate the intelligence, motivation, and maturity of students they perceive as low in task orientation and teachability [16, 25]. However, these boys may be similar in cognitive ability, as well motivated, and as mature as girls, but due to their temperament, differ only in how they respond to the demands of the school [18]. It is also possible that task orientation, especially activity and persistence may in reality be associated with student's increasing motivation. Although the present results cannot give affirmative evidence of teachers' underestimating the EC of boys with low task orientation, it is obvious that these boys do not match with teachers' ideas of what an appropriately behaved student should be. Thus, the present results raise doubts about the position of boys' and their 'goodness of fit' climate [64, 109, 118] in the school context.

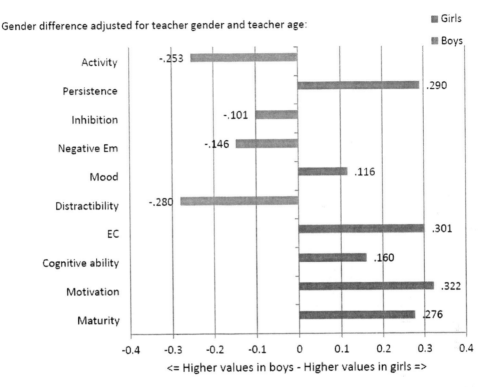

Figure 2. Gender differences (expressed in units of standard deviations) in temperament and EC traits adjusted for teacher gender and teacher age (positive values indicate higher values in girls; negative values indicate higher values in boys). Note. All p-values < .001. Negative Em = Negative emotionality.

Interactive Effects of Student and Teacher Gender and Teacher Age

As shown in Figures 3a and 3b, the results revealed a gender congruency-related effect in predicting the teacher-perceived student's temperament, EC, and teachability, which occurred only with male teachers and favoured boys and disfavoured girls. The findings highlight the role of male teachers and their pedagogy considering the school life of both genders.

Although boys were perceived lower in persistence and EC and higher in distractibility and inhibition than girls by teachers of both genders, the gender gap narrowed between boys and girls when a boy student was rated by a male teacher. This means that male teachers perceived girls' and boys' persistence, EC, distractibility, and inhibition as closer to each other than female teachers. Furthermore, the results indicate that male teachers perceive boys more positively than female teachers and view them as more capable in EC and teachability than female teachers do. In addition, male teachers' ratings of girls' activity and negative emotionality were higher, and persistence and EC lower, in comparison with female teachers' ratings for girls.

The current results are supportive to Bettinger and Long's [101] and Dee's [84, 100] findings, where same-gender matching improved in addition to teacher's perceptions of student capacity and performance, also student's achievement and engagement to the teacher's subject. The findings might also reveal the positive role model effect [88, 90, 100, 101] or situation where the same-gender teacher would have more capacity to understand the characteristic of the same-gender student. Consequently, it might be asked whether male teachers are also prone to practicing a more understanding and gentle pedagogy in the classroom for boys compared to girls, or in comparison with female teachers' pedagogy with boy students. In contrast, when compared to female teachers, male teachers are likely to be stricter and more critical with regard to their perceptions of girls' traits. They may also underestimate girls' persistence and EC or female teachers may overestimate girls' persistence and EC as well. This was contrary to our hypothesis that male teachers might practise a more gentle and relaxing pedagogy with their students, whether boys or girls. However, this seems to be true only for boys. On the other hand, our results are in line with Dee's [84] findings, where particularly female students were seen as more inattentive by the male teacher, although both female and male students were seen as disruptive by another gender teacher. Furthermore, the present findings suggest that when a boy's teacher was an older male, teacher ratings of inhibition were higher, and ratings of mood lower, compared to a female teacher's ratings for boys or girls [figures or tables not shown here]. Generally, the older the teacher, the more mature he/she perceived a student to be. The results considering the influence of teachers' age were also contrary to the hypothesis.

The hypothesis was that, in general, teachers' age would increase their negative views of students' temperament, especially task orientation, and decrease their perception of students' EC and teachability, independent of the teacher's gender. In addition to cultural gender stereotypes and expectations [14, 55], the results may be revealing in terms of the professional development and lifespan of a teacher. The association between teachers' age and students' teacher-perceived maturity may suggest that a teacher's professional and general life experience increases his/her general confidence in a student, and probably also allows him/her to be certain about a student's ability. However, male teachers' ageing, in particularly, decreased their perception of boys' mood and increased their perception of boys' inhibition.

It might be that ageing increases male teachers' strictness and intolerance with boys, while this seems not to be true with female teachers. This might have a significant influence also on the teacher–student relationship and interaction with boys [21, 117]. Previously, boys have been found to be more pressured than girls to change their inhibited, shy behaviour [119, 120], which appears to have been the case for a long time in the Finnish cultural and educational climate. Thus, a possible mechanism explaining our findings is that older male teachers might carry stronger cultural expectations, which reflect more traditional stereotypes of male gender. It is also possible, that due to these cultural gender role expectations and pressures, older male teachers might become somewhat disappointed and frustrated, if a boy student does not reach and fulfill the tacit gender role expectations of society and its generally accepted educational climate. However, because the cross-sectional study design, it cannot be said, whether teachers' perceptions of students' temperament change with ageing, or is it a question of generational differences between younger and older teachers. Further research-based evidence with longitudinal research design is necessary for more reliable implications.

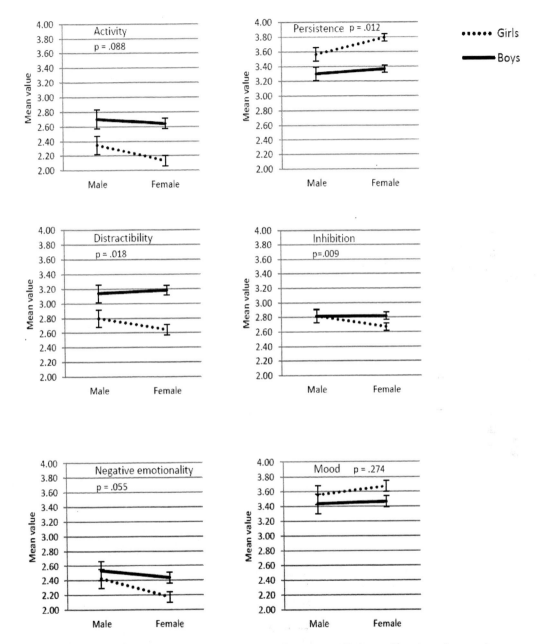

Figure 3.a. Interaction effects of multilevel regression models predicting students' teacher-rated temperament by teacher's gender and student's gender. The vertical bars denote the ± standard error of the mean (SEM).

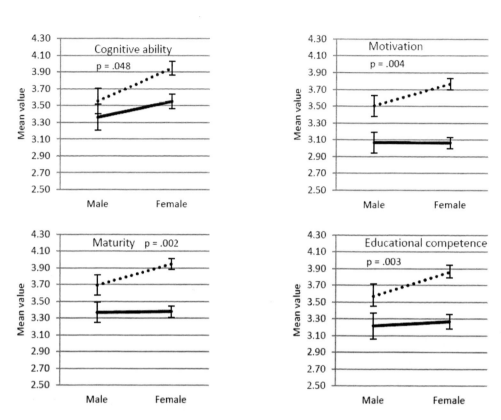

Figure 3.b. Interaction effects of multilevel regression models predicting students' teacher-rated educational competence (EC; including the dimensions of cognitive ability, motivation, and maturity) by teacher's gender and student's gender. The vertical bars denote the ± standard error of the mean (SEM).

Summary

The four major findings were as follows: There was (1) a significant gender difference between girls' and boys' temperament, EC, and teachability, which favoured girls and was independent of teachers' gender; (2) a significant gender congruency-related effect in predicting the teacher-perceived student's temperament, EC, and teachability, which however occurred only with male teachers and favoured boys and disfavoured girls; (3) a significant interactive effect of teacher's gender, student's gender, and teacher's age in the perceptions of student's temperament, especially inhibition and mood, which however occurred only with male teachers and only with respect to boys; and (4) a significant main effect of teacher's age in the perceptions of student's EC, especially maturity, which was independent of teacher's and student's gender.

GENDER DIFFERENCES IN THE ASSOCIATION OF TEMPERAMENT, EDUCATIONAL COMPETENCE AND TEACHABILITY WITH SCHOOL ACHIEVEMENT

Figure 4. presents the gender differences in the association between teacher-perceived temperament, EC and teachability with school achievement in terms of Math and ML grades. Teachers rated average ML grades significantly lower in boys, and almost two-thirds (62%) of this difference could be explained by gender differences in teacher-perceived temperament and educational competence. The gender difference in ML was the strongest after being adjusted for inhibition and (positive) mood. Gender differences in Math, by contrast, emerged only when gender differences in teacher-perceived educational competence (i.e., EC, motivation and maturity) and in certain temperament traits (e.g., activity, persistence and distractibility) were taken into account, being the strongest after being adjusted for motivation. This suggests that girls' lower Math grades (compared to boys) are compensated for by their higher standing on teacher-perceived educational competence and temperament traits associated with better grades.

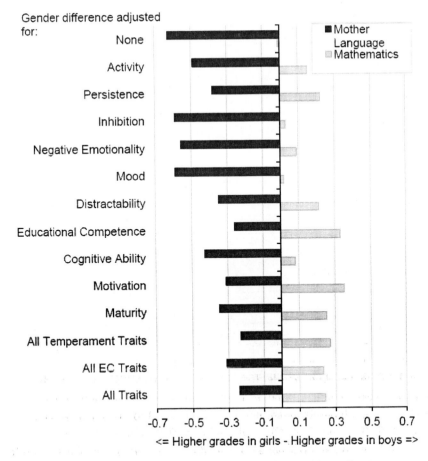

Figure 4. Gender differences (expressed in units of standard deviations) in Mother Language and Mathematics adjusted for student characteristics (positive values indicate higher grades in boys, negative values indicate higher grades in girls).

However, when girls and boys with similar teacher-perceived educational competence and temperament characteristics are compared, boys achieve higher Math grades. Considering ML this was in line with the original hypothesis and with previous studies confirming boys' lower teacher-assigned grades in comparison with those of girls in stereotypically feminine subject area, such as reading, spelling and writing [121, 122].

The results for Math imply that temperament traits may suppress some gender differences in school achievement that might surface if boys and girls had similar temperament characteristics. The results support the current concern over male students' learning circumstances, the 'goodness of fit-climate' [32, 109, 118] and general well-being in the school environment.

Generally, the gender differences were stronger in ML than in Math. Although the intensities of the effects were stronger in Math than in ML considering all temperament and EC traits, the results were more varied in ML and more uniform in Math. This was true regarding both genders. However, previous research is not consistent on this issue [27, 34, 40, 63, 111, 112].

In Finland, the subject-related pedagogy of ML may not expect students to have as exact working habits as is expected in Math. Thus the results may reveal more about the teacher-perceived gender-related expectations of teachable and ideal students than about the demands of the subject-related working habits that certain temperament traits could disturb. However, the results expand previous findings by offering evidence of the broader influence of teachers' gender-related perceptions of student temperament on students' Math and ML grades as examined at the same time.

Interactive Effects of Student and Teacher Gender and Teacher Age

There were no significant interaction effects between teacher gender or age and student characteristics in predicting Math grade. Instead in ML, it was not possible to demonstrate the role of teacher gender owing to the lack of male teachers, which also reveals the numerical imbalance between female and male teachers in Finland.

However, in ML (tables and figures not shown here), female teachers gave more weight to positive mood in boys than in girls. The results concerning teachers' age suggested that younger teachers give more weight than older teachers to student temperament and teacher-perceived educational competence when grading the students' school achievement. Student negative emotionality, educational competence and motivation were less strongly related to ML grades in older compared to younger teachers. This was also the case for maturity and inhibition in boys but not in girls. This finding might be related to the results presented by Van Houtte [71], who reported that older teachers showed more trust in their pupils independently of the pupils' teacher-perceived teachability. Perhaps older teachers are better at separating temperament from their assessment of the student so that temperament assumes a lesser role than in the assessments made by younger teachers.

In addition, it is possible that with age, the teacher becomes more aware of his/her professional strength and is in keeping with ones owns temperamental characteristics and behavioral style, which further assist him/her to understand student's uniqueness better, and also the general mechanism of how different temperaments interact with each other.

Summary

In summary, boys had lower ML grades but higher Math grades than girls, independently of teacher-perceived temperament and EC, the gender differences being stronger for ML than for Math. In addition, there were interaction effects between student and teacher characteristics, indicating that (a) positive mood predicted ML grades more strongly in boys than in girls; (b) teachers' age was more strongly associated with lower ML grades in boys compared to girls, independently of teacher-perceived EC, motivation and maturity; (c) inhibition and maturity were stronger predictors of boys' (but not girls') ML grades among older teachers compared to younger teachers (inhibition increased and maturity decreased ML grades more markedly in boys than in girls); and (d) negative emotionality, EC and motivation were more strongly related to student ML grades among younger teachers than among older teachers.

Comparisons between girls and boys indicated that gender differences in Math grades emerged only when some student characteristics (educational competence, persistence and distractibility in particular) were adjusted for. In other words, the boys' underlying advantage over girls in Math was suppressed by their less favorable teacher-perceived educational competence and temperament traits.

On average, girls had higher ML grades than boys, and almost two-thirds (62%) of this difference was accounted for by gender differences in teacher-perceived temperament and educational competence.

CONCLUSION

Along with previous literature, the present research evidence highlights the significance of innate temperament in relation to school environment and student's academic outcomes. Particularly, teachers' gender-related perceptions of an ideal and teachable model student seem to favor girls and disfavor boys. Teachers' temperament ratings carry a systematic variance both by their own gender and the students' gender, and also by their own age, which might further bias teacher-perceived school grades. However, because of cross-sectional research, the current study cannot give affirmative evidence for this. Boys received systematically lower ML grades, partly because of gender differences in temperament. The higher Math grades of boys compared to girls were suppressed by gender differences in temperament and educational competence favoring girls.

The current research evidence emphasize the actual and international concern regarding boys' school well-being and the education system's possibility to create affirmative "goodness of fit" – school climate that is supportive and equitable for both genders [18, 32, 35, 64]. In spite of the excellent PISA-results [7, 8, 9, 10], almost nine percent of Finnish students drop out from postgraduate studies after ninth grade, which is one percent more than a year ago [123] and consists mostly of boys [123]. Both international and domestic research in Finland leads to the critical question: "How to be a boy in today's school?" With all its societal and health implications, the most far-reaching consequence of "poorness of fit" in the school environment is boys' increased risk to drop out from society.

Girls' superior performance compared with boys raise questions whether there are general school expectations which advantage girls rather than boys. Also the nature of the subject and the divisions of the content teachers are tending to stress in their teaching and in their assessments are important topics. The teacher assigned ML grade, for example, consists of several fields, but which of them are in the focus? Are creative writing, literature, verbal presentation, and general neatness with good humour and positive mood in the centre stage when rating good performance? Are the girls' and boys' ways to express themselves something special that only a teacher with the same gender could understand?

It is noteworthy that the teacher-ratings of ML were all done by females. The feminization of the teacher profession has been seen as a wide concern in number of countries [98, 99] being topical issue also in Finnish education. In terms of temperament teacher gender did not extend its effect on students' school achievement. Thus, at least these results do not bring out any reason for the concern of the preponderance of female teachers in Finnish education. However, it does not eliminate the importance of female and male teachers' proportional balance in other educational practices.

Another socially important question is girls' underachievement in later professional education and career despite their excellent school success and advantage in comparison with boys. What happens to the "high grade girls" after the junior high school years or after the graduation? Although girls appear to meet the expectations and demands set by school environment better than boys, the school reports' promises of girls' predominance and preferable careers do not seem to continue after school. Does this suggest to the gap between the school demands and societal demands? It appears that within girls the present school system may reward inappropriate characteristics, whereas within boys it drops them out because of trivial traits. As such the present school system might not acknowledge enough the most appropriate characteristics of both genders relative in the successful choice of the later career.

Although teacher training and the general school system are world-famous and high in quality in Finland, the present research evidence indicates some future challenges. The present findings suggest that Finnish teachers also need more information about the importance and influence of temperament in school context in order to differentiate cognitive skills from behavioural styles, and consequently to ensure equitable school treatment for all students. This knowledge would be important for teacher's personal and practical knowledge because temperament differs from intelligence, cognitive ability, maturity and motivation [40], and because school reports have significant and far-reaching roles in students' academic lives.

The present research suggests more consideration regarding the prevailing assessment practice in the Finnish education system where student's learning process is in the central position. The assessment is not only based on exam results but on the teacher's evaluation of student's learning process (i.e., has the result achieved by the "right" way). The Finnish National Board of Education enables this practice in its operative statement of the National Core Curriculum for Basic Education [110]. Practically, this means that although the student would have achieved the highest grade from the school exam, teachers have the legal right to diminish (as well as improve) student's school grade to the tune of one grade, depending on how successful they perceive student's learning process. Student's innate temperament, however, has been found to be significantly associated to this learning process. That means that in terms of temperament research and theory, there is no "right" way to study, but the possibility to follow one's own temperament and behavioral style in studying is the most effective way for every student. The forcing of this learning process in a certain direction does not increase the efficiency of studying. Strong expectations and demands towards the "right" learning process are especially detrimental to the students with inhibited, shy or slow-to-warm-up temperaments or students with relatively high or low temperamental levels in general (e.g., high activity, low persistence or high distractibility).

Especially difficult are teachers' verbal assessments in school reports considering student's learning process because teachers' perceptions of students' temperaments are involved in these evaluations. Verbal assessments are aimed to focus on the student's working styles but they refer to the student's innate temperamental characteristics, like "you are active and eager", "you work target-oriented and motivated", "you are good at concentrating for a long time for the given task", "you finish your tasks persistently", "you come to school happy and in a good mood", "you are socially active in group working", etc. Although it may be important particularly for the younger students to receive feedback related their learning styles, this kind of feedback falls on individual personality, which may, particularly if it is negative, even bother and obscure the student's ability to realize his/her actual cognitive strengths. It is especially problematic if temperament-related assessment remains as a part of teacher's evaluation practice across student's later school years extending its associations also with teacher-assigned school grades. This might further influence the student's later choice of a career.

Although students' education and teaching for the certain learning processes are essential functions of the school, these teaching areas would be advisable, however, be kept apart from assessment, school grades and GPAs, at least in terms of temperament. If it is seen necessary to evaluate student's learning process, students should receive separate school grades from academic achievement and working styles.

Finally, temperament should not be thought only in terms of risk issues in school context but as enrichment and as a possibility to enhance the interaction and the teaching and learning circumstances between teachers and students considering both genders. Teachers with temperament knowledge may have a greater tolerance for their students' behavior and more sensitivity to recognize students' gender-specific differences including the talented and the underachievers.

Most of all, temperament conscious teacher training and teaching practice would work as a useful and practical tool in societies attempting to prevent boys' possible exclusion and to improve girls' later professional careers to be in accordance with their actual abilities.

REFERENCES

[1] Jussim, L., and Harber, K. D. (2005). Teacher expectations and self-fulfilling prophecies: Knowns and unknowns, resolved and unresolved controversies. *Personality and Social Psychology Review*, 9, 131−155.

[2] Hamre, B. K., and Pianta, R. C. (2001). Early teacher-child relationships and the trajectory of children's school outcomes through eighth grade. *Child Development*, 72(2), 625-638.

[3]   Lingard, B., Martino, W., and Mills, M. (2009). *Boys and Schooling Beyond Structural Reform*. New York: Palgrave Macmillan.

[4]   Ashley, M., and Lee, J. (2003). *Women teaching boys – caring and working in the primary school*. London: Trentham Books Limited.

[5]   EACEA (2010). *Gender Differences in Educational Outcomes: Study on the Measures Taken and the Current Situation in Europe*. Brussels: Education, Audiovisual and Culture Executive Agency (EACEA P9 Eurydice).

[6]   Tilastokeskus (2011). Suomen virallinen tilasto (SVT): *Erityisopetus* [verkkojulkaisu]. ISSN=1799-1595. Helsinki: Tilastokeskus [viitattu: 21.11.2011]. Retrieved from http://www.stat.fi/til/erop/index.html.

[7]   OECD (2010). *PISA 2009 Results: What Students Know and Can Do: Student Performance in Reading, Mathematics and Science (Volume I)*, OECD Publishing. Retrieved from http://dx.doi.org/10.1787/ 9789264091450-en

[8]   OECD 2007a OECD (2007a). *PISA 2006 Science competencies for tomorrow'sworld: Volume 1, analysis*. Paris: OECD.

[9]   OECD 2007b OECD (2007b). *PISA 2006 Science competencies for tomorrow's world: Volume 2, data*. Paris: OECD.

[10]   OECD (2004). *Learning for tomorrow's world: First results from PISA 2003*. Paris: OECD.

[11]   Mullola, S., Ravaja, N., Lipsanen, J., Hirstiö-Snellman, P., Alatupa, S., and Keltikangas- Järvinen, L. (2010). Teacher-perceived temperament and educational competence as predictors of school grades. *Learning and Individual Differences*, *20*(3), 209 - 214.

[12]   Mullola, S., Ravaja, N., Lipsanen, J., Alatupa, S., Hintsanen, M., Jokela, M., and Keltikangas- Järvinen, L. (2011). Gender differences in teachers' perceptions of students' temperament, educational competence, and teachability. *British Journal of Educational Psychology*, in press. DOI:10.1111/j.2044-8279.2010.02017.x

[13]   Mullola, S., Jokela, M., Ravaja, N., Lipsanen, J., Hintsanen, M., Alatupa, S., and Keltikangas- Järvinen, L. (2011). (Mullola et al., 2011b). Associations of student temperament and educational competence with academic achievement: The role of teacher age and teacher and student gender. *Teaching and Teacher Education, 27* (5), 942-951.

[14]   Kerr, M. (2001). Culture as a context for temperament: Suggestions from the life courses of shy Swedes and Americans. In T. D. Wachs and G. A. Kohnstamm (Eds.), *Temperament in context* (pp. 139–152). Mahwah, NJ: Lawrence Erlbaum Associates.

[15]   Kerr, M., Lambert, W. W., and Bem, D. J. (1996). Life course sequelae of childhood shyness in Sweden: comparison with the United States. *Developmental Psychology*, *32*(6), 1100–1105.

[16]   Keogh, B. K. (1994). Temperament and teachers' views of teachability. InW. B. Carey, and S. C. McDevitt (Eds.), *Prevention and early intervention: Individual differences as risk factors for the mental health of children* (pp. 246-254). New York: Brunner/Mazel.

[17]   Keogh, B. K. (1983). Individual differences in temperament: a contribution to the personal, social, and educational competence of learning disabled children. In J. D. McKinney, and L. Feagans (Eds.), *Current topics in learning disabilities*, Vol. 1 (pp. 33-55). Norwood NJ: Ablex Publishing Corporation.

[18] Keogh, B. K. (2003). *Temperament in the classroom: Understanding individual differences.* Baltimore: Paul H. Brookes Publishing Co.

[19] Stipek, D. (2002). Communicating expectations. In D. Stipek (Ed.), *Motivation to learn: Integrating theory and practice* (pp. 210–229). Boston, MA: Allyn and Bacon.

[20] DiLalla, L. F., Marcus, J. L., and Wright-Phillips, M. V. (2004). Longitudinal effects of preschool behavioral styles on early adolescent school performance. *Journal of School Psychology, 42*, 385-401.

[21] Rudasill, K. M., and Rimm-Kaufman, S. E. (2009). Teacher-child relationship quality: the roles of child temperament and teacherechild interactions. *Early Childhood Research Quarterly, 24*, 107- 120.

[22] Martin, R. P. (1989). Activity level, distractibility, and persistence: critical characteristics in early schooling. In G. A. Kohnstamm, J. E. Bates, and M. K. Rothbart (Eds.), *Temperament in childhood* (pp. 451-462). Chichester, England: John Wiley and Sons, Ltd.

[23] Martin, R. P., Nagle, R., and Paget, K. (1983). Relationships between temperament and classroom behavior, teacher attitudes, and academic achievement. *Journal of Psychoeducational Assessment, 1*, 377- 386.

[24] Guerin, D. W., Gottfried, A. W., Oliver, P. H., and Thomas, C. W. (2003). *Temperament: Infancy through Adolescence, The Fullerton Longitudinal Study, Longitudinal Research in the Social and Behavioral Sciences: An Interdisciplinary Series.* New York: Kluwer Academic/Plenum Publishers.

[25] Keogh, B. K. (1989). Applying temperament research to school. In G. A. Kohnstamm, J. E. Bates, and M. K. Rothbart (Eds.), *Temperament in childhood* (pp. 437-450). Chichester, England: John Wiley and Sons, Ltd.

[26] Rothbart, M. K., and Jones, L. B. (1998). Temperament, self-regulation, and education. *School Psychology Review, 27*, 479−491.

[27] Martin, R. P., and Holbrook, J. (1985). Relationship of temperament characteristics to the academic achievement of first grade children. *Journal of Psychoeducational Assessment, 3*, 131-140.

[28] Martin, R. P., Olejnik, S., and Gaddis, L. (1994). Is temperament an important contributor to schooling outcomes in elementary school? Modeling effects of temperament and scholastic ability on academic achievement. In W. B. Carey, and S. C. McDevitt (Eds.), *Prevention and early intervention: Individual differences as risk factors for the mental health of children* (pp. 59-68). New York: Brunner/Mazel.

[29] Buss, A. H., and Plomin, R. (1975). *A temperament theory of personality development.* New York: Wiley.

[30] Buss, A. H., and Plomin, R. (1984). *Temperament: Early developing personality traits.* Hillsdale, NJ: Erlbaum.

[31] Goldsmith, H. H., Buss, A. H., Plomin, R., Rothbart, M. K., Thomas, A., Chess, S., et al. (1987). Roundtable: what is temperament? Four approaches. *Child Development, 58*, 505-529.

[32] Thomas, A., and Chess, S. (1977). *Temperament and development.* New York: Brunner/Mazel.

[33] Goldsmith, H. H., Lemeny, K. S., Aksan, N., and Buss, K. A. (2000). Temperamental substrates of personality development. In V. J. Molfese, and D. L. Molfese (Eds.),

Temperament and personality development across the life span (pp. 1-32). Mahwah, NJ: Lawrence Erlbaum Associates.

[34] Guerin, D. W., Gottfried, A. W., Oliver, P. H., and Thomas, C. W. (1994). Temperament and school functioning during early adolescence. *Journal of Early Adolescence, 14*(2), 200-225.

[35] Kristal, J. (2005). *The temperament perspective: Working with children's behavioral styles.* Baltimore: Paul H. Brookes Publishing.

[36] Davis, H., and Carr, M. (2002). Gender differences in mathematics strategy use: the influence of temperament. *Learning and Individual Differences, 13*, 83-95.

[37] Elliot, A. J., and Thrash, T. M. (2002) Approach-avoidance motivation in personality: Approach and avoidance temperaments and goals, *Journal of Personality and Social Psychology, 82* (5), 804-818.

[38] Caspi, A. (1998). Personality development across the life course. In W. Damon (Ed.-in-Chief) and N. Eisenberg (Vol. Ed.), *Handbook of child psychology: Vol. 3. Social, emotional, and personality development* (5th ed., pp. 311–388). New York: John Wiley and Sons.

[39] Caspi, A., and Shiner, R. L. (2006). Personality development. InW. Damon, R. M. Lerner, and N. Eisenberg (Eds.), *Social, emotional and personality development (6th ed.).Handbook of child psychology,* Vol. 3 (pp. 300-365) Hoboken, NJ: John Wiley and Sons.

[40] Strelau, J. (1998). *Temperament: A psychobiological perspective.* New York: Plenum Press.

[41] Oliver, P. H., Guerin, D. W., and Gottfried, A. W. (2007). Temperamental task orientation: relation to high school and college educational accomplishments. *Learning and Individual Differences, 17*, 220-230.

[42] Keogh, B. K. (1982). Children's temperament and teachers' decisions. In R. Porter, and G. M. Collins (Eds.), *Temperamental differences in infants and young children. Ciba foundation symposium,* Vol. 89 (pp. 269-285). London: Pitman.

[43] Lerner, J. V., Lerner, R. M., and Zabski, S. (1985). Temperament and elementary school children's actual and rated academic performance: a test of a "goodness-of-fit" model. *Journal of Child Psychology and Psychiatry and Allied Disciplines, 26*(1), 125-136.

[44] Else-Quest, N. M., Hyde, J. S., Goldsmith, H. H., and Van Hulle, C. A. (2006). Gender differences in temperament: a meta-analysis. *Psychological Bulletin, 132*(1), 33-72.

[45] Sanson, A. V., Smart, D. F., Prior, M., Oberklaid, F., and Pedlow, R. (1994). The structure of temperament from age 3 to 7 years: age, sex, and sociodemographic influences. *Merrill-Palmer Quarterly, 40*, 233-252.

[46] Ahadi, S. A., Rothbart, M. K., and Ye, R. (1993). Children's temperament in the US and China: Similarities and differences. *European Journal of Personality, 7*, 359–377.

[47] Coplan, R. J., Barber, A. M., and Lagacé-Séguin, D. G. (1999). The role of child temperament as a predictor of early literacy and numeracy skills in preschoolers. *Early Childhood Research Quarterly, 14*(4), 537-553.

[48] Eaton, W. O., and Enns, L. R. (1986). Sex differences in human motor activity level. *Psychological Bulletin, 100*(1), 19–28.

[49] Maccoby, E. E., and Jacklin, C. N. (1974). *The psychology of sex differences.* Stanford, CA: Stanford University Press.

[50] Mendez, J. L., McDermott, P., and Fantuzzo, J. (2002). Identifying and promoting social competence with African American preschool children: Developmental and contextual considerations. *Psychology in the Schools, 39*(1), 111–123.

[51] Kwok, O., Hughes, J. N., and Luo, W. (2007). Role of resilient personality on lower achieving first grade students' current and future achievement. *Journal of School Psychology, 45,* 61–82.

[52] Rothbart, 1981 Rothbart, M. K. (1981). Measurement of temperament in infancy. *Child Development, 52,* 569–578.

[53] Hall, J. A., and Halberstadt, A. G. (1986). Smiling and gazing. In J. S. Hyde and M. C. Linn (Eds.), *The psychology of gender: Advances through meta-analysis* (pp. 136–158). Baltimore: John Hopkins University Press.

[54] LaFrance, M., Hecht, M. A., and Paluck, E. L. (2003). The contingent smile: A meta-analysis of sex differences in smiling. *Psychological Bulletin, 129*(2), 305–334.

[55] Zhou, Q., Lengua, L. J., and Wang, Y. (2009). The relations of temperament reactivity and effortful control to children's adjustment problems in China and the United States. *Developmental Psychology, 45*(3), 724–739.

[56] Nigg, J. T., Goldsmith, H. H., and Sachek, J. (2004). Temperament and attention-deficit hyperactivity disorder: The development of a multiple pathway model. *Journal of Clinical Child and Adolescent Psychology, 33*(1), 42–53.

[57] Bongers, I. L., Koot, H. M., Van Der Ende, J., and Verhulst, F. C. (2003). The normative development of child and adolescent problem behavior. *Journal of Abnormal Psychology, 112,* 179–192.

[58] Lemery, K. S., Essex, M. J., and Smider, N. A. (2002). Revealing the relation between temperament and behavior problem symptoms by eliminating measurement: Expert ratings and factor analyses. *Child Development, 73*(3), 867–882.

[59] Rosenfield, S. (2000). Gender and dimensions of the self: Implications for internalizing and externalizing behavior. In E. Frank (Ed.), *Gender and its effects on psychopathology* (pp.23–36). Washington, DC: American Psychiatric Press.

[60] Schoen, M. J., and Nagle, R. J. (1994). Prediction of school readiness from kindergarten temperament scores. *Journal of School Psychology, 32*(2), 135-147.

[61] Orth, L. C., and Martin, R. P. (1994). Interactive effects of student temperament and instruction method on classroom behavior and achievement. *Journal of School Psychology, 32*(2), 149-166.

[62] Ham, B.-J., Lee, Y.-M., Kim, M.-K., Lee, J., Ahn, D.-S., Choi, M.-J., et al. (2006). Personality, dopamine receptor D4 exon III polymorphisms, and academic achievement in medical students. *Neuropsychobiology, 53*(4), 203-209.

[63] Newman, J., Noel, A., Chen, R., and Matsopoulos, A. S. (1998). Temperament, selected moderating variables and early reading achievement. *Journal of School Psychology, 36*(2), 215-232.

[64] Chess, S., and Thomas, A. (1999). *Goodness of fit: Clinical applications from infancy through adult life.* Philadelphia, PA: Brunner/Mazel.

[65] Keogh, B. K., Pullis, M., and Cadwell, J. (1982). Teacher Temperament Questionnaire-Short Form. *Journal of Educational Measurements, 29,* 323−329.

[66] Windle, M., and Lerner, R. M. (1986). Reassessing the dimensions of temperamental individuality across the life span: the Revised Dimensions of Temperament Survey (DOTS-R). *Journal of Adolescent Research, 1*(2), 213-230.

[67] Pullis, M. E., and Cadwell, J. (1982). The influence of children's temperament characteristics on teachers' decision strategies. *American Educational Research Journal, 19*(2), 165-181.

[68] Guerin, D. W., and Gottfried, A. W. (1994). Developmental stability and change in parent reports of temperament: a ten-year, longitudinal investigation from infancy through preadolescence. *Merrill-Palmer Quarterly*, 40(3), 334-355.

[69] Saft, E. W., and Pianta, R. C. (2001). Teachers' perceptions of their relationships with students: Effects of child age, gender, and ethnicity of teachers and children. *School Psychology Quarterly, 16*(2), 125–141.

[70] Hintsanen, M., Alatupa, S., Pullmann, H., Hirstiö-Snellman, P., and Keltikangas-Järvinen, L. (2010). Associations of self-esteem and temperament traits to self- and teacher-reported social status among classmates. *Scandinavian Journal of Psychology, 51*, 488–494.

[71] Van Houtte, 2007 Van Houtte, M. (2007). Exploring teacher trust in technical/vocational secondary schools: male teachers' preference for girls. *Teaching and Teacher Education, 23*, 826-839.

[72] Kohnstamm, 1989; Kohnstamm, G. A. (1989). Temperament in childhood: Cross-cultural and sex differences. In G. A. Kohnstamm, J. E. Bates, and M. K. Rothbart (Eds.), *Temperament in childhood* (pp. 483–508). Chichester, England: John Wiley and Sons, Ltd.

[73] Radke-Yarrow, Richters, and Wilson, 1988; Radke-Yarrow, M., Richters, J., and Wilson, W. E. (1990). Child development in a network of relationships. In R. A. Hinde and J. Stevenson-Hinde (Eds.), *Relationships within families: Mutual influences* (pp. 48–67). Oxford: Clarendon Press.

[74] Stevenson-Hinde, J., and Hinde, R. A. (1986). Changes in associations between characteristics and interactions. In R. Plomin and J. Dunn (Eds.), *The study of temperament: Changes, continuities, and challenges* (pp. 115–129). Hillsdale, NJ: Lawrence Erlbaum Associates.

[75] Stevenson-Hinde, J. (1990). Individuals in relationships. In R. A. Hinde and J. Stevenson-Hinde (Eds.), *Relationships within families: Mutual influences* (pp. 68–80). Oxford: Clarendon Press.

[76] Lewis, M. (1989). Culture and biology: The role of temperament. In P. R. Zelazo and R. G. Barr (Eds.), *Challenges to developmental paradigms: Implications for theory, assessment, and treatment* (pp. 203–223). Hillsdale, NJ: Lawrence Erlbau Associates.

[77] Rothbart, M. K., and Bates, J. E. (2006). Temperament. In W. Damon, R. Lerner, and N. Eisenberg (Eds.), *Handbook of child psychology: Vol. 3. Social, emotional, and personality development* (6th ed., pp. 99–166). Hoboken, NJ: John Wiley and Sons.

[78] Windle, M., Iwawaki, S., and Lerner, R. M. (1988). Cross-cultural comparability of temperament among Japanese and American preschool children. *International Journal of Psychology, 23*, 547–567.

[79] Yang, K. (1986). Chinese personality and its change. In M. H. Bond (Ed.), *The Psychology of the Chinese People* (pp. 106–170). New York: Oxford University Press.

[80] Boivin, M., Hymel, S., and Bukowski,W. M. (1995). The roles of social withdrawal, peer rejection, and victimization by peers in predicting loneliness and depressed mood in childhood. *Development and Psychopathology, 7*(4), 765–785.

[81] Chen, X., Rubin, K. H., and Li, B. (1995). Social and school adjustment of shy and aggressive children in China. *Development and Psychopathology, 7*(2), 337–349.

[82] Chen, X., Rubin, K. H., and Sun, Y. (1992). Social reputation and peer relationships in Chinese and Canadian children: A cross-cultural study. *Child Development, 63*, 1336–1343.

[83] Caspi, A., Elder, G. H., Jr., and Bem, D. J. (1988). Moving away from the world: Life-course patterns of shy children. *Developmental Psychology, 24*(6), 824–831.

[84] Dee, T. S. (2005). A teacher like me: Does race, ethnicity, or gender matter? *American Economic Review, 95*(2), 158–165.

[85] Maccoby, E. E. (1990). Gender and relationships: A developmental account. *American Psychologist, 45*(4), 513–520.

[86] Lahelma, E. (2000). Lack of male teachers: A problem for students or teachers? *Pedagogy, Culture and Society, 8* (2), 173–186.

[87] Carrington, B., and Skelton, C. (2003). Re-thinking 'role models': Equal opportunities in teacher recruitment in England and Wales. *Journal of Education Policy, 18*(3), 253–265.

[88] Cushman, P. (2008). So what exactly do you want? What principals mean when they say 'male role model'. *Gender and Education, 20*(2), 123–136.

[89] Drudy, S. (2008). Gender balance/gender bias: The teaching profession and the impact of feminisation. *Gender and Education, 20*(4), 309–323.

[90] Francis, B. (2008). Teaching manfully? Exploring gendered subjectivities and power via analysis of men teachers' gender performance. *Gender and Education, 20*(2), 109–122.

[91] Lam, Y. H. R., Tse, S. K., Lam, J. W. I., and Loh, E. K. Y. (2010). Does the gender of the teacher matter in the teaching of reading literacy? Teacher gender and pupil attainment in reading literacy in Hong Kong. *Teaching and Teacher Education, 26*, 754-759.

[92] Chudgar, A., and Sankar, V. (2008). The relationship between teacher gender and student achievement: evidence from five Indian states. *Compare, 38*(5), 627-642.

[93] Krieg, J. M. (2005). Student gender and teacher gender: what is the impact on high stakes test scores? *Current Issues in Education, 8*(9). Retrieved from http://cie.ed.asu.edu/volume8/number9/ [On-line].

[94] UNESCO. (2005). *EFA global monitoring report 2005: The quality imperative.* Paris: UNESCO.

[95] Warwick, D. P., and Jatoi, H. (1994). Teacher gender and student achievement in Pakistan. *Comparative Education Review, 38*(3), 377-399.

[96] Michaelowa, K. (2001). Primary education quality in francophone sub-Saharan Africa: determinants of learning achievement and efficiency considerations. *World Development, 29*(10), 1699-1716.

[97] Driessen, G. (2007). The feminization of primary education: effects of teachers' sex on pupil achievement, attitudes and behaviour. *Review of Education, 53*(2), 183-203.

[98] Carrington, B., and McPhee, A. (2008). Boys' 'underachievement' and the feminization of teaching. *Journal of Education for Teaching, 34*(2), 109–120.

[99] Skelton, C. (2002). The 'feminisation of schooling' or 're-masculinising primary education'? *International Studies in Sociology of Education, 12*(1), 77–96.

[100] Dee, T. S. (2007). Teachers and the gender gaps in student achievement. *The Journal of Human Resources, 42*(3), 528–554.

[101] Bettinger, E. P., and Long, B. T. (2005). Do faculty serve as role models? The impact of instructor gender on female students. *American Economic Review, 95*(2), 152–157.

[102] Ehrenberg, R. G., Goldhaber, D. D., and Brewer, D. J. (1995). Do teachers' race, gender, and ethnicity matter? Evidence from the National Educational Longitudinal Study of 1988. *Industrial and Labor Relations Review, 48*(3), 547–561.

[103] Carrington, B., Tymms, P., and Merrell, C. (2008). Role models, school improvement and the 'gender gap' – Do men bring out the best in boys and women the best in girls? *British Educational Research Journal, 34*(3), 315–327.

[104] Sokal, L., Katz, H., Chaszewski, L., and Wojcik, C. (2007). Good-bye, Mr. Chips: Male teacher shortages and boys' reading achievement. *Sex Roles, 56*, 651–659.

[105] Ashley, M., and Lee, J. (2003). *Women teaching boys*. Stoke-on-Trent: Trentham Books.

[106] Salvano-Pardieu, V., Fontaine, R., Bouazzaoui, B., and Florer, F. (2009). Teachers' sanction in the classroom: effect of age, experience, gender and academic context. *Teaching and Teacher Education, 25*, 1-11.

[107] HildebR&T, S. A., and Eom, M. (2011). Teacher professionalization: motivational factors and the influence of age. *Teaching and Teacher Education, 27*(2), 416-423.

[108] Hargreaves, A. (2005). Educational change takes ages: life, career and generational factors in teachers' emotional responses to educational change. *Teaching and Teacher Education, 21*, 967-983.

[109] Keogh, B. K. (1986). Temperament and schooling: meaning of "goodness of fit"? In J. V. Lerner, and R. M. Lerner (Eds.), *Temperament and social interaction in infants and children: New directions for child development* (pp. 89-108) San Francisco: Jossey-Bass.

[110] FNBE (2004). *National Curriculum for Basic Education 2004. National core curriculum for basic education intended for pupils in compulsory education*. Vammala: Opetushallitus / The Finnish National Board of Education (FNBE). Retrieved from http://www.oph.fi/english/education/ overview_of_the_education_system

[111] Maziade, M., Cote, R., Boutin, P., Boudreault, M., and Thivierge, J. (1986). The effect of temperament on longitudinal academic achievement in primary school. *Journal of the American Academy of Child Psychiatry, 25*, 692-696.

[112] Rudasill, K. M., Gallagher, K. C., and White, J. M. (2010). Temperamental attention and activity, classroom emotional support, and academic achievement in third grade. *Journal of School Psychology, 48*, 113-134.

[113] Alatupa, S., Karppinen, K., Keltikangas-Järvinen, L., and Savioja, H. (Eds.). (2007). *Koulu, syrjäytyminen ja sosiaalinen pääoma - Löytyykö huono-osaisuuden syy koulusta vai oppilaasta?* [School, drop out, and social capital]. Helsinki: Sitran raportteja 75, Edita Prima Oy.

[114] Martin, R. P., and Bridger, R. C. (1999). *The temperament assessment battery for children - Revised: A tool for the assessment of temperamental traits and types of young children*. Unpublished manual.

[115] Walker, S., Berthelsen, D., and Irving, K. (2001). Temperament and peer acceptance in early childhood: Sex and social status differences. *Child Study Journal, 31*(3), 17192.

[116] Stuhlman, M. W., and Pianta, R. C. (2002). Teachers' narratives about their relationships with children: Associations with behavior in classrooms. *School Psychology Review*, *31*(2), 148–163.

[117] Silver, R. B., Measelle, J. R., Armstrong, J. M., and Essex, M. J. (2005). Trajectories of classroom externalizing behavior: Contributions of child characteristics, family characteristics, and the teacher-child relationship during the school transition. *Journal of School Psychology*, *43*, 39–60.

[118] Pullis, M. (1989). Goodness of fit in classroom relationships. In W. B. Carey and S. C. McDevitt (Eds.), *Clinical and educational applications of temperament research* (pp. 117–120). Berwyn, PA: Swets North America.

[119] Kagan, J., Reznick, J. S., and Snidman, N. (1987). The physiology and psychology of behavioral inhibition in children. *Child Development*, *58*, 1459–1473.

[120] Kerr, M., Lambert, W. W., Stattin, H., and Klackenberg-Larsson, I. (1994). Stability of inhibition in a Swedish longitudinal sample. *Child Development*, *65*, 138–146.

[121] Kenney-Benson, G. A., Pomerantz, E. M., Ryan, A. M., and Patrick, H. (2006). Sex differences in math performance: the role of children's approach to schoolwork. *Developmental Psychology*, *42*(1), 11-26.

[122] Pomerantz, E. M., Altermatt, E. R., and Saxon, J. L. (2002). Making the grade but feeling distressed: gender differences in academic performance and internal distress. *Journal of Educational Psychology*, *94*(2), 396-404.

[123] Tilastokeskus (2010). Suomen virallinen tilasto (SVT): *Koulutukseen hakeutuminen* [verkkojulkaisu]. ISSN=1799 - 4500. Helsinki: Tilastokeskus [viitattu: 21.11.2011]. Retrieved from http://www.stat.fi/ til/khak/index.html.

[124] Hintsanen, M., Alatupa, S., Jokela, M., Lipsanen, J., Hintsa, T., & Leino, M. (2012). Associations of Temperament Traits and Mathematics Grades in Adolescents: Dependent on the Rater but Independent of Motivation and Cognitive Ability. *Learning and Individual Differences, in press.*

In: Psychology of Gender Differences
Editor: Sarah P. McGeown

ISBN: 978-1-62081-391-1
© 2012 Nova Science Publishers, Inc.

Chapter 7

SEX, GENDER IDENTITY AND ADOLESCENT'S ACADEMIC MOTIVATION AND CLASSROOM BEHAVIOUR

Myfanwy Bugler, Helen St. Clair-Thompson*
and Sarah P. McGeown
Department of Psychology, University of Hull, Hull, UK

ABSTRACT

Sex differences or gender differences have long been investigated within the school environment; however the distinction between the two is often unclear. Whilst sex refers to differences between males and females at the biological level, gender refers to the characteristics commonly associated with being male or female. This study examines the importance of gender identity to understand differences in adolescent's academic motivation and classroom behaviour. Six hundred and nineteen adolescents (311 female, 308 male; aged 11 – 16) completed questionnaires measuring their academic motivation and gender identity (i.e., the extent to which they identified with masculine and feminine traits). In addition, teachers completed a questionnaire for each adolescent, reporting on negative classroom behaviours.

Sex differences were found in academic motivation, with girls reporting higher levels of motivation. However variation in adolescent's reported levels of motivation were better predicted by their gender identity than their sex.

For both males and females, identification with feminine traits was more closely associated with academic motivation than identification with masculine traits. With regard to behaviour, sex differences were found in negative classroom behaviours, with teachers reporting higher levels of problematic behaviour among boys. Variation in negative behaviours was predicted by both sex and gender identity (in particular a masculine identity).

In addition, for boys in particular, identification with masculine traits was closely associated with negative classroom behaviours. The importance of differentiating

---

* E-mail: myfanwybugler@gmail.com.

between sex and gender identity to investigate sex differences in motivation, behaviour and attainment are considered.

Finally, the merit of further educational research with the aim of disarming the hegemonic masculinities that could be preventing boys from achieving is discussed.

INTRODUCTION

There is compelling evidence that there are sex differences in academic motivation, classroom behaviour and educational attainment in favour of girls and that the gap between boys and girls attainment is widening (Department for Education, 2010; Gibb, Fergusson and Horwood 2008; Houghton, Wheldall and Merrett; Logan and Johnston, 2010; Younger and Warrington, 2005).

The differential attainment between boys and girls could be explained by differences in their nature, in that girls generally work harder, are more focused and need less encouragement than boys (Barber, 1996).

Another plausible explanation is more sociological and focuses on boys and girls as members of a same sex group reasoning and behaving in terms of popularity. This theory identifies adolescent culture as an explanation for differing attainment levels of boys and girls, arguing that boys, more than girls, view educational attainment as not 'cool' (Francis, 2000; Warrington, Younger and Williams, 2000).

Attention then is focused on the group that the individual belongs to independently of the individual's own beliefs (Van Houtte, 2004). Thus, a culture of what it is to be a boy and to be a girl may govern, to some extent, educational attainment during adolescence.

Sex Differences in Motivation

Sex differences in academic motivation and attitudes to school are consistently found among children and adolescents, in both primary and secondary schools (Davies, 1984; Darom and Rich, 1988; Francis, 2000; Logan and Johnston, 2010; Martino and Meyenn, 2002; Martin, 2004; Martin, 2005; Warrington, Younger and Williams, 2000; Younger and Warrington, 2005). Indeed, the evidence for sex differences in academic motivation is compelling and is generally not in boys favour.

Martin (2004) investigated school motivation of boys and girls and found sex differences in favour of girls in most positive motivation constructs although the effect sizes were relatively small, which is consistent with other research (Keys and Fernandes, 1993; Blatchford, 1996). In addition, sex differences favouring girls were found across all subjects and were as large in Maths and Science as in English (Martin, 2004; Marsh, Martin and Cheng, 2008). However, girls are not without their problems in terms of academic motivation but there is a difference in degree in that boys lack of motivation for schoolwork tends to be greater and more global (Martin, 2004; Marsh et al., 2008).

Indeed Martin (2004) posits that just as girls are generally more positively motivated, they are also more inclined to adopt a learning/mastery focus, plan schoolwork, manage their study time effectively and persist when faced with challenges. However, girls also show heightened anxiety (a maladaptive dimension of motivation) towards schoolwork. Similarly,

Martin and Marsh (2005) reported sex differences in positive aspects of motivation, but also found that girls were more likely to report higher levels of maladaptive feelings towards school work (i.e., anxiety).

Logan and Medford (2011) found that the relationship between reading motivation and reading attainment was significantly stronger among boys than girls and suggested that boys' underachievement in reading may be partially a result of their lack of motivation and engagement in literacy tasks. However, it is important to note that whilst some studies report sex differences in academic motivation, other studies report no differences in this area (Lepper et al., 2005). Indeed, Hyde (2005) reported that the sexes may be more similar than different. Sex differences in academic motivation therefore may depend, to some extent, on how the academic domain in question is perceived by boys and girls and their self-competence in that domain (Jacobs, Lanza, Osgood, Eccles and Wigfield, 2002). Indeed, it is more common to consistently find sex differences in motivation within various academic subjects, such as English, Mathematics or Sport (Eccles et al., 1993; Jacobs et al., 2002; Williams, Burden and Lanvers, 2002) than in the concept of general academic motivation. It has been reported that students' beliefs about their academic capabilities, or self-efficacy beliefs, are important components of motivation and influence academic achievement. Self-concept beliefs differ from self-efficacy beliefs in that self-concept includes judgments of self-worth, whereas self-efficacy beliefs are judgments of capability to accomplish tasks or succeed in activities. One theory that has been widely used to understand sex differences in motivation is self-efficacy theory (Eccles, Adler, Futterman, Goff, Kaczala, and Meece, 1983). This research has focused on academic domains that are traditionally sex-typed as male or female domains such as maths, science, sports and language arts. A substantial amount of research in these domains reports that boys show higher self-efficacy and expectancy beliefs than girls regarding their attainment in maths and science with girls expressing stronger self-beliefs in their competence in language arts (Eccles et al. 1983; Anderman and Young, 1994; Pajares, 1999; Pintrich and DeGroot, 2002; Zimmerman and Martinez Pons, 1990; Pajares and Valiante, 2001; Whitley, 1997). In summary, it has been found that girls generally have greater academic motivation (when taken as a global construct). In addition, girls also find it easier to achieve in school environments (Sukhnandan, Lee and Kelleher, 2000), value the presentation of school work more, spend more time improving the quality of presentation of their work (McDonald, Saunders and Benefield, 1999), show concern about teachers opinions (Bray, Gardner and Parsons, 1997) and have a greater level of enjoyment of school (Arnot, Gray, James, Rudduck and Duveen, 1998). In addition, girls have been described as predisposed to working harder and to be more persistent in their learning regardless of their level of interest in the work (Martin, 2004; Oakhill and Petrides, 2007) whilst boys work less hard and are more easily distracted (Barber, 1996; Warrington et al. 2000). When these studies are viewed together, there appears to be quite convincing evidence that girls, on average, are more motivated academically (although sex differences in motivation may change depending on academic subject).

Sex Differences in Behaviour

Research studies also show strong evidence of sex differences in disruptive classroom behaviour. Indeed, considerable primary and secondary school research suggests that male students are, on average, more disruptive than female students across the majority of disruptive behaviours (Arbuckle and Little, 2004; Beaman, Wheldall and Kemp, 2007; Borg and Falzon, 1989; Cameron, 1998; Cullingford, 1993; Gibb, Ferguson and Horwood, 2008; Houghton et al., 1988; Little, 2005; Merrett and Wheldall, 1984; Wheldall and Merrett, 1988; Wright and Dusek, 1998). These behavioural differences are evident from a young age. For example, research from the early years (Years Prep to Year 4) suggests that additional management strategies are needed for 5% of male students and 2% of female students in an average class (Stephenson, Martin and Linfoot, 2000). Kaplan, Gheen and Midgley (2002) posit that motivational orientations and achievement are related to disruptive behaviour and suggest that achievement and disruptive behaviour produce reciprocal effects; students who receive low grades tend to be more disruptive. Younger and Warrington (1996) found teachers reported that classroom ambience, tone of interactions, and atmosphere for teaching and learning were more likely to be heavily influenced by boys than girls, and that the demands of boys detracted from the learning opportunities of girls as they created a disruptive atmosphere for learning with their conscious attention seeking. In a large scale study in 251 British secondary schools, more boys than girls were identified as troublesome students; these results were consistently found across academic subjects and across different year groups (Houghton, Wheldall and Merrett, 1988). This was supported by research conducted by Beaman and Wheldall (1997) which also reported that boys were consistently nominated by teachers as the most troublesome. Behavioural strategies have been put in to the classroom environment in order to help manage these behaviours. However, Oswald (1995) in a study of 2354 children (from Reception – Year 7) in South Australia found a progressive rise in the percentage of students who failed to respond to discipline strategies. The proportion of troublesome students rose from 6% in Reception (Kindergarten) to 16% in Year 7 (with the exception of Year 6 which showed a decline from Year 5 figures). Consistent sex differences in behaviour management challenges were also found, with boys being identified much more frequently as troublesome. Again, when viewed together, these studies collectively highlight that negative classroom behaviours are more prevalent among males than females.

Sex versus Gender Identity

In order to understand why girls outperform boys academically, it is important to understand which psychological factors explain boys' and girls' educational attainment. Educational research has consistently shown that one of the most important predictors of educational attainment is students' individual characteristics. Indeed, one factor which is known to be a strong predictor of educational attainment is intelligence (Gottfredson, 2002; Gustafsson and Undheim, 1996). Research investigating sex differences in intelligence have found no or negligible sex differences in overall cognitive ability (Feingold, 1988; Halpern, 2000; Hedges and Nowell, 1995; Hyde, Fennoma and Lamon, 1990); therefore cognitive ability cannot be an adequate explanation for sex differences in educational attainment.

An alternative approach towards considering the differential attainment between boys and may be sociological; focusing on the developing sub cultures of boys and girls during adolescence. Socialisation and achievement experiences may play a pivotal role in the development of sex differences in motivation (Meece, Glienke and Burg, 2006) and impact on later educational attainment. Eccles et al's., (1983) expectancy-value model includes a parental socialisation component which highlights important pathways by which parents affect and influence children's motivation as important role models.

Parental involvement in children's activities has been reported to differentially affect the choices that girls and boys make (Larson, Dworkin and Gillman, 1995). Also significant associations have been found between parents' sex stereotypes, children's sex stereotypes and children's choice of activity (McHale, Shanahan, Updegraff, Crouter and Booth, 2004). This suggests that parents may shape sex differences in motivation by modelling sex-typed behaviour, communicating different expectations and goals for boys and girls and encouraging participation in different activities and skills. Thus gender appropriate play and choice in childhood will be well established in adolescence and would provide a perfect foundation for the development of gender identity and its potential effect on the motivation, behaviour and attainment of boys and girls.

Recent research has reported differences in parents' educational expectations for boys and girls (Lyon, Barnes and Sweiry, 2006). This study involved 7,000 11 to 16 year olds and found that only 72 percent of boys' parents wanted them to stay on at school compared to 82 percent of girls' parents. Parents of boys (19 percent) were more likely to want their sons to go on to an apprenticeship or training course than parents of girls (8 percent), whereas 60 percent of girls' parents were more likely to want their child to attend university compared to 49 percent of boys' parents. Interestingly the children reflected these aspirations with 22 percent of boys wanting a full time job at 16 compared to 15 percent of girls, and 22 percent of boys wanting to study full time compared to 27 percent of girls. Although these findings are interesting they do not show causality as there is no evidence that parents' differing expectations play a causal role in the different attainment of boys and girls. Nevertheless, parental attitudes, post-school opportunities, gender roles portrayed in the media and existing inequalities by gender in the family and workplace have all been shown to influence young people's attitudes and aspirations, thereby influencing their behaviour and performance at school (Tinklin et al., 2001).

Gender identity as a product of adolescent culture offers a plausible explanation for the differential attainment of boys and girls observed during the secondary school years. Boys more than girls may be influenced by their peer group, and as a group boys consider educational attainment as 'not cool' (Francis, 2000; Warrington et al. 2000; Whitelaw, Milosevic and Daniels, 2000).

Attention then is paid to the effect of the group that the individual belongs to independently of the individual's beliefs (Warrington et al., 2000; Whitelaw et al., 2000; Van Houtte, 2004). Possibly some boys may value study and academic attainment but not act accordingly for fear of rejection by the group (Warrington et al., 2000; Whitelaw et al., 2000).

Academic attainment does not make adolescents more popular with their peers (Coleman, 1961; Sebald, 1981; Thirer and Wright, 1985; Suitor and Reavis, 1995; Landsheer et al., 1998; Williams and White, 1983), they may consider educational attainment important but in comparison to more gendered activities such as sport (which boys rate highly) and physical appearance (which girls rate highly), educational attainment is relatively less important (Coleman, 1961; Suitor and Reavis, 1995).

For adolescents popularity within their peer group is vitally important and educational attainment does not sit well with or suit the male image (Van Houtte, 2004). For girls it is acceptable for them to work hard at school as long as they appear to be 'cool' outside school (Francis, 2000; Warrington et al., 2000).

Achieving academically and being cool may be possible in girls' culture, whilst for boys being cool and achieving at school may be incompatible (Van Houtte, 2004; Warrington et al., 2000). Indeed a positive attitude to educational attainment is antithetical to male or macho behaviour and popularity in a male group is conditional on appropriate male values (Epstein, Elwood, Jey and Maw, 1998; Power, Whitty, Edwards and Wigfall, 1998). It is reasonable to suggest therefore that these differences in peer culture may influence sex differences in academic motivation and behaviour.

Gender Identity Studies

Due to the overwhelming evidence that boys as a group are underachieving, research has explored the influence of gender identity on boys' attitudes and academic motivation, academic attainment, beliefs and behaviour (Connell, 1998; Jackson, 2002; 2003) and suggests that schools are crucial in the development of gender identity as they offer a complex medium through which gender identity is developed via discipline, group influence and subjects offered (Connell, 1998; Jackson, 2002, 2003). Thus school culture builds on established stereotypes and may reinforce gender identity during adolescence. Children spend a substantial proportion of their waking time in school and the significance of peer-group pressure in schools and the implications of this on boys' behaviour has been widely debated (Renold 2000; 2004; Swain, 2004).

Gender related knowledge and the ability to distinguish between males and females develops in early childhood (Banse, Gawronski, Rebetez, Gutt and Morton, 2010) and increases with age creating a core knowledge about the social world, hence gender stereotypes of a specific culture typically reflect the predominant gender roles of that culture (Diekman and Eagly, 2000). These role-congruent stereotypes influence the spontaneous differential developmental behaviour patterns of boys and girls (Banse et al., 2010; Greenwald, Nosek and Banaji, 2008). This early acquisition of stereotype knowledge is highly over learned and is relatively resistant to change (Devine, 1989; Wilson, Lindsey and Schooler, 2000). Masculinity defines success as achievement through independent working and competition which means that boys are less likely to seek help, ask for support or work collaboratively with others (Younger and Warrington, 1996). It is important that boys understand how masculinity is socially constructed and then look at how this construction can sit uncomfortably with success and motivation at school and in particular subject areas (Gilbert and Gilbert, 2001). Swain, (2000, 2003) posits that boys from very different socio-cultural backgrounds will report this need to conform to peer pressure, to be part of the group and adopt group norms and expectations.

It has been suggested that it is crucially important for many boys to be accepted by other boys, they need to identify with and comply with peer group norms, so that they are part of a greater whole (Skelton, 2001; Martino and Pallotta-Chiarolli, 2003) rather than apart from the whole. This acceptance is dependent on group norms, an acceptable identity, and acceptable aspects of behaviour associated with being a boy (Jackson, 2002; 2003).

It is argued that to be a boy requires the rejection of the feminine, and undertaking academic work is often perceived to be more feminine than masculine; therefore many boys avoid academic achievement because they believe it will compromise their 'laddish' image (Jackson, 2002; 2003). Academic attainment is not necessarily a problem, as long as boys appear to avoid academic work (Jackson, 2002). Younger and Warrington (2005) posit that one of the benefits of single-sex schooling is that boys are able to work hard without the fear of appearing 'feminine' in front of their peers. Some boys however, particularly those in the higher sets, conform to the norm of a group where hard work is accepted, and have learnt to ignore the pressure from their peers (Mac an Ghaill, 1994).

In addition some boys have a different definition of their sexuality and are caring and gentle and are at ease in the company of girls and women (Mac an Ghail, 1994; Martino and Pallotta-Chiarolli, 2003). As not all boys act in the same macho way, indeed the same may be said of girls. There are different types of girls and as many perspectives on femininity as there are perspectives on masculinity (Frosh et al, 2002; Reay, 2001). These differing images of femininity and masculinity all affect motivation, attitude and attainment (Young and Warrington, 2005). Some girls are high achievers and work hard, are conscientious and well-motivated, whilst others are not and have adopted the 'laddish' attributes of their male peers (Jackson, 2004). There are also girls who are disengaged and may not reach their potential academically (Jackson 2004).

However, the impact of the peer group appears to be significantly different with regard to girls and boys (Chung 2005; Swain 2004). The aim of this study is to investigate sex differences in academic motivation and classroom behaviour, but specifically to examine whether differences between males and females can be better predicted by their sex or gender identity. It was predicted that girls would have higher academic motivation and that boys would show higher levels of disruptive classroom behaviour.

However, it was hypothesised that motivation and behaviour would be better predicted by adolescents' gender identity (i.e., the extent to which they identified with masculine or feminine traits) than by their sex. In addition, it was predicted that a masculine identity would be more closely associated with negative classroom behaviour than a feminine identity and that a feminine identity would be more closely associated with academic motivation than a masculine identity.

METHOD

Participants

The sample comprised 619 students (311 girls and 308 boys) from two secondary schools in the U.K. Students in Years 7 – 11, aged 11 – 16 years (Mean age 14.04. SD 1.68) participated. All participants were English speaking, some students were supported by teaching assistants to help transcribe and read the questionnaire due to statements of dyslexia and dyspraxia.

School Information

School 1 was an inner city comprehensive school with 1412 students on roll and in an area of social need and unemployment. The percentage of students achieving Level 2 threshold (the equivalent of 5 + A* - C GCSE's) was 79%. The percentage of students achieving at least one entry level qualification was 99%.

School 2 was an inner city comprehensive school in a tourist city with 861 students on roll. The percentage of students achieving Level 2 threshold (the equivalent of 5 + A* - C GCSE's) was 92%. The percentage of students achieving at least one entry level qualification was 100%.

Materials

Academic Motivation: Motivation and Engagement Scale-High School (SMES-HS)

The Student Motivation and Engagement Scale (Martin, 2001, 2003f, 2007c, 2010) is an instrument that measures secondary school students' motivation. It assesses motivation using 4 dimensions; booster thoughts (self-belief, valuing school work and learning focus), booster behaviours (planning, task management and persistence), mufflers (anxiety, failure avoidance and uncertain control) and guzzlers (self-sabotage and disengagement). With regard to booster thoughts, self-belief refers to student's confidence in their ability to do well in their school work. Valuing of school work refers to the extent to which student's believe that what they learn is useful, important and relevant. Learning focus refers to the extent to which student's are focused on learning, problem solving and developing their skills. With regard to booster behaviours, planning refers to the extent to which student's plan their school work; task management refers to the way student's organise their study time, whilst persistence refers to how much student's will persist with challenging materials. With regard to mufflers, anxiety refers to feelings of nervousness or worrying relating to academic work, failure avoidance refers to the extent to which student's are motivated by avoiding failure and uncertain control refers to student's feelings of uncertainty about how to perform well academically. Finally, guzzlers refer to self-sabotage, the extent to which students self-handicap themselves by not trying, and disengagement, the extent to which student's feel they want to give up with academic work. There are a total of 44 items in the questionnaire. For each item the students agree/disagree with a series of statements on a 7 point Likert-type scale (ranging from "I disagree strongly" to "I agree strongly"). A score is calculated for each of the 11 motivation and engagement constructs by totalling the responses on the appropriate items.

Classroom Behaviour: Connors' Teacher Rating Scale – Revised (Short Version)

Subject teachers were asked to complete a Conners' Teachers Rating Scale Revised (CTRS - R) Short Version for each child. There are a total of 28 items assessing four dimensions of behaviour in the classroom: Cognitive problems/inattention, oppositional behaviour, hyperactivity and ADHD Index. Cognitive problems/inattention refers to difficulties with concentration, completing tasks and organisational skills. Oppositional behaviour refers to breaking rules, not respecting authority and being easily annoyed. Hyperactivity refers to difficulty sitting still, staying on task, being restless or impulsive and finally, ADHD Index identifies behaviours associated with children 'at risk' for ADHD. For each item teachers are asked to rate the extent to which the behaviour has been displayed by the child over the previous weeks. Teachers are required to respond to each statement using the 4 point Likert scale. Teacher rating scales provide a simple and economic method of obtaining relevant information. They use a common vocabulary for describing academic, social and emotional behaviours in the classroom which is readily understood by other professionals. The CTRS is economical of teacher time, has norms based on large samples of children and adolescent's of different ages and social backgrounds. Standard scores were used to analyse the relationship between motivation and classroom behaviour. However, the CTRS has different norms for boys and girls and is therefore standardised to level out sex differences in behaviour. Therefore teachers' actual ratings (raw scores) were used to examine sex differences in behaviour.

Gender Identity: The Children's Sex Role Inventory (CSRI) Short Form

The CSRI was used to assess gender roles (Boldizar, 1991). This instrument measures traditional masculine traits (e.g., competitiveness: 'When I play games, I really like to win'), feminine traits (e.g., compassion: 'I care about what happens to others') and neutral traits to act as fillers (e.g., friendly 'I have many friends). It is a self-report survey and uses a Likert scale ('4 = very true of me', '3 = mostly true of me', '2 = a little true of me' and '1 = not true of me at all'). Neutral items were excluded from the analysis. The CRSI does not refer to motivation or behaviour; questions refer specifically to stereotypical masculine and feminine traits.

Procedure

The assessments were carried out during the school day and students were assessed in their form rooms with a subject teacher present. Students were encouraged to answer all questions and use the full range of the Likert scale and to answer the questions honestly. If students were unsure of the meaning of a question or struggled to read some of the words they were helped by teaching staff.

RESULTS

Sex Differences in Academic Motivation, Classroom Behaviour and Gender Identity

A series of ANOVAs were carried out to investigate sex differences in these constructs.

After applying Benjamini and Hochberg's (1995) False Discovery Rate to control for multiple comparisons, there were still significant sex differences ($p < 0.05$) in the following areas, with girls reporting higher levels of academic motivation: Valuing; $F(1,616) = 4.66$, $p < 0.05$, $\eta_p^2 = .007$, learning focus; $F(1,616) = .8.89$, $p < 0.05$, $\eta_p^2 = .014$, task management, $F(1,616) = 5.75$, $p < 0.05$, $\eta_p^2 = .009$, persistence, $F(1,616) = 4.82$, $p < 0.05$, $\eta_p^2 = .008$, anxiety, $F(1,616) = 39.03$, $p < 0.01$, $\eta_p^2 = .060$, and uncertain control, $F(1,616) = 5.92$, $p < 0.05$, $\eta_p^2 = .010$. Following conventional approaches for η_p^2 in analysis of variance, a small effect size is .02, a medium effect size is $> .06$ and a large effect size is $> .10$. Therefore it is important to note that many of these differences were very small, except for anxiety where the difference was a medium effect size. Significant sex differences ($p < 0.05$) in behaviour were found, with boys receiving higher teacher ratings for oppositional behaviour; $F(1, 616) =$

4.55, $p < .05$ $\eta_p^2 = .007$; cognitive problems/inattention; $F(1,616) = 6.34$, $p < 0.05$, $\eta_p^2 = .010$, hyperactivity; $F(1,616) = 27.36$, $p < 0.01$, $\eta_p^2 = .042$ and ADHD; $F(1,616) = 23.21$, $p < 0.01$, $\eta_p^2 = .036$. Whilst the sex differences in oppositional behaviour and cognitive problems/inattention were very small, the sex differences in hyperactivity and ADHD type behaviours were small-medium in terms of effect size. In addition, significant sex differences were found in masculine traits; $F(1,616) = 14.97$, $p < 0.01$, $\eta_p^2 = .020$, and feminine traits; $F(1,616) = 157.88$, $p < 0.01$, $\eta_p^2 = .200$ in accordance with stereotypical perceptions. Whilst the sex difference in masculine traits was small, the sex difference in feminine traits was very large.

Table 1. Sex differences in academic motivation, classroom behaviour and gender identity (means and standard deviations)

	Male	Female
Self-belief	45.68(12.58)	46.83 (11.10)
Valuing	47.89 (12.26)	49.83 (10.14) *
Learning focus	42.62 (12.52)	45.49 (11.48) *
Planning	50.44 (9.87)	51.03 (9.88)
Task management	48.14 (10.30)	50.08 (9.88) *
Persistence	47.67 (11.11)	49.58 (10.52) *
Anxiety	47.23 (10.01)	52.22 (9.89) **
Failure avoidance	53.44 (10.35)	52.69 (10.25)
Uncertain control	51.43 (9.41)	53.32 (9.61) *
Self-sabotage	52.29 (10.44)	50.39 (14.72)
Disengagement	52.70 (11.87)	52.14 (12.43)
Oppositional	2.56 (3.03) *	2.06 (3.00)
Cognitive problems/inattention	4.57 (4.02) *	3.76 (4.14)
Hyperactivity	3.92 (4.48) **	2.34 (2.96)
ADHD	7.58 (8.25) **	4.78 (5.99)
Masculine traits	53.88 (4.59) **	52.47 (4.47)
Feminine traits	25.66 (5.47)	30.86 (4.82) **

Note: * $p < .05$, ** $p< .01$. Asterisks indicate where significantly higher scores were found, after Benjamini and Hochberg corrections.

Association between Gender Identity and Motivation

Correlations were carried out to examine the strength of association between masculine traits, feminine traits and the different aspects of academic motivation (see Table 2). Masculine traits were significantly and positively correlated with all positive constructs of motivation (all booster thoughts and behaviours) and significantly and negatively correlated with uncertain control and self-sabotage. However, many of these associations were weak. Feminine traits were also positively and significantly associated with all positive constructs of motivation (all booster thoughts and behaviours); however anxiety, failure avoidance and uncertain control were also positively associated with feminine traits. See Table 2. Whilst these latter associations were relatively weak, the correlations between feminine traits and booster thoughts and behaviours were relatively strong. The correlations were converted into a corresponding Fisher's z coefficient in order to investigate whether there were differences in the strength of these associations. Significant differences were found in the strength of association between positive aspects of motivation and masculine or feminine traits (self belief; $z = 1.99$, $p < 0.01$, valuing; $z = 2.48$, $p < 0.01$, learning focus; $z = 3.72$, $p < 0.01$, planning; $z = 2.23$, task management; $z = 2.48$, $p < 0.01$, persistence; $z = 3.97$, $p < 0.01$). In all cases, feminine traits were more closely associated with these positive aspects of motivation than masculine traits. In addition, feminine traits were also more closely associated with some negative aspects of motivation, (anxiety $z = 2.23$, $p < 0.01$ and failure avoidance $z = 1.99$, $p < 0.01$).

Table 2. Correlations examining associations between masculine and feminine traits and motivational constructs (both males and females)

	SB	V	LF	PL	TM	P	A	FA	UC	SS	D
M	.18**	.16*	.16**	.17**	.19**	.15**	.07	.00	-.14*	-.09*	-.05
F	.26**	.26**	.30**	.25**	.29**	.31**	.17**	.09*	.10*	-.07	.07

Note: M = Masculine Traits, F = Feminine Traits, SB =Self-belief, LF = Learning Focus, V = Valuing, PL = Planning, TM = Task Management, P = Persistence, A = Anxiety, FA = Failure Avoidance, UC = Uncertain Control, SS = Self-sabotage, D = Disengagement, ** $p < .01$, * $p < .05$.

Association between Gender Identity and Behaviour

Following this, correlations were carried out to examine the strength of association between masculine traits, feminine traits and the different aspects of classroom behaviour (see Table 3).

Table 3. Correlations examining associations between masculine and feminine traits and behaviour constructs (whole group)

	Oppositional	Cog/inatt	Hyperactivity	ADHD
Masculinity	-.09*	-.16**	-.11**	-.08
Femininity	-.04	-.06	-.04	-.02

Note: ** $p < .01$, * $p < .05$.

Whilst masculine traits correlated significantly with many different aspects of classroom behaviour (with the exception of ADHD typed behaviour), feminine traits did not. However, whilst these correlations were significant, they were very weak.

The correlations were converted into a corresponding Fisher's z coefficient in order to investigate whether there were differences in the strength of these associations. Masculine and feminine traits did not differ significantly in the extent to which they were associated with classroom behaviour ($p > .05$).

Association between Gender Identity and Motivation: Comparisons between Males and Females

Correlations were then carried out to examine differences between males and females in how masculine traits and feminine traits correlated with different aspects of academic motivation (see Table 4).

Table 4. Correlations examining associations between masculine and feminine traits and motivational constructs in boys and girls

	SB	V	LF	PL	TM	P	A	FA	UC	SS	D
Males											
M	.18**	.14*	.17**	.15**	.24**	.21**	-.04	.00	-.12*	-.03	-.07
F	.33**	.30**	.31**	.30**	.28**	.35**	.09	.14*	.04	-.10	-.10
Females											
M	.19**	.22**	.18**	.20**	.18**	.13*	-.03	-.01	-.13*	-.15**	-.04
F	.18**	.19**	.24**	.24**	.27**	.26**	.04	.09	.09	.02	-.02

Note: M = Masculine Traits, F = Feminine Traits, SB =Self-belief, LF = Learning Focus, V = Valuing, PL = Planning, TM = Task Management, P = Persistence, A = Anxiety, FA = Failure Avoidance, UC = Uncertain Control, SS = Self-sabotage, D = Disengagement, ** $p < .01$, * $p < .05$.

For both boys and girls, significant associations between both masculine and feminine traits and positive motivational constructs were found (see Table 4). For boys, identification with feminine traits was more closely associated with their academic motivation than their identification with masculine traits. However for girls, both masculine and feminine traits correlated with academic motivation to a similar degree.

Association between Gender Identity and Behaviour: Comparisons between Males and Females

Table 5. Correlations examining associations between masculine and feminine traits and behaviour constructs in boys and girls

	Oppositional	Cog/inatt	Hyperactivity	ADHD
Boys				
Masculinity	-.23**	-.21**	-.19**	-.16**
Femininity	-.07	-.07	-.07	-.08
Girls				
Masculinity	.00	-.11	.01	.02
Femininity	-.05	-.11	-.07	-.04

Note: ** $p < .01$, * $p < .05$.

Among males, masculine traits were significantly inversely associated with all negative classroom behaviours, whilst feminine traits were unrelated. Among females however, neither masculine nor feminine traits were significantly associated with negative classroom behaviours. (See Table 5).

Predicting Sex Differences Using Sex and Gender Identity

Those constructs in which significant sex differences were found (see Table 1) were entered into a series of regression analyses to examine whether sex or gender identity were better predictors of scores on these constructs.

Table 6. Regression analysis predicting motivational constructs with sex, masculinity and femininity as predictors

	Sex	Sex, masculine and feminine traits
Valuing		
Sex	.083*	-.009
Masculinity		.089*
Femininity		.241**
R^2	.007	.077
Learning focus		
Sex	.119*	.006
Masculinity		.075
Femininity		.276**
R^2	.014	.095
Task management		
Sex	.096*	.000
Masculinity		.115*
Femininity		.251**
R^2	.009	.093
Persistence		
Sex	.088*	-.047
Masculinity		.053
Femininity		.318**
R^2	.008	.103
Anxiety		
Sex	.244**	.186**
Masculinity		-.074
Femininity		.104*
R^2	.060	.068
Uncertain control		
Sex	.098*	-.001
Masculinity		-.186**
Femininity		.156
R^2	.010	.042

Note: * $p < .05$, ** $p < .01$. Values for sex, masculinity and femininity represent Final Beta values.

When entered alone, sex predicted significant variance in these constructs (column 1), explaining more variance in anxiety than in the other motivational constructs. However when gender identity was included as a predictor (column 2), sex no longer explained variance in the motivational constructs (with the exception of anxiety).

Instead feminine traits, and to a lesser extent masculine traits, explained variance in all motivation dimensions (with masculine traits explaining more variance than feminine traits in uncertain control).

This suggests that variation in academic motivation may be better accounted for by gender identity than sex. It is important to note however that whilst the predictors of sex and gender identity did predict some variance in academic motivation, they did not predict a large amount of the variance.

When entered alone sex predicted significant variance in all constructs, with the exception of oppositional behaviour (column 1). When entering masculine and feminine traits as predictors, sex was still a significant predictor of all aspects of motivation; whilst masculine traits predicted significant variance after accounting for sex for cognitive problems/inattention, in all other aspects of behaviour, sex was the only predictor.

As before, it is important to note however that whilst the predictors of sex and gender identity did predict some variance in classroom behaviours, they did not predict a large amount of the variance.

Table 7. Regression analysis predicting behavioural constructs with sex, masculinity and femininity

	Sex	Sex, masculine and feminine traits
Oppositional behaviour		
Sex	.051	.022
Masculinity		-.081
Femininity		-.028
R^2	.003	.009
Cognitive/inattention		
Sex	-.101*	-.105*
Masculinity		-.157**
Femininity		-.045
R^2	.010	.041
Hyperactivity		
Sex	-.206**	-.226**
Masculinity		-.116
Femininity		-.004
R^2	.042	.055
ADHD		
Sex	-.190**	-.182**
Masculinity		-.065
Femininity		-.041
R^2	.036	.044

Note: * $p < .05$, ** $p < .01$ Values for sex, masculinity and femininity represent Final Beta values.

DISCUSSION

The present study examined gender identity and its ability to predict adolescents' academic motivation and classroom behaviour, and also the association between masculine and feminine traits, academic motivation and behaviour. In concordance with the literature in this area, girls reported higher levels of academic motivation in the positive dimensions of valuing, learning focus, task management and persistence. However, the variation in the reported levels of academic motivation was better predicted by gender identity than by sex. In addition girls reported higher levels of anxiety and uncertain control; whilst gender identity was a better predictor of uncertain control, sex was a better predictor of anxiety. Interestingly, both boys and girls identification with feminine traits were more closely associated with academic motivation than identification with masculine traits. This is supported by the literature in this area as girls have been reported to show higher levels of academic motivation than boys (Martin, 2004; Martin and Marsh, 2005; Martino and Meyenn, 2002; Meece et al., 2006; Younger and Warrington, 2005) therefore it would be predicted that a feminine orientation would be more closely related to academic motivation.

Sex differences were found in negative classroom behaviour with teachers reporting higher levels of problem behaviour among boys. Overall, the sex differences found in negative classroom behaviours were wider than the sex differences found in the positive aspects of academic motivation. Indeed, variation in negative behaviour was better predicted by sex than gender identity (although masculine traits also explained variance in cognitive problems/inattention). In addition, when boys and girls scores were combined, identification with masculine traits was significantly associated with most negative classroom behaviours, whereas identification with feminine traits was unrelated. These results are consistent with considerable research in this area which reports male students as being more disruptive in the classroom (Borg, 1998; Houghton et al., 1988; Kaplan et al., 2002; Wheldall and Merrett, 1988).

In addition sex differences were found in masculine and feminine traits in accordance with stereotypical perceptions; girls identified more closely with feminine traits whilst boys identified more closely with masculine traits. However, it is important to note that the sex difference found in masculine traits was considerably narrower than the difference found in feminine traits; boys and girls differ more widely in their identification with feminine traits (or traits traditionally considered to be feminine). Interestingly, when examining the mean scores for both males and females on the CSRI, it is clear that both males and females identified more closely with the masculine traits in the questionnaire than the feminine traits (mean scores for feminine traits were almost half that of male traits). This may be due, in part, to cultural changes throughout the last two decades (the questionnaire was published twenty years ago). It may be the case that females, whilst identifying more with the feminine traits, are also rejecting a lot of the traits considered to be traditionally feminine.

When analyses were carried out separately for males and females, for males, identification with feminine traits was more closely associated with their academic motivation than their identification with masculine traits. Indeed, there was a greater distinction for boys compared to girls, in how their identification with masculine and feminine traits correlated with their academic motivation. For girls, whilst feminine traits were, in general, more closely related to their academic motivation, the distinction between masculine and feminine traits (as evidenced by the magnitude difference in the strength of associations with academic motivation) was not as wide. Similarly with behaviour, whilst boys' identification with masculine traits was significantly correlated with all negative behaviours, this same pattern was not found among females; greater association with masculine traits was not significantly related to negative classroom behaviours. As already discussed, gendered behaviours, attitudes and values may be the result of childhood socialisation in line with cultural norms of masculinity and femininity (Epstein, Elwood, Jey, and Maw, 1998; Weaver-Hightower, 2003). Research has suggested that a plausible explanation for the lower performance of boys relative to girls involves reference to a culture of 'laddishness' or 'macho' behaviour (Francis,

1999; Jackson, 2002) which acts as an impediment to academic attainment (Mac an Ghaill, 1994; Younger and Warrington, 1996; Francis, 2000; Martino, 1999; Warrington et al., 2000). Indeed, boys are more likely than girls to be ridiculed by their peers for working hard at school and frequently resort to 'laddish' behaviour such as challenging authority, diverting attention and pretending not to care about schoolwork in order to gain acceptance from their peer group (Younger, Warrington and Williams, 1999). As argued, theories regarding boys' educational attainment have focused on ways in which masculinities are constructed, sustained and reinforced in schools and in society. It is argued that boys need to be part of a hegemonic group; this hegemonic masculinity then is the standard-bearer of what it means to be a man or boy in a school context (Frosh, Phoenix and Pattman, 2002; Kessler, Ashendon, Connell, and Dowsett, 1982) and it is within these hegemonic masculinities that boys define their identities against other groups (Mac an Ghaill, 1994). Hegemonic masculinity has been reported to be at odds with academic work and being seen to work hard academically is antithetical to hegemonic masculinity (Frosh et al, 2002). Many boys learn to establish their masculinity in opposition to femininity (Mac an Ghail, 1994) rejecting anything feminine and research suggests that academic work is perceived by young students as feminine and if boys want to avoid being labelled feminine they need to disengage from academic work, or appear to disengage from academic work (Epstein, 1998; Frosh et al., 2002). Being cool is a priority for boys and is established within the context of a hierarchical set of social relations with their peers in which there is constant jostling of hegemonic and subordinate masculinities (Kessler et al, 1985; Connell, 1987). Doing homework or going to the library become markers of a subordinate form of masculinity. Rejecting such practices which lead to academic attainment is also a means by which the 'cool' boys can establish themselves as rebels in their rejection of school values (Martino 1999). The findings of this study support the literature which suggests that there are sex differences in academic motivation (Martin, 2005; Martin and Meyenn, 2002; Marsh, Martin and Chang, 2008; Younger and Warrington, 2005) and classroom behaviour (Arbuckle and Little, 2004; Beaman et al., 2007; Little, 2005) and offer an alternative explanation in terms of gender identity rather than sex in explaining variation in academic motivation and classroom behaviour.

Suggestions for Future Research

It is important to note that whilst sex and gender identity were correlated with adolescent's academic motivation and behavior, and predicted variance in their academic motivation and behavior, the variance explained by these qualities was relatively small. It is possible that other predictors such as cognitive skills, academic ability and other personality characteristics would also predict adolescent's motivation and behavior. Future research could include a range of additional assessments to tease out the relative importance of sex/gender identity versus other traits in predicting motivation and behavior in the classroom.

In addition, the results of this study have important implications for educational practice because motivation is a dimension that can be modified and as such can be targeted by intervention (Martin, 2005). Also as a close association has been found between motivation and attainment and classroom behaviour and attainment (Gibb et al., 2008) it would seem pertinent to investigate intervention methods aimed at improving both motivation and classroom behaviour in order to raise attainment. In addition as hegemonic masculinities are socially constructed and reinforced at the school level these can also be addressed within the school context by changing the emphasis of the 'cool boys' being dominant to an acceptance that learning is not an antithesis to masculinity. This may prevent the gradual psychosocial disengagement of boys which begins in early schooling and evolves over the years in response to transactions between the individual and the school environment. Children as well as adults can deconstruct gender binaries and evaluate hegemonic masculinity and this capacity may be the basis for educational intervention (Connell and Messerschmidt, 2005).

CONCLUSION

This study examined gender identity as a predictor for sex differences in adolescent motivation and behaviour and furthermore examined the relationship between masculine and feminine traits, academic motivation and classroom behaviour. The results suggest that a feminine gender identity is a better predictor of academic motivation whilst a masculine identity is more closely associated with negative classroom behaviour. The results of this study not only have substantive and methodological implications for researchers studying issues relevant to boys' lower levels of motivation and poor classroom behaviour, but also to educators working in contexts where masculinities are developed and enhanced; focusing on challenging hegemonic masculinities may result in increased academic motivation, better behaviour and greater attainment among boys.

REFERENCES

Anderman, E. M., and Young, A. J. (1994). Motivation and strategy use in science: Individual differences and classroom effects. *Journal of Research in Science Teaching, 31*(8), 811-831. doi: 10.1002/tea.3660310805.

Arbuckle, C., and Little, E. (2004). Teachers' perceptions and management of disruptive classroom behaviour during the middle years (year's five to nine). *Australian Journal of Educational and Developmental Psychology, 4,* 59-70.

Arnot, M., Gray, J., James, M, Rudduck, J. and Duveen, G. (1998). Recent Research on Gender and Education Performance. Ofsted.

Banse, R., Gawronski, B., Rebetez, C., Gutt, H., and Morton, J. B. (2010). The development of spontaneous gender stereotyping in childhood: relations to stereotype knowledge and stereotype flexibility. *Developmental Science, 13* (2), 298-306. doi: 10.1111/j.1467-7687.2009.00880.x.

Barber, M., (1996). The learning game: arguments for an education revolution (Londons, Victor Gonlancz.

Beaman, R., Wheldall, K., and Kemp, C. (2007). Recent research on troublesome classroom behaviour: A review. *Australian Journal of Special Education, 6,* 45-60. doi: 10.1080/10300110701189014.

Blatchford, P. (1996). Pupils' views on school work and school from 7 to 16 years, *Research Papers in Education,* 11(3), 263-288.

Borg, M. (1998). Secondary school teachers' perceptions of pupils' undesirable behaviours. *Journal of Educational Psychology, 68,* 67-79.

Bray, R., Gardener, C. and Parsons, N. (1997). Can Boys Do Better? Leicester: Secondary Heads Association.

Cameron, R., J., (1998). School discipline in the United Kingdom: Promoting classroom behaviour which encourages effective teaching and learning. *School Psychology Review, 27,* 33-44.

Chung, D. 2005. Violence, control, romance and gender equality: Young women and heterosexual relationships. *Women's Studies International Forum 28,* 445–55. doi: 10.1016/j.wsif.2005.09.005.

Coleman, J. (1961). The adolescent society. The social life of the teenager and its impact on education. (New York, Free press).

Connell, R. W. (1982). Class, patriarchy and Satre's theory of practice. *Theory and Society,* 11, 305-320.

Connell, R. W. Gender and power, Sydney, Australia: Allen and Unwin.

Connell, R.W., (1998). Teaching boys: new research on masculinity and gender strategies for schools. *Teacher's College Record, 98,* 206-235.

Connell, R. W., and Messerschmidt, J. W. (2005). Hegemonic Masculinity: Rethinking the concept. *Gender and Society, 19(6),* 829-859 doi: 10.1177/0891243205278639.

Cullingford, C. (1993). Children's view on gender issues in school. *British Educational Research Journal* 19(5), 555–63.

Darom, E. and Rich, Y. (1998). Sex-differences in attitudes toward school: student self-reports and teacher perceptions. *British Journal of Educational Psychology,* 58(3), 350-355.

Davies, L. (1984). Pupil power. Deviance and gender in school. London, Falmer Press.

Department for Education (2010). GCSE and equivalent attainment by pupil characteristics in England, 2009/10. Downloaded on the 22nd of July 2011 from:http://www.education.gov. uk/rsgateway/DB/SFR/s000977/sfr37- 2010.pdf.

Devine, P. G. (1989). Stereotypes and prejudice: their automatic and controlled components. *Journal of Personality and Social Psychology, 56,* 5-18.

Diekman, A. B., and Eagly, A. H. (2000). Stereotypes as dynamic constructs: women and men of the past, present and future. *Personality and Social Psychology Bulletin, 26,* 1171-1188.

Eccles, J. S., Adler, T. F., Futterman, R., Goff, S. B., Kaczala, C. M., and Meece, J. L. (1983). Expectancies, values and academic behaviours. In J. T. Spence (Ed), *Achievement and achievement motives* (75-146. San Francisco: Freeman.

Eccles, J. S., Wigfield, A., Harold, R. D., and Blumenfield, P. (1993). Age and gender differences in children's self and task perceptions during elementary school. *Child Development, 64,* 830-847.

Eccles, J. S. (1994). Understanding women's educational and occupational choices: Applying the Eccles et al. model of achievement-related choices. *Psychology of Women Quarterly,* 18, 585-609.

Eccles, J. S., Wigfield, A., and Schiefele, U. (1998). Motivation to succeed. In Damon (Series Ed.) and N. Eisenberg (Volume Ed.), *Handbook of child psychology, 5th edition, social, emotional and personality development,* 1017-1095. New York, Wiley.

Epstein, D., Elwood, J., Jey, V., and Maw, J. (1998). Failing boys? Issues in gender and achievement. Buckingham, PA: Open University Press.

Feingold, A. (1998). Cognitive gender differences are disappearing. *American Psychologist, 43,* 95-103. doi: 10.1037/0003-066X.43.2.95.

Fergusson, D.M., Horwood, J.L,. (1995). Early disruptive behaviour, IQ and later school achievement and delinquent behaviour. *Journal of Abnormal Child Psychology, 23, (2), 183-199.* doi: 10.1007/BF01447088.

Francis, B. (1999). Lads, lasses and (new) Labour: 14-16 year-old students' responses to the 'laddish' behaviour and boys' underachievement' debate, *British Journal of Sociology of Education, 20,* 355-371.

Francis, B (2000) Boys, Girls and Achievement: *Addressing the classroom issues, London: Routledge / Falmer.*

Frosh, S., Phoenix, A., and Pattman, R. (2002). Young masculinities. *Basingstoke, Palgrave.*

Gibb, S.J., Fergusson, D.M., and Horwood, L.J. (2008). Effects of single-sex and co-educational schooling on the gender gap in educational achievement. *Australian Journal of Education, 52*(3), 301-317.

Gilbert, P. and Gilbert, and R., (2001). Masculinity, inequality and post-school opportunities: disrupting oppositional politics about boys' education. *International Journal of Inclusive Education, 5*(1), 1-13.

Gottfredson, L. S. (2002). Highly general and highly practical. In R. J. Sternberg and E. L. Grigorenko (Eds.), The general factor of intelligence: How general is it? 331-380. Mahwah, NJ: Erlbaum.

Gottfried, A. E. (1985). Academic intrinsic motivation in elementary and junior high school students. *Journal of Educational Psychology, 77,* 631–645.

Greenwald, A. G., Noesk, B. A., and Banaji, M. R. (2003). Understanding and using the Implicit Association Test: 1. An improved scoring algorithm. *Journal of Personality and Social Psychology, 85,* 197-216. doi: 10.1037/0022-3514.85.2.197.

Gustafsson, J. E., and Undheim, J. O. (1996). Individual differences in cognitive functions. In D. C. Berliner and R. C. Calfee (Eds.). Handbook of educational psychology (pp. 186-242). New York: Prentice Hall International.

Halpern, D. F., (2000). Sex differences in cognitive abilities (3rd ed.). Mahwah, NJ: Lawrence Erlbaum.

Hedges, L.V., and Nowell, A. (1995). Sex differences in mental test scores, variability, and numbers of high-scoring individuals. *Science, 269, 41-45.*

Houghton, S., Wheldall, K., and Merrett, F. (1988). Classroom behaviour problems which secondary school teachers say they find most troublesome. *British Educational Research Journal, 14,* 297–312.

Ho, C. L., and Leung, J. P. (2002). Disruptive classroom behaviours of secondary and primary school. *Educational Research Journal, 17*(2), 219-233.

Hyde, J.S., Fennoma, E., and Lamon, S.J., (1990). Gender differences in mathematics performance: A meta-analysis. *Psychological Bulletin, 107,* 139-155.

Hyde, J.S. (2005). The gender similarities hypothesis. *American Psychologist,* 60, 581-592.doi: 10.1037/0003-066X.60.6.581.

Hyde, J. S., and Lynn, M. C. (2006). Gender similarities in mathematics and science. *Science,* 314, (5799), 599-600.

Jacobs, J. E., and Eccles, J. S. (2002). The impact of mothers' gender-role stereotypic beliefs on mothers' and children's ability perceptions. *Journal of Personality and Social Psychology*, 63(6), 932-944.

Jackson, C. (2002) 'Laddishness' as a Self-Worth Protection Strategy, *Gender and Education*, 14, pp. 37–51. doi: 10.1080/0954025012009887 0.

Jackson, C. (2003) Motives for 'Laddishness' at School: fear of failure and fear of the 'feminine', *British Educational Research Journal*, 29, 583-598 doi:10.1080 /0141192 032000099388.

Jackson, C. (2004). 'Wild' girls? An exploration of 'ladette' cultures in secondary schools. *Paper presented at the British Educational Research association conference, Manchester, September, 2004.*

Kaplan, A., Gheen, M., and Midgley, C., (2002). Classroom goal structure and student disruptive behaviour. *British Journal of Educational Psychology*, 72, 191- 211.doi: 10.13481000709902158847.

Keys, W. and Fernandes, C. (1993). What do students think about school? Research into factors associated with positive and negative attitudes towards school and education (Slough, National Foundation for Educational Research).

Kessler, S. J., Ashenden, D. J., Connell, R. W., and Dowsett, G. w. (1982). Ockers and disco-maniacs. Sydney, Australia: Inner City Education Centre.

Landsheer, H., Maassen, G., Bisschop, P. and Adema, I., (1998). Can higher grades result in fewer friends? A re-examination of the relation between academic and social competence, *Adolescence*, 33 (129), 185-191.

Larson, R., Dworkin, J., and Gillman, S. (1995). Facilitating adolescents' constructive use of time in one-parent families. *Applied Developmental Science*, 5(3), 143-157.

Lepper, M.R., Henderlong-Corpus, J.H., and Iyengar, S.S. (2005). Intrinsic and extrinsic motivational orientations in the classroom: age differences and academic correlates. *Journal of Educational Psychology*, 97(2), 184-196. doi: 10.1037/0022-0663.97.2.184.

Little, E., (2005). Secondary School Teachers' Perceptions of Problem Behaviours. *Educational Psychology*, 25(4), 369-377. doi:10.1080/01443410500041516.

Logan, S., and Johnston, R. (2010). Investigating gender differences in reading. *Educational Review*, 62(2), 175-187. doi: 10.1080/0013191100 3637006.

Logan, S. and Medford, E. (2011). Gender differences in strength of association between motivation, competency beliefs and reading skill. *Educational Research*, 53(1), 85-94. doi: 10.1080/00131881.2011. 552242.

Lyon, N., Barnes, M. and Sweiry, D. (2006). Families with Children in Britain; Findings from the 2004 Families Children Survey (FACS).

Mac an Ghaill, M. (1994) The Making of Men: masculinities, sexualities and schooling, *Buckingham: Open University Press.*

McDonald, A., Saunders, L., and Benfield, P. (1999). Boy's achievement progress, motivation and participation: Issues raised by the recent literature. Slough, UK: National Foundation for Education Research.

McHale, S. M., Shanahan, L., Updegraff, K. A., Crouter, A. C., and Booth, A. (2004). Developmental and individual differences in girls' sex-typed activities in middle childhood and adolescence. *Child Development*, 75, 1575-1593.

Marsh, H.W., Martin, A. J., and Cheng J. H. S. (2008). A multilevel perspective on gender in classroom motivation and climate: potential benefits of male teachers for boys. *Journal of Educational Psychology, 100* (1), 78-95. doi: 10.1037/0022-0663.100.1.78.

Martin, A.J., (2001). The Student Motivation Scale: A tool for measuring and enhancing motivation. *Australian Journal of Guidance and Counselling, 11,* 1-20. www.agca.com.au/article.php?id=5.

Martin, A.J., (2004). School motivation of boys and girls: Differences of degree, differences of kind, or both? *Australian Journal of Psychology, 56,* 133-146. doi: 10.1080/00049530412331283363.

Martin, A. J. (2005). Exploring the effects of a youth enrichment program on academic motivation and engagement. *Social Psychology of Education, 8,* 179-206, doi:10.1007/s11218-004-6487-0.

Martin, A.J., Marsh, H.W. (2005). Motivating boys and motivating girls: Does teacher gender really make a difference? *Australian Journal of Education, 49,* 320-334. ISSN: 0004-9441.

Martin, A. J., Marsh, H. W., and Cheng, J. H. S. (2008). A multilevel perspective on gender in classroom motivation and climate: potential benefits of male teachers for boys. *Journal of Educational Psychology, 100*(1), 78-95, doi: 10.1037/0022-0663.100.1.78.

Martino, W. (1999). 'Cool boys', 'party animals', 'squids' and 'poofters': interrogating the dynamics and politics of adolescent masculinities in school, *British Journal of Sociology of Education, 20,* 239-263.

Martino, W. and Meyenn, B., (2002). War, guns and cool, tough things': interrogating single-sex classes as a strategy for engaging boys in English. Cambridge *Journal of Educational Psychology, 32.* 303-324, doi: 10.1080/0305764022000024177.

Martino, W. and Pallotta-Chiarolli, M. (2003) *So What's a Boy? Addressing Issues of Masculinity and Schooling, Buckingham: Open University Press.*

Meece, J. L., Glienke, B. B., and Burg, S. (2006). Gender and motivation. *Journal of School Psychology, 44,* 351-373. doi: 10.1016/j.jsp.2006. 04.004.

Merrett, F. and Wheldall, K. (1984). Classroom behaviour problems which junior school teachers find most troublesome. *Educational Studies, 10, 87-92.*

Merrett, F. and Wheldall, K. (1993). How do teachers learn to manage classroom behaviour? A study of teachers' opinions about their initial training with special reference to classroom behaviour management. *Educational Studies, 19* (1), 91-106.

Oakhill, J. V., and Petrides, A. (2007). Sex differences in the effects of interest on boys' and girls' reading comprehension. *British Journal of Psychology. 98,* 223-235. doi:10.1348 /000712606X117649.

Oswald, M. (1995). Difficult to manage students: A survey of children who fail to respond to student discipline strategies in government school. *Educational Studies, 21,* 265-276.

Pajares, F. (1999). Self-efficacy beliefs in academic settings. *Review of Educational Research, 66*(4), 543-578.

Pajares, F. and Valiante, G. (2001). Influence of self-efficacy on elementary students' writing. *Journal of Educational Research, 90*(6), 353-360.

Pintrich, P. R., and De Groot, E. V. (2002). Motivational and self-regulated learning components of classroom academic performance. *Journal of Educational Psychology, 82,* 33-40 doi: 10.1037/0022-0663.82.1.33.

Power, S., Whitty, G., Edwards, T. and Wigfall, V. (1998). Schoolboys and schoolwork: gender identification and academic achievement, *International Journal of Inclusive Education, 2*(2), 135-153.

Reay, D. (2001). 'Spice girls' 'nice girls', 'girlies' and 'tomboys': gender discourses, girls' cultures and femininities in primary classroom. *Gender and Education, 13*, 153-166.

Renold, E. (2002). 'Presumed innocence': (hetero) sexual, homophobic and heterosexist harassment amongst children in the primary school, *Childhood, 9 (4), 415-433,* doi: 10.1177/0907568202009004004.

Renold, E. (2004). 'Other' boys: negotiating non-hegemonic masculinities in the primary school. *Gender and Education, 16*(2), 248-266. doi: 10.1080/09540250310001690609.

Sebald, H. (1981). Adolescents' concept of popularity and unpopularity, comparing 1960 with 1976, *Adolescence, 16*(61), 187-193.

Skelton, C., Francis, B., and Valkanova, Y. (2007). Breaking down the stereotypes: Gender and achievement in schools. Manchester, UK: Equal Opportunities Commission.

Skelton, C. and Francis, B. (2011). Successful Boys and Literacy: Are "Literate Boys" Challenging or Repackaging Hegemonic Masculinity? *Curriculum Inquiry, 41*(4), 457-479, doi: 10.1111/j.1467-873X.2011.00559.x.

Spinath, B., Spinath. F, M., Harlaar, N., and Plomin, R. (2006). Predicting school achievement from general cognitive ability, self-perceived ability and intrinsive value. *Intelligence, 34,* 363-374. doi: 10.1016/j.intell.2005.11.004.

Stephenson, J., Martin, A.J., and Linfoot, K. (2000). Behaviours of concern to teachers in the early years of school. *International Journal of Disability, Development and Education, 47,* 225-235, doi: 10.1080/713671118.

Suitor, J. and Reavis, R. (1995). Football, fast cars, and cheerleading: adolescent gender norms, 1978-1989, *Adolescence, 30*(118), 265-272.

Swain, J. (2000) 'The Money's Good, The Fame's Good, The Girls are Good'; the role of playground football in the construction of young boys' masculinity in a junior school', *British Journal of Sociology of Education, 21,* 95-110.

Swain, J. (2004). The resources and strategies that 10–11-year-old boys use to construct masculinities in the school setting. *British Educational Research Journal, 30,* 167–85, doi: 10.1080/01411920310001630017.

Thirer, J. and Wright, S. (1985). Sport and social status for adolescent males and females, *Sociology of Sport Journal, 2, 164-171.*

Tinklin, T.(2001). Gender differences and high attainment. *British Educational Research Journal, 29* (3), 2003. doi: 10.1080/0141192031000155971.

Van Houtte, M. (2004). Why boys achieve less at school than girls: The differences between boys' and girls' academic culture. *Educational Studies, 30,* 159-173. doi: 10/1080.0305569032000159804.

Warrington, M., Younger, M., and Williams, J. (2000). Student attitude, image and the gender gap. *British Educational Research Journal, 28,* 827-843.

Weaver-Hightower, M. (2003). The 'boy turn' in research on gender and education. *Review of Educational Research, 73*(4), 471-498.

Wheldall, K., and Merrett, F., (1988). Which classroom behaviours do primary school teachers say they find most troublesome? *Educational Review, 40,* 13-27.

Whitelaw, S., Milosevic, L. and Daniels, S. (2000). Gender, behaviour and achievement: a preliminary study of pupil perceptions and attitudes. *Gender and Education, 12*(1), 87-113.

Whitley, B. E. J. (1997). Gender differences in computer-related attitudes and behaviour: A meta-analysis. *Computers in Human Behaviour, 13*(1), 1-22.

Williams, J. and White, K. (1983). Adolescent status systems for males and females at three age levels, *Adolescence, 18 (70), 381-389.*

Williams, M., R. Burden, and Lanvers, U. (2002). 'French is the language of love and stuff': Student perceptions of issues related to motivation in learning a foreign language. *British Educational Research Journal 28*(4), 503–28.doi: 10.1080/0141192022000005805.

Wilson, T. D., Lindsey, S., and Schooler, T. Y. (2000). A model of dual attitudes. *Psychological Review, 107,* 101-12, doi: 10.1037/0033-295X107.1.101.

Wright, J., A., and Dusek, J., B., (1998). Compiling school base rates for disruptive behaviours from student disciplinary referral data. *School psychology Review,* 27, 138-147.

Younger, M., and Warrington, M., (1996). Differential achievement of girls and boys at GCSE: some observations from the perspective of one school. *British Journal of Sociology of Education, 17,* 299-314.

Younger, M. Warrington, M. and Williams, J. (1999). The gender gap and classroom interactions: reality and rhetoric? *British Journal of* Sociology of Education, 20,*327343.http://proquest-.umi.com/pqdweb-?did=*
46093171-andsid=1-andFmt=4-andclientId=25727-andRQT=309-andVName=PQD.

Younger, M.,and Warrington, M., (2000). The other side of the gender gap. *Gender and Education, 12*(4), 493-508. doi: 10.1080/09540250020004 126.

Younger, M., and Warrington, M., (2005). Raising boys' achievement. University of Cambridge Faculty of Education. Research Report.

Zimmerman, B. J., and Martinez Pons, M. (1990). Student differences in self-regulated learning: Relating grade, sex and giftedness to self-efficacy and strategy use. *Journal of Educational Psychology, 82*(1), 51-59.

In: Psychology of Gender Differences
Editor: Sarah P. McGeown

ISBN: 978-1-62081-391-1
© 2012 Nova Science Publishers, Inc.

Chapter 8

A REVIEW OF GENDER DIFFERENCES IN SELF-ESTEEM

Virgil Zeigler-Hill[1] and Erin M. Myers[2]*
[1]Oakland University, Michigan, US
[2]Western Carolina University, North Carolina, US

ABSTRACT

Self-esteem is a multi-faceted construct that describes an individual's feelings of self-worth. It has often been assumed that men and boys possess all-around higher levels of self-esteem than women and girls but the relationship between gender and self-esteem has been shown to be complex. The purpose of the present chapter is to review the studies that have compared males and females on various aspects of self-esteem. When self-esteem is conceptualized at the global level, males report slightly higher levels of self-regard than females across the life span with the largest difference occurring during adolescence.

This small but consistent self-esteem advantage for males does not, however, emerge for all forms of self-esteem. When self-esteem is conceptualized at the domain-specific level, males report higher levels of self-worth on some domains (i.e., athletic, physical appearance, self-satisfaction, and personal self-esteem) but lower levels of self-worth on others (i.e., moral-ethical and behavioral conduct self-esteem). Despite the clear gender differences in some domain-specific self-appraisals, there are also several domains in which males and females report roughly equivalent levels of self-esteem (i.e., academic, affect, social acceptance, and family self-esteem).

Few sex differences have emerged for the markers of self-esteem fragility but women have been found to be more likely than men to base their feelings of self-worth on meeting external contingencies such as gaining the approval of others. In sum, it appears that there are meaningful gender differences in the experience of self-esteem but these differences are complex and depend upon the way in which self-esteem is conceptualized.

---

*E-mail: zeiglerh@oakland.edu.

INTRODUCTION

Self-esteem has emerged as one of the most popular and enduring topics in psychology with more than 25,000 publications devoted to this construct during the last 30 years. This extensive literature has examined the potential causes, consequences, and correlates of self-esteem. Interest in self-esteem has not been limited to academic circles as it has also been an extremely popular topic in the mainstream media. This widespread interest in self-esteem is evident to anyone browsing the shelves of the self-help section at their local bookstore because they are likely to see a number of books with the word "self-esteem" emblazoned across their covers. One issue that has captured the interest of both scholars and the broader public has been gender differences in self-esteem. More specifically, there has been considerable attention paid to whether men and boys report higher levels of self-esteem than women and girls. The aim of this chapter is to provide an overview of the existing empirical literature in an attempt to clarify the complex relationship between gender and self-esteem.

The construct of self-esteem was first described by William James (1890) and was used to capture the sense of positive self-regard that develops when individuals consistently meet or exceed their important goals. More than a century later, the definition of self-esteem that was offered by James remains relevant such that self-esteem is still often thought of as a positive attitude that individuals hold toward themselves that reflects the extent to which they feel competent and successful (Coopersmith, 1967). Self-esteem has received considerable attention in recent decades due – at least in part – to the idea that self-esteem is a predictor of important life outcomes. The predictive ability of self-esteem has been debated in recent years (e.g., Baumeister, Campbell, Krueger, and Vohs, 2003; Swann, Chang-Schneider, and McClarty, 2007; Trzesniewski et al., 2006) but a wide array of studies have shown that high levels of self-esteem are associated with a variety of desirable outcomes including happiness (Furnham and Cheng, 2000), psychological health (Taylor and Brown, 1988), and overall life satisfaction (Diener and Diener, 1995), whereas low levels of self-esteem are associated with negative outcomes such as poor health, criminal behavior, and limited economic prospects (Trzesniewski et al., 2006). An important feature of high self-esteem is that it has been shown to exhibit protective properties for those who possess it. For example, individuals with high levels of self-esteem have been shown to be more resilient following negative experiences such as social rejection or achievement failure (see Zeigler-Hill, 2011 for a review).

Self-esteem can be conceptualized in a variety of ways but the term is most commonly used to describe *global* self-esteem (i.e., overall feelings of self-worth; Brown and Marshall, 2006; Rosenberg, 1965). A considerable number of measures have been developed to measure global self-esteem (see Blascovich and Tomaka, 1991 or Bosson, 2006 for reviews) with this list including instruments such as the Rosenberg Self-Esteem Scale (Rosenberg, 1965), the Coopersmith Self-Esteem Inventory (Coopersmith, 1967), the Self-Liking and Self-Competence Scale (Tafarodi and Swann, 2001), and the Single-Item Self-Esteem Scale (Robins, Hendin, and Trzesniewski, 2001). There are a number of important differences between these instruments but one feature they all have in common is that they simply ask individuals to report how they feel about themselves. For example, the Rosenberg Self-Esteem Scale asks respondents to rate their level of agreement with items such as "I feel that I'm a person of worth, at least on an equal plane with others" and "On the whole, I am satisfied with myself." This direct measurement approach is sensible considering that self-esteem is considered to be a subjective evaluation of the self.

GENDER DIFFERENCES IN GLOBAL SELF-ESTEEM

It has often been assumed that gender differences in self-esteem exist such that men and boys would report more positive attitudes about themselves than women and girls. Early studies concerning gender differences in self-esteem often had conflicting results with some studies confirming these initial speculations by showing that males had higher scores than females (Allgood-Merten and Stockard, 1991; Feather, 1991; Fertman and Chubb, 1992) but other studies found either no gender difference in self-esteem level (Greene and Wheatley, 1992; Simpson, Gangestad, and Lerma, 1990) or showed that females reported higher self-esteem than males (Connell, Spencer, and Aber, 1994; Ma and Leung, 1991). These conflicting findings failed to provide any sort of coherent answer about the existence of a gender difference for self-esteem. The reasons for the wide variation in these early results seem to be that those studies relied on relatively small samples and did not adequately control for potential moderators such as age, racial-ethnic background, or socioeconomic status. Early attempts to resolve these conflicting findings relied on a narrative review process (e.g., Maccoby and Jacklin, 1974; Wylie, 1979) but these attempts were less than satisfactory. These initial attempts to determine whether gender differences in self-esteem exist have been followed by more sophisticated meta-analytic approaches. At this point, a number of meta-analyses have been conducted that compare the self-esteem levels of men and women (Feingold, 1994; Hall, 1984; Kling, Hyde, Showers, and Buswell, 1999; Major, Barr, Zubek, and Babey, 1999; Twenge and Campbell, 2001). These meta-analyses have consistently found that men and boys report slightly higher levels of self-esteem than women and girls. It is important to note that the effect size for the self-esteem advantage observed for males tends to fall within the range of "small" (i.e., $ds < .20$). Although men and boys report higher levels of self-esteem than women and girls, this gender difference is not consistent across the life span. Boys and girls do not differ in their levels of self-esteem until adolescence which is the point when boys begin reporting higher levels of self-esteem than girls (Kling et al., 1999; Major et al., 1999; Twenge and Campbell, 2001). Not only is adolescence the first time that this gender difference emerges but this is also the period of life when the difference is the largest. Across all ages, the effect size tends to be rather small such that males report levels of self-esteem that are less than one-fifth of a standard deviation greater than those reported by females of their age but during adolescence this difference is nearly one-third of a standard deviation (i.e., $d = .33$; Kling et al., 1999; Major et al., 1999; Twenge and Campbell, 2001). The pronounced gender difference in self-esteem during adolescence has led to a great deal of speculation concerning the reason for this pattern (see Kling et al., 1999 for a review). One reason for the drop in the self-esteem of girls during adolescence – as well as the rise in the self-esteem of boys – may be subtle forms of sexism that occur in the classroom (American Association of University Women, 1990; Sadker and Sadker, 1994). This sexism may emerge through behaviors such as teachers treating boys and girls differently. For example, teachers tend to have more interactions with boys, provide boys with more focused feedback concerning their performance, select boys more often to answer questions during class, and attribute the poor performance of boys to a lack of effort rather than a lack of ability as is often assumed for girls. These subtle – and sometimes not-so-subtle – differences in the treatment of boys and girls in the classroom may lead girls to feel less academically competent than boys (Harter, Waters, and Whitesell, 1997). As important as feelings of academic competence may be for self-esteem, they are not the only reason that the self-esteem of boys and girls begins to diverge during adolescence. Another factor that likely contributes to this pattern is physical appearance. Numerous studies have shown that individuals who feel physically attractive tend to possess higher levels of self-esteem (e.g., Feingold, 1992; Harter, 1990). This is important because there is a pronounced decline in the attitudes of girls about their appearance during adolescence, whereas boys tend to maintain relatively positive attitudes about their appearance during this period (Harter, 1993). The negative shift in the attitudes of girls about their appearance is likely due to the physical changes they experience during puberty (e.g., increased body fat) as well as their heightened self-consciousness. This increase in self-consciousness may be particularly toxic for the self-esteem of adolescent girls as they begin to focus on the discrepancy between their actual appearance and their ideal appearance. The importance of physical appearance may be especially maladaptive for adolescent girls when it is combined with cultural pressure for women and girls to be thin (e.g., Brumberg, 1997). Another potential explanation for the gender difference in self-esteem concerns the gender roles than are assigned to males and females. Masculine characteristics have often been shown to be positively correlated with self-esteem for both men and women, whereas the link between feminine characteristics and self-esteem has been much weaker and less consistent (e.g., Whitley, 1983). Self-confidence, for example, is often considered to be a masculine characteristic (Broverman, Vogel, Broverman, Clarkson, and Rosenkrantz, 1972; Ruble, 1983) but similar displays of self-confidence for women and girls may be viewed as violating prescriptive gender norms concerning female modesty (e.g., Rudman, 1998; Rudman and Glick, 1999, 2001). Individuals learn about gender roles during the earliest years of their lives from a variety of sources including their parents, extended families, teachers, and media. One important source of information concerning gender roles is the gender-segregated play groups that children often form because these groups tend to enforce gender role conformity by exerting social pressure through mechanisms such as teasing those who violate gender roles (e.g., Moller and Serbin, 1996; Sroufe, Bennett, Englund, Urban, and Shulman, 1993). Groups of boys and girls tend to develop different orientations with boys often focusing on agentic pursuits (e.g., developing leadership skills), whereas girls are more likely to focus on communal activities (e.g., sharing ideas and experiences; Maccoby, 1990). The differences in communication and social influence styles that are observed for boys and girls may contribute to later differences in self-esteem because boys learn to be more direct and assertive than girls (McCloskey and Coleman, 1992).

GENDER DIFFERENCES IN DOMAIN-SPECIFIC SELF-ESTEEM

Another way of thinking about self-esteem is to consider domain-specific forms of self-esteem. Domain-specific self-esteem refers to feelings of self-worth in a specific area of life such as physical appearance or academic competence. This way of thinking about self-esteem is important because the attitudes that individuals hold about themselves may vary quite dramatically between domains. For example, it is easy to imagine someone who feels quite good about himself when considering his attractiveness but who may have rather negative attitudes about himself with regard to his academic performance. Domain-specific self-esteem is associated with global self-esteem but the two constructs are not interchangeable (e.g., Harter, 1990; Marsh, 1992; Pelham and Swann, 1989). It has been argued that domain-specific self-esteem may actually show more pronounced gender differences than those observed for global self-esteem (e.g., Hattie, 1992; Sondhaus, Kurtz, and Strube, 2001; Tiggemann and Rothblum, 1997). One reason to expect that gender differences may be more pronounced for domain-specific self-esteem is that males and females often receive different feedback within certain domains of life. For example, women and girls are more likely than men and boys to receive negative feedback from the social environment concerning their appearance.

As a result, it is possible that these negative experiences may translate into women and girls reporting lower levels of physical appearance self-esteem than their male counterparts. A recent meta-analysis examined gender differences for 10 domain-specific areas of self-esteem (Gentile et al., 2009): physical appearance, athletic, academic, social acceptance, family, behavioral conduct, affect, personal self, self-satisfaction, and moral-ethical. As expected, men and boys reported higher scores than women and girls for the following four domains: athletic self-esteem ($d = .41$), physical appearance self-esteem ($d = .35$), self-satisfaction self-esteem ($d = .33$), and personal self-esteem ($d = .28$). In contrast, women and girls actually had higher scores than men and boys for moral-ethical self-esteem ($d = -.38$) and behavioral conduct self-esteem ($d = -.17$). No gender differences emerged for academic self-esteem, affect self-esteem, social acceptance self-esteem, or family self-esteem. It is not terribly surprising that men and boys show the greatest self-esteem advantage for athletic self-esteem and physical appearance self-esteem because their experiences in these areas of life tend to be much more positive than those of women and girls. Athletic participation has been shown to be associated with higher levels of self-esteem for both males and females (Taylor, 1995; Wilkins, Boland, and Albinson, 1991) but athletic opportunities are generally more available for males than females which allow men and boys greater access to this source of self-esteem. As described earlier, women and girls report lower levels of satisfaction with their appearance than men and boys (e.g., Allgood-Merten, Lewinsohn, and Hops, 1990; McCaulay, Mintz, and Glenn, 1988; McDonald and Thompson, 1992). The dissatisfaction that women and girls feel regarding their appearance has actually gotten worse during recent decades (e.g., Brumberg, 1997; Kilbourne, 1994; Wiseman, Gray, Mosimann, and Ahrens, 1992). In fact, the levels of satisfaction that women and girls experience with regard to their physical appearance are so consistently low that it has been referred to as *normative discontent* (Rodin, Silberstein, and Striegel-Moore, 1985).

In contrast to what has been observed for global self-esteem and domains such as athleticism and physical appearance, women and girls reported higher scores than men and boys for moral-ethical self-esteem and behavioral conduct self-esteem. This finding reflects the fact that women and girls tend to perceive themselves as behaving better than men and boys (e.g., Bosacki, 2003; Wu and Smith, 1997). Females also tend to show higher levels of moral maturity than their male counterparts (Wark and Krebs, 1996) and are more likely to focus on how they will care for others when confronted with moral dilemmas (Gilligan and Attanucci, 1988; Wark and Krebs, 1996). This is important because this shows that there are certain areas of life where women and girls feel quite positively about themselves. It also suggests that it is helpful to examine specific domains of self-esteem when considering group-level differences in feelings of self-worth.

GENDER DIFFERENCES IN FRAGILE SELF-ESTEEM

There has been a growing consensus in recent years that high self-esteem is a heterogeneous construct consisting of both a *secure* form and a *fragile* form (see Kernis, 2003 for a review). Secure high self-esteem – which can be traced to the work of humanistic psychologist Carl Rogers (1959, 1961) – reflects positive attitudes toward the self that are realistic, well-anchored, and resistant to threat. Individuals with secure high self-esteem tend to have a solid basis for their feelings of self-worth that does not require constant validation. The well-anchored feelings of self-worth that serve as the foundation for secure high self-esteem allow these individuals to recognize and acknowledge their weaknesses without feeling threatened by their own lack of perfection. As a result, individuals with secure high self-esteem are able to experience success and failure in their daily lives without these experiences influencing their global feelings of self-worth. In contrast, fragile high self-esteem refers to feelings of self-worth that are vulnerable to challenge, require constant validation, and rely upon some degree of self-deception. Individuals with fragile high self-esteem have been found to be preoccupied with protecting and enhancing their vulnerable feelings of self-worth which leads them to take credit for their successes but deny their own failures and lash out at individuals or groups who represent a threat to their feelings of self-worth (see Kernis, 2003 for a review). Researchers rely on a number of markers to distinguish those with fragile high self-esteem from those with secure high self-esteem: low implicit self-esteem (Bosson, Brown, Zeigler-Hill, and Swann, 2003; Jordan, Spencer, Zanna, Hoshino-Browne, and Correll, 2003), contingent self-esteem (Crocker and Wolfe, 2001; Deci and Ryan, 1995), and unstable self-esteem (Kernis, Grannemann, and Barclay, 1989). Although these markers are distinct, each is similar in that it suggests that fragile high self-esteem should be associated with outcomes such as interpersonal style (Zeigler-Hill, Clark, and Beckman, in press) and defensiveness (Kernis, Lakey, and Heppner, 2008).

Low Implicit Self-Esteem. The vast majority of research concerning self-esteem has focused on individuals' self-reported and consciously accessible feelings of self-worth which are referred to as *explicit* self-esteem. Despite this focus on explicit attitudes, more recent evidence has suggested that *implicit* self-esteem (i.e., attitudes about the self that may fall outside of conscious awareness) may play a role in understanding behavior (see Zeigler-Hill and Jordan, 2010 for a review). Although research concerning implicit self-esteem is still in its earliest stages, the existing literature suggests that individuals are capable of simultaneously holding attitudes toward the self at the implicit and explicit levels that are inconsistent with each other (e.g., Bosson et al., 2003). On those occasions when implicit and explicit self-esteem diverge, the result is discrepant self-esteem. The form of discrepant self-esteem that has garnered the vast majority of theoretical and empirical attention to this point has been discrepant high self-esteem which refers to high levels of explicit self-esteem but low levels of implicit self-esteem (e.g., Bosson et al., 2003; Jordan et al., 2003). The positive attitudes toward the self that are expressed by individuals with discrepant high self-esteem are thought to be fragile and vulnerable to threat as a result of the underlying insecurities and self-doubts associated with their low levels of implicit self-esteem. In contrast to the gender differences that have been observed for explicit self-esteem, there is no clear and consistent evidence that the implicit self-esteem of males differs from that of females (Pelham et al., 2005; Riketta, 2005). This suggests that men and women may not differ in the implicit attitudes they hold about themselves. However, additional research needs to be conducted before a more definitive conclusion is reached concerning gender differences in implicit self-esteem.

Contingent Self-Esteem. Contingent self-esteem refers to the tendency to base one's feelings of self-worth on internal or external standards that are highly sensitive to success or failure (Crocker and Wolfe, 2001; Deci and Ryan, 1995). In other words, contingent self-esteem represents what an individual believes he or she must do or be in order to have value and worth as a person. Contingent self-esteem is considered to be a fragile form of self-esteem because it can only be maintained when certain standards are met (Deci and Ryan, 1995; Kernis, 2003). Research has consistently shown that women report possessing self-esteem that is at least somewhat more contingent than the self-esteem of men (Sanchez and Crocker, 2005; Crocker, Luhtanen, Cooper, and Bouvrette, 2003). For example, women were more likely to acknowledge basing their self-esteem on domains such as gaining the approval of others and feeling physically attractive. These findings are consistent with earlier arguments that men and boys are more likely to derive their self-esteem from feelings of autonomy and superiority whereas women and girls tend to derive their feelings of self-worth from their connections to others (Josephs, Markus, and Tafarodi, 1992). This pattern likely reflects the fact that women and girls are socialized to be interdependent (Cross and Madson, 1997; Markus and Oyserman, 1989; Wood, Christensen, Hebl, and Rothgerber, 1997). The contingent self-esteem reported by women and girls may serve as a partial explanation for their high rates of depression, anxiety, and eating disorders (Cambron, Acitelli, and Pettit, 2009).

Unstable Self-Esteem. The vast majority of self-esteem research has focused on how individuals generally feel about themselves but researchers have recognized that feelings of self-worth often change over time (Rosenberg, 1986). The term *self-esteem instability* is used to describe these fluctuations in moment-to-moment feelings of self-worth (Kernis et al., 1989; Rosenberg, 1986). Self-esteem instability is most often conceptualized as fluctuations in state self-esteem across repeated measurements by using the within-subject standard deviation of these assessments (see Kernis, 2005 for a review). Unstable high self-esteem is considered to be a form of fragile self-esteem because frequent changes in feelings of self-worth suggest these positive self-evaluations are at least somewhat uncertain (see Kernis, 2005, for a review). There have been few studies that directly compared the self-esteem instability of males and females but the scarce evidence that exists suggests that there is no reliable gender difference for this feature of self-esteem (e.g., Trzesniewski, Donnellan, and Robins, 2003). Further research is needed to be certain about whether males and females are indeed equal in terms of self-esteem instability. However, it is important to note that the associations that self-esteem instability has with other variables have sometimes been moderated by gender. For example, the interpersonal style of men with unstable high self-esteem reflects a blend of hostility and dominance, whereas the interpersonal behavior of women with unstable high self-esteem is characterized by affiliation and dominance (Zeigler-Hill et al., in press). Gender has been found to play a similar moderating role in the connection between self-esteem instability and aggression (Webster, Kirkpatrick, Nezlek, Smith, and Paddock, 2007; Zeigler-Hill and Wallace, in press).

CONCLUSION

Self-esteem is a construct with multiple facets and gender differences have been shown to exist for some – but not all – of those facets. For example, men and boys have been found to report slightly higher levels of global self-esteem than women and girls. This difference is not terribly large but it is consistent across studies. At the level of domain-specific self-esteem, the results become a bit more complicated with males reporting higher levels of self-esteem than females on some domains (i.e., athletic self-esteem, physical appearance self-esteem, self-satisfaction self-esteem, and personal self-esteem), lower levels of self-esteem on other domains (i.e., moral-ethical self-esteem and behavioral conduct self-esteem), and no difference on the remaining domains (i.e., academic self-esteem, affect self-esteem, social acceptance self-esteem, and family self-esteem). Relatively few gender differences have been noted for the markers of fragile self-esteem but it is clear that women and girls report being more likely than men and boys to base their feelings of self-worth on external domains such as the approval of others and physical appearance. Taken together, these findings suggest that there are important gender differences that exist for various aspects of self-esteem and that these differences should be considered when comparing males and females in other areas of life.

REFERENCES

Allgood-Merten, B., and Stockard, J. (1991). Sex role identity and self-esteem: A comparison of children and adolescents. *Sex Roles, 25*, 129-139.

Allgood-Merten, B., Lewinsohn, P.M., and Hops, H. (1990). Sex differences and adolescent depression. *Journal of Abnormal Psychology, 99*, 55-63.

American Association of University Women. (1990). *Shortchanging girls, shortchanging America: Full data report*. Washington, D.C: Author.

Baumeister, R. F., Campbell, J. D., Krueger, J. I., and Vohs, K. D. (2003). Does high self-esteem cause better performance, interpersonal success, happiness, or healthier lifestyles? *Psychological Science in the Public Interest, 4*, 1-44.

Blascovich, J., and Tomaka, J. (1991). Measures of self-esteem. In J. P. Robinson, P. R. Shaver, and L. S. Wrightsman (Eds.), *Measures of personality and social psychological attitudes* (Vol. 1, pp. 115-160). New York: Academic.

Bosacki, S.L. (2003). Psychological pragmatics in preadolescents: Sociomoral understanding, self-worth, and school behavior. *Journal of Youth and Adolescents, 32*, 141-155.

Bosson, J. K. (2006). Assessing self-esteem via self-reports and nonreactive instruments: Issues and recommendations. In M. Kernis (Ed.), *Self-esteem issues and answers: A sourcebook of current perspectives* (pp. 88-95). New York: Psychology Press.

Bosson, J. K., Brown, R. P., Zeigler-Hill, V., and Swann, W. B., Jr. (2003). Self-enhancement tendencies among people with high explicit self-esteem: The moderating role of implicit self-esteem. *Self and Identity*, *2*, 169-187.

Brown, J. D., and Marshall, M. A. (2006). The three faces of self-esteem. In M.H. Kernis (Ed.), *Self-esteem issues and answers: A sourcebook of current perspectives* (pp. 4-9). New York: Psychology Press.

Broverman, I.K., Vogel, S.R., Broverman, D.M., Clarkson, F.E., and Rosenkrantz, P.S. (1972). Sex role stereotypes: A current appraisal. *Journal of Social Issues*, *28*, 59-78.

Brumberg, J.J. (1997). *The body project*. New York: Random House.

Cambron, M.J., Acitelli, L.K., and Pettit, J.W. (2009). Further development of the interpersonal contingencies model: Our reply to the Mezulis and Funasaki and Burwell and Shirk commentaries. *Sex Roles*, *61*, 778-782.

Connell, J.P., Spencer, M.B., and Aber, J.L. (1994). Educational risk and resilience in African-American youth: Context, self, action, and outcomes in school. *Child Development*, *65*, 493-506.

Coopersmith, S. (1967). *The antecedents of self-esteem*. San Francisco: Freeman.

Crocker, J., Luhtanen, R. K., Cooper, M. L., and Bouvrette, A. (2003). Contingencies of self-worth in college students: Theory and measurement. *Journal of Personality and Social Psychology*, *85*, 894-908.

Crocker, J., and Wolfe, C. T. (2001). Contingencies of self-worth. *Psychological Review*, *108*, 593-623.

Cross, S.E., and Madson, L. (1997). Models of the self: Self-construals and gender. *Psychological Bulletin*, *122*, 5-37.

Deci, E. L., and Ryan, R. M. (1995). Human autonomy: The basis for true self-esteem. In M. H. Kernis (Ed.), *Efficacy, agency, and self-esteem* (pp. 31-49). New York: Plenum Press.

Diener, E. and Diener, M. (1995).Cross-cultural correlates of life satisfaction and self-esteem. *Journal of Personality and Social Psychology*, *68*, 653-663.

Feather, N.T. (1991). Human values, global self-esteem, and belief in a just world. *Journal of Personality*, *59*, 83-107.

Feingold, A. (1992). Good-looking people are not what we think. *Psychological Bulletin*, *111*, 304-341.

Feingold, A. (1994). Gender differences in personality: A meta-analysis. *Psychological Bulletin*, *116*, 429-456.

Fertman, C.I., and Chubb, N.H. (1992). The effects of a psychoeducational program on adolescents' activity involvement, self-esteem, and locus of control. *Adolescence*, *27*, 517-526.

Furnham, A., and Cheng, H. (2000). Perceived parental behaviour, self-esteem and happiness. *Social Psychiatry and Psychiatric Epidemiology*, *35*, 463-470.

Gentile, B., Grabe, S., Dolan-Pascoe, B., Twenge, J. M., Wells, B. E., and Maitino, A. (2009). Gender differences in domain-specific self-esteem: A meta-analysis. *Review of General Psychology*, *13*, 34-45.

Gilligan, C., and Attanucci, J. (1988). Two moral orientations: Gender differences and similarities. *Merrill-Palmer Quarterly*, *34*, 223-237.

Greene, A.L., and Wheatley, S.M. (1992). "I've got a lot to do and I don't think I'll have the time": Gender differences in late adolescents' narratives of the future. *Journal of Youth and Adolescence*, *21*, 667-686.

Hall, J.A. (1984). *Nonverbal sex differences*. Baltimore, MD: The Johns Hopkins University Press.

Harter, S. (1990). Causes, correlates and the functional role of global self-worth: A life-span perspective. In R.J. Sternberg and J. Kolligian, Jr. (Eds.), *Competence considered* (pp. 67-98). New Haven, CT: Yale University Press.

Harter, S. (1993). Causes and consequences of low self-esteem in children and adolescents. In R. Baumeister (Ed.), *Self-esteem: The puzzle of low self-regard* (pp. 87-111). New York: Plenum Press.

Harter, S., Waters, P.L., and Whitesell, N.R. (1997). Lack of voice as a manifestation of false self-behavior among adolescents: The school setting as a stage upon which the drama of authenticity is enacted. *Educational Psychologist, 32*, 153-173.

Hattie, J. (1992). *Self-concept*. Hillsdale, NJ: Erlbaum.

James, W. (1890). *The principles of psychology* (Vol. 1). New York: Holt.

Jordan, C. H., Spencer, S. J., Zanna, M. P., Hoshino-Browne, E., and Correll, J. (2003). Secure and defensive high self-esteem. *Journal of Personality and Social Psychology, 85*, 969-978.

Josephs, R.A., Markus, H.R., and Tafarodi, R.W. (1992). Gender and self-esteem. *Journal of Personality and Social Psychology, 63*, 391-402.

Kernis, M. H. (2003). Toward a conceptualization of optimal self-esteem. *Psychological Inquiry, 14*, 1-26.

Kernis, M. H. (2005). Measuring self-esteem in context: The importance of stability of self-esteem in psychological functioning. *Journal of Personality, 73*, 1-37.

Kernis, M. H., Grannemann, B. D., and Barclay, L. C. (1989). Stability and level of self-esteem as predictors of anger arousal and hostility. *Journal of Personality and Social Psychology, 56*, 1013-1023.

Kernis, M. H., Lakey, C. E., and Heppner, W. L. (2008). Secure versus fragile high self-esteem as a predictor of verbal defensiveness: Converging findings across three different markers. *Journal of Personality, 76*, 477-512.

Kilbourne, J. (1994). Still killing us softly: Advertising and the obsession with thinness. In P Fallon, M.A. Katzmanm and S.C. Wooley (Eds.), *Feminist perspectives on eating disorders* (pp. 395-418). New York: Guilford Press.

Kling, K. C., Hyde, J. S., Showers, C. J., and Buswell, B. N. (1999). Gender differences in self-esteem: A meta-analysis. *Psychological Bulletin, 125*, 470-500.

Ma, H.K., and Leung, M.C. (1991). Altruistic orientation in children: Construction and validation of the Child Altruism Inventory. *International Journal of Psychology, 26*, 745-759.

Maccoby, E.E. (1990). Gender and relationships: A developmental account. *American Psychologist, 45*, 513-520.

Maccoby, E.E., and Jacklin, C.N. (1974). *The psychology of sex differences*. Stanford, CA: Stanford University Press.

Major, B., Barr, L., Zubek, J., and Babey, S. H. (1999). Gender and self-esteem: A meta-analysis. In W. B. Swann Jr., J. H. Langlois, and L. A. Gilbert (Eds.), *Sexism and stereotypes in modern society: The gender science of Janet Taylor Spence* (pp. 223-253). Washington, DC: American Psychological Association.

Markus, H., and Oyserman, D. (1989). Gender and thought: The role of the self-concept. In M. Crawford and M. Gentry (Eds.), *Gender and thought: Psychological perspectives* (pp. 100-127). New York: Springer-Verlag.

Marsh, H.W. (1992). *The Self Description Questionnaire I: Manual*. Macarthur, Australia: University of Western Sydney.

McCaulay, M., Mintz, L., and Glenn, A.A. (1988). Body image, self-esteem, and depression-proneness: Closing the gender gap. *Sex Roles, 18*, 381-391.

McCloskey, L.A., and Coleman, L.M. (1992). Difference without dominance: Children's talk in mixed- and same-sex dyads. *Sex Roles, 27*, 241-257.

McDonald, K., and Thompson, J.K. (1992). Eating disturbance, body image dissatisfaction, and reasons for exercising: Gender differences and correlational findings. *International Journal of Eating Disorders, 11*, 289-292.

Moller, C., and Serbin, L.A. (1996). Antecedents of toddler gender segregation: Cognitive consonance, gender-typed toy preferences and behavioral compatibility. *Sex Roles, 35*, 445-460.

Pelham, B.W., Koole, S.L., Hardin, C.D., Hetts, J.J., Seah, E., and DeHart, T. (2005). Gender moderates the relation between implicit and explicit self-esteem. *Journal of Experimental Social Psychology, 41*, 84-89.

Pelham, B. W., and Swann, W. B., Jr. (1989). From self-conceptions to self-worth: On the sources and structure of global self-esteem. *Journal of Personality and Social Psychology, 57*, 672-680.

Riketta, M. (2005). Gender and socially desirable responding as moderators of the correlation between implicit and explicit self-esteem. *Current Research in Social Psychology, 11*, 14-28.

Robins, R. W., Hendin, H. M., and Trzesniewski, K. H. (2001). Measuring global self-esteem: Construct validation of a single item measure and the Rosenberg Self-Esteem scale. *Personality and Social Psychology Bulletin, 27,* 151-161.

Rodin, J., Silberstein, L.R., and Striegel-Moore, R.H. (1985). Women and weight: A normative discontent. In T.B. Sonderegger (Ed.), *Psychology and gender: The Nebraska Symposium on Motivation* (pp. 267-307). Lincoln, NE: University of Nebraska Press.

Rogers, C. R. (1959). A theory of therapy, personality, and interpersonal relationships, as developed in the client-centered framework. In S. Koch (Ed.), *Psychology: A study of science* (Vol. 3, pp. 184-256). New York: McGraw-Hill.

Rogers, C. R. (1961). *On becoming a person: A therapist's view of psychotherapy*. Boston: Houghton Mifflin.

Rosenberg, M. (1965). *Society and the adolescent self-image*. Princeton, NJ: Princeton University Press.

Rosenberg, M. (1986). Self-concept from middle childhood through adolescence. In J. Suls and A. G. Greenwald (Eds.), *Psychological perspectives on the self* (pp. 107-136). Hillsdale, NJ: Lawrence Erlbaum.

Ruble, T. L. (1983). Sex stereotypes: Issues of change in the 1970s. *Sex Roles, 9*, 397-402.

Rudman, L.A. (1998). Self-promotion as a risk factor for women: The costs and benefits of counterstereotypical impression management. *Journal of Personality and Social Psychology, 74*, 629-645.

Rudman, L.A., and Glick, P. (1999). Feminized management and backlash toward agentic women: The hidden costs to women of a kindler, gentler image of middle managers. *Journal of Personality and Social Psychology, 77*, 1004-1010.

Rudman, L.A., and Glick, P. (2001). Prescriptive gender stereotypes and backlash toward agentic women. *Journal of Social Issues, 57*, 743-762.

Sadker, M., and Sadker, D. (1994). *Failing at fairness: How our schools cheat girls*. New York: Touchstone.

Sanchez, D.T., and Crocker, J. (2005). Investment in gender ideals and well-being: The role of external contingencies of self-worth. *Psychology of Women Quarterly, 25*, 134-144.

Simpson, J.A., Gangestad, S.W., and Lerma, M. (1990). Perceptions of physical attractiveness: Mechanisms involved in the maintenance of romantic relationships. *Journal of Personality and Social Psychology, 59*, 1192-1201.

Sondhaus, L., Kurtz, R., and Strube, M. (2001). Body attitude, gender, self-concept: A thirty year perspective. *The Journal of Psychology, 135*, 413-429.

Sroufe, L.A., Bennett, C., Englund, M., Urban, J., and Shulman, S. (1993). The significance of gender boundaries in preadolescence: Contemporary correlates and antecedents of boundary violation and maintenance. *Child Development, 64*, 455-466.

Swann, W. B., Jr., Chang-Schneider, C., and McClarty, K. L. (2007). Do people's self-views matter? Self-concept and self-esteem in everyday life. *American Psychologist, 62*, 84-94.

Tafarodi, R. W., and Swann, W. B., Jr. (2001). Two-dimensional self-esteem: Theory and measurement. *Personality and Individual Differences, 31*, 653-673.

Taylor, D.L. (1995). A comparison of college athletic participants and nonparticipants on self-esteem. *Journal of College Student Development, 36*, 444-451.

Taylor, S. E., and Brown, J. D. (1988). Illusion and well-being: A social psychological perspective on mental health. *Psychological Bulletin, 103*, 193–210.

Tiggemann, M., and Rothblum, E.D. (1997). Gender differences in internal beliefs about weight and negative attitudes towards self and others. *Psychology of Women Quarterly, 21*, 581-593.

Trzesniewski, K., Donnellan, B., Moffitt, T., Robins, R., Poulton, R., and Caspi, A. (2006). Low self-esteem during adolescence predicts poor health, criminal behavior, and limited economic prospects during adulthood. *Developmental Psychology, 42*, 381-390.

Trzesniewski, K.H., Donnellan, M.B., and Robins, R.W. (2003). Stability of self-esteem across the lifespan. *Journal of Personality and Social Psychology, 84*, 205-220.

Twenge, J. M., and Campbell, W. K. (2001). Age and birth cohort differences in self-esteem: A cross-temporal meta-analysis. *Personality and Social Psychology Review, 5*, 321-344.

Wark, G.R., and Krebs, D.L. (1996). Gender and dilemma differences in real-life moral judgment. *Developmental Psychology, 32*, 220-230.

Webster, G., Kirkpatrick, L., Nezlek, J., Smith, C.V., and Paddock, E.L. (2007). Different slopes for different folks: Self-esteem instability and gender as moderators of the relationship between self-esteem and attitudinal aggression. *Self and Identity, 6*, 74-94.

Whitley, B.E., Jr. (1983). Sex role orientation and self-esteem: A critical meta-analytic review. *Journal of Personality and Social Psychology, 44*, 765-778.

Wilkins, J.A., Boland, F.J., and Albinson, J. (1991). A comparison of male and female university athletes and nonathletes on eating disorder indices: Are athletes protected? *Sport Behavior, 14*, 129-143.

Wiseman, C.V., Gray, J.J., Mosimann, J.E., and Ahrens, A.H. (1992). Cultural expectations of thinness in women: An update. *International Journal of Eating Disorders, 11*, 85-89.

Wood, W., Christensen, P.N., Hebl, M.R., and Rothgerber, H. (1997). Conformity to sex-typed norms, affect, and the self-concept. *Journal of Personality and Social Psychology, 73*, 523-535.

Wu, Y., and Smith, D.E. (1997). Self-esteem of Taiwanese children. *Child Study Journal, 27*, 1-19.

Wylie, R.C. (1979). *The self-concept* (Vol. 2). Lincoln, NE: University of Nebraska Press.

Zeigler-Hill, V. (2011). The connections between self-esteem and psychopathology. *Journal of Contemporary Psychotherapy, 41*, 157-164.

Zeigler-Hill, V., Clark, C. B., and Beckman, T. E. (in press). Fragile self-esteem and the interpersonal circumplex: Are feelings of self-worth associated with interpersonal style? *Self and Identity*.

Zeigler-Hill, V., and Jordan, C. (2010). Two faces of self-esteem: Implicit and explicit forms of self-esteem. In B. Gawronski and B. K. Payne (Eds.), *Handbook of implicit social cognition: Measurement, theory, and applications* (pp. 392-407). New York: Guilford Press.

Zeigler-Hill, V., and Wallace, M. T. (in press). Self-esteem instability and psychological adjustment. *Self and Identity*.

In: Psychology of Gender Differences
Editor: Sarah P. McGeown

Chapter 9

GENDER DIFFERENCES IN PSYCHOLOGICAL CAPITAL

Hang Yue Ngo[*] and Ming Shuang Ji

Department of Management
The Chinese University of Hong Kong, China

ABSTRACT

Psychological capital (PsyCap) has been defined as an individual's psychological capacities that are measurable, open to development, and manageable. It consists of four components: self-efficacy, hope, resilience, and optimism.

Individuals are presumed to vary in their levels of PsyCap, yet scant research has examined such variation. In this chapter, we explore the gender differences in PsyCap. Drawing on gender role theory and social identity theory, we attempt to explain why men and women may have different levels of PsyCap.

Several hypotheses are developed as regard the effects of gender, gender role orientation, and strength of gender identification. A data set collected from 362 Chinese employees is used to test the hypotheses. Regression analysis shows that all our predictors have significant effects on PsyCap and its various components.

INTRODUCTION

During the past decade, increasing research attention has been paid to positive organizational behavior (POB). POB refers to 'the study and application of positively oriented human resource strengths and psychological capacities that can be measured, developed, and effectively managed for performance improvement' [Luthans, 2002a:59]. Extending the POB framework for research, Luthans and Youssef [2004] introduced the construct of psychological capital (PsyCap) as a measure comparable and complementary to measures of human, social, and intellectual capital. The construct can be defined as 'an

---

[*]E-mail: hyngo@baf.msmail.cuhk.edu.hk.

individual's positive psychological state of development' [Luthans, Youssef, and Avolio, 2007a:3]. It can be seen as a constellation of motivational and behavioral tendencies derived from four components: (1) self-efficacy (i.e., the belief in one's own ability to succeed in a given task and domain), (2) hope (i.e., the motivation to achieve goals and the ability to recognize ways of doing so), (3) resilience (i.e., positive adaptation to setbacks and negative events), and (4) optimism (i.e., the tendency to make stable, internal attributions for positive events and unstable, external attributions for negative events) [Caza, Bagozzi, Woolley, Levy, and Caza, 2010; Luthans et al., 2007a]. These 'state-like' psychological capacities have been found to be predictive of individual's attitudes and behaviors in the workplace.

In current literature, individuals are presumed to vary in their levels of PsyCap, yet little research has examined the variation. In particular, owing to gender role socialization and differential life experiences, men and women tend to differ in the development of these psychological capacities. The primary objective of this chapter is to explore the gender differences in this regard. Informed by gender role theory and social identity theory, we attempt to explain why men and women may have different levels of PsyCap. Several hypotheses are proposed that specify the effects of gender, gender role orientation, and strength of gender identification on PsyCap and its various components. A data set collected from 362 employees working in three different firms in China is used to test the hypotheses.

China provides an excellent setting to conduct the study. For centuries, China has been a patriarchal society with clear demarcation of gender roles. Despite communist ideology and social policies that promoted gender equality during Mao's rule (1949-1976), the traditional patriarchal values and gender-based division of labor has resurfaced after the economic reforms [Ngo, 2001; Summerfield, 1994]. As observed by Currier [2007], the new policies promoted by the Chinese government implicitly and explicitly encourage women to return home, to take on traditional gender roles, and to leave the public sphere as the domain of men. Strong gender norms and role differentiation have become visible in contemporary China. Some recent studies showed that Chinese men and women hold different gender role attitudes, family and career orientations, and work values [Granrose, 2007; Pimentel, 2006; Peng, Ngo, Shi, and Wong, 2009; Zhang, 2006]. It is important to investigate how rapid social and economic changes influence gender roles and the psychological well-being of men and women in the country.

This chapter is organized as follows. In the next section, we review the literature on PsyCap, gender role theory, and social identity theory. Based on the theories, we then develop our hypotheses regarding the source of gender differences in PsyCap. It is followed by the methodology of the present chapter. After that, we present the empirical results. The last section concludes the chapter, as well as discusses its contributions, limitations, and future research directions.

LITERATURE REVIEW

Psychological Capital

The construct of PsyCap is drawn from theory and research on POB. Simply put, PsyCap represents who individuals are (i.e., their psychological self) and what they can become

[Luthans, Avey, Clapp-Smith, and Li, 2008a]. Some scholars [e.g., Caza, Bagozzi, Woolley, Levy, and Caza, 2010] consider it as a constellation of motivational and behavioral tendencies of individuals, while others [e.g., Luthans, 2002a; Luthans, Norman, Avolio, and Avey, 2008b] view it as 'state-like' psychological capacities that can be measured, developed, and effectively managed for improving individual performance. In the current literature, four different components of PsyCap have been identified, which are conceptually and psychometrically distinct [Luthans et al., 2008b; Peterson, Walumbwa, Byron, and Myrowitz, 2009].

The first component is *self-efficacy,* which is drawn from Bandura's [1997] social cognitive theory. Self-efficacy refers to an individual's belief in his or her abilities to successfully complete a task within a specific context [Chen, Gully, and Eden, 2001; Stajkovic and Luthans, 1998]. Individuals with low self-efficacy are easily convinced that efforts to address difficult challenges are futile, while those with high self-efficacy tend to perceive challenges as surmountable given sufficient effort [Bandura, 1982; 2008].

The second component is *hope*. Snyder, Irving, and Anderson [1991: 287] define it as 'a positive motivational state that is based on an interactively derived sense of successful (a) agency (goal-directed energy) and (b) pathways (planning to meet goals)'. This construct includes both the drive an individual experiences to accomplish a specific task or a goal (i.e., agency), and his/her psychological resources to find multiple, alternative paths to achieving the desired goals (i.e., pathways). Hopeful people are more likely to have established functional goals, providing themselves with directed motivation to work towards these goals on a daily basis [Snyder, 2002].

The third component, *resilience*, can be defined as 'the capacity to rebound or bounce back from adversity, uncertainty, conflict, failure, or even positive change, progress, and increased responsibility'[Luthans, 2002b: 702]. It is characterized by positive coping and adaptation in the face of adverse and stressful events [Masten and Reed, 2002]. Resilient persons tend to have: (1) a firm acceptance of reality, (2) a deep belief, often buttressed by strongly held values, that life is meaningful, and (3) an astounding ability to improvise and adapt to significant changes in their lives [Avey, Patera, and West, 2006; Coutu, 2002].

The last component is *optimism*. As argued by Seligman [1998], optimism is both a positively-oriented future expectation and an attributional style. People who are optimistic interpret specific positive events through personal, permanent, and pervasive causes and negative events through external, temporary, and situation- specific causes [Avey, Luthans, and Youssef, 2010; Seligman, 1998]. They expect good things to happen to them, and believe that they have the skills and abilities to cause positive events in the future [Carver and Scheier, 2002].

It has been argued that the above psychological capacities share self-directed motivating mechanisms and processes [Peterson et al., 2009]. As such, they are expected to exert significant effects on individual's work attitudes and behaviors. Previous studies have demonstrated that PsyCap is positively related to job satisfaction, organizational commitment, job performance, organizational citizenship behaviors, leadership, and absenteeism [Avey et al., 2006; Avey et al., 2010; Caza et al., 2010; Larson and Luthans, 2006; Luthans, Avey, and Norman, 2007; Peterson et al., 2009; Youssef and Luthans, 2007]. For that reason, PsyCap has become an important construct in organizational behavior (OB) research during the past decade. We believe that an investigation of gender differences in PsyCap would provide additional insights into this stream of research.

Gender Role Theory

Gender role theory holds that people tend to, and are expected to, engage in activities that are consistent with their culturally defined gender roles [Eagly, 1987; Eagly, Karau, and Makhijani, 1995; Foley, Ngo, and Wong, 2005]. Apart from external social pressures that drive people to perform behaviors congruent with gender roles, individuals also internalize cultural expectations regarding their gender and are intrinsically motivated to act in a way consistent with their gender roles. As such, female behaviors are usually expressive, characterized by a concern for others, and have an interpersonal orientation. On the other hand, male behaviors are typically instrumental, reflected by the traits of independence, proactivity, and self-confidence [Kidder, 2002; Loi, Ngo, and Foley, 2004].

Started at early stage of human development, gender role socialization encourages adherence to prevailing gender stereotypes. Through various agents of socialization (such as the family, schools, peers, and mass media), individuals learn the behaviors that a society defines as appropriate for their gender. As a consequence of gender role socialization, men and women hold different personality traits, interests, and values [Block, 1976; Eddleston, Veiga, and Powell, 2006]. In particular, they often place different priorities on work and family roles, and have different levels of involvement in the public and private spheres. Besides, men and women tend to develop different skills and capabilities that are in line with gender role expectations. Based on the arguments of gender role theory, the sex differences in PsyCap stem mainly from gender role socialization. Men are socialized to be assertive, aggressive, and task-oriented, and hence they are likely to process a higher level of PsyCap than women, who are socialized to be tender, emotional, and more concerned with people. Such gender differences are particularly marked in societies with a clear demarcation of gender roles [Foley et al., 2005].

Social Identity Theory

Social identity theory posits that individuals tend to classify themselves and others into various social groups, such as organizational membership, professional affiliation, gender, and ethnic group. Social identification refers to the perception of oneness with or belongingness to a group classification [Ashforth et al., 2008]. Through identification, individuals define themselves as members of social categories and ascribe to themselves characteristics that are typical of these categories. Arguably, the process of social identification helps to satisfy individuals' needs for belonging, inclusion, order, structure, and predictability [Fiol, 2002]. It also helps individuals to maintain a positive self-concept, which is composed of a self identity and a social identity [Tajfel, 1981] Ashford and Meal [1989] contended that social identification has some motivational and behavioral consequences. For example, a high level of identification always leads a person to engage in behaviors that are congruent with the identity and express the identity.

It is worthy to note that gender is an important social category, and it permeates the way people think, perceive, and behave within their social interaction. As pointed out by Alvesson and Billing [2009:101], 'most people probably gender themselves and are gendered by others and strive to keep a sense of masculinity or femininity intact, using gender-appropriate behaviors and meanings to do so in order to confirm a gender identity'. According to Tajfel and Turner [1986], gender identity represents the integration of gender group membership into one's self-view. For strong gender identity women, being female is a central component of the self. These women tend to consider gender as a positive self-regard, and are likely to endorse their gender roles [Leslie and Gelfand, 2008]. On the other hand, weak gender identity women tend to perceive the self as largely detached from gender group membership, and the influence of gender role norms on them would be limited. In a nutshell, the strength of gender identification would be an important factor in understanding individuals' motivations, perceptions, and behaviors under certain social conditions [Becker and Wagner, 2009; Foley, Ngo, and Loi, 2006].

HYPOTHESES

As discussed above, because of gender role socialization, men and women tend to process different personality and behavioral traits. In a study of gender differences in dispositional traits, Block [1976] reported that males are more dominant, and have a stronger and more potent self-concept. On the contrary, females are more fearful and timid, more susceptible to anxiety, less confident in task performance, and more likely seek help and reassurance. One may thus expect that men and women would be different in their psychological capacities and behavioral tendencies. In countries like China where gender roles are clearly distinct, such gender differences are likely to be substantial.

Caza et al. [2010] suggested that although no researchers have directly examined male-female differences in PsyCap, related research findings offer some suggestive evidence that they may be remarkable gender differences. Take the example of resilience. A meta-analysis of clinical studies reported that being female is a significant risk factor for post-traumatic stress [Brewin, Andrews, and Valentine, 2000]. Based on this research, Bonanno [2004] asserted that men would be more resilient than women.

Moreover, women are presumed to have lower self-efficacy in various domains than do men, because of their general disadvantages in the society and their lack of confidence in their ability [Bandura, 1982]. The career psychology literature provides evidence that men have higher career self-efficacy than women [Lent and Hackett, 1987]. In addition, some educational studies also demonstrated the gender differences in self-efficacy regarding learning [Busch, 1995; Pintrich and De Groot, 1990].

In a study of career planning and exploration among adolescents, Patton, Bartrum and Creed [2004] pointed out that males possessed a greater sense of optimism as compared to females. Previous research also showed that women tend to attribute success more externally than do men, while men emphasize the importance of their ability in achieving success [Beyer, 1990]. Hence, it seems plausible that men are more optimistic than women.

Turning to the gender differences in the level of hope, mixed results have been reported. In an earlier study, Snyder and his associates [1991] found no gender differences in level of reported hope among various samples. However, in another study, Snyder et al. [1996] reported that men had a higher score in their measure of hope compared to women. We expect that, owing to gender role differentiation and the gender stratification pattern in the society, Chinese men would have a higher level of hope than Chinese women.

Based on the above discussion regarding male-female differences in various components of PsyCap, we developed the following hypothesis.

Hypothesis 1: Men and women are different in their psychological capital. Compared to men, women are lower in their levels of self-efficacy, hope, resilience and optimism.

The male-female differences in PsyCap may not be due to biological sex *per se*, but due to some factors that vary with gender. One such factor is gender role orientation, which is related to individual psychological functioning and well-being [Karniol, Gabay, Ochion, and Harari, 1998; Sharpe and Heppner, 1991; Whitley, 1984]. As suggested by Bem [1974], gender role orientation represents the extent to which an individual believes that he or she possesses traits that are associated with traditional gender stereotypes. In current literature, two independent dimensions of gender role orientation have been identified. The first one is masculinity, which pertains to the beliefs about the extent to which one possesses traits associated with males such as aggressiveness, ambition, dominance and independence. The other one is femininity, referring to the beliefs about the extent to which one possesses traits associated with females such as compassion, sensitivity to the needs of others, understanding, and warmth [Bem, 1974; Eagly, Wood, and Diekman, 2000]. These two dimensions have been found to exert significant effects on individual's orientations and social behaviors [Chow, 1987; Karniol et al., 1998; Whitley, 1983].

In a study of gender role orientation and career choice, Gianakos [1995] reported that masculine persons prefer careers that offer challenging opportunities and have a strong self-efficacy in career decision-making. Long [1989] also found that self-efficacy in career is related to gender role orientation among a group of working women. Specifically, high-masculine women reported a higher level of self-efficacy in career as well as lower levels of anxiety and strain, as compared to low-masculine women. Additionally, Meuller and Dato-On [2008] found that gender role orientation is an important predictor of entrepreneurial self-efficacy, regardless of one's sex.

Some other studies also provide initial evidence that gender role orientation would be associated with various components of PsyCap. For example, Stets [1995] noted that a masculine identity is linked to the mastery identity [i.e., 'I am a competent person', indicating a high level of self-efficacy]. Eichinger, Heifetz, and Ingraham [1991] reported that masculinity generated a stronger feeling of personal accomplishment than femininity, even for working women. It follows that high-masculine persons would have a higher level of self-efficacy than high-feminine persons. Ptacek, Smith, and Dodge [1994] further found that gender role orientation explained gender differences in coping with stress. A positive relationship between masculinity and resilience is thus expected. Given that masculinity pertains to ambition, assertiveness, dominance, and independence, such an orientation would be conducive to the development of hope and optimism for individuals. Based on the above arguments, we put forward the following hypothesis:

Hypothesis 2: Gender role orientation is related to psychological capital. Specifically, masculinity is positively related to the levels of self-efficacy, hope, resilience, and optimism.

According to social identity theory, an individual's self-concept is made up of a personal identity and a social identity. Gender is an important and primary social category for people to identify with. A strong identification with one's gender group may help to fulfill self-esteem and self-consistency needs.

As argued by Highhouse, Thornbury, and Little [2007], gender identification serves as a means of expressing oneself and acquiring social approval, and thereby it facilitates an individual's adjustment in the social world as well as the maintenance of a positive self-concept [Taifel, 1981]. Following this argument, we expect gender identification would be related to the development of an individual's psychological capacities.

The strength of gender identification refers to how strongly a person identities oneself with one's gender group [Becker and Wanger, 2009], and his or her gender becomes an important reflection of who he or she is. Individuals who are strongly identified with their gender group tend to submit to the prevailing gender norms and accept the gender role ideology.

As their behaviors are congruent with the cultural and social expectations regarding gender roles, they would receive more compliments and feel less social pressure (e.g., threats of social sanctioning, rejection, and disapproval). Hence, they are likely to have better psychological adjustment in social interaction, and enjoy a higher level of psychological well-being [Sharpe and Heppner, 1991]. Such condition is conducive for the development of a positive self-concept and PsyCap among them.

On the contrary, for individuals who are less identified with their gender, they are reluctant to conform to existing gender stereotypes and engage in behaviors that are congruent with the gender role expectations in society. As they refuse to endorse the prevailing gender norms and ideology, they are more likely to experience social sanctioning, rejection, and disapproval from others in social interaction. This in turn brings about stress and strains for them, which adversely affects their psychological functioning and the development of positive psychological capacities. For example, as a result of their unpleasant experiences caused by incompatible gender role expectations, they would have lower levels of self-efficacy, hope, and optimism, as compared to those who are strongly identified with their gender group. Based on the above argument, we hypothesize that:

Hypothesis 3: The strength of gender identification is positively related to psychological capital. Specifically, highly identified individuals have higher levels of self-efficacy, hope, resilience, and optimism.

DATA

The data for this chapter were collected from 362 employees of three large companies in China in 2009. These companies are engaged in different industries, including energy, telecommunication, and manufacturing of multimedia electronics. With the permission of senior management and the help of the human resource departments in these companies, a self-administered questionnaire was distributed to the selected employees, the majority of whom are technical, marketing, and administrative staff. On the cover page of the questionnaire, we explained the purpose of the study and assured confidentiality of responses. We further protected the respondents' anonymity by asking them to return the completed questionnaire directly to us in a sealed envelope. Of the respondents, 49.6% were male and 50.4% were female. As regard marital status, 72.7% of them were married. Their average organizational tenure was 9.48 years. The distribution of the respondents among the three companies were 133 (36.7%), 124 (34.3%), and 105 (29.0%), respectively.

MEASURES

The questionnaires were developed using some well-established scales from Western researchers, and were then translated and administered in Chinese. Back translation was conducted where the original English version was translated into Chinese and then translated back into English to ensure proper translation. Respondents used a six-point Likert-type scale (1 = 'strongly disagree', 6 = 'strongly agree') to respond to the items in the following measures, except for gender.

Gender. Gender was measured as a dummy variable coded 0 if the respondent was a male and coded 1 if the respondent was a female.

Gender role Orientation. The two dimensions of gender role orientation, masculinity and femininity were assessed using a short version of Bem Sex-Role Inventory [Bem, 1981]. Respondents were asked to rate the extent to which 10 masculine items (e.g., 'independent', 'assertive', and 'having leadership abilities') and 10 feminine items (e.g., 'affectionate', 'sympathetic', and 'warm') described themselves. The scale has been used in previous study conducted in China and has demonstrated acceptable reliability [Zhang, Morvilitis, and Jin, 2001]. The masculine items were averaged to obtain a masculinity score, with a coefficient alpha of 0.778. Similarly, the feminine items were averaged to obtain a femininity score, with a coefficient alpha of 0.852.

Strength of gender identification. We used a six-item scale to measure this variable. Three items were adopted from Foley et al. [2006] and the other three terms were developed by us. An example of item is: 'I identity with other members of my gender group.' This new scale had a coefficient alpha of 0.807.

Psychological capital. We used different scales to measure the four dimensions of PsyCap. First, self-efficacy was measured using the eight-item scale developed by Chen, Gully, and Eden [2001]. A sample item is: 'I am confident that I can perform effectively on many different tasks.' This scale had a coefficient alpha of 0.864. Second, hope was measured by three items selected from the scale developed by Synder et al. [1996]. A sample item is: 'I can think of many ways to achieve my work goals.' The coefficient alpha of this three-item scale was recorded as 0.752. Third, resilience was measured by a four-item scale developed by Wagnild and Young [1993]. An example of item is: 'I usually take stressful things at work in stride.' The coefficient alpha of this scale was 0.77. Fourth, optimism is measured by a four-item scale developed by Scheier and Carver [1985]. A sample item is: 'I always look on the bridge side of things regarding my job.' The coefficient alpha of this scale was 0.763. Finally, an overall measure of PsyCap was obtained by averaging the above four scales.

RESULTS

Table 1. displays the means, standard deviations, and correlations of the study variables. The respondents reported a high level of PsyCap ($\bar{x}$ = 4.65) and a moderate level of strength of gender identification ($\bar{x}$ = 3.97). The mean score of femininity ($\bar{x}$ = 4.55) was higher than that of masculinity ($\bar{x}$ = 4.18). PsyCap was negatively correlated with gender (r = -0.19), and positively correlated with masculinity (r = 0.51), femininity (r = 0.26), and strength of gender identification (r = 0.35). T-tests were conducted to show the gender differences in PsyCap and its various components. Significant differences between males and females were found in PsyCap (t = 3.61, p < 0.01), self-efficacy (t = 2.27, p < 0.05), hope (t = 4.20, p < 0.001), and resilience (t = 4.26, p < 0.001), but not in optimism (t = 1.05, n.s.). These findings provided initial support for Hypothesis 1. Table 2 reports the results of regression analyses on PsyCap. We used gender, masculinity, femininity, and strength of gender identification to predict PsyCap (i.e., Model 1) and its various components in different models (i.e., Models 2-5). All the models were statistically significant as indicated by the F-value. In Model 1 where PsyCap was the dependent variable, we found that the coefficient for gender was significant and negative (β = -0.14, p < 0.001). Similar effect of gender (β = -0.18, p < 0.001 and β = -0.18, p < 0.001) was obtained in Models 3 and 4 in which hope and resilience were the dependent variables. However, the effect of gender was not significant (β = -0.08 and -0.02) in Models 2 and 5 in which self-efficacy and optimism were the dependent variables. In view of the above findings, Hypothesis 1 was partially supported.

Table 1. Means, standard deviations and correlations

Variables	$\bar{x}$	s.d.	1.	2.	3.	4.	5.	6.	7.	8.
Gender (female=1)	0.50	0.50								
Masculinity	4.18	0.78	-0.11*							
Femininity	4.55	0.78	0.03	0.32**						
Strength of gender identification	3.97	1.03	0.00	0.27**	0.26**					
PsyCap	4.65	0.73	-0.19**	0.51**	0.26**	0.35**				
Self-efficacy	4.96	0.71	-0.12*	0.46**	0.27**	0.26**	0.83**			
Hope	4.66	0.94	-0.21**	0.42**	0.15**	0.25**	0.87**	0.69**		
Resilience	4.60	0.89	-0.22**	0.44**	0.24**	0.32**	0.86**	0.66**	0.59**	
Optimism	4.38	0.95	-0.06	0.39**	0.24**	0.31**	0.78**	0.53**	0.48**	0.54**

Notes: N ranges from 359 to 362. * p < 0.05; ** p < 0.01.

Table 2. Regression analysis on PsyCap and its components

Variables	Model 1: PsyCap	Model 2: Self-efficacy	Model 3: Hope	Model 4: Resilience	Model 5: Optimism
Gender (female =1)	-0.14***	-0.08	-0.18***	-0.18***	-0.02
Masculinity	0.40***	0.38***	0.36***	0.34***	0.30***
Femininity	0.08	0.12*	0.01	0.07	0.09
Strength of gender identification	0.22***	0.13**	0.16**	0.21***	0.21***
Adjusted R^2	0.32	0.24	0.22	0.26	0.19
F value	43.25***	29.40***	26.60***	33.08***	22.38***
N	357	358	357	358	357

Note: * p < 0.05; ** p < 0.01; *** p < 0.001.

Hypothesis 2 states that gender role orientation is related to PsyCap. Specifically, it predicts a positive impact of masculinity on various components of PsyCap. The results in Model 1 show that masculinity, but not femininity, had a significant and positive effect on PsyCap ($\beta = 0.40$, $p < 0.001$). As revealed in Models 2 to 5, masculinity also exerted a strong and positive effect on the four components of PsyCap ($\beta = 0.38$, 0.36, 0.34, and 0.30, respectively, all $p < 0.001$). Hypothesis 2 was thus supported.

Hypothesis 3 predicts a positive relationship between strength of gender identification and PsyCap. We found that in Model 1 this independent variable had a significant and positive effect on PsyCap ($\beta = 0.22$, $p < 0.001$). As showed in Models 2 to 5, strength of gender identification also had a positive effect on self-efficacy ($\beta = 0.13$, $p < 0.01$), hope ($\beta = 0.16$, $p < 0.01$), resilience ($\beta = 0.21$, $p < 0.001$), and optimism ($\beta = 0.21$, $p < 0.001$). In other words, Hypothesis 3 was supported by our data.

CONCLUSION

As a central construct in the area of POB, PsyCap has attracted a great deal of research attention over the past decade. Most of the previous studies focused on the outcomes of PsyCap. Although PsyCap is expected to vary from person to person, no research has examined the gender differences in this regard. In this chapter, we explore whether or not men and women are different in their levels of PsyCap, as well as to explain such gender differences. Informed by gender role theory and gender identity theory, we expect that gender, gender role orientation, and gender identification are important determinants of PsyCap. Regression analyses were used to test the hypotheses. We collected our data in China, which is a male-dominated society with a clear demarcation of gender roles. Thus, it provides an ideal setting for our empirical investigation.

The results of t-tests and regression analyses revealed that men and women were different in their levels of PsyCap. The effect of gender, however, was not particularly strong when other predictors were included in the regression models. Overall speaking, men have a higher level of PsyCap than women. For the various components of PsyCap, we found that gender had a significant effect on hope and resilience only, but not on self-efficacy and optimism. More importantly, our regression analyses indicated that gender role orientation is a salient predictor of PsyCap. We found that masculinity, but not femininity, had a strong and positive effect on PsyCap and all its components. We further found that strength of gender identification also has a key role to play. This predictor exerted a significant and positive effect on PsyCap and its various components. Taken together, all our hypotheses have been supported by the data.

As with any research, this study has several limitations that should be acknowledged. First, our data collection relied on self-reports, and thus the results may be contaminated by common method bias. Another limitation involves the generalization of our results. Given that our data set was drawn from technical, marketing, and administrative employees in three large Chinese firms, our sample may not be representative of the general working population in China. Third, in evaluating the effects of gender role orientation, we focused mainly on masculinity and femininity. In addition to these two gender roles, there are other gender roles such as androgyny that could be examined. Lastly, our measures of various dimensions of PsyCap were crude and had a lower reliability than desired.

This chapter has made two important contributions to the current literature. In the first place, by exploring the gender differences in PsyCap, it provides a gender perspective on POB. Specifically, we evaluate the relative effects of gender, gender role orientation, and strength of gender identification on individual's levels of PsyCap, and hence fill a research niche. In view of our findings, future studies on gender differences in psychological capacities should consider the possible effects of gender role orientation and gender identification, apart from the effect of biological sex. In addition, gender role orientation may also interact with other variables to influence individual's development of PsyCap. More studies are thus called for to examine the possible interaction effects. Second, our investigation opens an avenue for research on demographic antecedents of PsyCap. The impacts of some demographic variables, such as ethnicity, age, marital status, and educational attainment, should be examined in future research, particularly from the perspective of social learning theory and social identity theory. It is important to find out how and why people develop their PsyCap in different social environments.

To conclude, the results of this chapter provided the first evidence of gender differences in PsyCap. We found that gender, gender role orientation, and strength of gender identification are important factors that explain individuals' variations in their levels of PsyCap. To extend the generalizability of our findings, the present study could be replicated in other social and cultural settings.

REFERENCES

Alvesson, M., and Billing, Y. D. (2009). *Understanding gender and organizations* (second edition). Los Angeles, CA: Sage.

Ashforth, B. E., Harrison, S. H., and Corley, K. G. (2008). Identification in organizations: An examination of four fundamental questions. *Journal of Management, 34,* 325–374.

Ashforth, B. E., and Mael, F. (1989). Social identity theory and the organization. *Academy of Management Review, 14,* 20–39.

Avey, J. B., Luthans, F., and Youssef, C. M. (2010). The additive value of positive psychological capital in predicting work attitudes and behaviors. *Journal of Management, 36,* 430–452.

Avey, J. B., Patera, J. L., and West, B. J. (2006). Positive psychological capital: A new lens to view absenteeism. *Journal of Leadership and Organizational Studies, 13,* 42–60.

Bandura, A. (1982). Self-efficacy mechanism in human agency. *American Psychology, 37,* 122–147.

Bandura, A. (1997). *Self-efficacy: The exercise of control.* New York: Freeman.

Bandura, A. (2008). *An agentic perspective on positive psychology.* New York: The Science of Human Flourishing.

Becker, J. C., and Wanger, U. (2009). Doing gender differently--The interplay of strength of gender identification and content of gender identity in predicting women's endorsement of sexist beliefs. *European Journal of Social Psychology, 39,* 487–508.

Bem, S. L. (1974). The measurement of psychological androgyny. *Journal of Consulting and Clinical Psychology, 42*, 155–162.

Beyer, S. (1990). Gender differences in the accuracy of self-evaluations of performance. *Journal of Personality and Social Psychology, 59*, 960–970.

Block, J. H. (1976). Issues, problems, and pitfalls in assessing sex differences: A critical review of the psychology of sex differences. *Merrill-Palmer Quarterly, 22*, 283–308.

Bonanno, G. A. (2004). Loss, trauma, and human resilience: Have we underestimated the human capacity to thrive after extremely aversive events? *American Psychologist, 59*, 20-28.

Brewin, C. R., Andrews, B., and Valentine, J. D. (2000). Meta-analysis of risk factors for posttraumatic stress disorder in trauma-exposed adults. *Journal of Consulting and Clinical Psychology, 68*, 748–766.

Busch, T. (1995). Gender differences in self-efficacy and attitudes toward computers. *Journal of Educational Computing Research, 12*, 147–158.

Carver, C. S., and Scheier, M. S. (2002). Optimism. In Snyder, C. R., and Lopez, S. J. (Eds.), *Handbook of positive psychology* (pp.231-243). Oxford, UK: Oxford University Press.

Caza, A., Bagozzi, R. P., Woolley, L., Levy, L., and Caza, B. B. (2010). Psychological capital and authentic leadership: Measurement, gender, and cultural extension. *Asia-Pacific Journal of Business, 2*, 53–70.

Chen, G., Gully, S. M., and Eden, D. (2001). Validation of a new general self-efficacy scale. *Organizational Research Methods, 4*, 62–83.

Chow, E. N. (1987). The influence of sex-role identity and occupational attainment in the psychological well-being of Asian American women. *Psychological of Women Quarterly, 11*, 69–82.

Coutu. D. J. (2002). How resilience works. *Harvard Business Review, 80*, 46–55.

Currier, C. L. (2007). Refining 'labor' in Beijing: Women's attitudes on work and reform. *Asia Journal of Women's Studies, 13*, 71–108.

Eagly, A. H. (1987). *Sex differences in social behavior: A social-role interpretation.* Hillsdale, HJ: Erlbaum.

Eagly, A. H., Karau, S. J., and Makhijani, M. G. (1995). Gender and the effectiveness of leaders: A meta-analysis. *Psychological Bulletin, 117*, 125–145.

Eagly, A. H., Wood, W., and Diekman, A. B. (2000). Social role theory of sex differences and similarities: A current appraisal. In Eckes, T., and Trautner, H.M. (Eds.), *The developmental social psychology of gender* (pp.123–174). New Jersey: Lawrence Erlbaum Associate.

Eddleston, K. A., Veiga, J. F., and Powell, G. N. (2006). Explaining sex differences in managerial career satisfier preferences: The role of gender self-schema. *Journal of Applied Psychology, 91*, 437–445.

Eichinger, J., Heifetz, L. J., and Ingraham, C. (1991). Situational shifts in sex-role orientation: Correlates of work satisfaction and burnout among women in special education. *Sex Roles, 25*, 425–440.

Fiol, C. M. (2002). Capitalizing on paradox: The Role of language in transforming organizational identities. *Organization Science, 13*, 653–667.

Foley, S., Ngo, H. Y., and Loi, R. (2006). Antecedents and consequences of perceived gender discrimination: A social identity perspectives. *Sex Roles, 55*, 197–208.

Foley, S., Ngo, H. Y., and Wong, A. (2005). Perceptions of discrimination and justice: Are there any gender differences in outcomes? *Group and Organization Management, 30,* 421-450.

Gianakos, I. (1995). The relation of sex-role identity to career decision-making self-efficacy. *Journal of Vocational Behavior, 46,* 131–143.

Granrose, C. S. (2007). Gender differences in career perceptions in the People's Republic of China. *Career Development International, 12,* 9–27.

Highhouse, S., Thornbury, E. E., and Little, I.S. (2007). Social-identity functions of attraction to organizations. *Organizational Behavior and Human Decision Processes, 103,* 134–146.

Karniol, R., Gabay, R., Ochion, Y., and Harari, Y. (1998). Is gender or gender-role orientation a better predictor of empathy in adolescence? *Sex Roles, 39,* 45-59.

Kidder, D. L. (2002). The influence of gender on performance of organizational citizenship behaviors. *Journal of Management, 28,* 629–648.

Larson, M., and Luthans, F. (2006). The potential added value of psychological capital in predicting work attitudes. *Journal of Leadership and Organization Studies, 13,* 44–61.

Lent, R., and Hackett, G. (1987). Career self-efficacy: Empirical status and future directions. *Journal of Vocational Behavior, 30,* 347–383.

Leslie, L. M., and Gelfand, M. J. (2008). The who and when of internal gender discrimination claims: An interactional model. *Organizational Behavior and Human Decision Processes, 107,* 123-140.

Loi, R., Ngo, H. Y., and Foley, S. (2004). The effect of professional identification on job attitudes: A study of lawyers in Hong Kong. *Organizational Analysis, 12,* 109–128.

Long, B. C. (1989). Sex-role orientation, coping strategies, and self-efficacy of women in traditional and nontraditional occupations. *Psychology of Women Quarterly, 13,* 307–324.

Luthans, F. (2002a). The need for and meaning of positive organizational behavior. *Journal of Organizational Behavior, 23,* 695–706.

Luthans, F. (2002b). Positive organizational behavior: Developing and managing psychological strengths. *Academy of Management Executive, 16,* 57–72.

Luthans, F., Avey, J. B., Clapp-Smith, R., and Li, W. (2008a). More evidence on the value of Chinese workers' psychological capital: A potentially unlimited competitive resource? *International Journal of Human Resource Management, 19,* 818-827

Luthans, F., Avey, J. B., and Norman, S. M. (2007b). Positive psychological capital: Measurement and relationship with performance and satisfaction. *Personal Psychology, 60,* 541–572.

Luthans, F., Norman, S. M., Avolio, B. J., and Avey, J. B. (2008). The mediating role of psychological capital in the supportive organizational climate--employee performance relationship. *Journal of Organizational Behavior, 29,* 219–238.

Luthans, F., and Youssef, C. M. (2004). Human, social, and now positive psychological capital management: Investing in people for competitive advantage. *Organizational Dynamics, 33,* 143–160.

Luthans, F., Youssef, C. M., and Avolio, B.J. (2007a). *Psychological capital: Developing the human competitive edge.* Oxford, UK: Oxford University Press.

Masten, A. S,. and Reed, M. G. J. (2002). Resilience in development. In Snyder, C. R., and Lopez, S. J. (Eds.), *Handbook of positive psychology* (pp.74-88). Oxford, UK: Oxford

University Press. Mueller, S. L., and Dato-On, M. C. (2008). Gender-role orientation as a determinant of entrepreneurial self-efficacy. *Journal of Developmental Entrepreneurship, 13,* 3–20.

Ngo, H. Y. (2002). Trend in occupational sex segregation in urban China. *Gender, Technology and Development, 6,* 175–196.

Patton, W., Bartrum, D. A., and Creed, P. A. (2004). Gender differences for optimism, self-esteem, expectations and goals in predicting career planning and exploration in adolescents. *International Journal for Educational and Vocational Guidance, 4,* 193–209.

Peng, K. Z., Ngo, H.Y., Shi, J., and Wong, C.S. (2009). Gender differences in the work commitment of Chinese workers: An investigation of two alternative explanations. *Journal of World Business, 44,* 323–335.

Peterson, S., Walumbwa, F. O., Byron, K., and Myrowitz, J. (2009). CEO positive psychological traits, transformational leadership, and firm performance in high-technology start-up and established firms. *Journal of Management, 35,* 348–368.

Pimentel, E. E. (2006). Gender ideology, household behavior, and backlash in urban China. *Journal of Family Issues, 27,* 341–365.

Pintrich, P. R., and Groot, D. E. V. (1990). Motivational and self-regulated learning components of classroom academic performance. *Journal of Educational Psychology, 82,* 33–40.

Ptacek, J. T., Smith, R. E., and Dodge, K. L. (1994). Gender differences in coping with stress: When stressor and appraisals do not differ. *Personality and Social Psychology Bulletin, 20,* 421-432.

Scheier, M., and Carver, C. (1985). Optimism, coping and health: Assessment and implications of generalized outcome expectancies. *Health Psychology, 4,* 219–247.

Seligman, M. E. P. (1998). *Learned optimism.* New York: Pocket Books.

Sharpe, M. J., and Heppner, P. P. (1991). Gender role, gender-role conflict, and psychological well-being in men. *Journal of Counseling Psychology, 38,* 323–330.

Snyder, C. R., Harris, C., Anderson, J. R., Holleran, S. A., Irving, L. M., Sigmon, S. T., Yoshinobu, L., Gibb, Langelle, C., and Harney, P. (1991). The will and the ways: Development and validation of an individual-differences measures of hope. *Journal of Personality and Social Psychology, 60,* 570–585.

Snyder, C. R., Sympson, S. C., Ybasco, F. C., Borders, T. F., Babyak, M. A., and Higgins, R. L. (1996). Development and validation of the state hope scale. *Journal of Personality and Social Psychology, 70,* 321–335.

Snyder, H. R. (2002). Hope theory: Rainbows in the mind. *Psychological Inquiry, 13,* 249–276.

Snyder, H. R., Irving, L., and Anderson, J. (1991). Hope and health. In Snyder, C. R., and Forsyth, D. R. (Eds.), *Handbook of Social and Clinical Psychology* (pp.285-305). Elmsford, NY: Pergamon.

Stajkovic, A. D., and Luthans, F. (1998). Self-efficacy and work-related performance: A meta-analysis. *Psychological Bulletin, 124,* 240–261.

Stets, J. E. (1995). Role identities and person identities: Gender identity, mastery identity, and controlling over one's partner. *Sociological Perspectives, 38,* 129–150.

Stets, J. E., and Burke, P. J. (2000). Identity theory and social identity theory. *Social Psychology Quarterly, 63,* 223–237.

Summerfield, G. (1994). Economic reforms and the employment of Chinese women. *Journal of Economic Issues, 28,* 715–732.

Tajfel, H. (1981). *Human groups and social categories: Studies in social psychology.* Cambridge: Cambridge University Press.

Tajfel, H., and Turner, J. C. (1986). The social identity theory of intergroup behavior. In Worchel, S. and Austin, W. G. (Eds.), *Psychology of intergroup relations* (pp.7–24). Chicago: Nelson-Hall Publishers.

Wagnild, G., and Young, H. (1993). Development and psychometric evaluation of the resilience scale. *Journal of Nursing Measurement, 1,* 165–178.

Whitley, B. E. Jr. (1984). Sex-role orientation and psychological adjustment: Two meta-analyses. *Sex Roles, 12,* 207–225.

Whitley, B. E. (1983). Sex role orientation and self-esteem: A critical meta-analytic review. *Journal of Personality and Social Psychology, 44,* 765–778.

Youssef, C. M., and Luthans, F. (2007). Positive organizational behavior in the workplace: The impact of hope, optimism, and resiliency. *Journal of Management, 33,* 774–800.

Zhang, J., Morvilitis, J. M., and Jin, S. H. (2001). Measuring gender orientation with the Bem sex role inventory in Chinese culture. *Sex Roles, 44,* 237–251.

Zhang, N. J. (2006). Gender role egalitarian attitudes among Chinese college students. *Sex Roles, 55,* 545-553.

In: Psychology of Gender Differences
Editor: Sarah P. McGeown

ISBN: 978-1-62081-391-1
© 2012 Nova Science Publishers, Inc.

Chapter 10

WORKING MEMORY LOAD ELICITS GENDER DIFFERENCES IN MENTAL IMAGERY

R. Nori,[1,*] *L. Piccardi*[2,3], *L. Palermo,*[3,4]
C. Guariglia[3,4] *and F. Giusberti*[1]

[1]Dipartimento di Psicologia, Università degli Studi di Bologna, Bologna, Italy
[2]Dipartimento di Scienze della Salute, Università degli Studi de L'Aquila, Italy
[3]I.R.C.C.S., Fondazione Santa Lucia, Roma, Italy
[4]Dipartimento di Psicologia, Università Sapienza degli Studi di Roma, Italy

ABSTRACT

Findings concerning gender differences in solving imagery tasks are controversial: sometimes they show that men outperform women and sometimes they show no difference between them. These findings have been interpreted by considering personality factors and evolutionary theories about the use of different strategies to solve imagery tasks. To interpret these results, the visuo-spatial working memory (VSWM) load required to perform these tasks should be considered. According to Coluccia and Louse (2004), the VSWM load could be a determining factor in increasing or levelling off individual differences. But, until now few studies have considered this explanation of gender differences. The aim of this study was to determine whether women perform worse than men on tasks requiring a high VSWM load, as proposed by Coluccia and Louse. Specifically, based on Kosslyn's model (1995) we analyzed three different aspects of mental imagery ability, that is, generation, inspection and transformation, involving different VSWM loads.

The Visual Mental Imagery Battery (VMIB) was performed by 190 participants (95 males; 95 females); it includes two generation tasks, two inspection tasks and three transformation tasks. We found no significant gender differences in performance of either the generation or the inspection tasks. On the transformation tasks, however, men outperformed women in both mental rotation and mental folding.

Thus, on the basis of these results gender differences were absent on tasks with a lower VSWM load (i.e., generation and inspection), but men outperformed women on

*E-mail: raffaella.nori@unibo.it, Phone: +390512091885. Fax: +39051243086.

tasks with a higher VSWM load (i.e., transformation tasks), which involve elaborating and comparing mental images. Therefore, further investigation of VSWM would be useful to clarify the controversial results reported in imagery task studies.

Keywords: Working memory, gender differences, mental imagery, cognitive load

INTRODUCTION

Visuo-spatial imagery ability, which involves generating and maintaining the representation of an object and simultaneously imagining what the object would look like if it were rotated at angles, is important in everyday activities and in technical-scientific or technological professions (e.g., aviation, driving, architecture, engineering, etc.).

It is also important in studying gender and individual characteristics because strong sex differences have been reported in various studies (see review by [1]; [2]). Some controversial results indicate that men outperform women or that women outperform men or that there are no performance differences between them.

For example, on average men perform better than women on mental rotation tasks, which require the ability to mentally judge how an object would look in 2D or 3D space (effect size from .48 to .90: [3]; [4]; [5]; [6]). By contrast, a small female advantage has been found in memory for object locations (effect size from .27 to .31: [7]; [5]).

On spatial visualization tasks, which require exploring a complex figure and finding a simple figure in it or deciding which shape will emerge when an unfolded figure is folded, men perform slightly better than women (effect size from .13 to .19: [3]) or no differences are found.

Different accounts of gender differences in visuo-spatial imagery ability have been proposed. For instance, *biological theories* affirm that sex hormones influence visuo-spatial ability. In fact, hormone manipulation affects some aspects of cognition (i.e., visuo-spatial memory) and sexual behaviour (e.g., [8]). Findings reported in the animal literature suggest that spatial behaviour is affected by early exposure to testosterone during development (see review by [9]). By contrast, the *environmental factors theory* hypothesizes that different amounts of time spent in visuo-spatial activity by males and females could explain these differences.

Indeed, from childhood males play games that involve high visuo-spatial skills, such as videogames and Lego constructions (e.g., [10]). Based on an *evolutionistic theory*, Silverman and Earls [11] hypothesized that the social roles of early women and men might explain present-day differences between the sexes. For example, selection pressures might have contributed to the development of men's spatial abilities to help them hunt (i.e., follow a track or find their way) and to the development of women's spatial tasks to help them identify the shapes and colours of edible plants and to locate objects in an array. The *difference in spatial strategy theory* suggests that differences between the sexes are determined by the strategy chosen to solve visuo-spatial problems (i.e., [12]). Specifically, self-reports of strategies used in mental rotation tasks support the idea that males use a "holistic" strategy, that is, they visualize and transform the object as a unified whole, whereas females use an "analytic" strategy in which they analyze each single part of the object to be rotated by comparing it with the corresponding part of the rotated object (e.g., [13]).

Another interpretation comes from psychological studies of *personality factors*. According to Lawton [14], [15], males are more confident about their visuo-spatial ability than females, who are more anxious than males when performing spatial tasks. This "spatial anxiety" ([14], [15]) could reduce the capability to use cognitive resources necessary to solve visuo-spatial problems.

Recently, Coluccia and Louse [1] tried to explain the controversial findings on gender differences based on the cognitive demands of visuo-spatial imagery tasks advancing the *working memory load theory*. According to these authors, the above-mentioned theories cannot account for all results, especially those that show no gender differences. According to the working memory load theory, each cognitive task requires different involvement of visuo-spatial working memory (VSWM). For example, mental rotation tasks make high demands on VSWM, because they require at least two processes, maintaining the image and transforming it. By contrast, memory for location objects requires only one process, generation of the target image. According to Coluccia and Louse, gender differences emerge only when a high VSWM load is required, that is, in tasks that require elaborating, integrating and transforming the visually imagined material. This interpretation is in line with much evidence confirming that men perform better than women on mental rotation tasks (e.g., [16]) and tasks that require rapid transformations of mental imagery.

In Cornoldi and Vecchi's model of VSWM functioning (Continuum model: [17], [18]; [19]), which hypothesizes differences in active and passive processing; cognitive load is determined by task requirements. In this model, a visual or spatial sequential/simultaneous task can be passive (i.e., when it requires the simple recall of previously acquired information) or active (i.e., when it requires integration and manipulation of information to produce an output that is substantially different from the original input). Kosslyn's model ([20], [21]) of visual mental imagery subdivides mental imagery processes into three components that involve different VSWM loads: generation is the ability to compose patterns in mental images based on stored information (the lowest cognitive load), inspection is the ability to interpret patterns in images (medium cognitive load) and transformation is the ability to alter patterns in images, such as in mental rotation (the highest cognitive load). Reinterpreting Kosslyn's model in light of the Continuum model, the first two processes (generation and inspection) involve passive working memory components, whereas the last one (transformation) requires active manipulation of information, or a high working memory load. Several studies analyzed gender differences in relation to the cognitive transformation process and reported contrasting results:) men were more accurate and faster than women (e.g., [22]; [23]); and ii) men and women were equally accurate but men were faster (e.g., [24]; [25]).

Therefore, gender differences might emerge when active transformation processes are involved ([26]), but we do not know whether gender differences emerge in the generation process, which requires the lowest VSWM load, or in the inspection process, which requires the medium VSWM load.

To our knowledge, until now no study has directly examined gender differences by considering the three cognitive processes proposed in Kosslyn's model and their cognitive load in VSWM, supporting the Continuum model. The aim of this study was to determine whether men and women perform differently on tasks requiring a high, medium or low VSWM load. We expected to find gender differences showing a male advantage in transformation but not in generation and inspection processes.

METHOD

Participants

The present study was designed in accordance with the ethical principles for human experimentation in the Declaration of Helsinki and with the local ethical committee. All subjects gave their informed written consent to participate in the study. We recruited 190 participants (95 males; 95 females) to take part in the experiment. They were between 18 and 30 years of age (M = 22.97 years; SD = 2.85 years) and had a mean educational level of 13.01 (SD = 1.54 years; range = 8-18 years). The research was conducted at I.R.C.C.S. Fondazione Santa Lucia, in Rome.

Materials

The Visual Mental Imagery Battery (VMIB) assesses the ability to generate, inspect and transform a mental image; it considers the three cognitive processes involved in mental imagery according to Kosslyn's model [20] with different VSWM cognitive load levels.

Generation Tasks

Categorical Test (a shorter version of the task reported in [27]).

This test allows assessing the ability to generate an image using categorical information. It consisted of 20 items. Each item consists of two paper stimuli plus a blank sheet of paper (inter-stimulus) presented in succession (see Figure 1a).

In the first stimulus, a line-delineated square frame (20 cm x 20 cm) with a circle in the centre was presented for 3 sec. Then a blank sheet of paper was presented for 3 sec. followed by the second stimulus, which consisted of the same frame plus a black square (side 4 mm).

The radius of the circle presented in the first stimulus could have one of four different dimensions: 3 cm, 4.7 cm, 5.3 cm or 7 cm. Items were presented in central vision. The subject's task was to mentally superimpose the second stimulus over the first one and to judge whether the square was inside or outside the circle. In ten trials the small square was inside the circle and in ten trials it was outside the circle. In this test, each participant had to complete 20 trials. The score was either 1 (correct) or 0 (incorrect); the highest score was 20.

Coordinate Test (a shorter version of the task reported in [27]).

This test requires generating an image based on metric coordinates. It includes 20 items, each composed of two paper stimuli plus a blank sheet of paper (inter-stimulus) presented in succession (see Figure 1b).

In the first stimulus, a line-delineated square frame (side 20 cm) with a circle in the centre and a black square inside or outside the circle (side 4 mm) was presented for 3 sec. Then a blank sheet of paper was presented for 3 sec. followed by the second stimulus, which was the same as the first stimulus but contained another black square (side 4 mm) in a different position.

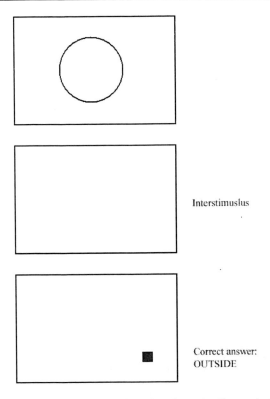

Interstimuslus

Correct answer:
OUTSIDE

Figure 1.a. Generation Tasks; Example of a stimulus taken from the Categorical Test.

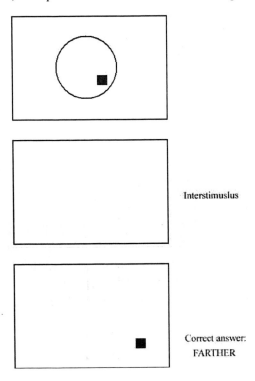

Interstimuslus

Correct answer:
FARTHER

Figure 1.b. Generation Task; Example of a stimulus taken from the Coordinate Test.

In the first stimulus, the radius of the circle was 2.4 cm, 4.1 cm, 5.3 cm or 7 cm long. In the first and the second stimulus, the black square could be inside or outside the circle. Items were presented in central vision. The participant's task was to mentally superimpose the second stimulus over the first one and to judge whether the black square in the second stimulus was nearer to or farther from the circumference of the circle than the black square in the first stimulus. In ten trials, the second black square was nearer to the circumference of the circle and in ten trials it was farther. Each participant completed 20 trials. The score was either 1 (correct) or 0 (incorrect); the highest score was 20.

Inspection Task

Object Inspection Test

Participants observed a picture for 20 seconds; then picture was removed and the examiner asked them to answer questions about the picture they had just observed (i.e., "Was the dog's tail pointing up or down?"; Figure 2). The test requires generating the image of the picture and inspecting it. In this test, each participant completed 20 trials. The score was either 1 (correct) or 0 (incorrect); the highest score was 20.

Letter Inspection Test

Participants were asked to imagine writing a letter and placing it with respect to the lines of a sheet of paper (i.e., "Imagine writing the letter "d" in lower case. Does the "d" occupy one or two rows?"). The test requires generating and inspecting a well-known object, in which the working memory load is lower because the inspection concerns previous and well-established knowledge. In this test, each participant completed 20 trials. The score was either 1 (correct) or 0 (incorrect); the highest score was 20.

Figure 2. Inspection Task. Example of a stimulus taken from the Object Inspection Test.

Transformation Tasks

Mental Folding Test (based on [28]; [29]).

Participants were asked to mentally fold an unfolded cube and to indicate whether the arrows marked on the two sides of the cube could touch each other (see Figure 3a). Each participant performed 20 trials; the maximum score was 20 (1 point for each correct answer).

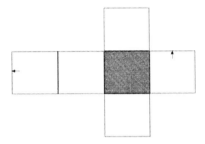

Figure 3a. Transformation Tasks; Mental Folding Test.

Mental Rotation Test (based on Thurstone's primary mental ability test cards; [30]; [29]).

This test involves mentally rotating a figure printed at the top of the sheet, comparing it in a multiple-choice task in which five figures are depicted and choosing those that correspond to the target rotation (see Figure 3b). Each participant performed 20 trials. The maximum score was 20 (1 point for each correct answer).

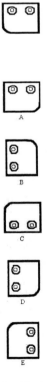

Figure 3.b. Transformation Tasks; Mental Rotation Test.

Mental Assembly Test (a shorter version of the test used in [29]).

In this test, the participant had to mentally assemble three segments of an object (i.e., a missile, a streetlamp, an asparagus shoot, a tower, and a pencil) and then judge whether their mental assembly corresponded with the subsequently presented picture. Stimuli were presented sequentially (on a vertical or horizontal axis, see Figure 3c). Each segment of the object was presented for 3 sec., then the whole picture was presented until the participant answered "yes" or "no".

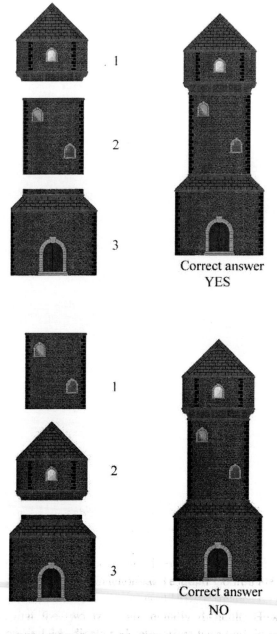

Figure 3.c. Transformation Tasks; Mental Assembly Test.

Procedure

Participants were tested individually. As soon as they entered the room, they had to complete a questionnaire regarding gender, education and handedness. To assess the three processes of mental imagery described in Kosslyn's model and to interpret the results in light of the VSWM load, we asked the participants to solve seven visual mental imagery tests included in the above-described VMIB.

The seven tests were administered in random order. In agreement with Robert and Savoie [31], in each test we considered only accuracy because it is the best measure of cognitive load.

RESULTS

Generation Tasks

We performed 2 x 2 mixed ANOVA (Gender x Generation Tasks) on hits and found a non significant main effect of Gender [F (1, 188) = 1.06, p = .34, η2 = .006], a significant Generation tasks main effect [F (1, 188) = 73.83, p < .0001, η2 = .28; Categorical Test: M = 14.71; SD = 2.71; Coordinate Test: M = 16.68; SD = 2.71] and a non significant Gender x Generation Tasks interaction [F (1, 208) = .53, p = .46, η2 = .003]. Means and Standard Deviations are reported in Table 1.

Inspection Tasks

A 2 x 2 mixed ANOVA (Gender x Inspection Tasks) on hits revealed a non significant main effect of Gender [F (1, 188) = .18, p = .67, η2 = .001], a significant Inspection Tasks main effect [F (1, 188) = 35.50, p <.001, η2 = .15; Object Inspection Test: M = 18.85, SD = 1.33; Letter Inspection Test: M = 19.91, SD = 1.19] and a non significant Gender x Inspection Tasks interaction [F (1, 188) = 1.11, p = .29, η2 = .006].

Means and Standard Deviations are reported in Table 1.

Table 1. Means and Standard Deviations on accuracy by gender and type of visuo-spatial tasks

Groups	Generation tasks		Inspection tasks		Transformation tasks		
	Categorical Test	Coordinate Test	Object Inspection Test	Letter Inspection Test	Mental Folding Test	Mental Rotation Test	Mental Assembly Test
Males (n.= 95)	14.94 (2.51)	16.75 (2.73)	18.94 (1.09)	19.48 (1.23)	16.71 (2.61)	17.63 (2.61)	19.29 (1.45)
Females (n.= 95)	14.47 (2.36)	16.62 (2.70)	18.76 (1.53)	19.53 (1.16)	15.37 (3.00)	15.73 (4.19)	19.48 (.97)

Transformation Tasks

A 2 x 3 mixed ANOVA (Gender x Transformation tasks) on hits showed a significant main effect of Gender [F (1, 188) = 12.96, p < .001, $\eta2$ = .06], that is, men outperformed women (see Table 1). The Transformation tasks main effect was significant [F (2, 188) = 115.23, p < .001, $\eta2$ = .38]. A post-hoc Neuman Keuls multiple comparison test showed that the Mental Folding Test (M = 16.06, SD = 2.88) was more difficult than the Mental Rotation Test (M = 16.68, SD = 2.88) and the Mental Assemby Test (M = 19.38, SD = 1.24) and that the latter was the easiest. The interaction between Gender and the Transformation tasks was also significant [F (2, 376)= 10.65, p< .001, $\eta2$ = .05]. The Neuman Keuls post-hoc comparison showed that women performed worse than men on the Mental Rotation and Mental Folding Tests (p_s < .001), whereas no significant gender differences emerged in the Mental Assembly Test (p = .56) (see Table 1).

DISCUSSION

We developed the Visual Mental Imagery Battery (VMIB) to determine whether men and women perform differently on imagery tasks because of the VSWM load. The VMIB assesses the ability to generate, inspect and transform a mental image.

In Kosslyn's model ([20], [21]), visual mental imagery is subdivided into three different cognitive processes (i.e., generation, inspection and transformation). On the basis of this model and Cornoldi and Vecchi's model of VSWM (the Continuum model; [17], [18], [19]), the three imagery processes seem to involve different VSWM loads; generation requires the lowest cognitive load and transformation the highest.

The different performance of men and women on the VMIB supports the idea that the VSWM load is a crucial factor in explaining gender differences. Indeed, as reported by Coluccia and Louse [1], men outperform women when the VSWM load increases. Our results also indicate the importance of considering task demands as crucial variables in interpreting gender difference (see also [23]). In fact, each task can be considered in terms of the cognitive load necessary to perform it. Generation tasks require the use of information retrieved from long-term memory. For example, in Coordinate Test participants have to observe a very simple image (i.e., a circle) and then retrieve it from long-term memory by superimposing it over a new image needed to solve the task. This task requires only passive generation of mental imagery because participants do not have to actively process the elements, Kosslyn [20] hypothesized that the image generation process might present different levels of difficulty because multipart images are more complex to generate than non-multipart images. Indeed, according to Kosslyn it requires more time and cognitive effort to generate multipart images than simple ones.

Our data are consistent with these speculations. Men and women obtained the same results on these passive tasks. Furthermore, Categorical Test and Coordinate Test used here were selected by Palermo et al. [27], who found comparable performance on categorical and coordinate tasks, suggesting that the two tasks are equally difficult. However, here we observed a difference in performing coordinate and categorical tests both in men and women without differences between sexes. Two different explanations of this data can be hypothesized: 1. In this chapter, we presented only a part of the test battery used by Palermo et al. [27] and this could have altered the results; 2. Women and men might use different strategies to solve categorical tests and one of them probably requires greater involvement of VSWM. For example, women might solve categorical tests by memorizing a single part of the figure instead of the whole figure and this might have created the difference in performance on the two tasks.

On the inspection tasks, participants have to keep in mind and look at previously acquired images. In this case, people have to "zoom" their mental image retrieving by long-term memory for permitting at their "mental eye" of focusing on the specific details necessary to solve the task. In this case, individuals change the size of their image, that is, they enlarge it, and according to Kosslyn ([20], [21]) this mental process requires a greater effort than simply retrieving a mental image. Moreover, this task is easier when participants have to inspect a familiar image (i.e., a letter) than an unfamiliar one (i.e., an object) even if in both cases they retrieve them from long-term memory. Men and women also perform similarly on inspection tasks.

Gender differences emerge when participants have to transform a mental image, that is, when they have to rotate or fold objects. According to the literature, these tasks require manipulating mental images, which involves a high VSWM load (e.g., [32]; [33]), which elicits gender differences. According to Coluccia and Louse's working memory load theory ([1]), gender differences emerge only when a high VSWM load is required. In fact, many studies have shown that females have a low VSWM span (e.g., [34]; [35]; [36]; [37]). This can be detected particularly in active tasks that require the processing (i.e., transformation) of imagined visual material (e.g., [38]; [39]). Our findings support the strict relationship between VSWM active processes. The poor performance of women was also reported in previous studies (e.g., [40]; [39]; [23]). However, we observed no performance difference between men and women in the mental assembly test. We believe that this task is primarily based on an inspection, not a transformation, process. We asked the participants to memorize different parts of an object. In this task, the image is not really transformed. Different parts of it are collected (generation ability) and then inspected by means of comparison with another figure (inspection ability). Our findings suggest that the Mental Assembly Test should be added to the list of visuo-spatial imagery inspection tasks, not to the transformation tasks. Another possible explanation could be that the women used a verbal, not a mental imagery, strategy to solve the Mental Assembly Test. Indeed, the Mental Assembly Test is the only one in which a verbal strategy could be adopted. On the other hand, women's use of a verbal strategy to perform visuo-spatial tasks is not new in the literature. Heft [41] observed that although his participants pointed out the importance of landmarks in an environmental task, their performance did not differ if landmarks were present in the environment. To explain this result, the author reported that the participants also declared they had used environmental features and had memorized turns in the no-landmark condition, demonstrating that the environment in which they moved allowed them to extrapolate cues using a verbal strategy also in the no-landmark condition. Also in Piccardi [42] study, healthy participants admitted having used verbal labelling (right–left) to recall turns and crossings in a virtual maze. Therefore, we can hypothesize that also in the present study women took advantage of a verbal strategy, thus solving the task more innately.

In conclusion, as proposed by Coluccia and Louse [1], VSWM load seems to be an important factor in explaining gender differences in spatial ability. Our results also suggest that the weight of active and passive VSWM processes should be considered in visual mental imagery models.

In our study, we found a weakness in the women's VSWM system only when it was overloaded with excessive active requests, that is, in the mental imagery transformation process (i.e., Mental Rotation Test and Mental Folding Test). In the light of this finding, it can be hypothesized that gender differences emerge only in transformation tasks in which the cognitive load is particularly high. Future research should try to determine whether women could take advantage of specific training for mental transformation tasks and perform comparably to men.

REFERENCES

[1]   E. Coluccia and G. Louse. *Journal of Environmental Psychology* 24, 329–340 (2004).
[2]   C. A. Lawton in J. Chrisler and D. McCreary, *Handbook of gender research in psychology*, Springer, New York (2010).
[3]   M. C. Linn and A. C. Petersen. *Child Development 56*, 1479-1498 (1985).
[4]   M. S. Masters and B. Sanders. *Behavior Genetics 23*, 337-341 (1993).
[5]   I. Silverman, J. Choi and M. Peters. *Archives of Sexual Behavior* 36, 261-268 (2007).
[6]   D. Voyer, S. Voyer and M. P. Bryden. *Psychological Bulletin* 117, 250-270 (1995).
[7]   D. Voyer, A. Postma, B. Brake and J. Imperato-McGinley. *Psychonomic Bulletin and Review* 14, 23-38 (2007).
[8]   C. L. Williams, A. M. Barnett and Meck, W. H. *Behavioral Neuroscience* 104, 84-97 (1990).
[9]   L. S. Liben, E. J. Susman, J. W. Finkelstein, V. M. Chinchilli, S. Kunselman, J. Schwab, J. Semon Dubas, L. M. Demers, G. Lookingbill, M. R. D'Arcangelo, H. R. Krogh and H. E. Kulin. *Developmental Psychology* 38, 236-253 (2002).
[10] M. Baenninger and N. S. Newcombe. *Sex Roles* 20, 327-344 (1989).
[11] I. Silverman and M. Eals in J. H. Barkow, L. Cosmides and J. Tooby (Eds.), *The adapted mind: Evolutionary psychology and the generation of culture,* Oxford University Press, London (1992).
[12] G. Grön, A. P. Wunderlich, M. Spitzer, R. Tomczak and M. W. Riepe. *Nature Neuroscience* 3, 404-408 (2000).
[13] J. Glück and S. Fitting. *International Journal of Testing* 3, 293-308 (2003).
[14] C. A. Lawton. *Sex Roles 30,* 765-779 (1994).
[15] C. A. Lawton. *Journal of Environmental Psychology* 16, 137-145 (1996).
[16] D. M. Saucier, S. M. Green, J. Leason, A. MacFadden, S. Bell and L. J. Elias *Behavioral Neuroscience* 116, 403-410 (2002).
[17] C. Cornoldi and T. Vecchi in M. Heller, *Touch, representation, and blindness*, Oxford University Press, Oxford, UK (2000).
[18] C. Cornoldi and T. Vecchi. *Visuo-spatial working memory and individual differences,* Psychology Press, Hove, UK (2003).
[19] C. Cornoldi in F. Marucci, *Le immagini mentali,* La Nuova Italia, Roma (1995).
[20] S. M. Kosslyn, M. Behrmann and M. Jeannerod. *Neuropsychologia* 33, 1335–1344 (1995).

[21] S. M. Kosslyn. *Cognitive Neuropsychology* 22, 333–347 (2005).
[22] S. C. Levine, J. Huttenlocher, A. Taylor and A. Langrock. *Developmental Psychology* 35, 940-949 (1999).
[23] A. Bosco, A. M. Longoni and T. Vecchi. *Applied Cognitive Psychology* 18, 519-532 (2004).
[24] D. F. Lohman and P. D. Nichols. *Learning and Individual Differences* 2, 67-93 (1990).
[25] S. Loring-Meier and D. F. Halpern. *Psychonomic Bulletin and Review* 6, 464-471 (1999).
[26] D. F. Halpern. *Sex differences in cognitive abilities,* Erlbaum, Mahwah, NJ (2000).
[27] L. Palermo, I. Bureca, A. Matano and C. Guariglia. *Neuropsychologia* 46, 2802-2807 (2008).
[28] J. W. French, R. B. Ekstrom and L. Price. *Manual for kit of reference tests for cognitive factors*, Educational Testing Service, Princeton, NJ (1963).
[29] L. Palermo, L. Piccardi, R. Nori, F. Giusberti and C. Guariglia. *Cognitive Neuropsychology* 27, 15-33 (2010).
[30] L. L. Thurstone. *Psychological tests for the study of mental abilities.* University of Chicago Press Chicago (1937).
[31] M. Robert and N. Savoie. *European Journal of Cognitive Psychology* 18,. 378-397 (2006).
[32] D. Pearson, R. De Beni and C. Cornoldi in M. Denis, R.H. Logie, C. Cornoldi, M. de Vega and J. Engelkamp, *Imagery, language and visuo-spatial thinking* (pp. 1-27). Psychology Press Hove, UK (2001).
[33] S. Garden, C. Cornoldi and R. H. Logie. *Applied Cognitive Psychology* 16, 35-50 (2002).
[34] J. T. E. Richardson in R. H. Logie and M. Denis, *Mental images in human cognition,* Elsevier, London (1991).
[35] D. F. Halpern. *Sex differences in cognitive abilities.* Lawrence Erlbaum Associates Hillsdale, NJ, US (1992).
[36] C. A. Lawton and K. A. Morrin. *Sex Roles* 40, 73-92 (1999).
[37] Z. Cattaneo, A. Postma and T. Vecchi. *Quarterly Journal of Experimental Psychology* 59, 904-919 (2006).
[38] T. Vecchi and C. Cornoldi. *Giornale Italiano di Psicologia* 25, 491–530 (1998).
[39] T. Vecchi and L. Girelli. *Acta Psychologica* 99, 1-16 (1998).
[40] J. M. Clark and A. Paivio. *Educational Psychology Review* 3, 149-170 (1991).
[41] H. Heft. *Journal of Applied Social Psychology* 9, 47-69 (1979).
[42] L. Piccardi. *Cognitive Neuropsychogy.* 26, 247–265 (2009).

In: Psychology of Gender Differences
Editor: Sarah P. McGeown

ISBN: 978-1-62081-391-1

Chapter 11

ITEM TYPE, TIMING CONDITIONS, AND GENDER DIFFERENCES ON THE MENTAL ROTATIONS TEST

Daniel Voyer and Randi A. Doyle*
University of New Brunswick, New Brunswick, Canada

ABSTRACT

The present study investigated gender differences in the pattern of responses as a function of item types on the Mental Rotations Test (MRT). Accordingly, 425 undergraduate students completed the MRT either with unlimited time or with a 10-minute time limit. For each item, the responses were coded on whether they reflected two correct (CC), one correct and one wrong, two wrong, one correct and one blank, one wrong and one blank, or two blank answers. Three different analyses were then conducted examining the influence of gender and timing conditions on performance. The first analysis considered gender differences in the prevalence of each of these outcomes. The second analysis focused on gender differences in CC outcomes as a function of distractor type (structural or mirror) and occlusion in the items (occluded, non-occluded). Finally, the third analysis explored gender differences in the prevalence of each outcome as a function of test item location. Results replicated previous findings relevant to the magnitude of gender differences on the MRT by showing the expected overall male advantage on CC outcomes. However, results relevant to other outcomes also supported the notion that women are more reluctant to guess than are men. In addition, the magnitude of gender differences was found to be larger for occluded than non-occluded items, emphasizing the role of the three-dimensional nature of the stimuli on gender differences on the MRT. Finally, results of the third analysis emphasized minute differences between items that account in part for variance in performance between men and women. Implications of the results for explanations of gender differences on the MRT are discussed.

---

*Phone: 506-453-4974; Fax: 506-447-3063; e-mail: voyer@unb.ca.

This research was funded by a grant from the Natural Sciences and Engineering Research Council of Canada (NSERC) to D. Voyer. The authors thank Nicholas Larade for his assistance in data collection and scoring.

INTRODUCTION

According to Gardner (1993), spatial ability refers to the ability to perceive, transform and modify one's internal, imaginary visual world. It follows from this general definition that the importance of spatial abilities in a wide-range of activities is undeniable. For example, it is believed that we engage our spatial abilities when participating in sports (Newcombe, Bandura and Taylor, 1983), completing mathematics calculations (Holmes and Adams, 2006), and when navigating through our environment (Castelli, Corazzini and Geminiani, 2008). Spatial abilities are thus important to our everyday functioning. However, as in most skills, individual differences are prevalent in spatial abilities. In particular, it is generally accepted that men tend to perform better than women on tasks involving spatial abilities (Kimura, 1999; Voyer, Voyer and Bryden, 1995). Males' superior performance includes both speed and accuracy on measures of spatial ability (Moffat, Hampsom and Hatzipantelis, 1998; Voyer, et al., 1995). The magnitude of these gender differences has led some researchers to speculate that they might partly explain the under-representation of women in fields believed to involve spatial abilities, such as science, technology, engineering, and mathematics (STEM; Lubinski and Benbow, 2007).

One aspect of spatial abilities that is also widely recognized is that they don't have one unitary ability, but rather they have separate components. This statement was particularly supported by the findings of the meta-analysis conducted by Linn and Petersen (1985). These authors reported that the magnitude of gender difference was largest for tasks of mental rotation, followed by spatial perception tasks, and finally, by spatial visualization tasks; findings that were replicated by Voyer et al. (1995).

Although Linn and Petersen (1985) defined each of these components and argued on their distinct character, this aspect is not within the scope of the present chapter. Instead, it focuses exclusively on the area where the largest gender differences have been observed, that is, mental rotation. Mental rotation can be defined as "the ability to rotate quickly and accurately two- or three-dimensional figures, in imagination" (Voyer et al., 1995, p. 250). When discussing mental rotation, the study conducted by Shepard and Metzler (1971) often comes to mind. Indeed, theirs was likely the first investigation of mental rotation. These researchers aimed to determine whether reaction time would be affected by angular separation when deciding if a pair of three-dimensional images were the same or different. Their now classic and oft-replicated findings showed an essentially linear increase of response time as a function of angle of rotation. This led to the conclusion that participants were mentally rotating the figures, hence the term "mental rotation".

Vandenberg and Kuse (1978) adapted the three-dimensional block images created by Shepard and Metzler (1971) to develop a pen-and-paper version of the mental rotation task. They called this 20-item measure the Mental Rotations Test (MRT) and gender differences on this test are well documented (see e.g., Voyer et al., 1995). Following the deterioration of the Vandenberg and Kuse (1978) MRT after repeated copying by researchers, Peters et al. (1995) revised this pen-and-paper test using a computer-assisted drawing program. This revised version of the MRT follows the original format of the Vandenberg and Kuse test in that it consists of a target three-dimensional block configuration on the left and four response alternatives on the right for each of 24 items.

Two of the alternatives are correct answers as they are the same object as the target but rotated in space, and two of these alternatives are distractors. After completing their revision, Peters et al. (1995) administered the MRT to over 600 undergraduate students and reported, among other findings, that men outperformed women on the test with gender accounting for almost 20% of the variance in scores. Cross-cultural studies have reflected similar magnitudes of gender differences in spatial abilities.

For example, Amponsah and Krekling's (1997) investigation of gender differences in visual-spatial abilities revealed comparable gender differences in performance on the Vandenberg and Kuse (1978) MRT amongst both Ghanaian and Norwegian samples, with men showing a significantly better performance than women.

Gender Differences in Mental Rotation

One particularly intriguing aspect of the MRT is that it has been reported as producing the largest magnitude of gender differences among spatial measures (Linn and Petersen, 1985; Voyer et al., 1995). Among the many possibilities that have been investigated to explain this finding, recent studies suggest that the type of item used in a mental rotation task affects the magnitude of gender differences. For example, Alexander and Evardone (2008) examined gender differences in performance on a mental rotations task that involved mentally rotating three-dimensional human figures as opposed to the typical block images. Compared to gender differences on the Peters et al. (1995) version of the MRT, the magnitude of gender differences was approximately cut in half when mentally rotating three-dimensional human figures. Although the authors considered social and hormonal factors as possible sources of these reduced gender differences, specific causes remained unclear. Similarly, Rilea (2008) examined gender differences in speed and accuracy when mentally rotating two-dimensional polygons compared to gender differences with two-dimensional human stick figures. Men outperformed women with polygons but no gender differences were obtained with human stick figures. The author proposed that differences in task difficulty likely accounted for these findings. In the same vein, Jansen-Osmann and Heil (2007) found significant gender differences in mental rotation only for polygons, not for various other stimuli, including the Shepard and Metzler (1971) drawings. They concluded from their findings that gender differences in pen-and-paper tests of mental rotation are unlikely to be due to a generalized male advantage in speed of mental rotation.

Item Types

In contrast to these studies that compared MRT items to other types of stimuli, Voyer and Hou (2006) considered variations in item types within the test itself. These authors emphasized the fact that, among the 24 items on the MRT, a structural difference defines both distractors (structural items hereafter) on 10 items, both distractors are a mirror image of the target (mirror items hereafter) on 12 items, and one distractor differs structurally from the target whereas the other is a mirror image of the target (mixed items hereafter) for 2 items. In addition, in the Peters et al. (1995) version of the MRT, the rotation of the objects results in partial occlusion of the correct alternatives or distractors in 7 of the 24 items. In considering item types, Voyer and Hou (2006) argued that variations in items due to the type of distractors (mirror or structural) or to occlusion would affect task difficulty. In particular, a correct alternative might appear as structurally different from the target whereas a distractor could be misperceived as similar to the target because of occlusion. From this perspective, Voyer and Hou (2006) inferred that occlusion reflected an aspect relevant to the purely three-dimensional nature of the MRT stimuli and speculated that their finding that gender differences were larger for occluded than non-occluded items was due to this aspect. Similarly, it was expected that structural items would be easier to complete than mirror items because the identification of the distractors on these items would require only basic object recognition processes, whereas mirror items would require both basic recognition processes and mental rotation. However, these authors did not find an effect of distractor type on the magnitude of gender differences. They concluded from their findings that the three-dimensional nature of the stimuli used in the MRT is likely critical to the large magnitude of gender differences observed on this test.

Guessing Behavior

Although the above discussion emphasizes test components as critical to the magnitude of gender differences on the MRT, test-taker behavior should not be overlooked. Specifically, investigation of guessing behavior on the MRT has produced some interesting findings. In particular, Voyer (1997) suggested that the examination of item outcomes on the MRT allows for some conclusions on guessing on the MRT. Specifically, a given item on the MRT can result in two correct (CC), one correct and one wrong (CW), two wrong (WW), one correct and one blank (CB), one wrong and one blank (WB), or two blank (BB) responses. Voyer (1997) initially proposed that the number of CW, CB, WB, and WW outcomes would reflect a high propensity to guess on the MRT. However, Voyer and Saunders (2004) refined this approach by suggesting that items with a blank (CB, WB) likely reflect reluctance to guess, whereas wrong guesses in CW and WW items would reflect propensity to guess, and BB items would be affected by time constraints. This hypothesis was supported by their factor analytic findings. However, across their two experiments, Voyer and Saunder's (2004) expectations that men would show greater propensity to guess (more CW and WW items than women) was not supported, whereas the expectation that women would be more reluctant to guess (more CB and WB items than men) was clearly supported.

Time Pressure

The various possible outcomes on the MRT are valuable in understanding factors accounting for gender differences on the MRT as they demonstrate the role of guessing behavior in test completion. Guessing behavior is often seen as one component of performance factors (Goldstein, Haldane, and Mitchell, 1990).

Another aspect relevant to performance factors concerns the influence of time pressure on performance on the MRT. Although, recent work suggests that the magnitude of gender differences on the MRT is not significantly different when the test is administered with and without time constraints (Masters, 1998; Voyer, Rodgers, and McCormick, 2004 but see Voyer, 2011), this conclusion is typically based on the exclusive examination of CC outcomes.

In contrast, when outcomes other than CC were examined, Voyer et al. (2004) concluded that guessing increases as time available decreases. Specifically, these authors controlled the amount of time available to respond to each item on the MRT (15, 20, 25, 30, 40 s, or unlimited) across two experiments. They observed that the number of CW items increased as time available decreased, although this was more pronounced in women than in men in Experiment 1 of their study.

However, the results obtained by Voyer et al. (2004) were based on a procedure where all participants attempted each item, regardless of its placement in the test, whereas it is a common observation that most unattempted items (BB outcomes) are found at the end of the test under timed conditions. Considering that the last four items on the MRT are non-occluded, and all but one is structural, they should be among the easiest items on this test. Thus, when participants are given a limited amount of time to complete the whole MRT (as opposed to individual items), this could contribute to variations in performance level that relate more to item type than to item placement.

Accordingly, the present study examined performance on the MRT item-by-item as a function of the presence or absence of time pressure in test completion. The progression of gender differences was also examined in this way.

Current Study

As such a systematic item analysis of the MRT of the type proposed here has never been performed; it was accomplished in three separate analyses. The first two analyses established the fit of the present data with previous findings, whereas the third analysis constituted a novel approach. Specifically, in the first analysis, data were examined in a way similar to the analysis of variance presented by Voyer and Saunders (2004), but with the addition of timing conditions as a factor. Thus, CC outcomes, and the proportion BB, CW, CB, WB, and WW outcomes as a function of non-CC outcomes were examined across genders and timing conditions (10 minutes, unlimited). Of course, it was expected that men would obtain more CC outcomes than would women. In addition, it was predicted that findings reported by Voyer and Saunders (2004) would generally be replicated. Thus, women should be more reluctant to guess (more CB and WB items) than men. However, in keeping with Voyer et al. (2004), it was also expected that the decline in BB outcomes would be accompanied by an increase in CW outcomes in the unlimited time condition when compared to the 10 minutes condition and that this effect would be more pronounced in women than in men. In the second analysis, the approach used by Voyer and Hou (2006) was implemented. Accordingly, CC outcomes were used to examine the influence of distractor type (structural, mirror) and occlusion on gender differences on the MRT. It was predicted that the findings observed by Voyer and Hou (2006) on CC items would be replicated. Thus, a gender by occlusion interaction should emerge for CC outcomes. However, if item placement is more important than item type, the influence of occlusion should be less pronounced without than with time pressure, as the last occluded item is the 17th one in the test. On average, this would allow participants to attempt more non-occluded items without than with time pressure, thereby improving their performance for non-occluded items.

Findings contradicting this expectation would support the importance of item type over placement. Finally, for the third data analysis, the proportion of each outcome (CC, BB, CW, CB, WB, and WW) was examined for each test item as a function of gender and timing conditions. The only empirical basis for predictions comes from the Peters (2005) study. Specifically, in two of the three studies presented by this author, the proportion of attempted items and magnitude of gender differences was examined over the course of items in the two sets of 12 items forming the MRT.

The number of attempted items decreased and the magnitude of gender differences increased as participants got closer to the end of each part, although magnitude data were collapsed across the two parts. Unfortunately, Peters (2005) did not use a condition without any time constraints, preferring a longer time limit. He also did not present raw performance data as a function of item.

The present study used a time limit (10 minutes total) to allow direct comparison with the findings reported by Voyer and Saunders (2004) and Voyer (1997). Although this duration was intermediate between the two extremes used by Peters (2005: 6 and 12 minutes total), it should be sufficiently long to demonstrate that even under these conditions, further improvement in performance should occur without time limit when compared to a relatively long time limit. In fact, the meta-analysis conducted by Voyer (2011) demonstrated that any time limit results in an increase in the magnitude of gender differences in tests of mental rotations when compared to the absence of time limit. In any case, it is tentatively predicted that item type distribution differences between the two parts of the MRT will reduce the prevalence of gender differences and guessing in the last few, non-occluded, items when the test is administered without time limit.

METHOD

Participants

A sample of 425 undergraduate students (198 males and 227 females) was recruited from Introductory Psychology classes. Volunteer participants were aged between 17 and 49 years ($M = 20.09$; $SD = 4.25$), although one female participant declined to report her age. Preliminary analyses showed that there was no correlation between age and performance on the MRT (Pearson $r = -.057$, $p > .23$, $N = 424$) and mean age did not vary across gender and timing conditions (all p's > .22).

Participants were compensated for their time with one bonus mark towards their Introductory Psychology course grade. Participation was voluntary, informed consent was obtained, and approval to conduct this experiment was obtained from the institutional research ethics board.

Materials

The Peters et al. (1995) revised Mental Rotations Test was used in the present study. This multiple choice test consists of 24 items; each item includes a three-dimensional block image as target to the left and four response alternatives to the right.

Response alternatives consist of images of block configurations rotated in space, two of which are rotated versions of the target (correct alternatives) and two of which are distractors. Following the definitions provided by Voyer and Hou (2006), occluded items were those in which a section of at least one of the block configuration for a distractor or correct alternative was not visible or the three-dimensional nature of any section of the block configuration was unclear due to occlusion.

Classification of items on the basis of distractor type was based on whether the distractors differed from the target in structure or they were mirror images of the target.

Finally, mixed items were those where one distractor was a mirror image and the other was structurally different from the target. This approach produced eight non-occluded mirror items (items 1, 2, 5, 6, 12, 16, 19, and 20), four occluded mirror items (items 9, 10, 11, and 15), eight non-occluded structural items (items 3, 4, 7, 8, 13, 21, 22, and 24), two occluded structural items (items 14 and 17), one non-occluded mixed item (item 23), and one occluded mixed item (item 18). An example of each type of item can be found in Figure 1 of the Voyer and Hou (2006) article.

Procedure

The MRT was completed in a quiet room designed for pen and paper testing. Before completing the test, participants were required to indicate their age and gender on a sheet attached to the MRT. The experimenter read aloud the instructions on the cover page of the test. Participants then performed the three sample problems provided in the test to ensure that they understood the task.

Following standard MRT instructions, participants were reminded that two answers were required on each item and that they should refrain from guessing. Participants were randomly assigned to either a limited time condition in which they had 10 minutes to complete the entire test or an unlimited time condition in which they were instructed to take as much time as they needed.

The time limit of 10 minutes was selected to make the results directly comparable to those obtained by Voyer and Saunders (2004) and Voyer (1997). Random assignment resulted in 86 males and 109 females tested without time limits whereas 112 males and 118 females were tested with the 10 minutes limit.

In the unlimited time condition, test completion time was measured, although only 49 (25.1%) of the participants (18 males, 31 females) were made aware of this aspect as the timing component was mentioned in the instructions. Whether participants were aware that they were timed had no significant effect and did not interact with gender on completion time or performance accuracy (smallest $p > .31$).

In addition, there was no significant effect of gender on completion time ($p > .78$). Accordingly, these aspects will not be considered further in data analyses. Participants in the unlimited time condition were tested individually to minimize the influence of implicit time pressure that might occur when other participants finish sooner.

As this factor is not as critical under timed conditions, those in that condition were tested in groups of at most four. In this case, they were seated in a small cubicle and they were separated from other test-takers by a screen on each side. Although this approach could be seen as a difference in treatment confounded with time limit, Voyer and Sullivan (2003: Experiment 2) showed that individual versus group testing had no significant effect on performance on the MRT regardless of timing conditions. This factor is thus unlikely to account for the results reported here.

RESULTS

As previously mentioned, three separate data analyses were computed. Analysis 1 involved the examination of CC outcomes, and the percentage of BB, CW, CB, WB, and WW outcomes as a function of non-CC outcomes across genders and timing conditions (10 minutes, unlimited). Analysis 2 involved the use of CC outcomes to examine the influence of distractor type (structural, mirror) and occlusion (occluded, non-occluded) on gender differences on the MRT as a function of timing conditions. Finally, Analysis 3 investigated the proportion of each outcome (CC, BB, CW, CB, WB, and WW) separately for each test item as a function of gender and timing conditions. The .05 probability was used as base significance level in all analyses. In addition, significant interactions were followed by simple main effects analyses as outlined in Winer (1962). Finally, as the last analysis involved a repeated measures variable with more than two levels, a Greenhouse-Geisser correction was applied in the estimation of significance levels when the sphericity assumption was violated.

Analysis 1: MRT Outcomes as a Function of Gender and Timing Conditions

Scoring. Each item on the MRT was coded in terms of whether it represented a CC, BB, CW, CB, WB, or WW outcome. The number of CC outcomes totaled across the 24 items was left untransformed, reflecting the raw score on the MRT. However, Voyer and Saunders (2004) pointed out that, as males are expected to obtain more CC outcomes than women do, this would leave more non-CC outcomes for women, possibly producing incorrect conclusions on gender differences. Accordingly, for non-CC outcomes, the observed number of outcomes for BB, CW, CB, WB, and WW was divided by the number of non-CC outcomes obtained to compensate for potential gender differences in the overall number of such outcomes. This value was then multiplied by 100 to reflect a percentage. The score presented for BB, CW, CB, WB, and WW outcomes thus reflects the percentage of a given outcome as a function of the overall number of non-CC responses.

Analysis of Variance. Data analysis was computed by means of a multivariate analysis of variance with the number of CC outcomes and the proportion of BB, CW, CB, WB, or WW outcomes as the dependent variables. Gender and timing conditions (10 minutes, unlimited) were the independent variables. Results revealed a significant multivariate main effect of timing condition, $F(6, 416) = 29.99$, $p < .01$, based on Pillai's Trace. Univariate tests of significance showed a significant effect of timing conditions on CC, $F(1, 421) = 64.13$, $p < .01$; CW, $F(1, 421) = 49.42$, $p < .01$; CB, $F(1, 421) = 4.62$, $p < .05$; and BB, $F(1, 421) = 153.57$, $p < .01$. This effect did not achieve significance on WW and WB outcomes (smallest $p > .16$). Examination of the relevant means in Table 1 indicates that there were more CC and CW outcome for the unlimited than for the 10 minutes condition whereas CB and BB outcome were more frequent for the 10 minutes condition than for the unlimited time condition.

Table 1. Mean and Standard Deviation (SD) for the Number of CC Outcomes and the Percentage of CW, WW, CB, WB, and BB Outcomes on the Mental Rotations Test as a Function of Gender and Timing Conditions

Outcome		Men	SD	Women	SD	d
CC	10 minutes	15.74	5.46	11.30	5.89	0.73
	Unlimited	19.96	4.59	15.83	6.08	0.71
BB	10 minutes	29.48	33.36	31.12	32.22	-.05
	Unlimited	0	0	2.07	7.92	-0.34
WW	10 minutes	2.20	5.45	3.72	7.18	-0.24
	Unlimited	3.56	12.65	3.94	7.28	-0.04
CW	10 minutes	49.93	37.09	51.61	33.64	-.05
	Unlimited	74.11	41.11	75.61	28.61	-0.04
WB	10 minutes	1.33	3.69	2.01	4.44	-0.17
	Unlimited	0	0	2.18	6.10	-0.46
CB	10 minutes	9.09	14.41	11.55	14.45	-0.17
	Unlimited	2.33	12.30	11.62	20.69	-0.51

Note: CC: two correct responses; CW: one correct and one incorrect CB: one correct and one blank; WB: one incorrect and one blank; WW: two incorrect; BB: two blanks. The score for CW, WW, CB, WB, and BB outcomes represents a percentage of non-CC outcomes. d reflects the mean for men minus that for women divided by the pooled standard deviation (Cohen, 1977).

A significant multivariate effect of gender was also obtained, $F(6, 416) = 13.72$, $p < .01$, based on Pillai's Trace. Univariate tests of significance showed a significant effect of gender on CC, $F(1, 421) = 61.48$, $p < .01$, $p < .05$; CB, $F(1, 421) = 14.23$, $p < .01$; and WB, $F(1, 421) = 11.43$, $p < .01$ (other outcomes: smallest $p > .24$). Relevant means, also presented in Table 1, indicate that men obtained significantly more CC outcomes than women did, whereas women had a greater percentage of CB and WB outcomes than men did.

It is worth noting that the interaction between gender and timing conditions did not achieve multivariate significance, $F(6, 416) = 1.60$, $p > .14$, based on Pillai's Trace. In addition, CB was the only outcome where univariate significance was obtained, $F(1, 421) = 4.81$, $p < .05$ (other outcomes: smallest $p > .076$). Accordingly, Table 1 presents the means by gender and timing conditions. Simple main effect analyses indicated that, for CB, this interaction reflected the fact that gender differences in favor of women were significant in the unlimited condition, $F(1,421) = 16.26$, $p < .01$, but not in the 10-minutes condition, $F(1,421) = 1.38$, $p > .24$.

DISCUSSION

The purpose of Analysis 1 was to determine whether results of previous studies that investigated the pattern of responses on the MRT (e.g., Voyer et al., 2004; Voyer and Saunders, 2004) would replicate when timing conditions for the whole test were manipulated. Gender differences in favor of men were expected for CC outcomes. In addition, it was expected that Voyer and Saunders' (2004) findings for the other outcomes would be replicated so that women would be more reluctant to guess (more CB and WB items) than men. In addition, based on the results obtained by Voyer et al. (2004), it was also expected that the decline in BB outcomes would be accompanied by an increase in CW outcomes in the unlimited time condition when compared to the 10 minutes condition. This effect was expected to be more pronounced in women than in men.

The analysis confirmed the first prediction as men did obtain more CC outcomes than women did, on average. The data presented in Table 1 suggest that the effect size combined for the two timing conditions was about 0.72, which would be considered relatively large based on Cohen's (1977) classification. This finding can be added to the large body of evidence indicating gender differences in favor of men on the MRT. It is also noteworthy that examination of the effect sizes (d) in Table 1 shows that the 10 minutes and unlimited condition produced gender differences that are virtually equal in magnitude. This finding can thus be added to the research suggesting that time pressure does not affect significantly the magnitude of gender differences on the MRT (e.g., Masters, 1998; Resnick, 1993; Voyer et al., 2004; but see Voyer, 2011). However, this does not mean that all performance factors should be disregarded, as consideration of the other predictions revealed.

The second prediction was confirmed for the two outcomes that Voyer and Saunders (2004) presumed to reflect reluctance to guess. Specifically, women obtained a greater percentage of WB and CB outcomes than men did. It is thus legitimate to conclude that, when completing the MRT, women show some reluctance to guess, thereby emphasizing the part of the test instructions that discourages guessing, as opposed to the aspect of the instructions emphasizing the need for two answers on each item. This would support the notion that women tend to be cautious and reluctant to take chances when completing the MRT, as proposed by Goldstein et al. (1990). In fact, the finding that women produced some BB outcomes when given unlimited time to complete the task (see Table 1) would further support this point, especially considering that men produced no BB outcomes under those conditions. Further support for this interpretation comes from the fact that CB outcomes were the only ones that showed a significant gender by timing conditions interaction (although the underlying multivariate test was not significant). Essentially, gender differences on CB items were significant for the unlimited but not for the 10 minutes condition. The pattern of means for CB in Table 1 suggests that the percentage of CB outcomes remained essentially the same for women across timing conditions, whereas, in men, it was lower in the unlimited condition than in the 10 minutes condition. This supports the notion that men tended to produce CB items when they ran out of time, whereas time pressure did not make a difference for women. Thus, the conclusion that women are reluctant to guess regardless of timing conditions stems logically from the findings for CB outcomes. It also suggests that the overall greater percentage of CB outcomes in the 10 minutes than in the unlimited condition was due exclusively to a change in men's test-taking behavior.

The third prediction for Analysis 1 was also clearly confirmed, at least as far as its first component is concerned. Indeed, results showed that the percentage of BB outcomes decreased from the 10 minutes to the unlimited time condition (see Table 1), whereas the percentage of CW outcomes increased from the 10 minutes to the unlimited time condition. This findings supports the interpretation suggested by Voyer et al. (2004) that when participants are given more time to complete the MRT, they typically emphasize the aspect of test instruction requiring two answers per item, rather than the component discouraging guessing. However, their knowledge of the correct answers is not affected by the extra time available in the unlimited condition, resulting in a greater number of guesses. Contrary to what was expected from Voyer et al.'s (2004) findings, however, this finding was not more pronounced in women than in men. A number of aspects account for this finding in the present study. Specifically, this finding was only based on a marginal interaction of gender with timing conditions in the Voyer et al. (2004) study when they compared time limited conditions to an unlimited time condition, although their sample size of 210 participants gave them less statistical power than the sample of 425 used here. More importantly, Voyer et al. (2004) used an item-by-item presentation format with the items viewed by means of a projector. This ensured that every participant was exposed to all items in all timing conditions. In contrast, the present study used the whole test in paper format. This changed the nature of the task in that it left participants in control of the items on which they chose to spend time in the 10 minutes condition. For example, this might result in very few BB outcomes at the beginning of the test and many toward the end in the limited time condition (Peters, 2005). This would reflect the fact that participants ran out of time for later items. In contrast, in the Voyer et al. (2004) experiments, BB outcomes could occur anywhere in the test and would depend more on item difficulty than on item placement. This suggests that an analysis of the type implemented in Analysis 3 (below) in the context of the Voyer et al. (2004) procedure would be informative to settle this matter.

Aside from these considerations, the lack of gender differences for BB outcomes might be seen as puzzling considering reports that such unattempted items are typically more common in women than in men (e.g., Masters, 1998; Peters, 2005; Voyer, 1997). However, studies that have reported gender differences on BB outcomes also did not take into account the total number of non-CC outcomes produced by participants. In contrast, Voyer and Saunders (2004) took the overall number of non-CC outcomes into account and did not find significant gender differences on BB outcomes, a finding that was replicated here under similar circumstances. However, when the raw number of BB outcomes is used as the dependent variable, results show that women produce significantly more such outcomes than men do in the present data ($p < .05$). This means that women do tend to produce more BB outcomes than men do in general. However, the number of BB outcomes that women produce is proportionally similar to that produced by men when the total number of non-CC outcomes is taken into account. Thus, BB outcomes form the same percentage of non-CC outcomes in men and women. This suggests that reports of gender differences on unattempted items are somewhat misleading when other non-CC outcomes are not taken into account.

Analysis 2: CC Outcomes as a Function of Gender, Occlusion, and Distractor Type

Scoring. In Analysis 2, the approach proposed by Voyer and Hou (2006) was used to examine type of distractor and occlusion. Thus, in the primary analysis, the percentage of CC outcomes in each category was calculated for each variable combination (non-occluded mirror, non-occluded structural, occluded mirror, and occluded structural) by averaging the percentage of CC outcomes in each item category. Mixed items were considered separately, as was done by Voyer and Hou (2006). The score on these items (one occluded, one non-occluded) was also calculated as the percentage of CC outcomes.

Primary Analysis. The primary analysis for CC outcomes was computed by means of a mixed-design analysis of variance with the percentage of CC outcomes as the dependent variable. Gender, timing conditions (10 minutes, unlimited), distractor type (mirror, structural), and occlusion (occluded, non-occluded) were the independent variables.

Table 2. Mean and Standard Deviation (SD) for the Percentage of CC Outcomes on the Mental Rotations Test as a Function of Gender, Timing Conditions, and Occlusion

Condition / Occlusion	Males	SD	Females	SD	d
10 Minutes					
Non-occluded	70.96	23.04	54.13	25.51	0.65
Occluded	56.31	29.60	32.10	27.66	0.79
Unlimited					
Non-occluded	87.21	19.09	72.48	25.74	0.61
Occluded	70.88	25.10	49.97	30.10	0.70

Note: CC: two correct responses; CW: one correct response and one incorrect response; CB: one correct response and one blank; WB: one incorrect response and one blank; WW: two incorrect responses; BB: two blanks. The score for CW, WW, CB, WB, and BB outcomes represents a percentage per non-CC outcomes. *d* represents the difference between the mean of men minus that of women divided by the pooled standard deviation (see Cohen, 1977).

Results revealed a significant main effect of occlusion, $F(1, 421) = 304.49, p < .01$. This finding reflected the fact that participants obtained significantly better scores for non-occluded ($M = 69.93\%; SD = 26.31$) than for occluded items ($M = 50.62\%; SD = 31.14$).

A significant main effect of timing was also obtained, $F(1, 421) = 51.72, p < .01$. This finding reflected the fact that participants obtained significantly better scores in the unlimited time ($M = 68.75\%; SD = 24.94$) than in the 10 minutes condition ($M = 53.15\%; SD = 25.73$).

As expected, a significant main effect of gender was obtained, $F(1, 421) = 71.57, p < .01$, reflecting significantly better performance in men ($M = 70.25\%; SD = 23.11$) than in women ($M = 51.69\%; SD = 26.26$).

However, this main effect was qualified by a significant gender by occlusion interaction, $F(1, 421) = 11.03, p < .01$. Simple main effect analyses showed that men had significantly better performance than women for both non-occluded, $F(1, 421) = 46.09, p < .01$, and occluded items, $F(1, 421) = 70.52, p < .01$. Cohen's *d* (Cohen, 1977) was calculated to further elucidate this interaction by subtracting the mean for women from that for men and dividing this difference by the pooled standard deviation.

Accordingly, a positive *d* reflected a better score in men than in women whereas a negative value reflected the reverse direction of gender difference. Thus, examination of the effect sizes presented in Table 2 suggests that gender differences in favor of men were more pronounced for occluded than for non-occluded items. No other main effects or interactions achieved significance at the .05 level. In fact, it is noteworthy that all the interactions involving timing conditions were not even close to significance (all p's > .21).

Mixed Items Analysis. The analysis for mixed items was computed by means of a mixed-design analysis of variance with the percentage of CC outcomes as the dependent variable. Gender and occlusion (occluded, non-occluded) were the independent variables.

This analysis revealed a significant main effect of gender, $F(1, 421) = 29.10$, $p < .01$. This finding indicates that men ($M = 65.66\%$; $SD = 39.44$) had significantly better performance than women ($M = 48.68\%$; $SD = 40.17$) on mixed items.

A significant main effect of timing conditions was also obtained, $F(1, 421) = 96.39$, $p < .01$. This finding indicates that performance was significantly better in the unlimited condition ($M = 74.74\%$; $SD = 35.35$) than in the 10 minutes condition ($M = 41.34\%$; $SD = 38.60$) on mixed items.

The main effect of occlusion also achieved significance, $F(1, 421) = 17.02$, $p < .01$, but it was qualified by a timing condition by occlusion interaction, $F(1, 421) = 6.16$, $p < .05$. Simple main effect analyses showed that the effect of occlusion was significant in the 10 minutes condition, $F(1, 421) = 24.10$, $p < .01$, but not in the unlimited condition, $F(1, 421) = 1.24$, $p > .26$. For the 10 minutes condition, this finding reflected significantly better performance for occluded ($M = 50.22\%$; $SD = 50.11$) than for non-occluded items ($M = 32.47\%$; $SD = 46.93$).

The difference in performance between occluded ($M = 76.80\%$; $SD = 42.32$) and non-occluded items ($M = 72.68\%$; $SD = 44.68$) was not significant in the unlimited condition.

DISCUSSION

The purpose of Analysis 2 was to determine whether previous findings relevant to the influence of occlusion on the magnitude of gender differences on the MRT would replicate in the context of the manipulation of time pressure. Based on the findings observed by Voyer and Hou (2006) on CC items, a gender by occlusion interaction was expected, showing larger gender differences in favor of men for occluded than for non-occluded items. This analysis also provided an opportunity to determine whether the influence of item placement is more important than that of item type. If it is the case, the influence of occlusion should be less pronounced without than with time pressure as many non-occluded items are at the end of the MRT and might not be completed by a majority of participants when a time limit is imposed. Results clearly replicated those obtained by Voyer and Hou (2006), regardless of timing conditions. Specifically, occluded items were found to decrease the level of performance for participants regardless of gender. In addition, the results showed significantly larger gender differences in favor of men for occluded than for non-occluded items, although just as in Voyer and Hou (2006), this finding did not extend to mixed items. The timing conditions by gender by occlusion interaction required to provide clear support for the notion that item placement is more important than item type was not observed. It is therefore legitimate to argue against this position. However, this is not to say that item placement is not involved in the results. Specifically, the importance of item placement was supported by the finding that, among mixed items, participants obtained better performance on occluded ones than on non-occluded ones. Furthermore, the finding that this effect was significant for the 10 minutes but not for the unlimited time condition can be interpreted plausibly when taking into account the influence of item placement. Indeed, item 23 is a mixed non-occluded item that would be likely to produce more BB outcomes than the mixed occluded item 18 in the 10-minutes condition as it would be reached by fewer participants when time is limited. Thus, performance should be better on the mixed occluded item (item 18) in the 10-minutes condition because more participants attempted it than those who attempted item 23. This possibility will be examined more closely in Analysis 3, therefore it will be discussed further at that point. However, the finding that the somewhat better performance for the occluded item over the non-occluded item was not significant in the unlimited time condition does not allow interpretations in terms of item placement.

It is interesting to note that this effect was significant in the Voyer and Hou (2006) study, although they also used untimed administration of the MRT. Voyer and Hou (2006) explained this finding by noting that item 18 is the only one where the occluded alternative is one of the incorrect choices. This would make it more likely to be viewed as incorrect (i.e., perceived as a distractor), considering the interpretation that occluded items that are correct alternatives are likely to be misperceived as different from the target. Thus, item placement and specific characteristics of the items involved create some ambiguity in terms of the factors critical to performance on mixed items. Taken together, the results that lend some support for the role of item placement cannot be ignored. They suggest that development of a new version of the MRT where item types are equally represented throughout the test would allow a more thorough examination of the role of occlusion on the magnitude of gender differences on the MRT.

It would also allow having an equal number of items of each type, which might contribute to more stable estimates of performance for each distractor type by occlusion combination. Preliminary work has been undertaken in our laboratory with such a version of the MRT and early results are quite promising (Doyle and Voyer, in preparation). In summary, Analysis 2 showed that the results obtained by Voyer and Hou (2006) are robust across timing conditions.

Results relevant to item placement suggest some ambiguity concerning the role of this factor over item type in performance on the MRT. Accordingly, Analysis 3 was performed to take a closer look at the relation between gender, item placement, and item type.

Analysis 3: MRT Outcomes as a Function of Gender, Timing Conditions, and Item

Scoring. As in Analysis 1, each item on the MRT was coded in terms of whether it represented a CC, BB, CW, CB, WB, or WW outcome. Whether a given outcome was present for each participant was then determined across items. The score presented for CC, BB, CW, CB, WB, and WW outcomes in this analysis thus reflects the proportion of participants in each gender by timing conditions cell in the design that obtained the particular outcome. Thus, for example, a value of 0.32 for CB outcomes in men/unlimited time would indicate that 32% of the men obtained a CB outcome in the untimed condition.

Analysis of Variance. Data analysis was computed by means of a separate mixed-design analysis of variance for each of the outcomes (CC, BB, CW, CB, WB, or WW), with the proportion of participants that produced the relevant outcome as the dependent variable. Gender, test item (1 to 24), and timing conditions (limited, unlimited) were the independent variables.

As a step by step presentation of the results for each outcome would produce a lengthy and tedious results section, the findings are presented as a function of the specific effects tested, and outcomes where this effect was significant are the only ones typically mentioned. As a way of summarizing response behavior on each item of the MRT, the proportion of participants that produced CC, BB, WW, CW, WB, and CB outcomes are presented in Figures 1 to 6, respectively, as a function of timing conditions and gender.

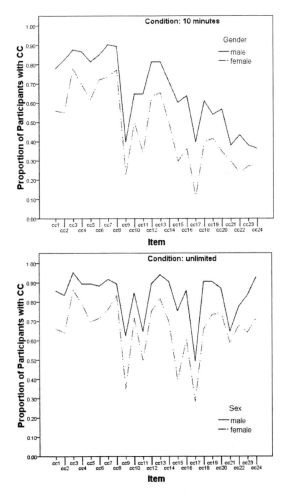

Figure 1. Proportion of men and women obtaining a CC outcome (two correct responses) as a function of item on the MRT for the 10 minutes condition (top) and the unlimited time condition (bottom).

In addition, the sphericity assumption was violated for the effects involving the variable "item" for all outcomes. Uncorrected degrees of freedom are shown in what follows for ease of presentation, although the test of significance was always based on Greenhouse-Geisser corrected degrees of freedom, as previously mentioned.

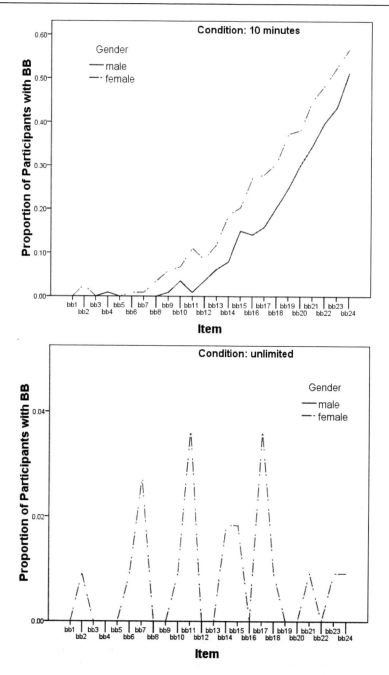

Figure 2. Proportion of men and women obtaining a BB outcome (two blanks) as a function of item on the MRT for the 10 minutes condition (top) and the unlimited time condition (bottom). Note that BB outcomes were not obtained for men in the unlimited time condition. In addition, the Y axis for the two graphs is not on the same scale to emphasize small differences in the unlimited time condition.

Main effect of item and item by timing conditions interaction. A significant effect of item was obtained on all outcomes (all p's < .01). Figures 1 to 6 provide summary data for this effect. Examination of Figures 1 to 6 suggests much variability in the pattern of response across items. CC outcomes (Figure 1) showed a significant linear trend, $F(1, 421) = 225.61$, $p < .01$.

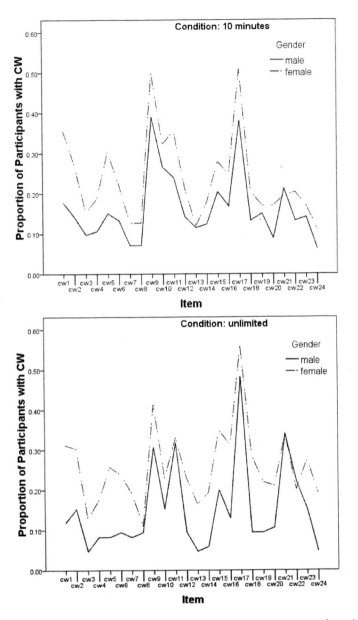

Figure 3. Proportion of men and women obtaining a CW outcome (one correct and one incorrect response) as a function of item on the MRT for the 10 minutes condition (top) and the unlimited time condition (bottom).

However, the finding that the decrease in the proportion of CC outcomes as participants progressed through the test was only found in the 10 minutes condition is reflected in a significant item by timing conditions interaction for CC outcomes, $F(23, 9683) = 14.16$, $p < .01$. It is interesting to note that clear drops in the proportion of CC outcomes were observed for items 9, 11, 15, and 17 regardless of timing conditions (see Figure 1).

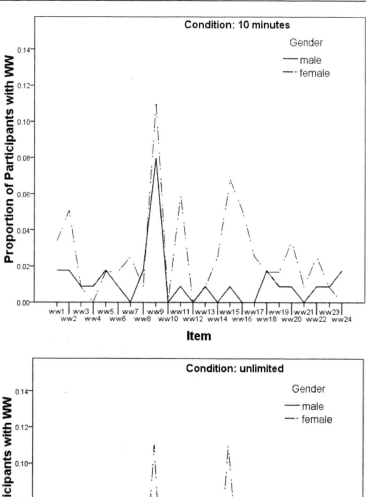

Figure 4. Proportion of men and women obtaining a WW outcome (two incorrect responses) as a function of item on the MRT for the 10 minutes condition (top) and the unlimited time condition (bottom).

The significant quadratic trend observed for BB outcomes, $F(1, 421) = 69.91$, $p < .01$, is evidenced in Figure 2, but only for the 10 minutes condition, as reflected in a significant item by timing conditions interaction for BB outcomes, $F(23, 9683) = 77.50$, $p < .01$.

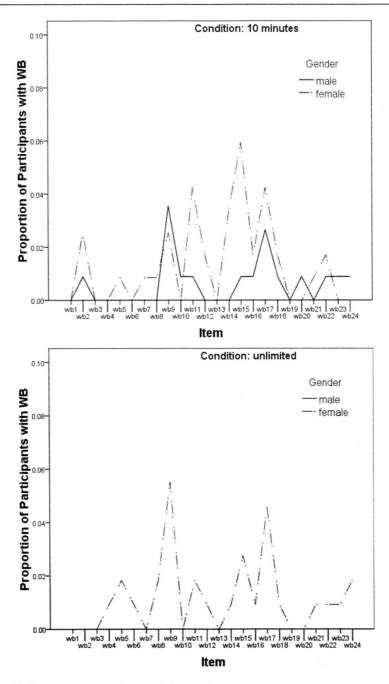

Figure 5. Proportion of men and women obtaining a WB outcome (one incorrect response and one blank) as a function of item on the MRT for the 10 minutes condition (top) and the unlimited time condition (bottom). Note that WB outcomes were not obtained for men in the unlimited time condition.

Indeed, BB outcomes were relatively infrequent until around item 8 for women and item 12 for men in the 10 minutes condition. After this, they increased in a relatively linear fashion for both genders. Thus, as suggested in the discussion for Analysis 1, when time was limited, BB outcomes were much less frequent at the beginning than at the end of the test.

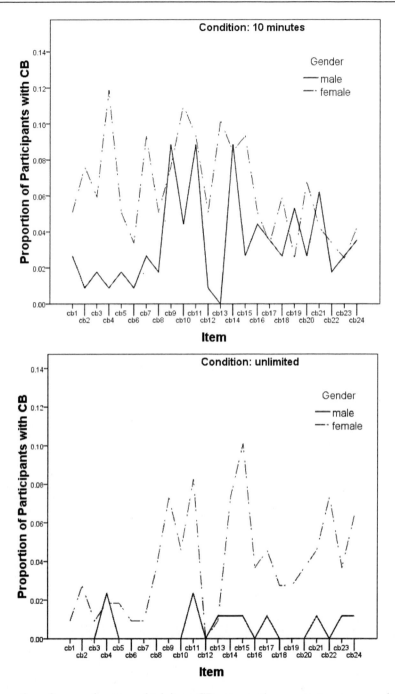

Figure 6. Proportion of men and women obtaining a CB outcome (one correct response and one blank) as a function of item on the MRT for the 10 minutes condition (top) and the unlimited time condition (bottom).

In addition, as suggested for Analysis 2, BB outcomes were also more frequent for item 23 than for item 18 in the 10-minutes condition. In contrast, these outcomes were quite infrequent and distributed throughout the test in the unlimited time condition. In fact, BB outcomes were not found at all in men when they were given unlimited time to complete the test. Finally, the item by timing conditions interaction was significant for CW outcomes, $F(23, 9683) = 2.27$, $p < .01$, but it was due to differences in the level of performance as a function of items rather than a differential trend as a function of timing conditions, as suggested by the data presented in Figure 3. It is worth noting that the drop in the proportion of CC items seen in Figure 1 for items 9, 11, 15, and 17 is generally paralleled by an increased proportion of CW outcomes (Figure 3). Other outcomes showed no discernable trends and the significant effect of item likely reflected inter-item differences in the occurrence of these outcomes. It is noteworthy that items 9 and 15 showed a sharp rise in the number of WW outcomes (Figure 4) and WB outcomes (Figure 5), particularly in women (WB outcomes were not observed at all in men for the unlimited time condition). Such a rise was additionally found for items 11, 17, and 21 on CB outcomes (Figure 6).

Main effect of gender and gender by timing conditions interaction. The main effect of gender was significant on all the outcomes in this analysis (all p's $< .02$). However, unlike what was done in Analysis 1, it was not possible to compensate for the overall number of non-CC items when calculating scores for the BB, WW, CW, CB, and WB outcomes in Analysis 3. As previously mentioned, women are bound to produce more non-CC outcomes than men do, and gender differences on non-CC outcomes are uninterpretable in Analysis 3. Therefore, only the results relevant to the CC outcome can be interpreted. In this case, as expected from the first two analyses, men ($M = 0.732$, $SD = 0.254$) produced a significantly greater proportion of CC outcomes than did women ($M = 0.562$, $SD = 0.266$).

The gender by item interaction was of great interest here, as it would point to variations in the magnitude of gender differences across items. However, after Greenhouse-Geisser correction, this interaction was only significant for CC outcomes, $F(23, 9683) = 2.71$, $p < .01$. Table 3 presents the effect size, calculated as Cohen's d (Cohen, 1977) to elucidate the gender by item interaction for this outcome.

Despite the absence of a gender by item by timing condition interaction on CC, even before Greenhouse-Geisser correction ($p > .55$), the effects sizes were broken down by timing conditions for information purpose. For CC outcomes, although it is clear that there was much variability in the magnitude of gender differences, they were always in favor of men, except for items 21, 23, and 24, where they did not achieve significance in the 10 minutes condition (smallest $p > .067$ for these items) and for items 3, 4, 8, 21, and 22 in the unlimited time condition (smallest $p > .14$ for these items).

The fact that there was much seemingly unsystematic variability in the magnitude of the effect was demonstrated by the finding that a Spearman correlation revealed only a small, non-significant, negative overall relation between item location and the magnitude of gender differences (*Spearman r* = -.35, $p > .09$, $N = 24$). This correlation was equally non-significant in the 10 minutes condition (*Spearman r* = -.23, $p > .27$, $N = 24$) and in the unlimited time condition (*Spearman r* = 0.11, $p > .60$, $N = 24$). Interestingly enough, however, when the effect sizes were collapsed across the two parts of the MRT to produce a combined set of 12 items, the correlation between item location and Cohen's d suggested a significant decrease in the magnitude of the effect as participants progressed across items (*Spearman r* = -.72, $p < .01$, $N = 12$). When timing conditions were considered separately, this pattern was observed in the 10 minutes condition (*Spearman r* = -.64, $p < .05$, $N = 12$), but not in the unlimited time condition (*Spearman r* = -.45, $p > .14$, $N = 12$), although the correlation was still relatively large and negative in the latter condition.

Table 3. Effect Size (Cohen's d) for Gender Differences as a Function of Timing Conditions for CC Outcomes

Item	10 minutes	Unlimited	Overall
1	0.46	0.45	0.45
2	0.58	0.43	0.51
3	0.25	0.30	0.26
4	0.41	0.28	0.35
5	0.43	0.47	0.44
6	0.31	0.41	0.35
7	0.43	0.41	0.42
8	0.33	0.17	0.25
9	0.36	0.55	0.43
10	0.29	0.31	0.27
11	0.61	0.30	0.46
12	0.40	0.36	0.37
13	0.36	0.37	0.34
14	0.44	0.51	0.44
15	0.61	0.72	0.65
16	0.54	0.56	0.51
17	0.66	0.43	0.53
18	0.42	0.58	0.44
19	0.25	0.44	0.27
20	0.44	0.32	0.33
21	0.18	0.12	0.12
22	0.42	0.22	0.26
23	0.23	0.43	0.25
24	0.18	0.54	0.23

Note: Cohen's d (Cohen, 1977) was calculated as the mean proportion of CC outcomes for men minus that for women divided by the pooled standard deviation.

Main effect of timing conditions and item by gender by timing conditions interaction. The main effect of timing conditions achieved significance for CC, $F(1, 421) = 64.13$, $p < .01$, BB, $F(1, 421) = 126.36$, $p < .01$, and CB, $F(1, 421) = 16.99$, $p < .01$. Figures 1, 2, and 6, respectively relevant to CC, BB, and CB reflect this finding as showing significantly more CC outcomes in the untimed than in the 10 minutes condition, whereas BB and CB outcomes were more frequent in the 10 minutes than in the untimed condition. The condition by gender interaction did not achieve significance on any outcome (smallest $p > .07$ for BB outcomes), whereas the condition by item by gender interaction approached significance only for CB outcomes ($p < .062$).

DISCUSSION

Analysis 3 constituted the primary novel contribution of the present study to the literature. Indeed, to our knowledge, analysis of the pattern of response considering the various possible outcomes across the whole MRT had not been attempted to date. There was thus only a slim basis for predictions of expected findings. The discussion presented here follows the expectation that item type rather than item placement is the critical factor in MRT performance. Thus, no systematic, linear relation was expected between item location and the magnitude of gender differences on the MRT.

However, it was also expected that the completion of the last few items would be compromised by the implementation of a time limit. The findings of the gender by item interaction generally supported the expectations that item placement would not be a critical factor in performance on the MRT. Indeed, only item 21 failed to produce significant gender differences in both timing conditions. This was not surprising as this item was structural, non-occluded and, as such, it was expected to produce small gender differences based on Voyer and Hou's (2006) findings.

However, the fact that this item is one of the few structural/non-occluded items that showed a drop in performance on CC outcomes, as seen in Figure 1, is rather puzzling. Indeed, one would expect item 21 to be relatively easy rather than so difficult that performance would drop in this noticeable fashion. However, this drop in the proportion of CC outcomes for item 21 was also accompanied by an increase in the proportion of CW and CB outcomes (see Figures 3 and 6, respectively). This could be accounted for by the fact that one of the distractors on this item, while being structurally different from the target, was still quite similar to it.

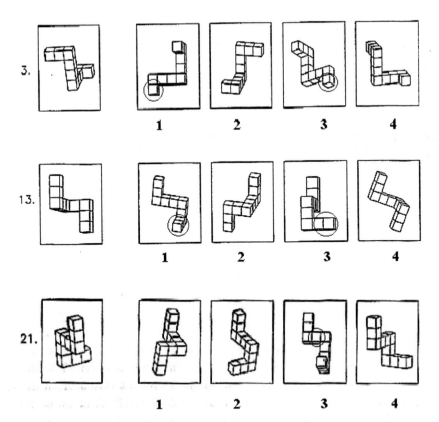

Figure 7. Examples of "different tail" (item 3), "no tail" (item 13) and "different alternatives" (item 21) type of structural alternatives. The critical points distinguishing incorrect alternatives from the target are circled in relevant alternatives.

Specifically, as seen in Figure 7, alternative 3 for item 21 is only structurally differentiated from the target by the fact that the horizontal section at mid-point of the block configuration (circled in Figure 7) included only one block, whereas the target included two blocks in that section. This would account for confusion that occurred in responding, and likely resulted in CW and CB outcomes, especially when time was limited. The lack of gender differences on this item suggests that this confusion was equally likely to occur in men and in women. Modification of this alternative or its removal from the test should be encouraged to produce a purer measure of mental rotation abilities. At the more global level, the shape of the curve in Figure 1 is quite informative and it is relatively similar for both timing conditions, except for the clear drop in the proportion of CC outcomes in later items for the 10 minutes condition (likely replaced mostly by BB items, as can be inferred from Figure 2).

Specifically, aside from the previously discussed item 21, sharp drops in performance can be seen for both genders on items 9, 11, 15, and 17. These four items have in common that they include an occluded alternative. Examination of Figure 3 suggests that for most of these four items, participants are also quite likely to produce a CW outcome, presumably as a result of the occlusion.

Other outcomes (see Figures 2, 4, 5, and 6) also show some increase in their proportion for these items, but CW outcomes are by far the most frequent. In fact, on items 9 and 17, more than 40% of women and about 35% of men produced a CW outcome in both timing conditions. This suggests that occlusion leads participants of both gender to show a greater propensity to guess on these items, thereby confirming the importance of item type on the pattern of response on the MRT.

Interestingly enough, the magnitude of the effect sizes for gender differences presented in Table 3 is not necessarily associated with the items that showed a drop in performance in Figure 1. Still, the largest overall effect size was observed for the occluded mirror item 15 ($d = 0.65$), whereas the smallest was obtained for the non-occluded structural item 21 ($d = 0.12$), as previously discussed. However, it is interesting to note that the overall effect size for items 21 to 24 would all be categorized as small by Cohen (1977). This would also be the case for items 23 and 24 in the 10 minutes condition, whereas their magnitude would be considered medium for the unlimited condition. This suggests that the time limit affects the performance of both men and women so that the gender differences are quite small for the last two items on the test under the 10-minutes conditions. However, when enough time is available to attempt all items, the expected male advantage emerges. The lack of significant correlations between item location and the magnitude of gender difference in the present study clearly fits with this interpretation. This supports the viewpoint that item location is critical for timed conditions only inasmuch as fewer women than men might reach the last few items when time is limited (see Figure 2). However, the gender by item interaction and the timing conditions by gender by item interaction failed to achieve significance for BB outcomes in the present study, suggesting that the proportion of men and women who left items blank was statistically similar across items.

In view of the above discussion, the findings of significant negative correlations for the magnitude of gender differences when item location was combined for the two parts of the MRT is rather puzzling. It cannot even be explained in the context of Peters' (2005) findings as he found a positive correlation between these two factors. Admittedly, the present approach was concerned with replicating the results obtained by Voyer and Saunders (2004) and did not attempt a replication of Peters' (2005) method as the MRT was administered in a single block instead of in two parts timed separately as Peters did. It is thus impossible to compare the present findings directly with those obtained by Peters (2005). Nevertheless, the findings of the correlational analysis in which the two parts are combined compared to when the whole test was considered, as in the present study, beg the question of whether the results obtained by Peters (2005) would replicate when each part of the test is considered separately in the timing approach he used.

GENERAL DISCUSSION

The purpose of the present study was to investigate possible gender differences in the pattern of response for various item types on the MRT. This was implemented in three separate analyses, the first two of which aimed at replicating previous findings while extending some of them to a comparison of conditions with and without time constraints.

All analyses replicated the well-established finding of gender differences in favor of men on MRT performance. In addition, Analysis 1 replicated the finding that women tend to show greater reluctance to guess than men do, if one assumes that CB and WB outcomes do indeed reflect reluctance to guess. In addition, as expected, BB outcomes, essentially reflecting unattempted items, were more frequent with a time limit than without it. This confirmed the notion that these outcomes provide a good measure of time pressure (Voyer and Saunders, 2004).

Analysis 2 replicated Voyer and Hou's (2006) findings concerning the deleterious effect of occlusion on MRT performance. In particular, results showed that gender differences on the MRT were larger for occluded than for non-occluded items. This emphasizes the role the three-dimensional nature of the stimuli in producing gender differences on the MRT. The fact that timing conditions did not affect the gender by occlusion interaction was taken as showing that item type was more important than item placement in determining performance on the MRT, although performance on mixed items mitigated this conclusion.

Finally, Analysis 3 constituted the novel aspect of the present study as it considered changes in the outcomes produced by participants as they progressed through the MRT with and without time constraints. The proportion of a given outcome varied widely across items as evidenced by the fact that the main effect of item was significant for all the outcomes. The drop in the proportion of CC outcomes and the increase in the number of CW outcomes for items 9, 11, 15, and 17 were particularly noticeable. However, the main effect of item was affected by timing conditions for CC and BB outcomes, showing essentially a linear decrease in performance across items for the former and a quadratic increase across items for the latter. Only CC outcomes showed a gender by item interaction, reflecting wide variations in the magnitude of gender differences across items.

Taken together the results of the three analyses showed some stable gender differences in response behavior on the MRT. They also showed that categorizing specific items based on underlying components, such as the presence of occlusion, provides a valuable tool that could lead to a better understanding of factors underlying gender differences on the MRT. However, collapsing various items together into subgroups does not seem to capture fully the wide fluctuations in performance and magnitude of gender differences on the MRT. For example, although items 9, 11, 15, and 17, were all occluded, only item 15 showed relatively large gender differences whereas the remaining items in this set showed gender differences of intermediate magnitude. In addition, the finding that item 21 was the only one where gender differences were not significant on CC outcomes was particularly important as it brought to light the fact that inclusion of one somewhat confusable alternative can have observable effects on performance. Considering that this item was structural non-occluded, which should be relatively easy, this clearly suggests that the item categorization proposed by Voyer and Hou (2006) still falls short in trying to determine fully what guides the fluctuations in performance across items, aside from time limits. This line of discussion actually brings into question whether the various items on the MRT each measure the same aspect of mental rotation abilities (Bors and Vigneau, 2011), as there seems to be subtle fluctuations in cognitive requirements across items. Closer examination of each item suggests that there are many such subtle differences that might account for fluctuations in performance. For example, in structural non-occluded items 3, 4, 7, and 8, the structural difference occur in the spatial relationship between a block that is either below the bottom axis of the configuration or on the same plane as in the target ("different tail" hereafter; see Figure 7 for an example). In contrast, for items 13 and 24, one block is omitted at the bottom of the block configuration ("no tail" hereafter; again, see Figure 7 for an example). Finally, for items 21 and 22, a subtle difference distinguished one block configuration from the target, as explained earlier for item 21 ("different alternatives" hereafter; again, see Figure 7 for an example). Although these are seemingly small differences in item type, they produce large changes in performance. Indeed, an analysis of variance including only these three types of structural non-occluded items with type (different tail, no tail, different alternatives), gender, and timing conditions as independent variable, and percentage of CC outcomes as dependent variable showed a large effect of item type ($p < .001$). This finding reflected significant differences in performances between the three levels of this new variable, with the following order of means: different tail ($M = 83.76\%$, $SD = 25.36$) > no tail ($M = 67.38\%$, $SD = 35.66$) > different alternatives ($M = 49.03\%$, $SD = 42.06$). Although this factor did not interact with gender or with timing conditions, this pattern of results clearly demonstrates the potential role of subtle item manipulations on performance on the MRT. This finding also opens the exciting possibility to investigate whether this factor (let us call it "type of structural alternatives") might interact with occlusion to affect the magnitude of gender differences. An investigation of these factors would provide further elements to understand factors underlying gender differences on the MRT. However, such an attempt with the present version of the MRT would be complicated by the fact that the various distractor type by occlusion combinations include an unequal number of items and the only two occluded structural items are of the "no tail" type of structural alternatives. Thus, one way to better understand performance and gender differences on the MRT might involve the construction and validation of a version of the MRT where various item types are balanced across the test, both in terms of number of each item type and in terms of the distribution of each item type from item 1 to item 24. Such an endeavor might be particularly fruitful in view of the present results. As a starting point, one might just balance the distractor type (mirror, structural) by occlusion items in a novel version of the test (which is what we have done in our preliminary work mentioned earlier). Another novel version of the MRT could also be constructed by considering only structural items and manipulating the type of structural alternatives. It would also be possible to implement these manipulations in chronometric studies of mental rotation using pairs of stimuli in a context similar to Shepard and Metzler's (1971) research. Regardless, of the approach used, these efforts would definitely advance our knowledge concerning the role of item type on performance on mental rotation problems.

The finding that timing conditions did not interact with gender in any of the analyses conducted here (except for one single case where the multivariate test was non-significant) is quite important. It supports the notion that time pressures are not necessary to findings of gender differences on the MRT, in agreement with the conclusion reached by Masters (1998) and in disagreement with that reached by Goldstein et al. (1990). Peters (2005) has brought interesting arguments concerning "unlimited" time conditions (which, as he rightfully argued, are not really unlimited as participants do complete the test in a finite time period). Specifically, his main argument was that studies that report a lack of gender differences under such conditions might reflect a ceiling effect due to the number of problems. However, it is plausible to argue that many studies that have failed to report gender differences with unlimited time conditions suffer from methodological or conceptual problems (see Masters, 1998 and Voyer et al., 2004 for some of these criticisms). Peters' (2005) interpretation disregards this aspect. In addition, the present findings can be added to an increasing body of evidence (e.g., Cooke-Simpson and Voyer, 2007; Masters, 1998; Resnick, 1993; Voyer and Hou, 2006; Voyer et al., 2004) indicating that gender differences on the MRT remain significant even when no time limit is imposed on its completion. This suggests that ceiling effects, if they are involved in conditions where participants can take all the time they need to attempt each item on the MRT, are at a different level for men and women. In other words, the ceiling is higher for men than for women and gender differences on the MRT reflect differences in level of spatial ability, as argued by Lohman (1986), rather than in speed of processing as was argued by Goldstein et al. (1990). It is still important to keep in mind that when more power was brought to bear on this question through meta-analysis, Voyer (2011) found that gender differences were significantly reduced on pen and paper tests of mental rotation when time limits were absent compared to when they were present, regardless of their actual duration. However, in considering the power inherent to meta-analysis when compared to individual studies, Voyer (2011) admitted that "differences in the magnitude of gender differences as a function of timing conditions are unlikely to achieve significance in the typical individual study" (p. 274). Relatively low power thus likely accounts for the overall absence of such effects in the present experiment, despite what can be considered a large sample for an individual study.

Usage of the term "unlimited" time should really be considered the short form to write "given as much time as they need to complete the test". From this perspective, the time that one actually requires to complete the MRT when given "unlimited" time should be informative. As previously mentioned, completion times were collected from all participants in the "unlimited" time condition and these data are quite revealing concerning the "limited" nature of the time required. Specifically, men required on average 1002.57 sec (16.71 min) and women needed an average of 1057.28 sec (17.62 min) to attempt all items on the MRT when given as much time as they needed. Although women required almost one more minute than did men for test completion (a non-significant difference, as previously reported), they could not reach the level of performance achieved by men. In fact, women still left a few items blank even when given "unlimited" time (see Figure 2), presumably reflecting reluctance to guess in this context, and their number of CW outcomes increased compared to the 10 minutes condition (reflecting a propensity to guess similar to men under these conditions). Again, this evidently suggests that gender differences on the MRT are a matter of level of spatial abilities, not processing speed.

The present study clearly demonstrated the importance of considering separate items and item subtypes on the MRT to better understand performance on this test. However, its generalizability is limited to a subset of the existing literature.

Specifically, the fact that the MRT was administered in one single block for a limit of 10 minutes in the time limited condition does not allow direct comparison with and generalization to studies (such as Peters, 2005) that used a two-parts administration and a shorter time limit. However, only conditions where participants are given as much time as they need to complete the MRT ensure that all items on the test are likely to be attempted. In contrast, any time limit increases the likelihood that late items will remain unattempted. Figure 2 (top part) in the present study clearly supports this point. Similarly, Peters (2005) still found gender differences in favor of men on the percentage of items attempted even with a limit of 6 minutes per part. This still leaves open the argument, made by Goldstein et al. (1990), that women would have done better if they could have attempted more items, although this argument has obtained little support (e.g., Masters, 1998). From this perspective, the consequence of the exact time limit imposed on participants is mostly in determining how many items will be attempted. Considering that the present study has shown little influence of time limit on gender differences in actual performance (CC outcomes, specifically), it would be legitimate to conclude that the lack of generalizability of our timed approach is of little consequence (but see Voyer, 2011). Nevertheless, the question of whether the present results would replicate with a shorter time limit remains open.

Considering the influence of item type and the fact that it is confounded with item placement (i.e., most mirror occluded items are at the end of part 1, and many non-occluded items are at the end of part 2), it is likely that two-block administration with a shorter time limit could affect the gender by occlusion interaction obtained here and in Voyer and Hou (2006). However, this finding would be an artifact of item placement and timing. This suggests that "unlimited" time administration allows a better assessment of the role of item type on MRT performance with the existing versions of this test. A version of this test where item type is randomized across items, as suggested previously, would overcome the confounding influence of item type and item placement to some extent.

CONCLUSION

In conclusion, the present chapter raises important issues concerning the role of item type and item placement in determining performance and gender differences on the MRT. Results generally emphasize the importance of item type.

In fact, the finding that subtle differences in response alternatives (such as in item 21) can have a major effect on performance could be seen as the most important one reported here. This leads to a conclusion that likely applies to any situation where one is assessing cognitive abilities.

Specifically, the role of specific items on performance on the MRT suggests that the underlying cognitive abilities required for its completion are much richer than what can be reflected in a single score. With this in mind, it is quite clear that much more research is required to disentangle factors relevant to item type and their potential role in producing gender differences on the MRT.

REFERENCES

Alexander, G. M., and Evardone, M. (2008). Blocks and bodies: Sex differences in a novel version on the mental rotations test. *Hormones and Behavior, 53*, 177-184.

Amponsah, B., and Krekling, S. (1997). Sex differences in visual-spatial performance among Ghanaian and Norwegian adults. *Journal of Cross-Cultural Psychology, 28*, 81-92.

Bors, D. A., and Vigneau, F. (2011). Sex differences on the mental rotation test: An analysis of item types. *Learning and Individual Differences, 21*, 129-132.

Castelli, L., Corazzini, L. L., and Geminiani, G. C. (2008). Spatial navigation in large-scale virtual environments: Gender differences in survey tasks. *Computers in Human Behavior, 24*, 1643-1667.

Cohen, J. (1977). *Statistical power analysis for the behavioral sciences.* (2nd ed.). New York: Academic Press.

Cooke-Simpson, A., and Voyer, D. (2007). Confidence and gender differences on the Mental Rotations Test. *Learning and Individual Differences, 17*, 181-186.

Doyle, R. A., and Voyer, D. (in preparation). Bodies and occlusion: Item types, cognitive strategies, and gender differences in mental rotation.

Gardner, H. (1993). *Frames of mind: The theory of multiple intelligences.* New York: Basic Books.

Goldstein, D., Haldane, D., and Mitchell, C. (1990). Sex differences in visual-spatial ability: The role of performance factors. *Memory and Cognition, 18*, 546-550.

Holmes, J., and Adams, J. W. (2006). Working memory and children's mathematical skills: Implications for mathematical development and mathematics curricula. *Educational Psychology, 26,* 339-366.

Jansen-Osmann, P., and Heil, M. (2007). Suitable stimuli to obtain (no) gender differences in the speed of cognitive processes involved in mental rotation. *Brain and Cognition, 64,* 217-227.

Kimura, D. (1999). *Sex and cognition.* Cambridge, MA: The MIT Press.

Linn, M. C. and Petersen, A. C. (1985). Emergence and characterisation of gender differences in spatial abilities: A meta-analysis. *Child Development, 56,* 1479-1498.

Lohman, D. F. (1986). The effect of speed–accuracy tradeoff on sex differences in mental rotation. *Perception and Psychophysics, 39*, 427-436.

Lubinski, D. S., and Benbow, C. P. (2007). Sex differences in personal attributes for the development of scientific expertise. In S. J. Ceci and W. M. Williams (Eds.), *Why aren't more women in science?* (pp. 79-100). Washington: American Psychological Association.

Masters, M. S. (1998). The gender difference on the Mental Rotations Test is not due to performance factors. *Memory and Cognition, 26,* 444-448.

Moffat, S. D., Hampsom, E., and Hatzipantelis, M. (1998). Navigation in a virtual maze: Sex differences and correlation with psychometric measures of spatial ability in humans. *Evolution and Human Behavior,* 19, 73–87.

Newcombe, N., Bandura, M. M., and Taylor, D. G. (1983). Sex differences in spatial ability and spatial activities. *Sex Roles, 9*, 377-386.

Peters, M. (2005). Sex differences and the factor of time in solving Vandenberg and Kuse mental rotation problems. *Brain and Cognition, 57*, 176-184.

Peters, M., Laeng, B., Latham, K., Jackson, M., Zaiyouna, R., and Richardson, C. (1995). A redrawn Vandenberg and Kuse mental rotations test: Different versions and factors that affect performance. *Brain and Cognition, 28*, 39-58.

Resnick, S. M. (1993). Sex differences in mental rotations: An effect of time limits? *Brain and Cognition, 21*, 71-79.

Rilea, S. L. (2008). A lateralization of function approach to sex differences in spatial ability: A reexamination. *Brain and Cognition, 67*, 168-182.

Shepard, R. N., and Metzler, J. (1971). Mental rotation of three-dimensional objects. *Science, 171*, 701-703.

Vandenberg, S. G., and Kuse, A. R. (1978). Mental rotation, a group test of three-dimensional spatial visualization. *Perceptual and Motor Skills*, 47, 599-604.

Voyer, D. (1997) Scoring procedure, performance factors, and magnitude of sex differences in spatial performance. *American Journal of Psychology, 110*, 259-276.

Voyer, D. (2011). Time limits and gender differences on paper-and-pencil tests of mental rotation: A meta-analysis. *Psychonomic Bulletin and Review, 18*, 267-277.

Voyer, D., and Hou, J. (2006). Type of items and the magnitude of gender differences on the mental rotations test. *Canadian Journal of Experimental Psychology, 60*, 91-100.

Voyer, D., Rodgers, M. A. and McCormick, P. A. (2004). Timing conditions and magnitude of gender differences on the Mental Rotations Test. *Memory and Cognition, 32*, 72-82.

Voyer, D. and Saunders, K. A. (2004). Examination of possible outcomes on the Mental Rotations Test: A factor analysis. *Acta Psychologica, 117*, 79-94.

Voyer, D. and Sullivan, A. M. (2003). The relation between spatial and mathematical abilities: Potential factors underlying suppression. *International Journal of Psychology, 38*, 11-23.

Voyer, D., Voyer, S., and Bryden, M. P. (1995). Magnitude of sex differences in spatial abilities: A meta-analysis and consideration of critical variables. *Psychological Bulletin, 117*, 250-270.

Winer, B. J. (1962). *Statistical principles in experimental design.* New York: McGraw-Hill.

In: Psychology of Gender Differences
Editor: Sarah P. McGeown

ISBN: 978-1-62081-391-1
© 2012 Nova Science Publishers, Inc.

Chapter 12

TRUST AND TRUSTWORTHINESS – A SURVEY OF GENDER DIFFERENCES

Holger A. Rau[*]

Duesseldorf Institute for Competition Economics (DICE), Duesseldorf, Germany

ABSTRACT

This chapter reviews articles about gender differences in trust and reciprocity. The literature about experimental trust games finds striking gender differences in participants' reciprocal behavior. Most papers report that female first movers in trust games trust less than male ones. In trust games there is ample evidence that female second movers are more trustworthy than male ones. Interestingly it can be found that reciprocal behavior of female decision makers is stronger in the environment of a real-effort task. The results of gift-exchange gender studies document that female workers' are discriminated in the laboratory and receive smaller wages than men in a double-auction market. In general there is a tendency in trust games that men trust more than women and women are more trustworthy than men. A real-effort task furthermore amplifies these results. In gift-exchange games it can be found that female principals show higher levels of reciprocity and female workers receive lower wages in some setups.

INTRODUCTION

Over the last thirty years Experimental Economics received increasing attention and economists realized that peoples' decisions can often not be explained with standard economic theory. For instance the seminal paper of Fehr and Schmidt (1999) documents that people not only care about their own outcome, they would rather give up money to generate equal outcomes. Other studies like the investment game (Berg et al. (1995)) emphasized that people reciprocate fair offers. These studies and myriads of other papers enabled economists

---

[*] E-mail address: *rau@dice.uni-duesseldorf.de.*

to rethink about models. That is, economists reinvented the so-called "Homo Oeconomicus" and included emotional components in economic decision-making models.

Some time ago, economists also carried out that there exists substantial gender differences in many economic decisions. Since economic outcomes crucially depend on the behavior of human decision makers, economists noticed that they not only have to focus on peoples' emotions but also on possible gender differences. Trust and reciprocity are one of the core elements of economic decision making. Most of these decisions would not work without people trusting other people. In business there exist lots of examples where trust and reciprocity play a superior role. For instance if two business partners decide about a joint investment project one party often has to act as a first mover, i.e. she has to decide whether to trust the other person and to invest a positive amount into the project. If the first mover invested her money the other person is in a comfortable position because she can easily exploit the first mover. However, the second mover can also show positive reciprocity and send back a positive fraction of the money which has been increased due to the joint project. Here, both parties would be better off. This example can also be applied when a lender has to decide whether she gives a credit to a private investor. As can be seen, the decision whether to trust a private investor has essential impacts: without banks trusting private investors many economic projects would not take place and therefore economic growth would slow down. However, if banks trust too much and investors do not behave reciprocally this might lead to bad loans and possibly to a financial crisis (this once more emphasizes the important role of first movers' beliefs about the behavior of the partner in a trust game). Principal-agent relations are another example for the important role of trust and reciprocity in economics. In business many principal-agent relations can often be characterized by incomplete contracts. That is, employers pay wages to employees without the guarantee that the expected effort level will be exerted. Thus, if employers pay a certain wage to their workers they act as first movers. Hence, workers can easily shirk and exert no or low effort levels. For this reason an efficient principal agent relation crucially depends on employees' reciprocity. These examples summarize the important role of trust and reciprocity in modern economic life. Thus, if there exist gender differences in trust and reciprocity it should have crucial impacts for the investments in projects and principal-agent relations should also be concerned. Therefore these differences cannot be ignored.

This chapter focuses on gender differences in experimental trust games, gift-exchange games, and related setups.[1] In the next sections the basic work horses to analyze this behavior are introduced. Afterwards the literature about gender differences in trust and reciprocity is reviewed.

TRUST GAMES

A common work horse to analyze trust and reciprocity in experiments are investment and trust games. The investment game has been introduced by Berg, McCabe, and Dickhaut (1995). It consists of two players: a "trustor" who acts as a first mover and a "trustee" who acts as a second mover. In their experiment the authors divided a group of students into two

[1] For a complete survey about gender differences in different economic setups see Croson and Gneezy (2009).

different rooms. In the "no history" treatment 32 subjects were sent along as subjects A in room A and 32 subjects were placed as subjects B in room B. Both types of subjects received $10 as a show-up fee. Afterwards every subject A had to decide about the investment sum (SA) of her endowment she was willing to send to a matched subject in room B. Subjects B made their decisions in a "double blind" condition which is a mechanism to ensure that subjects made their decisions anonymous such that both the experimentator and subjects A could not observe subjects' B decisions. Then every dollar sent to subject B was tripled such that subjects B received: 3SA. Subject B had to decide about the amount she was willing to send back to subject A. This amount can be denoted with: SB(3SA). Thus, the final payoffs of both players are the following:

Subject A (first mover): $P_A(S_A, S_B) = \$10 - S_A + S_B(3S_A)$

Subject B (second mover): $P_B(S_A, S_B) = 3S_A - S_B(3S_A)$

If the game is not repeated and played only once, backward induction predicts that a second mover who receives a positive amount (3SA > 0) will not return anything. This is why the second mover has not to fear punishment by subject A. A rational subject A should anticipate this, i.e. in the standard subgame perfect Nash equilibrium subject A will not invest anything. However, if second movers have social preferences and do not only care about monetary payoffs it could be that they send back positive amounts. If subjects A believe that subjects B reciprocate their offers then it might be a dominant strategy for first movers to send SA > 0.

Contrary to the standard economic equilibrium Berg et al. (1995) observe that subjects A on average send $5.16 to subjects B. They find that subjects B reciprocate this and return on average $4.66 to subjects in room A. Interestingly only two subjects of room A follow the standard economic predictions and send $0. In contrast there were 5 out of 32 subjects who send their entire endowment of $10 to the subject in room B. If subjects B receive small amounts $1 ≤ SA < $5 they often return SB ≤ SA. However, if subjects B receive large amounts they often send back amounts which are higher than SA. For instance, if subjects A send $5 subjects B return on average $7.17 and investments of $10 lead to a payback of $10.20. Berg et al.'s (1995) results highlight that second movers observing a kind action of first movers reciprocate this by returning high amounts. If first movers send high amounts they receive higher returns compared to the case when sending low amounts. Thus, second movers show positive reciprocity in the domain of high investments and negative reciprocity when receiving small investments.

Table 1. Avg. amount sent/ returned (generated with data of Croson and Buchan (1999))

Gender	Amount Sent	Amount returned	Proportion returned
Men	696.4	928.0	28.6
	(286.1)	(688.7)	(17.8)
Women	630.4	1215.1	37.4
	(260.6)	(603.1)	(13.8)
Total	680.1	1013.5	31.2
	(280.1)	(674.2)	(17.1)

There also exist simplified variants of the trust game where a first mover only has to make a binary choice. In contrast to Berg et al.'s (1995) setup the trustor in these noncontinuous designs cannot decide how much money to invest, they can only define whether to trust or not. If first movers trust they automatically invest a predetermined amount. When the trustor does not trust the trustee nothing happens and both subjects receive their endowment. Since first movers only have two options (trust or not trust) first movers who trust can never induce negative reciprocity[2] Hence, if we observe second movers who send back small amounts this can only be attributed to exploitance behavior. In the following I discuss papers analyzing gender effects for both types of trust games: continuous and binary choice trust games. In the next subsection trust game designs where the first movers do not know the gender of the second mover are discussed.

GENDER DIFFERENCES IN TRUST GAMES

In this subsection I discuss standard trust game studies, i.e. setups where no information about the interaction partner was given. The first mover and the second mover do not know anything about the partner's gender. Croson and Buchan (1999) investigate in an interesting inter cultural setup gender differences in trust and reciprocity. The authors use a continuous trust game à la Berg et al. (1995) and analyze subjects of four different countries (US, China, Japan, and Korea). In total 186 subjects participated in this study. All trustors were endowed with 1,000 experimental units. Table 1 presents the results of Croson and Buchan.

When focusing on gender effects with respect to trusting behavior of first movers, the authors find no significant differences between male and female trustors no matter of their nationality. However, table 1 illustrates that men on average send 696.4 units compared to female who slightly send smaller amounts (630.4). This result is in line with many other papers analyzing gender differences in trusting behavior of first movers in trust games. For instance Clark and Sefton (2001) and Cox and Deck (2006) confirm these results in binary choice trust games.[3] Although Croson and Buchan (1999) cannot find a significant difference in first mover behavior, they find a striking gender difference in terms of trust-worthiness of men and women. The authors report that men return on average 28.6 percent compared to 37.4 percent which is returned by women. A non-parametric Wilcoxon test reveals that this difference is highly significant ($p = 0.0183$). Thus, the authors find that women are more trustworthy than men. This result is supported by a couple of papers studying gender differences in trust games. For instance Croson and Buchan (1999), Chaudhuri and Gangadharan (2007), Snijders and Keren (2001) also find that female second movers send back significant higher amounts than male. Croson and Buchan (1999) furthermore find a positive correlation between the amounts received by a trustee and the amount which is sent by the trustor. However, their regressions reveal that there does not exist a cultural effect. Subjects' nationality had no effect on returning behavior of second movers at all. Another interesting study about gender differences in trust games is Chaudhuri and Gangadharan

---

[2] In continuous designs the reason for a second mover sending back a too low amount could be attributed to first mover offers which might be too low.

[3] There exist lots of other trust game designs who find no significant gender differences regarding first mover behavior. For example see Bohnet (2007), Schwieren and Sutter (2008).

(2007). The authors apply the design of Berg et al. (1995) and add an extension compared to Croson and Buchan (1999). Their study basically investigates whether there exists a correlation between the behavior as a first mover and a second mover when subjects have to decide in both roles. A further crucial difference to Croson and Buchan (1999) is that students are asked how much money they expect to get back when acting as a first mover. In total they invited 100 subjects to the laboratory. In the experiment everybody had to complete a decision as a first mover, followed by a decision as a second mover. Therefore the subjects were divided in room A and B and were matched twice. That is, every subject was matched to a certain person, when acting as a first mover. The same person was also matched to a different person when acting as a second mover. Subsequently, everybody received AU $10 and first acted in the role as a first mover (sender). The senders first had to decide how much money they were willing to send to their matched receiver in the other room. Afterwards everybody acted as a receiver and observed how much money was received by the matched first mover. The subjects then had to decide about the amount they were willing to return. Because subjects in this design have to think about both decisions (deciding as a first- and second mover) it might be that subjects were affected by this. To be more precise it is possible that subjects who send high amounts also return high amounts when acting as a second mover. However, the authors find no evidence for a correlation between sender- and receiver behavior. Chaudhuri and Gangadharan report that a non-parametric Spearman correlation test reveals a correlation coefficient of 0.1432 with a corresponding p-value of 0.1994 which is not significant. In contrast to Croson and Buchan (1999), Chaudhuri and Gangadharan (2007) find a gender difference in trusting behavior. Their results reveal that men trust more as first movers compared to women. On average they find that men send $5.30 compared to only $3.47 which was sent by women. This difference is statistically significant (non-parametric Wilcoxon ranksum test p-value = 0.0367).[4] For instance this results are also confirmed by Eckel and Wilson (2004), Snijders and Keren (2001), Buchan et al. (2004), and Migheli (2007) who also find that men trust more in environments where the gender of the interaction partner is unknown. Interestingly Chaudhuri and Gangadharan (2007) report a strong correlation between first-movers' expectations about second mover behavior and the amount sent by first movers (Spearman Correlation coefficient of 0.58, p-value <0.01). Thus, the authors line out that conditional trust can be an explanation for first movers transferring money. That is, senders transfer money because they expect their investments to be reciprocated by the second movers. When comparing the trustworthiness of receivers (i.e. the amounts returned by second movers) Chaudhuri and Gangadharan again find a strong gender effect. That is, their results emphasize that female receivers send back higher amounts compared to men. On average female second movers return 19.8 percent compared to men who only send back 14.7 percent. A Tobit regression supports a significant difference. Therefore Chaudhuri and Gangadharan's results are in line with the gender trust game literature.

The data of Blanco, Engelmann, Koch and Normann (2011) reveals another interesting gender effect. The authors find that gender differences in trust games might depend on the way the players make their decisions. That is, the players seem to behave differently when

---

[4] Although this difference is significant, the result is in line with Croson and Buchan (1999) because Croson and Buchan (1999) at least find that men slightly show more trust compared to women.

their decisions are obtained by the "strategy method"[5] compared to a standard setup where players directly make their decisions. The authors conducted a trust game variant with a binary choice option (sequential prisoner's dilemma), where players had to decide in both roles: as first movers and second movers as well. Similar to Chaudhuri and Gangadharan (2007) Blanco et al. (2011) are interested whether there exists a correlation between first-and second-mover behavior in the trust game. However, Blanco et al. (2011) rather test the impact of a belief elicitation task on the correlation between second- and first-mover choices. The crucial difference to Chaudhuri and Gangadharan (2007) is that the authors use the strategy method to elicit their data. That is, subjects do not know to whom they are matched to. Moreover, they first have to decide as a second mover (choose either cooperate or defect) being not matched to another player. Afterwards they also have to decide as a first mover not knowing to whom they will be matched. Subsequently every first-mover (second-mover) decision of a player is randomly matched to the second-mover (first-mover) decision of another player. Thus, there is an important difference when applying the strategy method: players hypothetically state what they would do if something happens. In order to show trustworthiness it might matter whether the players are able to put oneself in a hypothetical situation where a first mover hypothetically shows trusting behavior. The question whether a second mover shows trustworthiness also depends on the fact whether second movers are empathic. Applying the strategy method requires for the second movers that they hypothetically feel empathic about first movers who have sent positive investments. Therefore it might be possible that there exist gender differences in "hypothetical empathy". Figure 1 illustrates the game tree used in Blanco et al. (2011). A first mover either chooses cooperate (c) or defect (d). If she chooses d the second mover's decision does not matter: everybody receives 10. However, if the first mover chooses c, the second mover can either be trustworthy (choose c) or exploit the first mover (choose d). If the second mover is trustworthy both are better off (each player receives 14). If she chooses defect her payoff is higher (17) compared to choosing cooperate, however the first mover is worse off and only receives 7.

Blanco et al. implement four different treatments: (1) Baseline, (2) Belief Elicitation, (3) True Distribution and (4) True Distribution+. The Baseline treatment is the control treatment where players decide with the strategy method as a second mover and afterwards they decide as a second mover, not knowing to whom they will matched to. The Belief Elicitation condition is exactly the same as in the Baseline. The only difference is that they have to do a belief elicitation task after their first choice (as a second mover). More precisely, the players had to state their belief about how many of the other players will cooperate as a second mover. Subsequently the players had to make their choice as a first mover. The difference of the True Distribution and True Distribution+ treatments to the Belief Elicitation treatment is, that players are informed about the true distribution of actual second mover cooperators of the other nine players. Note that the True Distribution and the True Distribution+ treatments take USge of the same written instructions, the only difference is the oral information which was

---

[5] The strategy method which was proposed by Selten (1967) is a method where players are hypothetically asked what to do in different situations. For instance players have to state what they would do as a first mover and as a second mover as well. Subsequently pairs of players are matched and they receive a payoff as a consequence to their hypothetical decisions.

given during the True Distribution and the True Distribution+ treatment.[6] Table 2 summarizes Blanco et al.'s (2011) results.

Focusing on players behavior as first movers the authors find that on average half (48.20%) of the players trust. A deeper look into the data also does not reveal a difference between men and women. About half of all men (46.20%) and women (51%) trust as first movers. Thus, the result is in line with most of the gender trust games: no significant difference in first mover behavior of men and women can be found. This pattern changes when investigating second mover behavior: here, 55.60% of all players behave trustworthy. Focusing on the amount of men who showed trustworthy behavior reveals that again the same amounts of men are trustworthy. If we focus on the amount of females who showed trustworthiness we find an intense gender difference: more female (62.70%) do not exploit first movers, in contrast to only 46.20% men ($\chi 2 = 4.279$, d. f. = 1, p = 0.039). This gender difference is very stable in all treatments.[7] The data of Blanco et al. has strikingly shown that gender differences are sensitive to the way people make their decisions.

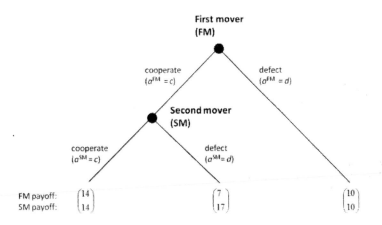

Figure 1. Sequential prisoner's dilemma game (as used in Blanco et al. (2011)).

Table 2. Overview of FM- and SM-behavior (generated with data of Blanco et al. (2011))

	Treatment				
	Baseline	Elicit Beliefs	T. Distrib.	T. Distrib. (+)	Avg.
First mover	31.3	50.0	57.1	42.9	46.2
Men	25.0	61.5	50.0	65.4	51.0
Women	27.5	55.0	52.5	57.5	48.9
Overall					
Second mover					
Men	56.3	44.1	50.0	35.7	46.2
Women	54.2	65.4	61.5	69.2	62.7
Overall	55.0	53.3	57.5	57.5	55.6

---

[6] During the "+" treatment the players were informed more precisely about the likelihood (depending on the actual distribution) of being exploited or not when choosing cooperate as a first mover.

[7] The effect can be found in 3 out of 4 treatments, only in the baseline treatment there is no difference.

Here, the strategy method only enabled women to show trustworthy behavior as second movers. In contrast, men always made the same decisions as first- and second movers. Therefore it may be the case that men's degree of empathy is too weak to "survive" the hypothetical strategy method. All surveyed studies only focused on environments where the subjects decided about money which was exogenously given to them at the beginning of the experiment. However, this assumption might be unrealistic to some extent. When considering economic setups which focus on fairness issues it may also be asked whether subjects would behave the same way if they had to decide about money which was earned by a real-effort task. In this regard I discuss the setup introduced by Heinz, Juranek and Rau (2011) where subjects have to do a real-effort task before deciding.

GENDER DIFFERENCES INDUCED BY A REAL-EFFORT TASK

In contrast to the studies discussed before we now focus on a study which analyzes endogenized money. That is, subjects in this experiment first had to a "real-effort" task which determines the size of their endowment. Heinz, Juranek, and Rau (2011) analyze whether a real-effort task may induce reciprocal behavior of subjects. In this regard they analyze with a modified dictator game whether there exist gender differences in terms of reciprocity induced by the working task.

In the standard dictator game, originally introduced by Kahneman, Knetsch, and Thaler (1986) a subject is endowed with a certain money amount. Afterwards the subject is asked how much she is willing to send to an anonymous receiver. Contrary to other games the receiver has no choice and the dictator's offer cannot be rejected by the receiver. Thus, the dictator has not to fear punishment by the other person. The standard predicted outcome is that dictators do not send anything. Nevertheless there exists a bulk of dictator game studies which report that dictators usually send about 15-20 percent (e.g. see Forsythe et al. (1994), Hoffman et al. (1996)). Interestingly Cherry, Frykblom, and Shogren (2002) show that dictators' generosity melts down when they first have to earn the money to decide about within a real-effort task. During the real-effort task dictators first had to answer questions of the GMAT-test. Afterwards subjects received either $10 or $40 depending on the amount of correctly solved questions. Although Cherry et al. (2002) do not find a stake-size effect, they report that dictator giving dramatically declined and 95 percent of their dictators made zero offers in the double blind environment. This result is striking and shows that an external factor like the real-effort task can significantly influence the outcome of the game.

Heinz, Juranek, and Rau (2011) extended the Cherry et al. (2002) setting to test real effort's impact on subjects' reciprocal behavior.[8] The authors modify Cherry et al.'s (2002) setup in that the receivers first have to do a real-effort task. Afterwards the dictators get to know about the corresponding money outcome and have to decide about the money which has to be dictated to the receivers. The main difference to Cherry et al. (2002) is that letting receivers work adds a strategic component to the setup. When receivers exert effort they play a trust game because they do not know how much money will be sent back by the dictators. If a receiver believes that the dictator is not trustworthy she should not work at all. Thus

---

[8] Note that similar setups also have been conducted by Ruffle (1998) and Oxoby and Spraggon (2006). However, both designs do not focus on gender differences.

dictators in that setup correspond to second movers of a trust game and receivers correspond to first movers. In their experiment Heinz et al. (2011) analyzed 352 subjects. The authors implemented two treatments: Windfall and Real Effort. After arriving, subjects were randomly assigned the role of a dictator or receiver. Afterwards dictators and receivers were placed into two different rooms.[9] Their Windfall treatment served as baseline treatment where subjects did not have to do a real-effort task. Instead they took part in a lottery in order to determine whether they were endowed with 5 or 10 Euros. In the Real Effort treatment subjects had to solve a GRE test. Subjects who had at least correctly answered 13 out of 20 questions received 10 Euros. If subjects were not successful they only received 5 Euros. Afterwards the dictators were asked to dictate the money endogenized by the receivers.

Table 3. Dictators' taking rates (generated with data of Heinz et al. (2011))

Gender	Stake Size	Windfall	obs.	Real Effort	obs.	Avg.	obs.
males	5 Euros	68.73 (24.40)	15	74.21 (27.73)	24	72.10 (26.31)	39
males	10 Euors	77.27 (21.62)	22	76.52 (25.65)	25	76.87 (23.38)	47
Avg.	--	73.81 (22.56)	37	75.39 (26.44)	49	74.71 (24.72)	86
females	5 Euros	72.68 (21.62)	28	63.33 (20.33)	21	68.67 (21.38)	49
females	10 Euors	76.11 (22.59)	18	63.26 (20.92)	23	68.90 (22.35)	41
Avg.	--	74.02 (21.82)	46	63.30 (20.40)	44	68.68 (21.70)	90

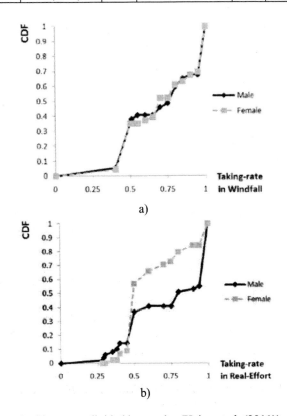

a)

b)

Figure 2. CDF of dictators' taking-rates divided by gender (Heinz et al. (2011)).

---

[9] Before subjects were separated they could see each other. This was done in order to sustain credibility for dictators that there really existed a receiver.

Heinz et. al (2011) find that on average men receive higher endowments and solve more questions correctly. However, this difference is only small and not significant. Nevertheless this could be evidence for a slightly higher level of trust of men. This is consistent with the other trust game papers without real-effort tasks. Interestingly the authors find striking gender differences in dictators' reciprocity. Table 3 reports the average taking rate of the dictators in the Windfall and Real Effort treatment.

It can clearly be seen that in the Real Effort treatment female dictators behave more trust-worthy than male dictators. Neglecting stake size, female dictators in Real Effort on average take 63.30 percent of the receivers compared to men who take 75.39 percent. A non-parametric Mann-Whitney test shows that this difference is statistically significant (p-value = 0.021). In the Windfall treatment where reciprocity cannot play a role there is no gender effect. On average men take 73.81 percent and women take nearly the same amount (74.02). Thus Heinz et al. (2011) highlight that a real-effort task induces reciprocal behavior for females only. Table 3 also reports that female dictators do not show a stake-size effect in Real Effort. Independent from receivers' performance female dictators always take around 63 percent. Figure 2 demonstrates the significant gender effect with CDF diagrams of the Windfall and the Real Effort treatments.

The left diagram shows that in the absence of a real-effort task, both male and female dictators behave quite the same. The CDFs do not differ at all. This result is statistically supported by a Kolmogorov Smirnov test (Max. D = 0.062, p-value = 1.000). Furthermore the CDF diagram shows that in the environment of a real-effort task female dictators behave significantly different compared to male dictators. Here, a Kolmogorov Smirnov test reveals that there exist a highly significant difference (Max. D = 0.362, p-value = 0.011). Heinz et al. (2011) show that a remarkable fraction (57%) of female dictators take the equal split. Whereas only 37% of male dictators equally share the endogenized money. The CDF also documents that a small amount (16%) of all female dictators take all the endogenized money. This stands in stark contrast to men, where 45% decide to take all the money.

Heinz et al.'s (2011) study therefore supports the findings of the gender trust game papers which mainly find that female second movers are more trustworthy and show higher amounts of reciprocity than men. It also shows that reciprocity can be induced by a real-effort task. Interestingly it can be seen that only women are sensitive to that. It is also surprising that receivers' performance does not play a role. The surveyed literature showed so far, that most of the papers find that men trust more than women. Although not every paper finds statistical support for this, at least small differences can be found to confirm this tendency. In the next subsection it will be analyzed whether these findings also hold for trust game setups where first movers receive information about their interaction partners.

GENDER DIFFERENCES IN TRUST GAMES WITH INTRODUCED INFORMATION

In contrast to the trust game gender studies of subsection 2.1 there also exist some studies where subjects get information about the interaction partner. For example they get to know about the gender of the other player. These studies involve a more realistic environment because in everyday life people mostly know their business partners. If peoples' actions are sensitive to the gender of their interaction partner this might have crucial implications. For instance if women trust only other women an implication for negotiations within companies would be to establish only female negotiators when negotiating with females. It is also interesting to analyze whether male and female trustors or trustees behave differently when their interaction partner is not of the same gender. If male receivers often exploit female trustors and if female senders anticipate this, it might be an indication for the origins of the gender wage gap. This could explain why women possibly behave more reluctantly compared to men in the presence of male negotiators.[10] In the following I discuss trust game studies which control for these interaction effects.

An interesting variant of the standard trust game is introduced by Eckel and Wilson (2004). They use a binary version of the standard trust game and vary the information condition of second movers. Therefore first movers were first presented a trust game and different kinds of icons of faces. Subsequently the first movers have to choose whether they want to trust or not and afterwards they also have to choose one of the faces. The faces represented different emotions: some of them showed smiling faces and others showed angry people. The authors thereby told the first movers that they had to choose with whom they want to interact. Eckel and Wilson (2004) find that most first movers want friendly partners to interact with. Regarding trusting behavior, their results are consistent to the evidence about trust games without information. Interestingly in the treatment where female first movers could not choose an interaction partner they trust less than men. However, if females could choose the partner to interact with, they show more trust compared to men. Contrary to the literature about no partner information, Eckel and Wilson (2004) find no gender difference in trustworthiness of second movers.

In their study Croson, Buchan and Solnick (2008) also extend the information given to the players in a trust game. Their study consists of a continuous trust game study which controls for gender interaction effects. The special feature of this experiment is that they control for the impacts when one interaction partner knows the gender of the other player. This information was given by informing participants about the first names of their interaction partners. The authors also focus on the outcome when both parties are informed about the other subject's gender. In total they had 754 subjects in their experiment. First and second movers were separated into two different rooms and the first movers were given envelopes and $10 to decide about. In this respect they used four treatments to test for the impacts of knowing the receiver's gender. In a control treatment ("number identification") subjects did not receive information about the first names of the interaction partners (subjects were only told a participation number of the partner). In contrast in the "mutual name identification" treatment the gender of the first- and the second mover was known. The authors also include two conditions called "asymmetric name identification" where only the first (second) mover is informed about the gender and the second (first) mover was only told the number of the other decision maker. Table 4 presents their results regarding the average amounts sent, when only the gender of the responder was known (first column). The second column documents their findings when only the gender of the sender was known. Finally the results when both genders are known are presented in the third column.

---

[10] Note that many studies also show that female subjects behave less competitive than males in negotiations (e.g. Gneezy, Niederle, and Vesterlud (2003), Sutter and Rützler (2010)).

Table 4. Average amounts sent (generated with data of Croson et al. (2008))

Condition and Responder					
	Sender's gender unknown		Sender's gender	Sender's gender unknown	
	Resonder's gender unknown		known	Resonder's gender unknown	
	Responder	Responder	Responder's	Responder	Responder
Sender	male	female	gender unknown	male	female
Male	8.17	8.42	7.20	8.08	7.85
	(2.96)	(2.33)	(3.74)	(2.98)	(3.18)
Female	7.08	7.13	7.31	6.68	5.84
	(2.79)	(3.00)	(2.80)	(3.16)	(3.17)
Total	7.69	7.68	7.25	7.39	6.82
	(2.90)	(2.78)	(3.32)	(3.13)	(3.31)

Table 5. Average amounts returned (generated with data of Croson et al. (2008))

Condition and Sender		Responder		
		Male	Female	Total
Sender's gender	Sender	26.0	28.2	27.1
known	Male	(19.8)	(26.1)	(22.8)
Responder's	Sender	17.8	36.6	26.9
gender unknown	Female	(17.0)	(16.2)	(19.0)
Responder's	Sender's	29.6	36.5	33.0
gender known	gender unknown	(16.9)	(15.1)	(16.3)
Sender's gender	Sender	32.5	35.9	34.2
known	Male	(20.0)	(16.9)	(18.6)
Reponder's	Sender	32.0	29.0	30.9
gender known	Female	(20.3)	(17.0)	(18.7)

Focusing on the first asymmetric treatment where only the gender of the responder (second mover) was known, the authors find that there exists no difference in the amount females and males received. Ignoring gender of senders, male responders receive on average $7.69 and female responders receive $7.68. Analyzing the other asymmetric treatment the authors find that when ignoring receivers' gender, male and female first movers get back nearly the same amounts (male: $7.20, female: $7.31). When both genders are known there is only a slight difference between the amounts male and female responders receive: male receive $7.39 and female $6.82. The gender of the sender does not play a role: male and female senders are both not affected by the gender of the corresponding responders. This holds for all three conditions. Thus, it can be summarize that, information about the gender of an interaction partner does not change the results. Instead the authors confirm in their baseline treatment (where no information about gender was given) the result that on average male first movers trust more than female first movers.[11] It will be interesting to analyze whether this

---

[11] They find that men send $7.45, whereas women do only send $6.08.

result also holds for the amount sent back by the responders when information about gender is given. Table 5 illustrates Buchan, Croson and Solnick's (2008) results regarding the amount sent back, when gender was known.

Analyzing the amounts send back, when only the gender of the sender was known, it appears that there is no difference between the amounts returned. Buchan et al. find that male senders (27.1%) and female senders (26.9%) get back the same amounts. No difference can be found for male and female second movers when the senders have the same gender as the second moves. That is, men send back 26% to male senders, whereas female senders only receive 17.8%. The same pattern can be observed for females: they send back 28.2% to male senders, whereas female senders receive 36.6%. Men and female responders again send back nearly the same amounts when their gender was known. Focusing on the gender interaction effects when both genders are known, it can be seen that on average male senders receive slightly more than female senders (male receive: 34.2% and female receive: 30.9%). Here, male second movers are not sensitive to the senders' gender: they send back 32% to both. However, female responders return more to male senders (35.9%) compared to female senders (29.0%) when both genders are known. Thus, it can be seen that subjects are sensitive to the information about the gender of their interaction partner when deciding about the amount to return. In contrast when focusing on sender behavior the information about the gender of the interaction partner has no influence on senders' decisions. In the next section the experimental setup of a principal-agent framework called "gift-exchange" game is introduced. Afterwards I discuss gender differences in trust and reciprocity in "gift-exchange" games.

GIFT-EXCHANGE GAMES

Many real-life business situations involve principal-agent relations where a manager is employed by a company. The economic literature about principal-agent relations is huge. For instance Akerlof (1982) introduced the gift exchange game and analyzed a setup where an employee is matched to an employer. The "gift-exchange" game is a well-known working horse model for incomplete labor contracts. In more detail the game usually consists of two players (principals and agents) and it involves two stages. In the first stage the wages are determined by the principals. In the second stage the agent chooses the effort he is willing to exert. In this framework exerting effort is costly to the employee and the wage payments reduce the principal's payoff at the same time. Analyzing the one-shot game[12] there exists an unique subgame-perfect Nash equilibrium. That is, the principals and the agents as well do not make a wage payment and no effort is exerted by the worker respectively. The reasoning for this equilibrium is easy: solving the game by backward induction requires for the agent to think about the employee's action after having received a positive wage payment. For instance if the employer pays $50 to the worker, the worker has no incentive to exert any positive amount of effort at the second stage of the game. This is due to the fact that the game ends after the second stage. If the employer solves this game by backward induction she anticipates this and will not make a positive wage payment at the first stage. Fehr,

---

[12] A one-shot game is a game that is played without repetition.

Kirchsteiger and Riedl (1993) were the first to experimentally test the gift-exchange game. In the following I present examples for the payoffs of principals and agents. Therefore I use the common cost and payoff functions introduced by Fehr, Kirchler, Weichbold and Gächter (1998).

Principal : $\pi_i = (v - w_i) \cdot e_i$

Agent : $u_j = w_j - c_0 - c(e_j)$

The definition of the principal's payoff prevents losses for the principal. The labor costs of the principal depend on the effort chosen by the agent. As long as the principal does not choose wages that are higher than v his payoff will always be positive.[13] The agent is free to choose a minimum effort level that does not imply any cost but she cannot choose zero effort. Fehr et al. (1998) assume that there is a convex relation between effort and the costs that arise for the agent. Table 6 presents the action space of the agents in the gift-exchange game.

Note that gift-exchange games are similar to trust-games. A crucial difference is that trust-games involve an efficiency factor which usually triples the invested amount of senders, after they have made their investments. The second movers receive the tripled investment to decide about the amount they are willing to send back. That is, the receivers in the trust game profit from the efficiency factor because it directly increases their endowment. In contrast in the gift-exchange game the efficiency factor multiplies the effort choices exerted by the workers. That is, the factor only increases the payoff an employer receives. The literature about experimental gift-exchange games mainly focuses on fairness issues. In this regard Fehr et al. (1993) find in their laboratory study that opposed to the theoretical predictions employers make positive wage payments to their workers. A surprising result is that employees reciprocate the wage payments of the employers and exert positive effort levels. Another astonishing finding of Fehr et al. (1993) is that the authors experimentally show that Akerlof's "Fair Wage-Effort Hypothesis" is right. Akerlof's (1982) "Fair Wage-Effort Hypothesis" postulates that there exist a positive monotonic correlation between the wages paid and the efforts exerted. Figure 3 presents Fehr et al.'s (1993) results regarding the evidence of the "Fair Wage-Effort Hypothesis.

The diagram clearly documents the positive correlation between wages paid and exerted average efforts. The result supports the idea that employees invest more effort when they have been paid higher wages. It thus, emphasizes the finding that employees positively reciprocate higher wages with higher efforts. In the next subsection I analyze gift-exchange setups and report whether there exist gender differences in terms of paid wages and exerted efforts.

Table 6. Agents' effort-cost-relation following Fehr et al. (1998)

e	0.1	0.2	0.3	0.4	0.5	0.6	0.7	0.8	0.9	1.0
c(e)	0	1	2	4	6	8	10	12	15	18

---

[13] Usually the principal's actions are restraint to wages lower than v.

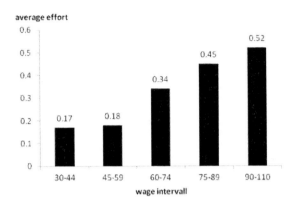

Figure 3. The Wage-Effort Relation (plot generated with data of Fehr et al. (1993)).

GENDER DIFFERENCES IN GIFT-EXCHANGE GAMES

The experimental literature about gender differences in gift-exchange games is relatively small. Nevertheless, there exist some interesting designs with astonishing results. This subsection focuses on three studies investigating gender differences in first-mover and second-mover behavior of gift-exchange setups. In this regard Chaudhuri and Sbai (2011) study a repeated gift-exchange setup with random matching. In more detail, at the beginning of the experiment their subjects were given fixed roles to either act as a first mover (employer) or as a second mover (employee). First of all employers had to decide about a wage payment to the employee and the same time the employers have to request an effort level (e^*) for the workers. Note that sending a suggestion is similar to "cheap talk" because independent of the demanded level the employees are free to choose any effort level. After the principal made her wage decision the worker can either reject (choose a zero effort ($e = 0$)) or accept (choose $e > 0$) the offer. In total the game was played for 10 periods. When deciding about the wages and effort participants did not know the gender of their interaction partner. The authors find no gender difference in first mover behavior, i.e. male principals pass the same average wage payment to receivers as female principals do. Figure 4 illustrates the development of male and female principals' average wage payments over time.

Figure 4 documents that male and female employers' wage payments decrease over time. The average wage payments cut in halve when comparing period 10 (about 2) with the beginning of the game (about 4.4). Focusing on exerted effort levels of employees (i.e. the workers' tendency to reciprocate) the authors find that female workers more often shirk than male workers, i.e. there are more women who exert less than the requested effort compared to male workers. Table 7 presents the frequency of male and female employees shirking.

Both men and women accept most contract offers. However, when accepting a contract employees usually shirk and make effort choices (e) below the demanded level (e^*). On average there are 80% of female employees who shirk compared to only 72% of male workers. A regression analysis reveals statistical significance of this difference. The authors furthermore outline that this difference decreases over time.

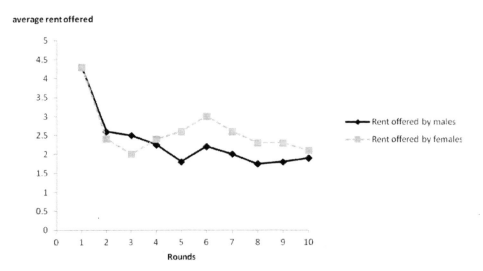

Figure 4. Average rents offered (plot generated with data of Chaudhuri and Sbai (2011)).

Table 7. Contracts offered (generated with data of Chaudhuri and Sbai (2011))

	Male		Female		Total
Contracts offered	210		170		380
Contracts rejected	14		9		23
Contracts accepted	196		161		357
Shirk (e < e*)	141	(72%)	130	(80%)	271
Work (e > e*)	55	(28%)	31	(19%)	86

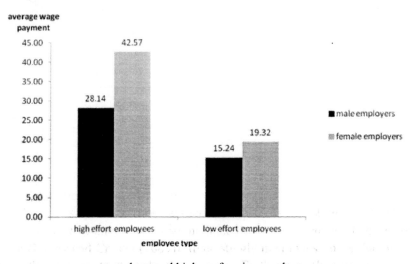

Figure 5. Average wage payments to low- and high-performing employees.

There also exists a gift-exchange setup which focuses on competitional effects between workers in a framework with two employees employed by the same employer. Benndorf and Rau (2011) analyze in a modified gift-exchange game whether the presence of a co-worker increases average efforts of employees. To induce competitional pressure they modify the standard gift-exchange game and use the setup introduced by Abeler, Altmann, Kube, and

Wibral (2010). In this setup there are two workers who act as first movers and simultaneously choose their effort level. Subsequently a principal can observe the effort levels of both workers and can decide about the wage payments for each employee. Because workers move before the employers they cannot shirk. Furthermore they are faced with competitive pressure because there is a co-worker who simultaneously chooses an effort level. Thus, the principal can reward the more productive worker. The authors compare their results to a treatment with the same move order. Note there exists a crucial difference: only one employee is matched to the employer. The setup is repeated for 12 periods. Benndorf and Rau report that average effort levels are only slightly smaller in the non-competitive treatment compared to the multiple workers treatment. However, they find an intense learning behavior of employees in the multiple workers treatment. That is, having the possibility to observe the performance of the co-worker significantly boosts the workers' effort levels. Benndorf and Rau (2011) find in their multiple worker treatment a strong increase in average effort in periods 1-6. This effect cannot be found in their control treatment.[14] The authors' data also reveals interesting gender effects. Although there is no gender difference in competitive behavior between the employees, a distinct gender effect can be found when focusing on the employers. Focusing on average payments in general[15] Benndorf and Rau find that female employers paid on average higher wages compared to male employers. To be more precise, employers in that setup could pay every integer between zero and 100 and female principals paid on average 30.94 compared to males who only paid 21.69. Since employers act as second movers they could exploit the workers (first movers) by making a zero wage payment. Thus, the result can be interpreted such as that female principals behave more reciprocally (or trustworthy) than male ones. Hence Benndorf and Rau's finding is in line with the evidence about reciprocity in trust games. Since wage payments can be interpreted as revealing reciprocity it is also interesting to analyze whether there also exists a gender difference of paid wages according to workers' performance. In more detail it will be exciting to examine whether employers differently evaluate the workers who outperform their co-workers. Figure 5 reports the average wage payments to employees who perform better (high effort employees) or weaker (low effort employees) than their co-worker.

First of all it appears that female employers on average pay higher wages compared to males. This is true for the wage payments which are received by low- and high-performing employees as well. Interestingly the difference in average wage payments by female and male employers is higher when focusing on the employees who exerted high effort levels. The wages paid by female employers are higher for 51% compared to the wages paid by male employers. In contrast the wages paid by female employers to low-performing workers are only higher for 27% compared to the males' choices. Thus, Benndorf and Rau find evidence that female principals show a higher magnitude of reciprocity.

Schwieren (2003) analyzes whether the "gender wage gap" can be observed in a laboratory gift-exchange game. The "gender wage gap"[16] describes the phenomenon of gender wage differentials between women and men of equal productivity. Schwieren employs the special double-auction gift-exchange setup introduced by Falk and Fehr (1999) to analyze

---

[14] The difference in learning behavior between their single worker and multiple worker treatment is significant.

[15] Note here, it is neglected whether an employee performed better (weaker) than his co-worker.

[16] See Weichselbaumer and Winter-Ebmer (2005) for a meta-study of the overwhelming empirical evidence of the gender wage gap.

whether women receive lower wages in the laboratory. Furthermore the author investigates whether differences in productivity (reciprocity) can be related to these differences. The Falk, Fehr (1999) design uses a double auction mechanism[17] with an excess supply of work, i.e. there are six employees and only four employers. Schwieren furthermore informs both: employers and employees about the gender of the interaction partners. In Schwieren's homogenous treatment all employers were men (women) and the employee were women (men). For instance, at the beginning of the experiment the experimentator told the participants : "All men are employers and all women are workers". The author finds that female workers were offered significant smaller average wages compared to male workers, no matter whether they are employed to a male or female employer. That is, male principals on average pay to male workers about 50. In contrast, if male principals employ female workers wage payment is only about 41. Interestingly female employees are also discriminated by female employers: female employees receive from female employers a wage of about 40. Whereas male employees receive average wage payments of about 63. Schwieren (2003) furthermore investigates whether male and female employees as well showed reciprocal behavior due to wage payments. That is, it is tested whether effort levels do correlate with wages paid. When splitting the data by sex, the author only finds a strong significant effect for male workers. That is, the exerted effort by male workers is significantly correlated with wages paid (Pearson correlation $r = 0.5$, one-sided p-value $= 0.002$). In contrast female workers' effort choices are only weakly correlated to wages paid (Pearson correlation $r = 0.25$, one-sided p-value $= 0.081$). Although there is a weaker correlation of effort levels and the wages paid, female employees do behave reciprocally. Schwieren (2003) shows that male and female workers reciprocate low wage payments less strongly than high wage payments. Since female employees more often receive small wage payments in contrast to men, they do not show the same reciprocal behavior. This finding emphasizes the importance of further factors which may have an effect on reciprocal behavior: the fact that employers knew that workers were female lead to smaller wage payments. Thus, female workers exerted low effort and received small wage payments in the following period.

CONCLUSION

The surveyed papers about gender differences in trust and gift-exchange games emphasize that there exist striking gender differences. Although there are some papers which do not find a significant difference in trusting behavior, most of the papers show that men in general trust more. That is, men usually send higher amounts to second movers compared to women. Note that this behavior can also be related to differences in risk attitudes. That is, many papers find that men behave more risk seeking in contrast to women who behave rather risk averse (e.g. see Gneezy and Croson (2009)). Interestingly men invest more than women but at the same time they are less trustworthy than women. Furthermore the results show that female second movers' reciprocity is amplified in the presence of a real-effort task. Here, only female dictators showed higher levels of reciprocity and return high amounts to workers. This finding is very interesting in the context of voluntary bonuses. If female bosses reward

---

[17] In a double-auction mechanism participants post bids and asks to a market. If employers and employees agree on the same price the contract is accepted and the employee decides about the effort level to exert.

their employees more often with voluntary bonuses this could have an impact on long term motivation of the employees. Another interesting finding is that the reversed gift-exchange game revealed that female employers in that setup behaved differently in terms of wage payments compared to men. This may also have significant effects on the incentive structure in a company if female bosses reward workers who outperform their co-workers. The results of Croson, Buchan, and Solnick (2008) and Schwieren (2003) strikingly showed that subjects in trust and gift-exchange games behave differently when knowing the gender of their interaction partners. These studies highlight the presence of the "gender wage gap" because it is showed that this phenomenon exists even in the laboratory. All these studies show a high degree of gender differences in trust and reciprocity. Thus, it follows that these results cannot be ignored when analyzing economic decision-making of trust and reciprocity.

REFERENCES

Abeler, J., Altmann, S., Kube, S., Wibral, M. (2010): "Gift Exchange and workers' fairness concerns.", *Journal of the European Economic Association,* 8: 1299-1324.

Akerlof, G., A., (1982): "Labor Contracts as Partial Gift Exchange.", *Quarterly Journal of Economics*, 97: 543-569.

Benndorf, V., Rau, H. A., (2011): "Competition on the Workplace: An Experimental Investigation.", Unpublished.

Berg, J., Dickhaut, J. W., McCabe, K. A., (1995): "Trust, Reciprocity, and Social History.", *Games and Economic Behavior*, 10: 122-142.

Blanco, M., Engelmann, D., Koch, A. K., Normann, H. T., (2011): "Preferences and Beliefs in Sequential Social Dilemma Problems.", Unpublished.

Bohnet, I., (2007): "Why Women and Men Trust Others.", *Economics and Psychology*: A Promising New Cross-Disciplinary Field, ed. Bruno S. Frey and Alois Stutzer, 89-110. Cambridge and London: MIT Press.

Chaudhuri, A., Gangadharan, L., (2007): "An Experimental Analysis of Trust and Trustworthiness.", *Southern Economic Journal*, 73, 959-985.

Chaudhuri, A., Sbai, E., (2011): "Gender differences in trust and reciprocity in repeated gift exchange games.", *New Zealand Economic Papers*, 45, 81-95.

Cherry, T., Frykblom, P., Shogren, J. F., (2002): "Hardnose the Dictator.", *American Economic Review*, 92, 1218-1221.

Clark, K., Sefton, M., (2001): "The Sequential Prisonser's Dilemma: Evidence on Reciprocation.", *Economic Journal*, 111, 51-68.

Croson, R., Buchan, N. R., (1999): "Gender and Culture: International Experimental Evidence from Trust Games.", *American Economic Review*, 89, 386-391.

Croson, R., Gneezy, U., (2009): "Gender Differences in Preferences.", *Journal of Economic Literature*, 47, 1-27.

Cox, J., C., Deck, C. A., (2006): "When are Women More Generous than Men?", *Economic Inquiry*, 44, 587-598.

Eckel, C., Wilson, R. K., (2004): "Whom to Trust? Choice of Partner in a Trust Game.", Unpublished.

Fehr, E., Kirchsteiger, G., Riedl, A., (1993): "Does Fairness Prevent Market Clearing? An Experimental Investigation.", *Quarterly Journal of Economics*, 108, 437-459.

Fehr, E., Falk, A., (1999): "Wage Rigidity in a Competitive Incomplete Contract Market.", *Journal of Political Economy*, 107, 106-134.

Fehr, E., Kirchler, E., Weichbold, A., Gächter, S., (1998): "When Social Norms Overpower Competition: Gift Exchange in Experimental Labor Markets.", *Journal of Labor Economics*, 16, 324-351.

Fehr, E., Schmidt, K., (1999): "A Theory of Fairness, Competition, and Cooperation", *Quarterly Journal of Economics*, 114, 817-868.

Forsythe, R., Horowitz, J. L., Savin, N. E., Sefton, M., (1994): "Fairness in Simple Bargaining Experiments", *Games and Economic Behavior*, 6, 347-369.

Gneezy, U., Nieder, M., Rustichini, A., (2003): "Performance in Competitive Environments: Gender Differences.", *Quarterly Journal of Economics*, 118, 1049-1074.

Heinz, M., Juranek, S., Rau, H. A., (2011): "Do Women Behave more Reciprocally than Men? Gender Differences in Real Effort Dictator Games.", *Journal of Economic Behavior and Organization*, forthcoming.

Hoffman, E., McCabe, K., Shachat K., Smith., V., (1996): "Preferences, Property Rights, and Anonymity in Bargaining Games.", *Games and Economic Behavior*, 7, 346-380.

Migheli, M., (2007): "Trust, Gender, and Social Capital: Experimental Evidence from Three Western European Countries.", Unpublished.

Oxoby, R. J., Spraggon, J., (2008): "Mine and yours: Property rights in dictator games.", *Journal of Economic Behavior and Organization*, 65, 703-713.

Ruffle, J. B., (1998): "More is Better, But Fair is Fair: Tipping in Dictator and Ultimatum Games.", *Games and Economic Behavior*, 23, 247-265.

Schwieren, C., (2003): "The gender wage gap - due to differences in efficiency wage effects or discrimination?", *Maastricht : METEOR, Maastricht Research School of Economics of Technology and Organization, Research Memoranda* 046.

Schwieren, C., Sutter, M., (2008): "Trust in Cooperation or Ability? An Experimental Study on Gender Differences.", *Economics Letters*, 99, 494-497.

Selten, R., (1967): "Die Strategiemethode zur Erforschung des eingeschränkt rationalen Verhaltens im Rahmen eines Oligopolexperiments.", Beiträge zur experimentellen Wirtschaftsforschung, ed. H. Sauerman, *Tübingen: Mohr.*, 136-168.

Snijders, C., Keren, G., (2001): "Do You Trust? Whom Do You Trust? When Do You Trust?", *Advances in Group Processes*, 18, 129-160.

Sutter, M., Rützler, D., (2010): "Gender Differences in Competition Emerge Early in Life ", *IZA Discussion Paper* No. 5015, 2010.

Weichselbaumer, D., Winter-Ebmer, R. (2005): "A Meta-Analysis of the International Gender Wage Gap", *Journal of Economic Surveys*, 19, 479-511.

In: Psychology of Gender Differences
Editor: Sarah P. McGeown

ISBN: 978-1-62081-391-1
© 2012 Nova Science Publishers, Inc.

Chapter 13

DOES HOUSEHOLD GENDER-STRUCTURE AFFECT PHYSICAL HEALTH?

Ari K. Mwachofi and Robert Broyles*
University of Oklahoma Health Sciences Center, US

ABSTRACT

At the micro-level, the household assembles and allocates health resources among its members and between competing wants. Household structure has an important influence on the production of health and on resource allocation. Few studies have examined the effect of household gender- structure on the production of health. The American household structure has changed radically from 71% being traditional married-couple in 1970s to only 49.57% in 2008. In 2008 4.59% of US households were single-male-headed, 12.46% were single-female-headed and 33.38% were non-family households. To be effective, policy formation and implementation has to keep abreast of such changes. The study focused on the household as the entity that is responsible for the production of health. The study examined household gender -structure as a health resource to determine its effect on the health status of household members.

Based on production economics, the study used a Grossman-type model of health production as the organizing frame of reference. Analysis was conducted using data derived from individual responses to the 2010 survey conducted by the Behavioral Risk Factor Surveillance System (BRFSS) of the US Centers for Disease Control and Prevention (CDC). The study used a sample of respondents from single-female-headed and single-male-headed households. Logistic regression analysis examined the relation between household structure and the likelihood of good physical health. Limited to respondents who experienced at least one day of poor physical health, the study used linear regression analysis to examine the influence of household gender-structure on variation in the number of days of poor physical health.

Household structure exerted a significant influence on health status. Relative to residents of single-male-headed households, those residing in single-female-headed households were significantly less likely to report their physical health as being excellent, very good or good. However, the results of the multivariate analysis indicated that

---

* E-mail address: *amwachof@ouhsc.edu.*

respondents from female-headed household experienced significantly fewer days of poor physical health. There is a significant relation between household structure and individual health. Health policy-formation should be cognizant of the special needs and strengths of single-female-headed households. There is need for greater more detailed exploration of the role of female household heads in health production, promotion and maintenance.

INTRODUCTION

At the micro-level, the foundation for improving, preserving, and promoting health is the household. The focus of this study is household structure and its effects on physical health. This study uses a Grossman's (1972, 2004) model of health as a consumption good (people enjoy good health) and as human capital stock- a production input (a healthy population yields a productive labor-force). Like other capital, health stock depreciates over time. However, the household can invest in health and produce health and so reduce its depreciation. Health production at the household level involves many factors and processes to include socioeconomic status (SES), individual behavior, demographic factors, social environment, economic environment, government policy, access to care, use of care and the individual's existing stock of health which is influenced by age, and other chronic conditions.

Decisions implemented by the head of the household are likely to affect the behavior of household members to include the promotion or preservation of health, the use of health care and adherence to provider prescriptions. The head of the household may also influence the accumulation and the distribution of health resources among household members and the allocation of household resources among competing household wants or needs such as education, health care, leisure, and other consumption goods and services.

Although only a few studies examine household gender structure and its effect on health, there are numerous studies of gender differences in health. Women experience higher morbidity but lower mortality than men do resulting in women's higher life expectancies (Verbrugge, 1985; Walters, McDonough, and Strohschein, 2002; Bambra et al., 2009; Osmani and Sen, 2003). Among many explanations proposed for this paradox include: differential exposure to health risks and vulnerability (McDonough and Walters, 2001; Denton et al 2004; Kaneda, Zimmer, Fang and Tang, 2009); variation in access to- and utilization of socio-economic resources (Chen, Chang and Yang, 2008; Denton Prus and Walters, 2004). It is also possible that differential health status is attributable to gender-power relations, which determine whether women's health needs are acknowledged, whether they have a voice or a modicum of control over their lives and their health, and whether they can realize their rights (Sen, Östlin, and George, 2007).

Married people enjoy better health than those who are single (Turaagabeci, Makamura, Kisuki and Takano, 2007; Umberson, 2002; August and Sorkin, 2010; Walson Weiss and Hughes, 1997; Olser, McGue, Lund and Christensen, 2008; Schoenborn, 2004). In traditional (married couple) households, women endure their own poor health but also the illnesses of family members because females are the main care-givers. They are expected to assume the responsibility of caring for those who are ill and may suffer more from that stress (Osmani and Sen, 2003). Other suggestions are that men suffer more and die soon because of socially constructed norms of femininity and masculinity that force men to adopt more unhealthy beliefs and personal health practices than those adopted by women (Courtenay, 2000).

In a study of the social production of health, Denton and Walters (1999) found that the structures of social inequality are the most important determinants of health and act independently through their influence on the behavioral determinants of health. Social structural factors such as being in the highest income category, working full-time, caring for family and having social support were more important predictors of good health for women than for men. Smoking and alcohol consumption were more important determinants of health status for men than for women. In a follow-up (Denton Prus and Walters, 2004) found gender differences in health and that social -structural and psychosocial determinants of health were more important for women while behavioral determinants were more important for men. Similarly in a community-based research on reproductive health Amin and Bentley (2002) found that gender inequalities have resulted in rural Indian women accepting high thresholds of suffering and failing to seek treatment for their symptoms. In order to reduce gender health inequality it is important to recognize the roles and contributions of females in the family as well as in society and for women to actively participate in all household decision making process.

Numerous studies have examined and documented the relationship between SES, health status and health production (Wilkinson, 1997, 1992, 1989; Rodgers, 1979; Lynch et al., 2000; Wilkinson and Marmot, 2003; Marmot and Wilkinson, 1999). Socioeconomic indicators are the single most pervasive determinants of health-seeking behavior, overriding age and gender (Ahmed, Tomson, Ptzold and Kabir 2005). The health–income relation varies throughout the life cycle and between genders. Limited to members of the labor force, Bender and Habermalz (2006) reported similar findings. Thornton (2002) examined the impact of medical care, socioeconomic status, lifestyle and environmental factors on the health status of the population of the US. The results indicated that SES and lifestyle factors were most important predictors of mortality rates while additional medical care was relatively ineffective in lowering mortality or increasing life expectancy.

Maternal education affects efficiency in the production of child health (Barrera, 1990). Utilizing the Grossman model, Fayissa and Gutema (2005) estimated a health production function for Sub-Saharan Africa. Their results indicate that an increase in per capita income, a decrease in illiteracy rate, and an increase in food availability were strongly associated with an improvement in life expectancy at birth. They concluded that a health policy that focuses on the provision of health services, to the exclusion of socioeconomic and environmental aspects may do little to improve health. Cultural practices and beliefs also influence health production (Clark, 1993; Halvorson, 2004) and so does social capital (Schultz, O'Brien and Tedesse, 2008).

Household Gender-Structure and Health Production

Past studies of the influence of the gender of the head of the household on health production used data from less developed countries and they primarily analyzed health production for children. They found gender differences in allocation of household resources. Handa (1996) found that a female decision maker generally increased the share of the household budget allocated to child and family goods. The study also found that female-headed households spend more on adult wear and less on health but that such expenditures are partially offset by the use of other health inputs. Bronte-Tinkew and DeJong (2004) assessed the influence of household structure and resource distribution on children's nutritional status in Jamaica. They compared the effect of different types of household structures (single-parent, two-parent, cohabiting and extended family) on child nutrition. They found that living in a single-parent household and a cohabiting household increased the odds of stunting for children. There were also indications that children in single-parent low-income families with siblings and low-income extended families with siblings were more likely to have low height for age.

Schmeer (2009) assessed whether the absence of a father due to migration is associated with increased child illness in poor, rural Mexico communities. The state-level models illustrated that the odds of children being ill were 39% higher for any illness and 51% higher for diarrhea when fathers were absent compared to when fathers were present. In the context of rural Mexico, fathers are important sources of support for ensuring the healthy development of young children.

Yoo and Lim (2009) estimated household income distribution at three stages: pre-transfer income, pre-transfer income plus social insurance benefits, and post-transfer income. They found that children in female-headed households were economically worse off than children in married-couple households both in the pre-transfer and post-transfer income stages. The greatest disadvantage appeared in the post-transfer income distribution. Compared to children in male-headed households, children in female-headed households gained small economic ground at both income stages. Since female-headed households are poorer it is usually assumed that children from such households have poorer nutrition and health.

A study of children's nutrition in the Dominican Republic found more calories and protein per adult-equivalent available in male-headed families (Johnson and Rogers, 1993). Despite the economic and dietary advantages for residents of male-headed households, the study found that children of female-headed households were taller and heavier for their age than those of two parent homes. Other anthropometric measures showed differences in the same direction even after controlling for the mother's schooling and employment outside the home. In a similar study in Kenya, Onyango, Tucker and Eisemon (1994) found that children in female-headed households consumed a greater variety of foods. However, among children of female-headed households, there was greater prevalence of stunting but lower prevalence of low weight for age. Other findings indicate that single-male-headed households spent a significantly greater proportion of their food budget on commercially prepared food than married male-headed and female-headed households (Kroshus 2008). There are also indications that a mother invests in the child's health and that step-mothers are not substitutes for birth-mothers in this domain (Caseand Paxson, 2001).

The influence on health exerted by gender head and household structure intersects with socioeconomic effects, a finding that is attributable to the close association between the two variables (Heard, Gorman and Kapinus, 2008). For example, household structure affects educational attainment, economic mobility and ultimately, children's health (Mahler and Winkelmann, 2004; Ginther and Pollak, 2003; Björklund, Ginther and Sundström, 2004; Heiland and Liu, 2006; McMunn, Nazroo, Marmot, Boreham and Goodman, 2001; Briones, Schwartz, Dillon and Mitrani, 2006). Furthermore, household structure influences: individual behaviors, patterns of access to care and outcomes (Gorman and Braverman, 2008 ;) and investment in children's health (Case and Paxson, 2001). On the other hand, a child's health has an effect on marital stability and family structure (Hughes and Waite, 2002), and family stability is a production input for a child's health and education (Kutty, 2008).

There is little evidence concerning the effects of household structure on adult health. One of very few studies of household structure and adult health was conducted in Japan. The findings suggest that women in multi-generational households reported more care-giving worries, but less future health and financial worries (Takeda, Kawachi, Yamagata, Hashimoto, Matsumura, Oguri and Okayama, 2004). Elderly women who take care of a husband or relatives do not care for themselves (or their health) as much as do older women who live alone (Pizzetti, Manfredini, and Lucchetti, 2005).

Study Objective and Data

Most of the previous examinations of the influence of gender head and household structure relied on data from less developed countries and were limited to the production of children's health rather than adult health. Unlike previous research, the purpose of this study is to focus on the health status of adults and use data assembled in the U.S. to examine the role of the gender head and household structure in influencing physical health.

The structure of the American household has changed from predominantly traditional married-couple family to other structures. Census data indicate that in the 1970s, traditional families comprised 71% of all households but that proportion had shrank to 53% in 2000 and to 49.57% in 2008 (US Census, 2000; American Community Survey, 2009). Data from the American Community Survey indicate that between 2006 and 2008 4.59% of households were headed by an adult male with no wife present, 12.46% were headed by females with no husband present, and 33.38% were non-family households (ACS, 2009). Thus the typical American household has changed radically over time. These changes imply that health policies directed to households need to change to meet new needs from new household structures.

METHOD

Study Model

The study adopts the household as the entity that influences consumption of health resources and the production of health. Household structure, composition, and social relations influence distribution of resources including food, income and other health resources (Messer, 1983; Guyer, 1981). Economic theory posits that in their role as producers, households choose and combine production inputs in a manner that will maximize their profits (profit maximization) and as consumers their decisions aim to maximize satisfaction (utility maximization). Because their utility or profit maximization is constrained by resource limitations (budget constraint), household production decisions are heavily dependent on perceptions of costs and benefits. Household gender-structure (e.g. female-headed, male-headed, or grandparent-headed) can influence perceptions of costs and benefits of health production inputs. Household structure also influences production of inputs used for the production of health including: food, housing, access to care, habits/individual behavioral choices – such as smoking, diet, exercise. Individual household characteristics may also influence efficiency in the production of health inputs and of health.

The household head is responsible for most household decision-making and for the organization and care of individual family members. Often the household head is the primary provider and distributor of household resources among household members and the allocator of resources among competing household wants. Such distribution of resources influences household health production. Illness adversely affects households through direct costs (medical treatment and related financial costs), indirect costs (productive time losses). There is evidence that medical costs can force households into poverty (McIntyre, Thiede, Dahlgren and Whitehead, 2006). Although households try to cope with these loses through labor substitution, they are not able to fully compensate such loses (Suerborn, Adams, and Hien, 1996).

The study applies the household production of health proposed by Berman et al. (1994) as useful framework for integrating, motivating and organizing perspectives of a variety of disciplines in analyzing determinants of health and health change. Berman et al (1994) define household production of health as: "A dynamic behavioral process through which households combine their (internal) knowledge, resources, and behavioral norms and patterns with available (external) technologies, services, information, and skills to restore, maintain, and promote the health of their members." (Berman et al., 1994, page 206). The advantage of this approach is that it recognizes the critical role of internal household resources and processes in promoting and maintaining health and reduces emphasis on formal health services (clinics, hospitals etc) as primary determinants of health rather than treating them as one of the many inputs for household production of health. From the perspective household health production, there are two phases to producing health: demand for health resources and health production which combines the inputs to produce health (the health production function).This study focuses on the health production function and it includes household structure as one of the health production inputs.

The study also applies the Grossman (1972) model which posits that health is a capital asset that provides services or benefits in multiple periods and depreciates with the passage of time. Health promoting activities, to include the use of health services, are viewed as an investment in the stock of health, suggesting that the change in health is given by the difference between the effects of health promoting activity and the use of health (Grossman, 1972; 2004; Reid, 1998; Jacobson, 2000; Chang, 2005; McCarthy, 2006). The benefits derived from health are of two types, namely consumption and production benefits. The consumption benefits of health consist of freedom from pain, a sense of physical wellbeing and an enhanced ability to enjoy daily life. The production benefits are directly related to the ability of the individual to perform economic and social functions. With regard to market based activities, the production benefits are frequently measured in terms of income, suggesting that improved health enables the individual to avoid lower wages resulting from disability or the loss of income due to illness-related absences from the work place.

Jacobson (2000) extended the Grossman model to include the household as the producer of health and shows that rather than attempting to equalize the health capital of different family members, the family will try to attain the equalization of rate of marginal consumption benefits to the rate of marginal net effective costs of health capital. Other studies (Bolin, Jacobson and Lindgren, 2002) used this extended model to analyze household health production in situations where family members have different preferences about allocation of family's resources. The researchers demonstrate that when allocation of health investments are based on decisions made strategically by man and wife the levels of health capital may not be Pareto-efficient. Another version of this model extended the analysis to situations where parties outside the family (e.g. employers) have incentives for investing in the health of a family member (Bolin, Jacobson and Lindgren, 2002a)

Applying an individual's health status as the output the study estimates parameters of a linear health production function:

$$H_j = f(HS_j, BC_j, HR_j, P_j, C_j) \ (1)$$

In equation 1, the subscript j identifies the individual as the unit of analysis. The dependent variable H_j represents a set of variables that measure the physical health status of the individual while HS_j is a vector of variables that serve as surrogates for the structure of the household. The vectors BC_j and HR_j consist of a set of measures that depict the budget constraint and the potential availability of health resources respectively. Finally, the vector P_j consists of a set of surrogates for activities that preserve or promote health while the vector Cj consists of a set of control variables depicting the presence of chronic conditions.

Data Source

The study utilized data from responses of adults 18 years and older to the 2010 survey conducted by the Behavioral Risk Factor Surveillance System (BRFSS) of the US Centers for Disease Control and Prevention (CDC). Assembled in the BRFSS survey are data that describe the individual's demographic characteristics, SES, access to care, life style risk factors, chronic conditions and social support. The set of dependent variables are based on self-reported assessment of the individual's health status. The study selected a subsample of individuals residing in households where there are no adult males (female-headed) and those that have no adult females (male-headed). This sample is used to compare health production in female-headed to production in male-headed households.

Based on past research, the study posits that the gender of the head of the household influences health production and the related effects on the individual's health status. The study tests the hypothesis that female-headed households are more efficient health producers than their male-headed counterparts. Thus the study expects to find that individuals in households that are headed by women will experience better health than individuals in male-headed households.

Summarized in Table 1 are the means, standard deviations and the definitions of the variables examined in this study. As indicated, the focus of analysis is on two surrogates for the health status of the individual. The first (good physical health) is a binary variable that identifies individuals who reported their physical health as excellent, very good or good. Respondents who reported their physical health as not good or poor formed the reference group. Logistic regression analysis was employed to examine the relation between the set of covariates and the binary dependent variable. Limited to those who experienced at least one day of poor physical health in the previous 30-day period, the study conducted multiple regression analysis to determine factors that influence the variation in the number of days that respondents experienced poor physical health.

Table 1. Descriptive Statistics

Variable Name	Variable Definition	Mean	Std. Dev
Good-physical	=1 if they reported excellent, very good or good physical health =0 otherwise.	0.59	0.49
Physical-days	number of days (in 30 day- period) they experienced poor physical health.	13.79	11.57
Household Structure			
Female-H	=1 if there are no adult males in the household=0 otherwise.	0.71	0.46
Children	Number of dependent children (under 18 years) in the household.	0.27	0.75
Adults	Number of adults in the household.	1.12	0.37
Demographics and Socioeconomic Status (SES).			
Old	=1 if aged 55 or older =0 otherwise		
Unemployed	=1 if they are not able to work or have lost a job=0 otherwise.	0.17	0.37
Poor	=1 if household annual income is less than $20,000.	0.35	0.48
College	=1 if has had at least 2 years of college =0 otherwise.	0.56	0.50
Access to Care			
Cost-Bar	=1 If have been unable to see a doctor due to cost =0 otherwise.	0.13	0.33
Social Support			
Cell-Phone	=1 if they have a cell phone available for personal use=0 otherwise.	0.67	0.47
Satisfied	=1 if they are satisfied with their lives.	0.85	0.36
Behavioral factors			
Exercise	=1 if in the past 30 days they participated in any activities or exercises =0 otherwise.	0.68	0.47
Ever-Smoke	=1 if they have smoked at least 100 cigarettes in their entire life =0 otherwise.	0.50	0.50
Drink1	=1 if they have had at least one drink in the past 30 days =0 otherwise.	0.41	0.49
No-Sleep-Days	Number of days they did not get enough sleep in the past 30 . days.	7.61	10.27
Health conditions			
Angina	=1 if they have ever been diagnosed with angina or coronary heart disease=0 otherwise.	0.08	0.27
Disability	=1 if they have a disability =0 otherwise.	0.33	0.47
Use-Equip	=1 if they require the use of assistive devices because of their disability=0 otherwise.	0.17	0.38

As shown in Table 1, the binary variable Female Head identifies households in which no adult males are present. The variable "old" is binary and it identifies individuals aged 55 years or older with younger respondents serving as the reference group. This variable is a surrogate measure of the stock of health capital. The stock of health capital depreciates over time but it is relevant in health production. Older people are expected to have experienced more depreciation of their stock of health unless they spent resources to invest in their health.

Socioeconomic factors are represented by the three variables – poor, unemployed and college. College identifies individuals who have at least two years of college education and unemployed identifies those unable to work and those who have lost their jobs. The variable poor identifies households with less than $20,000 in annual income. It is expected that those with a college education are more efficient producers of health. Poor captures the income/budget constraint relevant in household health production. Access to care is represented by the variable cost-bar which identifies individuals who were unable to access care because of costs. This variable also represents a surrogate for the restrictions imposed by the budget constraint.

Social support/interaction as an input in health production is represented by two binary variables. The first, satisfied, identifies individuals who are satisfied with their lives and the support they receive while the variable cell phone identifies individuals who have access to a cell phone for personal use and communication.

One of the inputs in household health production is the current stock of health capital. This input is represented by the variables angina, disability and use-equip. Angina identifies individuals who have been diagnosed with angina while disability identifies people with a disability. Use-equip identifies individuals whose disability necessitates the use of assistive devices.

The final input into the production process is individual behavior or activities that promote or preserve health. This input was measured by the binary variables Exercise, which identifies respondents who engage in vigorous physical activity. This variable is expected to have a positive effect on the production of health. No-sleep-days is the number of days that the individual did not get enough sleep in the previous 30-day period. The binary variable Ever-Smoke identifies individuals who smoked (100 cigarettes or more in their lifetime) and the variable Drink identifies individuals who consumed at least one drink of alcohol during the previous month. These variables are expected to have a negative effect on health status.

Analysis Method

To test this hypothesis, the study assigned households in the study sample to two groups: households with no male adults (assumed to be female-headed); and households with no female adults (assumed to be male-headed). The analysis was conducted in two stages. First, the study estimated the likelihood of good physical health as a function of the independent variables listed in the equation above. This analysis utilized logistic regression analysis. The second phase of the analysis was limited to respondents who reported at least one day of poor physical health. In this phase the study applied multiple regression analysis to assess factors that influence the variation in number of days that an individual experienced poor physical health. All analysis was conducted using SPSS.

RESULTS

Logistic regression analysis results are presented in table 2. Table 3 presents results from linear regression analysis which estimated variation in number of days (within a 30-day period) that respondents experience poor physical health. As indicated in table 2 logistic regression analysis included 85,137 observations and it correctly identified 72.6% of the respondents. The Nagelkerke R^2 is 0.265. As depicted in table 3, linear regression analysis of days of poor physical health included 32,999 observations and produced a coefficient of multiple determination of 0.299.

Table 2. Logistic regression- likelihood of good physical health

Variable	B	Wald	Sig	EXP (B)	95% C.I. for EXP(B)	
					lower	upper
Household Structure						
Female-Headed	-.206	128.171	000	814	785	843
Children	053	21.657	000	1.055	1.031	1.079
Adults	-.062	8.529	003	940	902	980
Socioeconomic Status (SES)						
Old	086	18.978	000	1.089	1.048	1.132
Poor	-.182	82.500	000	833	801	867
Unemployed	-.428	286.581	000	652	621	685
College	010	309	578	1.010	975	1.046
Cost-Bar	-.419	271.032	000	658	626	692
Social Support						
Satisfied	460	371.842	000	1.584	1.512	1.660
Cell-phone	-.003	031	861	997	960	1.034
Behavioral factors						
Drink	095	31.343	000	1.100	1.064	1.137
Ever-smoke	004	051	821	1.004	972	1.036
No-sleep days	-.028	1109.28	000	972	971	974
Exercise	250	189.163	000	1.284	1.239	1.331
Health conditions						
Angina	-.574	335.294	000	563	530	599
Disability	-1.131	3758.57	000	323	311	335
Use-Equip	-.744	875.420	000	475	452	499
Model Fit Statistics						
Nagelkerke R2 =.265		-2 Log likelihood= 95155.009				
% Correct prediction=72.6		Observations (N)= 85,137				

Contrary to expectations, the variable measuring household gender- structure (female-headed) exerted an adverse and statistically significant ($p<0.0001$) influence on the likelihood of good physical health. This finding implies that relative to those who reside in single-male-headed households, responds from single-female-headed households have a lower likelihood of reporting their physical health as excellent, very good or good. However, once ill, they reported significantly fewer days of illness than their counterparts residing in male-headed households (see table 3). These findings suggest that the question about female headed households being better health producers cannot be answered with these data. Logistic regression results indicate that male-headed households might be better health producers but the linear regression analysis indicates the opposite.

The number of children in the household related positively and significantly ($p<0.0001$) to the likelihood of good physical health. Furthermore, respondents from households with children also experienced fewer days of poor physical health. The number of adults in the household related negatively to the likelihood of good physical health and to the number of days of poor physical health. This finding implies that the more adults there are in the household, the shorter time it takes household members to recover from physical illness. This might be explained by the fact that the adults help to nurse the ill back to health.

Contrary to expectations, respondents aged 55 years or older had a significantly ($p<0.0001$) higher probability of reporting their health as excellent, very good or good. As expected, they experienced significantly ($p<0.0001$) more days of poor physical health.

Measures of socioeconomic status exerted a consistent and significant influence on health status. As expected, those with a college education had higher likelihood of good physical health but the effect is statistically insignificant. However, they experienced significantly ($p<0.0001$) fewer days of poor physical health. Individuals who were unemployed and those residing in poor households had a significantly ($p<0.0001$) lower likelihood of reporting good physical health and they also experienced significantly ($p<0.0001$) more days of poor physical health. These results are consistent with expectations and with results of past studies of SES and health status.

Respondents who were satisfied with their lives were more likely to experience good physical health and reported significantly fewer days of poor physical health than those who were less satisfied with their lives. However, the variable used to measure social interaction (cell-phone) indicated an insignificant influence on the likelihood of good physical health. However, linear regression results indicate that those with cell phones experienced significantly fewer days of poor physical health. Thus confirming that social interaction and support exert positive effects on health and well-being.

Table 3. Linear Regression: Days of poor physical Health

Variable	B	Beta	t	Sig
Household Structure				
Female-Headed	-.513	-.020	-4.184	000
Children	-.360	-.024	-4.688	000
Adults	-.465	-.015	-3.316	001
Socioeconomic Status (SES)				
Old	1.633	068	12.597	000
Poor	1.231	053	9.561	000
Unemployed	3.077	117	21.463	000
College	-.924	-.040	-7.953	000
Cost-Bar	069	002	475	635
Social Support				
Satisfied	-1.812	-.069	-13.378	000
Cell-phone	-.759	-.031	-6.279	000
Behavioral factors				
Drink	-1.350	-.058	-11.655	000
Ever-smoke	943	041	8.622	000
No-sleep days	118	114	22.752	000
Exercise	-2.793	-.119	-24.180	000
Health conditions				
Angina	1.522	043	8.990	000
Disability	4.285	187	35.046	000
Use-Equip	3.950	153	29.409	000
Model Fit Statistics R2= 0.299		Observations (N)= 32,999		

Measures of existing health stock (current health conditions) also performed as expected. Those with a disability or who had experienced angina or had conditions requiring the use of assistive devices had significantly lower likelihood of reporting excellent, very good or good physical health. Furthermore, they experienced significantly more days of poor physical health than respondents with no such conditions.

The results also indicate that physical exercise exerts a positive and statistically significant ($p<0.0001$) influence on the likelihood of good physical health and a negative effect on the number of days an individual experiences poor physical health. This finding is in concert with findings of past research about the health benefits of physical exercise. The results further indicate the importance of sleep to good health. Logistic regression results indicate that the number of days without proper sleep exert a negative and statistically significant ($p<0.0001$) effect on the likelihood of good physical health and are likely to increase the number of days an individual experiences poor physical health.

Results of the other individual behavioral variables are mixed. This is most likely due to inexact measurement. For example, drink includes people who had at least one drink in a thirty day period. This is an inexact measure because it includes a wide variety of drinking levels. The same is true of the ever-smoke which includes individuals who have smoked at least 100 cigarettes in their entire life. Individuals who had at least one alcoholic drink during the 30-day period had a significantly higher likelihood of reporting excellent, very good or good health than those who did not have a drink. Contrary to expectations, ever-smoke has a statistically insignificant effect on the likelihood of good physical health (expected it to be negative and significant). However, those who smoke experience significantly ($p<0.0001$) more days of poor physical health.

IMPLICATIONS AND LIMITATIONS

Prior to a discussion of tentative conclusions and possible policy implications, several limitations of the study should be noted. First, the study was based on cross-sectional data and, as a consequence, causality is neither possible nor implied. Second, self-reported health or days of poor health may suffer from faulty memories of respondents. In addition, measures based on self reported health status usually fail to capture the clinical dimensions of an individual's health status with precision. Accordingly, the examination of the number of days of poor health might benefit from an assessment of the individual's health status, grouped by diagnostic nomenclature. Finally, available data prevented a direct examination of the role played by the prior use of specific components of health care or a more complete spectrum of services that preserve or promote health.

Recognizing the limitations of the study, several tentative conclusions are possible. First, the household gender structure has a consistently significant effect on physical health. Individuals residing in single-female-headed households have a lower likelihood (than respondents living in single-male-headed households) of reporting their physical health as excellent, very good or good. However, for those who experienced days of poor physical health, residing in a single-female-headed household had a positive effect by reducing the number of days of such poor health. This factor could be explained by the fact that women have traditionally taken the role of caregivers so that they nurse those who are ill back to health. Moreover, in the process of bearing and raising children, women have frequently come into contact with healthcare providers thus learning care-giving skills and getting more familiar and at ease with caring for the ill. Males might be less at ease with nursing the ill because society views nursing the ill more as the responsibility or role of female than for males. This fact is supported by research findings on people's perception of nursing as being a female-oriented career; male nurses experiencing discrimination in nursing, and enduring stereotypes about nursing; and male nurses facing gender-based barriers even in nursing education programs (Ozdemir, Akansel and Tunk, 2008; Keogh and O'Lynn, 2007; Tracey and Nicholl, 2007; Roth and Coleman, 2008).

Socioeconomic status variables used in this study (employment, income, education) have the potential for improving health. There is evidence of intersection between socioeconomic status and gender (MacIntyre and Hunt, 1997) and, therefore, with household gender structure. Studies indicate that single-mothers experience higher poverty rates than other households. This fact is true of most developed countries but the US has the highest single mother poverty rates. In-or-near poverty rates for single parent families in 17 high income countries in 2007 ranged from 17% in Denmark to 50% in the US much higher than the 16-European country average of 31%. The high poverty rates among single parents puts children at risk. It is estimated that in the mid 2000s poverty rates among children in single mother families in the US and 15 high income countries ranged from 8% in Denmark to 49% in the US (Legal Momentum, 2010). Results of this study indicate that even after controlling for socioeconomic status, respondents residing in single-female-headed households have a lower probability of reporting their physical health as excellent, very good or good. This finding suggests that children living in single-female-headed households have a double health disadvantage - the probability of poor health from residing in this type of household and from being poor. This implies a need for policies that are supportive of single mothers raising children to ensure promotion and protection of children being raised in poverty.

The effects of the budget constraint indicate that the adoption of policy options that improve access might improve the health status of the economically disadvantaged. In particular, policy analysts might consider an expansion of programs that subsidize the use of health care, an option that promises to relax the limitations imposed by the budget constraint, and to increase the use of health resources leading to improvements in health status. Similarly, an increase in the number of providers who practice in disadvantaged areas might reduce access costs, increase access to care and thereby improve health. It should be noted that the adoption of policy options which subsidize the use of service or increase the availability of providers will likely increase the use of health services by the disadvantaged. Thus, if those in greatest need consume more health services, it is likely that an equitable distribution of health will be accompanied by an inequitable distribution of care.

Results from analysis of the effects of health protecting habits such as abstaining from alcohol and tobacco use on physical health were mixed. Indulging in alcoholic beverages seems to have a positive effect on the likelihood of good physical health but a negative relation with the number of days of poor physical health. Smoking has an insignificant effect on the likelihood of good physical health. However it has a positive effect on the number of days of poor physical health. A possible explanation for these apparent contradictions is the way the use of alcohol and smoking were measured by the questionnaire. Alcohol consumption is measured as consuming at least one drink during the previous month. Smoking is also measured as having smoked at least 100 cigarettes in a lifetime. This measure is inexact because it lumps together many levels of smoking. The results might be different for people who consume greater amounts of alcohol or indulge in more smoking. An active life style exerted a uniformly favorable influence on health status. These findings support policies and practices that encourage abstention from using tobacco and active lifestyles as viable options that promote good health.

The study also indicates that respondents reporting the presence of chronic conditions were more likely to report a poor health status and more days of poor health. Accordingly, the interaction between chronic illness and the physical health status suggest that both must be considered when developing treatment regimens. Such an approach may reduce the adverse effects of chronic illness while improving the physical health status of the individual.

The coefficients derived for the measures of social support were significant and consistent with expectations. Specifically, respondents who reported satisfaction with their lives, and the availability of cell-phone service for personal communications were more likely to report good health. Accordingly, the results suggest social support to be a favorable input in the production of health. Policies designed to improve the social interaction and support available to individuals should be given due consideration in policy formation.

REFERENCES

Ahmed S. M., Tomson G., Ptzold M. and Kabir Z. N. (2005) Socioeconomic status overrides age and gender in determining health-seeking behaviour in rural Bangladesh. *Bull World Health Organ.* 83 (2);81-160.

Amin A. and Bentley M. E. (2002) The Influence of Gender on Rural Women's Illness Experiences and Health-seeking Strategies for Gynaecological Symptoms. *Journal of Health Management*, 4(2),229-249.

August K. J. and Sorkin D. H. (2010). Marital status and gender differences in managing a chronic illness: The function of health-related social control. *Social Science and Medicine*, 71(10) 1831-1838.

Bambra C., Pope D., Swami V., Stanistreet D., Roskam A., Kunst A., and Scott-Samuel A. (2009). Gender, health inequalities and welfare state regimes: a cross-national study of 13 European countries *J. Epidemiol. Community Health* 63:38-44.

Barrera A. (1990) The role of maternal schooling and its interaction with public health programs in child health production. *Journal of Development Economics*, 32,(1), 69-91.

Bender, K. A. and Habermalz, S. (2006) Are There Differences in the Health– Socio-economic Status Relationship over the Life Cycle? Evidence from Germany *LABOUR*,22 (1),107-125.

Berman P., Kendall C., Bhattacharyya K. (1994) The household production of health: integrating social science perspectives on micro-level health determinants. *Social Science and Medicine*, 38 (2), 205-215.

Björklund, Anders and Ginther, Donna K. and Sundström, Marianne, 2004. "Family Structure and Child Outcomes in the United States and Sweden," IZA Discussion Papers 1259, Institute for the Study of Labor (IZA).

Bolin K., Jacobson L., Lindaren B. (2002a) Employer investments in employee health Implications for the family as health producer. *Journal of Health Economics,* 21, 563–583.

Bolin K., Jacobson L., Lindgren B. (2002) The *family as the health producer* – when *spouses act strategically. Journal of* Health *Economics,* 21: 475-495.

Borrell, C. Muntaner, C. Benach, J. and Artazcoz, L. *(2004)* Social class and self-reported health status among men and women: what is the role of work organisation, household material standards and household labour? *Social Science and Medicine,*58(10), 1869-1887.

Bronte-Tinkew, J. and DeJong, G. (2004) Children's nutrition in Jamaica: do household structure and household economic resources matter? *Social Science and Medicine,* 58(3), 499-514.

Bzostek S. and Beck, A. (2008) 2011. Bzostek, Sharon and Audrey Beck. "Familial Instability and Young Children's Physical Health." *Social Science and Medicine* 73.

Case, A. and Paxson, C. (2001)Mothers and others: who invests in children's health? *Journal of Health Economics,* 20 (3), 301-328.

Chang F. (2005) A theory of health investment under competing mortality risks. *Journal of Health Economics,* 24(3):449–463.

Chen, D., Chang, L. and, Yang, M. (2008) Evidence for gender inequality in Health: differential exposure hypothesis or differential vulnerability hypothesis? *Social Science and Medicine,* 67(10),1630-1640.

Clark, L. (1993) Gender and Generation in Poor Women's Household Health Production Experiences. *Medical Anthropology Quarterly, New Series, Racism, Gender, Class, and Health,* 7(4): 386-402.

Cooper H. (2002). Investigating socio-economic explanations for gender and ethnic inequalities in health. *Social Science and Medicine.* 54(5), 693-706.

Courtenay, W. H. (2000) Constructions of masculinity and their influence on men's well-being: a theory of gender and health. *Social Science and Medicine* 50,1385-1401.

DeLeire T. and Lopoo L. M., (2010). Family Structure and the Economic Mobility of. Children. Economic Mobility Project, Pew Charitable Trusts.

Denton M. and Walters V. (1999) Gender differences in structural and behavioral determinants of health: an analysis of the social production of health. *Social Science and Medicine,* 48 (9), 1221-1235.

Denton, M., Prus, S. and Walters, V. (2004) Gender differences in health: a Canadian study of the psychosocial, structural and behavioural determinants of health. *Social Science and Medicine* 58, (12), 2585-2600.

Fayissa, B. and Gutema, P. (2005) Estimating a health production function for Sub-Saharan Africa (SSA) *Applied Economics.* 37(2):155-164

Folland, S., Goodman, A. and Stano M. (2007) *The Economics of Health and Health Care.* 5th Edition, Pearson Prentice Hall.

Frank, R. H. (2008) Microeconomics and Behavior, 7th Edition2008 McGraw-Hill Higher Education.

Gita Sen, Piroska Östlin, Asha George (2007)Unequal, Unfair, Ineffective and Inefficient - Gender Inequity in Health: Why it exists and how we can change it. Report of the Women and Gender Equity Knowledge Network of the Commission on Social

Determinants of Health. Accessed 11-9-2011 from:*http://www.who.int/social_ determinants/resources/csdh_media/wgekn_final_repor_07.pdf.*

Ginther, Pollak R. A. and Ginther D. K. (2003) Does Family Structure Affect Children's Educational Outcomes? *NBER Working Paper.* NBER Working Paper No. w9628.

Gorman B. K. and Braverman, J. (2008) Family Structure Differences in Health Care Utilization among US. Children. *Social Science and Medicine* 67(11):1766-75.

Griffin J. M., Fuhrer R., Stansfeld S. A. and Marmot M. (2002) The importance of low control at work and home on depression and anxiety: do these effects vary by gender and social class? *Social Science and Medicine.* 54(5), 783-798.

Grossman, M. (1972) On the Concept of Health Capital and the Demand for Health. *Journal of Political Economy*, 80(2), 223-255.

Grossman, M. (2004) The demand for health, 30 years later: a very personal retrospective and prospective reflection. *Journal of Health Economics,* 23(4): 629–636.

Guyer, J. I. (1981) The Raw, the Cooked, and the Half-baked: A Note on the Division of Labor by Sex. Working Paper 4X. African Studies Center, Boston, University, Boston, Mass.

Halvorson, S. J. (2004) Women's management of the household health environment: responding to childhood diarrhea in the Northern Areas, Pakistan. *Health and Place*, 10 (1),43-58.

Handa, S. (1996) Expenditure behavior and children's welfare: An analysis of female headed households in Jamaica. *Journal of Development Economics*, 50(1), 165-187.

Heard H. E., Gorman B. K. and Kapinus C. A. (2008) Family Structure and Self-Rated Health in Adolescence and Young Adulthood. *Population Research and Policy Review* 27(6):773-797.

Heiland F. and Liu S. H. (2006). Family structure and wellbeing of out-of-wedlock children. *Demographic Research*, Max Planck Institute for Demographic Research, Rostock, Germany, vol. 15(4), 61-104.

Hughes M. and Waite L. (2002) Health in household context: Living arrangements and health in late middle age. *Journal of health and social behavior*, 43(1) 1-21.

Jacobson, L. (2000) The family as producer of health— an extended Grossman model. *Journal of Health Economics* ,19, 611–637.

Janz, N. K., and Becker, M. H. (1984) Health Belief Model a decade later. *Health Education and Behavior*, 11 (1),1-47.

Johnson, C. F. and Rogers, B. L. (1993) Children's nutritional status in female-headed households in the Dominican Republic. *Social Science and Medicine*, 37(11), 1293-1301.

Kaned T., Zimmer Z., Fang X., and Tang Z. (2009) Gender Differences in Functional Health and Mortality Among the Chinese Elderly:*Testing an Exposure Versus Vulnerability Hypothesis Research on Aging*, 31(3), 361-388.

Keogh B., O'Lynn C. (2007) Male nurses' experiences of gender barriers: Irish and American perspectives. *Nurse Educ.* 32(6):256-9.

Kroshus, E. (2008) Gender, Marital Status, and Commercially Prepared Food Expenditure. *Journal of Nutrition Education and Behavior*, 40(6), 355-360

Kutty N. K. (2008) A household production function model of the production child health and education - the role of housing-related inputs. Available at SSRN: *http://ssrn.com /abstract=1232602.*

Kwawu J. (1993) Gender and household health seeking behaviours. In: Gender, Health, and Sustainable Development. Proceedings of a workshop held in Nairobi, Kenya, 5-8 October 1993, edited by Pandu Wijeyaratne, Lori Jones Arsenault, Janet Hatcher Roberts, and Jennifer Kitts. Ottawa, Canada, International Development Research Centre [IDRC], 1994 Jan.:225-9.

Legal Momentum - the Women's Legal Defense and Education Fund (2010). Single Mothers Since 2000: Falling Farther Down. Available at: *http://www.legalmomentum.org/our-work/women-andpoverty/resources-publications/single-mothers-since-2000.pdf.*

Lynch, J. W., Davey Smith, G., Kaplan, G. A. and House, J. S. (2000) Income inequality and mortality: importance to health of individual income, psychosocial environment, or material conditions. *British Medical Journal*, 320(7423):1200-1204.

MacIntyre S. and Hunt K. (1997) Socio-economic Position, Gender and Health How Do They Interact? *J. Health Psychol.*, 2(3), 315-334.

MacKian S (2003) A review of health seeking behaviour: problems and prospects in Marmot, M., R. G. Wilkinson (eds.). Social Determinants of Health. New York: Oxford University Press. 1999.

Mahler P. and Winkelmann, R. (2004) Single Motherhood and (Un)Equal Educational Opportunities: Evidence for Germany," *Working Papers* 0512, University of Zurich, Socioeconomic Institute.

Marmot, M., R. G. Wilkinson (eds.). Social Determinants of Health. New York: Oxford University Press. 1999.

McCarthy R. (2006) On the dynamics of health capital accumulation. *Social Science and Medicine,* 63, 817–828.

McIntyre, D., Thiede, M., Dahlgren, G. and Whitehead, M. (2006) What are the economic consequences for households of illness and of paying for health care in low- and middle-income country contexts? *Social Science and Medicine*, 62 (4), 858-865.

Messer, E. 1983. The Household Focus in Nutritional Anthropology: An Overview. *Food Nutr. Bull.,* 5(4): 212-25.

McMunn A. M., Nazroo J. Y., Marmot M. G., Boreham R., Goodman R. (2001) Children's emotional and behavioural well-being and the family environment: findings from the Health Survey for England. *Soc. Sci. Med.* 53(4):423–440.

Onyango, A. Tucker, K. and Eisemon, T. (1994) Household headship and child nutrition: A case study in Western Kenya. *Social Science and Medicine*, 39, (12), 1633-1639.

Osler M., McGue M., Lund R., and Christensen K. (2008). Marital status and twins' health and behavior: an analysis of middle-aged Danish twins. *Psychosom Med.*, 70(4):482-7.

Osmani S. and Sen A. (2003).The hidden penalties of gender inequality: fetal origins of ill-health. *Economics and Human Biology*. 1, 105–121.

Ozdemir A., Akansel N., and Tunk G. C. (2008) Gender And Career: Female And Male Nursing Students' Perceptions Of Male Nursing Role In Turkey. *Health Science Journal*, 2(3) 153-161.

Ozdemir A., Akansel N., and Tunk G. C. (2008) Gender And Career: Female And Male Nursing Students' Perceptions Of Male Nursing Role In Turkey. *Health Science Journal*, 2(3) 153-161.

Pizzetti, P., Manfredini, M. and Lucchetti, E. (2005) Variations in late-age mortality by household structure and marital status in Parma, Italy. *Ageing and Society,* 25(6), 305-318.

Read, J. G. and Gorman, B. K. (2006) Gender inequalities in US adult health: The interplay of race and ethnicity. *Social Science and Medicine*, 62(5): 1045-1065.

Ried W. (1998) Comparative dynamic analysis of the full Grossman model *Journal of Health Economics,* 17: 383–425.

Robbins, M. S. Briones, E. Schwartz, J. S., Dillon, F. R. Mitrani, V. B. (2006) Differences in Family Functioning in Grandparent and Parent-Headed Households in a Clinical Sample of Drug-Using African American Adolescents. *Cultural Diversity and Ethnic Minority Psychology*, 12, (1), 84-100.

Rodgers G. B. Income and inequality as determinants of mortality: an international cross-section analysis. *Population Studies* 1979; 33: 343-5.

Roth J. E. and Coleman C. L. (2008). Perceived and real barriers for men entering nursing: implications for gender diversity. *J. Cult. Divers*, 15(3), 148-152.

Rout, H. S. (2006) Gender inequality in household health expenditure: the case of urban Orissa *NAGARLOK*, 38(3), 44-48.

Sauerborn R., Adams A. and Hien M. (1996) Household strategies to cope with the economic costs of illness. *Soc. Sci. Med.*, 43(3):291-301.

Schmeer, K. (2009) Father absence due to migration and child illness in rural Mexico. *Social Science and Medicine*, Volume 69, Issue 8, October 2009, Pages 1281-1286.

Schoenborn C. A. Marital status and health: United States, 1999–2002 Advance data from vital and health statistics; no 351. Hyattsville, Maryland: *National Center for Health Statistics*. 2004.

Schultz, J. A., O'Brien, M. and Tadesse, B. (2008) Social capital and self-rated health: Results from the US 2006 social capital survey of one community. *Social Science and Medicine*, 67, 606-617.

Scutella, R. and Wooden, M. (2008)The effects of household joblessness on mental health. *Social Science and Medicine*,67(1)88-100.

Sen G., Piroska Östlin P., and George A. (2007)Unequal, Unfair, Ineffective and Inefficient - Gender Inequity in Health: Why it exists and how we can change it. Report of the Women and Gender Equity Knowledge Network of the Commission on Social Determinants of Health. Accessed 11-9-2011 from: *http://www.who.int/social_ determinants/resources/csdh_media/wgekn_final_report_07. pdf.*

Takeda, Y., Kawachi, I., Yamagata, Z., Hashimoto, S., Matsumura, Y., Oguri, S., and Okayama, A. (2004). Multigenerational family structure in Japanese society: Impacrs on stress and health behaviors among women and men. *Social Science and Medicine*, 59, 69-81.

Thornton J.(2002) Estimating a Health Production Function for the US: Some New Evidence. *Applied Economics, 34*(1);59-62.

Tracey C., Nicholl H. (2007) The multifaceted influence of gender in career progress in nursing. *J. Nurs. Manag.*, 15(7),677-82.

Turagabeci, A. R., Nkakamura K., Kizuki M., and Takano, T. (2007) Family structure and health, how companionship acts as a buffer against ill health. *Health and Quality of Life Outcomes* 2007, 5:61 doi:10.1186/1477-7525-5-61.

Umberson D. (2002)Gender, marital status and the social control of health behavior. *Social Science and Medicine*, 34(8) 907-917.

Waldron I., Weiss C. C. and Hughes M. E. (1997). Marital status effects on health: are there differences between never married women and divorced and separated women? *Social Science and Medicine* 45(9):1387-97.

Walker, J. L. Holben, D. H. Kropf, M. L. Holcomb, J. P. and Anderson, H. (2007) Household Food Insecurity Is Inversely Associated with Social Capital and Health in Females from Special Supplemental Nutrition Program for Women, Infants, and Children Households in Appalachian Ohio. *Journal of the American Dietetic Association*, 107(11), 1989-1993.

Walters V., McDonough P., and Strohschein L. (2002) The influence of work, household structure, and social, personal and material resources on gender differences in health: an analysis of the 1994 Canadian National Population Health Survey. *Social Science and Medicine.* 54(5), 677-692.

Wilkinson R. G. Health inequalities: relative or absolute material standards? *British Medical Journal* 1997; 314:591-5.

Wilkinson R. G. and Marmot M. (Eds) 2003. Social Determinants of Health: the Solid Facts. Second Edition. World Health Organization, Copenhagen Denmark 2003.

Wilkinson R. G. Class mortality differentials, income distribution and trends in poverty 1921-1981. *Journal of Social Policy* 1989; 18 (3): 307-35.

Wilkinson R. G. National mortality rates: the impact of inequality? *American Journal of Public Health* 1992; 82: 1082-4.

Yoo, J. and Lim, L. (2009) The trend in the income status of children in female-headed families: A replication and update. *Children and Youth Services Review*, 31,(4),482-488.

In: Psychology of Gender Differences
Editor: Sarah P. McGeown

ISBN: 978-1-62081-391-1
© 2012 Nova Science Publishers, Inc.

Chapter 14

THE COVARIATES OF MENTAL HEALTH WITH SPECIAL REFERENCE TO HOUSEHOLD GENDER-STRUCTURE

Ari K. Mwachofi[1] and Robert Broyles

University of Oklahoma Health and Sciences Center, US

ABSTRACT

The World Health Organization (WHO) estimates that over 450 million people world-wide suffer from mental illnesses and many more have mental problems. Mental illnesses impose a heavy cost burden on households, governments and on society at large. The costs include: reduced supply of labor and its productivity, public support, limited educational attainment, incarceration, homelessness, medical complications, premature mortality and the heavy costs to family members who bear the emotional and financial burden of these illnesses. In the United States, the total annual cost for mental illness is estimated at $205 billion. Gender differences in mental health are well documented. However, little attention is given to household gender-structure and its effects on the production of mental health at the household level. Such information is necessary for effective policies that would improve the foundation of mental health production at the household level.

Recognizing the household as a micro-level production unit and as a critical foundation for health production and maintenance, the study applied production economics to analyze household gender-structure as an input in the production of mental health.

The study relied on the Investment Theory of Demand as the organizing frame of reference, and data derived from individual responses to the 2010 survey conducted by the Behavioral Risk Factor Surveillance System (BRFSS) of the US Centers for Disease Control and Prevention (CDC). The study estimated a health production function in two stages: a logistic regression analysis was conducted to examine the relation between household gender structure, other covariates and the likelihood of good mental health. For those reporting mental illness the study estimated the likelihood of being diagnosed with depression and anxiety disorders. Limited to those who experienced at least one day

---

[1] Email address: *amwachof@ouhsc.edu.*

of poor mental health in the previous month, the study conducted a multivariate analysis, estimating variations in the number of days the individual experienced poor mental health.

Relative to being in a male-headed household, being in a female-headed household exerted a significant adverse effect on mental health. It significantly (p<0.0001) increased the likelihood for being diagnosed with depression or an anxiety disorder. Being in a female headed household also significantly reduced the likelihood of good mental health. The analysis shows this to be true even after controlling for demographics, SES, access to care, social support, behavioral factors and current health conditions. Furthermore, multivariate analysis indicates that being in a female-headed household is associated with significant (p<0.0001) increases in the number of days an individual experienced poor mental health. Other significant predictors of mental health are: education, employment, social support, individual health behaviors (tobacco use, sleep, physical exercise) and chronic conditions such as asthma and having a disability.

Individuals residing in single-female-headed households have a significant mental health disadvantage. They have a higher likelihood of experiencing mental illnesses and for longer periods. It is important to gather more information about factors within the single-female-headed households that adversely affect mental health production. Such information would be invaluable in improving mental health at the household level and ultimately at the societal level.

INTRODUCTION

The WHO defines mental health as *"a state of well-being in which an individual realizes his or her own abilities, can cope with the normal stresses of life, can work productively and is able to make a contribution to his or her community. In this positive sense, mental health is the foundation for individual well-being and the effective functioning of a community"*. Estimates from the WHO indicate that over 450 million people world-wide suffer from mental disorders and many more have mental problems. One half of all mental disorders begin in childhood before the age of 14, and about 20% of the world's children are estimated to have mental disorders and problems (WHO, 2010). It is difficult to tackle the world-wide mental health problem for several reasons: there is scarcity and inequity in distribution of skilled human resources across the world; regions with high needs for mental health services have the lowest capacity for providing such services; lack of public health leadership in mental health; and there are many barriers to mental health services. Low-income countries experience the worst shortages in mental health professionals. In some countries there are 0.05 psychiatrists and 0.42 nurses per 100,000 people or one psychiatrist for every one to four million people (WHO, 2010).

Among the most intractable problems confronting the health analyst is the rising costs of mental health services. The total yearly cost for mental illness in the United States is estimated at $205 billion (National Mental Health Association, 2010). The costs of mental illness consist of direct and incidental components. Direct costs are usually measured by spending on the provision of mental health services. One quarter of hospital stays for adults in U.S. community hospitals involve mental health and substance abuse (MHSA) disorders. Individuals with mental health and substance abuse disorders have longer hospital stays. Adults with a principal MHSA diagnosis remain in the hospital for an average of 8 days compared with 5 days for other diagnoses. Hospitalizations for the 5 most common principal

MHSA diagnoses cost $9.9 billion nationally. Mental illnesses impose a heavy burden on public spending. It is estimated that 33% of all uninsured stays, 29% of Medicaid stays, and 26% of Medicare stays are related to MHSA disorders, compared with only 16 percent of privately insured stays. In 2004, over 66 percent of adult hospital stays with MHSA diagnoses were financed by the government (Owens, Myers, Elixhauser, and Brach, 2007).

Incidental costs of mental illness are imposed on society and include: losses in productivity due to reduced labor supply and premature mortality, the costs of public support, limited educational attainment, incarceration, homelessness, medical complications associated with serious mental illness, high prevalence of pulmonary disease resulting from higher smoking rates among the mentally ill, and the costs to family members who bear the emotional and financial burden of these illnesses. Serious mental illnesses reduce annual earnings by about $193.2 billion in US (Kessler, Heeringa, Lakoma, Petukhova, Rupp, Shoenbaum, Wang and Zaslavsky, 2008). These estimates understate the economic impact of mental illness since the costs for individuals hospitalized in institutions, incarcerated, or those who are homeless are not included in the calculations. For example, expenditures related to criminal justice, general health, mental health, and social welfare services over a four-year period for arrestees with serious mental illnesses in a large Florida county, amounted to $94,957,465, with a median cost of $15,134 per person. The highest expenditures were associated with individuals who were 40 years old with a psychotic disorder (Petrila, Andel, Constantine, and Robst, 2010). The World Health Organization (WHO) estimates indicate that in 2000, mental health contributed 12.3% of total global loss of disability adjusted life years (DALYs). This is indicative of the productivity losses world-wide and the urgent economic need to address mental health effectively.

Gender Differences in Mental Health

Mental health is determined by socio-economic, biological, and environmental factors (WHO, 2010). There is a strong inverse relationship between social position and health. Research finds evidence indicating that people in low socioeconomic positions experience two to two and half times more adverse health effects than those in the highest socioeconomic positions (Dohrenwend, 1990; Najman, 1993; Bartley and Owen, 1996). One's socioeconomic position determines access to resources which impact the social determinants of health including, education, income, social position, employment, early childhood, transportation and their health behaviors (health habits). There are gender-based differences in power and socioeconomic position. For example, WHO estimates that of the 50 million people affected by violent conflicts, civil wars, disasters, and displacement 80% are women and children; lifetime prevalence rates of violence against women ranges from 16% to 50%; at least one in five women suffer rape or attempted rape in their lifetime (WHO, 2006). Gender-based power and socioeconomic differences affect women's mental health negatively, making gender a structural determinant of health.

Gender differences in mental health are well documented. There are differences in the illness types, onset age, symptoms, coping mechanisms, treatment seeking behavior, diagnosis, treatment and responses to treatment (WHO, 2002). A major mental health gender difference in adulthood is higher prevalence of depression and anxiety among women while men have higher prevalence of substance abuse disorders and antisocial behaviors (WHO,

2006). Examination of patterns of mental health co-morbidity indicate that women have a higher mean level of internalizing (resulting in anxiety or depression diagnosis) while men showed a higher mean level of externalizing (resulting in substance abuse and antisocial disorders) (Eaton et al., 2011).

In almost all societies and social contexts depression is reported to be twice as common in women as in men. Prior to teenage, depression rates are similar between males and females. After thirteen years of age, depression affects proportionately more females than males (WHO, 2002). According to estimates of the WHO, 41.9% of disability from neuropsychiatric disorders among women is due to depression, while the proportion for men is 29.3% (WHO, 2006). Explanations for the differences in depression rates include: gender stereotyping in diagnosis; men have significantly higher levels of serotonin in their blood than women (serotonin is necessary for mood maintenance); girls are more unhappy with their body shapes than boys; girls experience more sexual abuse than boys; girls tend to have more negative reactions to abuse than boys (Burt and Stein, 2002; Hankin and Abramson, 1999; Nishizawa et al., 1997; Muck-Seler , Pivac, and Jakovljevic, 1999). Differences in mental health symptoms and coping mechanisms are: women tend to report more physical symptoms than men (Silverstein, 2002; Barsky, Peekna and Borus, 2001); women experiencing depression are more likely to be unmarried or to complain about marital problems (Kornstein et al., 2000); and they are also more likely to develop alcohol problems (Caldwell et al., 2002; Wang and Patten, 2002; Mascato et al.,1997).

There are also some disease specific differences. Symptoms of Schizophrenia (which affects about 2 million Americans, Spearing, 1999) differ by gender. Whereas men's symptoms appear earlier and more intensely than women's (USll et al., 2001), women tend to experience more depression and impairment in cognition, conceptualization, apathy and in speech (Danielsson, Flyckt and Edman, 2001). Furthermore, women respond differently to schizophrenia treatment. Consequently, women tend to require more complex treatment regimens (Kelly, Conley and Tamminga, 1999; Melkersson, Hulting, and Rane, 2001; Labelle, Light and Dunbar, 2001).

There is evidence suggesting that the underlying mechanism for Alzheimer's disease is different in men and women (Lapane et al., 2001). There are indications that that sex hormones (testosterone and estrogen) affect levels of the protein amyloid beta differently (the protein that contributes to development of plaque in the brain of those affected by Alzheimer's disease) (Mayeux at al., 1999; Gandy et al., 2001; Xu, et al., 1998). Although men carry a higher Alzheimer's disease mortality risk, women have a higher risk of developing the disease (Di Carlo et al., 2002; McDowell, 2001). Relative to men, women with schizophrenia report less need for provision of food, personal and home care, and other assistance with daily living activities (Ochoa et al., 2001). They also experience more severe damage to the white brain matter and changes in brain nucleus basalis of Meynert than men do (Sawada et al., 2000; Salehi, Martinez, and Swaab, 1998). Furthermore, women with Alzheimer's have lower insulin levels than men, making women more susceptible to diabetes (Craft et al., 1999).

Some differences relate to women's vulnerability due to power differentials between men and women. Subsequent to a traumatic experience, women's risk of post-traumatic stress disorder (PTSD) is twice as high as men's (Yonkers et al, 2003). Although women have a higher likelihood of experiencing assault, injury or sexual abuse by someone they know, they are less likely to abuse drugs at the time of the assault or need emergency treatment

(Holbrook et al, 2002). Women's rates of anxiety disorders are higher than men's (Yonkers et al., 2003).

Gender differences in mental health are compounded by differences in help-seeking patterns and gender stereotyping in diagnosis and treatment. For example, females have a higher likelihood of being diagnosed with depression and being prescribed psychotropic drugs while men are more likely to be diagnosed as having problems with alcohol (WHO, 2006). The differences make a gendered framework of analysis a useful instrument in analyzing health production at the household level.

Organizing Frame of Reference

Policy formation and implementation designed to reduce the costs of mental illness may benefit from a conceptual distinction between the demand for mental health and the demand for mental health services. Consistent with the Investment Theory of Demand, ITD, proposed by Grossman (1972), the demand for mental health services is derived from a demand for mental health or the freedom from mental illness. The ITD regards health as capital stock that provides services or benefits in multiple periods and depreciates with the passage of time. Health promoting activities, to include the use of health services, are viewed as an investment in the stock of health, suggesting that the change in health is given by the difference between the effects of health promoting activity and the use of health. Accordingly, the ITD emphasizes the preservation and promotion rather than the consumption of health.

The benefits that are derived from the stock of health are of two types, namely consumption and production benefits. The consumption benefits of health consist of freedom from pain, a sense of physical wellbeing and an enhanced ability to enjoy daily life. The production benefits are directly related to the ability of the individual to perform economic and social functions. With regard to market based activities, the production benefits are frequently measured in terms of income, suggesting that improved health enables the individual to avoid lower wages resulting from disability or the loss of income due to illness related to lower work productivity and increased absences from the work place.

The ITD assumes that individual behavior is constrained by technological and economic or financial factors. The technological constraint is represented by the health production function that links the use of health inputs, including health services, to the final output, health. The health production function exhibits diminishing marginal returns of health inputs. The economic or financial limits on the individual's behavior are imposed by the budget constraint which indicates that, as the price of health inputs declines or the individual's income increases, the individual is able to acquire more health resources. The acquisition of additional health inputs, when combined with the technological constraints imposed by the health production function, potentially results in an incremental improvement in the individual's stock of health.

The increment to an individual's stock of health also is contingent on the availability of health resources. The resources combined to produce health include health services, nutrition, housing, exercise equipment and the social support provided by members of the household or members of the individual's social environment. In addition, the theory of household production suggests that an essential ingredient is the time and effort committed by the individual or members of the household in the process of producing health and the allocation of household resources to health production and the distribution of such resources among members of the household. It is reasonable to assume that the head of the household allocates household resources among competing wants (including the process of producing health) and distributes such resources among household members.

Of particular importance in this study are the expected effects exerted on mental health status by the household gender-structure as represented by the gender of the household head. The expected direction of relation between each covariate and mental health status is described in more detail in the following discussion.

Household Structure

The household is a unit that acquires, assembles, allocates and consumes health resources, thereby producing health. Its structure, composition and social relations influence acquisition and distribution of resources including food, income and other health resources (Messer, 1983; Guyer, 198; Ngom, Wawire, Gandaho, Klissou, Adjimon, et al., 2000). Household structure influences access to resources used to produce health such as food, housing, immunization, access to care and behavioral · choices (e.g. smoking, diet and exercise). Often the household head is also the chief provider and distributor of household resources among family members and the allocator of resources among competing household wants, decisions that influence the production of health in the household. The head of the household may also be responsible for the organization and provision of care required by family members. For the purposes of this study, the influence of the gender of the head of the household on the production of mental health is of primary importance.

Kutty (2008) demonstrates that family stability is an important ingredient that influences a child's health and education. Empirical findings indicate that a child who lives in an unstable family that is characterized by violence, drunkenness and high mobility will experience poor mental health. Robbins, Briones, Schwartz, Dillon and Mitrani (2006) compared adolescents who resided in households headed by grandparents to those headed by parents. The results suggested a similar set of behavioral problems. In an examination of the investment in children's health, Case and Paxson (2001), found that the mother dominates decisions concerning investment in health and that step-mothers are not substitutes for birth-mothers in this domain.

Using data from less developed countries, several studies compared health decisions of male and female household heads. Handa (1996) found that the presence of a female decision maker generally increases the share of the household budget allocated to children and to family goods. The study also found that households headed by women spend more on adult wear and less on health but that such expenditures are partially offset by the use of other health inputs. Bronte-Tinkew and DeJong (2004) assessed the influence of household structure and resource distribution characteristics on children's nutritional status in Jamaica. They compared the impact of different types of household structures (i.e. single-parent, two-parent, cohabiting and extended families) on child nutrition so as to determine whether household structure and household resources interact to affect child nutrition. The results indicated that the physical stature of children living in a single parent home was less well developed than their counterparts who resided in a cohabiting household. There were also indications that children in single-parent low-income families with siblings and low-income extended families with siblings were more likely to have low height for age. In a study in rural Mexico communities, Schmeer (2009) found that the odds of children being ill were 39% higher for any illness and 51% higher for diarrhea when fathers were absent compared with those in which fathers were present in the household. Yoo and Lim (2009) found that children in female-headed households were more economically disadvantaged than children in married-couple families.

The gender of the head of the household has also been associated with differences in nutrition patterns. In a study of children's nutrition in the Dominican Republic, Johnson and Rogers (1993) found that male-headed households had higher incomes and more calories and protein per adult equivalent than was available in female-head households. Despite the economic and dietary advantages of male-headed households, children of female-headed households were taller and heavier for their age than those of two parent homes. In a similar study in Kenya, Onyango, Tucker and Eisemon (1994) compared child nutrition in female-headed versus male-headed households. They found that children in female headed households consumed a greater variety of foods. Despite a greater prevalence of stunting, there was a lower prevalence of low weight for age among children of female heads. Kroshus (2008) examined per capita household expenditure on commercially prepared food in relation to gender and marital status. The results indicated that households headed by unmarried men spent a significantly greater proportion of their food budget on commercially prepared food than their married male peers and female headed households. There are mixed results on the role of household gender-structure on the health of household members. Furthermore, most of the studies were conducted using data from low-income and less developed countries. Therefore, this study will use data from the US to determine the effect of household gender-structure on the production of mental health.

The Budget Constraint

Consistent with normative economic theory, the budget constraint reflects relative prices and the income of the individual or family unit. Holding relative prices constant, economic theory suggests that a more restrictive budget constraint is accompanied by a decline in the consumption of normal goods. The relation between socio-economic status (SES) (sometimes measured as income) and health is well documented (Kawachi et al., 1994; Wilkinson, 1997, 1992, 1989; Rodgers, 1979; Marmot and Wilkinson, 1999; Lynch et al., 2000; Raphael, 2001; Wilkinson and Marmot, 2003; Ahmed, Tomson, Ptzold and Kabir, 2005;). Bender and Habermalz (2006) found that the health–income relationship varied across the life cycle and between genders and labor force status. SES and lifestyle factors are the most important predictors of mortality rates in the US. Additional medical care is relatively ineffective in lowering mortality and increasing life expectancy (Thornton 2002). Accordingly, this study controls for income in order to isolate the effects of household gender-structure on mental health.

Health Resources

Health resources include not only health services, nutrition and housing but also the social support that is available to the individual. Several studies provide evidence in support of the proposition that social support is an ingredient in the process of improving health status (Ahearn and Hendryx ,2005; Netuveli et al., 2008; Awasthi and Mishra, 2007; Miller, Rohleder, and Cole, 2009; Yee, Cavigelli, Delgado, and McClintock, 2008; Pai and Barrett, 2007; Glei, Landau, Goldman, et al., 2005). Based on previous findings, this study controls for social support so as to examine the role of household gender-structure.

Study Objective and Data Source

Recognizing the importance of improving mental health and controlling the cost of mental illness, the purpose of this paper is to examine instrumental covariates of the individual's mental health status with particular attention to the structure of the household. Adopting the ITD as the organizing frame of reference, the study examines the parameter estimates of the linear function

$$H_j = f(BC_j, HR_j, HS_j, P_j, C_j) \qquad (1)$$

where the subscript j identifies the individual as the unit of analysis. The dependent variable H_j represents a set of variables that measure the mental health status of the individual while BC_j is a vector of variables that measure the budget constraint. The vectors HR_j and HS_j consist of a set of health resources and measures of the household structure respectively. Finally, the vector P_j consists of a set of surrogates for activities that preserve or promote mental health while the vector C_j consists of a set of control variables depicting the presence of chronic conditions.

The study relies on data derived from individual responses to the 2010 survey conducted by the Behavioral Risk Factor Surveillance System (BRFSS) of the US Centers for Disease Control and Prevention (CDC). Assembled in the BRFSS survey are data that describe the individual's, mental health status, demographic characteristics, SES, access to care, life style risks, the of presence chronic conditions, characteristics of the individual's household and measures of social support. The set of dependent variables are based on a self reported assessment of mental health status and limited activity resulting from poor mental health.

METHODS

The study selected a sub-sample of data from responses of the 2010 BRFSS. The subsample consisted of individuals residing in two types of households: those that had no male adults present (single-female-headed), and those with no adult females present (single-male-headed). Summarized in Table 1 are the means, standard deviations and the definitions of the variables examined in this study. There are four surrogates for the mental health status of the individual. The first, *Good Mental Health*, is a binary variable that identifies individuals who reported no days of poor mental health during the previous month. The second and third measures of mental health are the variables *depression* and *anxiety* which identify individuals diagnosed with depression and anxiety disorders respectively. Logistic regression analysis was employed to examine the relation between the set of covariates and these binary dependent variables. The fourth surrogate for mental health measured the number of days that the individual experienced poor mental health in the previous month. This measure only included individuals who had experienced at least one day of poor mental health during the previous month.

Table 1. Descriptive Statistics

Dependent Variables	Variable Definition.	Mean	Std. Dev
Good-mental	=1 if reported excellent, very good or good mental health.	0.67	0.47
Depression	=1 if diagnosed with depression.	0.21	0.41
Anxiety	=1 if diagnosed with an anxiety disorder.	0.15	0.36
Mental-days	number of days of poor mental health in the past 30-day period.	4.13	8.65
Household Structure			
Female-H	=1 if there are no adult males in the household.	0.71	0.46
Children	Number of dependent children (<18 years) in the household.	0.27	0.75
Adults	Number of adults in the household.	1.12	0.37
Demographics and Socioeconomic variables.			
young	=1 if aged 18 to 35 years.	0.08	0.27
Old	=1 if aged 75 years or older.	0.68	0.47
Poor	=1 if annual household income <$20,000.	0.35	0.48
Unemployed	=1 if they are not able to work or have lost a job.	0.17	0.37
Income75	=1 if annual household income is $75,000 or greater.	0.11	0.32
College	=1 of they have at least 2 years of college education.	0.56	0.50
Access to care			
Cost-Bar	=1 If have been unable to see a doctor due to cost.	0.13	0.33
Social and Emotional Support.			
Satisfied	=1 if they are satisfied with their lives.	0.85	0.36
Emotional	=1 if they always get social and emotional support.	0.46	0.50
Cell-Phone	=1 if they have a cell phone available for personal use.	0.67	0.47
Behavioral Factors			
Exercise	=1 they did physical activities or exercises such as running, walking calisthenics, or gardening.	0.68	0.47
Ever-Smoke	=1 if they have smoked at least 100 cigarettes in their lives.	0.50	0.50
Tobacco	=1 if other tobacco use such as snuff, chew tobacco etc .	0.02	0.15
No-Sleep-Days	Number of days they did not get enough sleep in the past 30-days.	7.61	10.3
Sleep-enough	=1 if they slept enough daily in the past 30 days.	0.41	0.49
Health Conditions			
Angina	=1 if ever diagnosed with angina.	0.08	0.27
Asthma	=1 if they have been diagnosed with asthma.	0.15	0.35
Disability	=1 if they have a disability.	0.33	0.47

The set of covariates included: household structure in which the respondent resided, demographics, socioeconomic status, access to healthcare, social and emotional support, individual behaviors that promote or harm health, and current health conditions indicative of the presence of chronic conditions. The *household structure* is measured by three variables. The first depicts the gender of a single head of the household. In Table 1, the binary variable Female Head identifies households in which a female is the head and no adult males are present. The reference category are individuals residing in single-male-headed households with no adult females present. Other household structure variables are: the number of adults and the number of children residing in the household.

Demographics and socioeconomic status was measured by several binary variables including: old, young, unemployed and college. Old identified individuals who are 55years or older while young identified individuals aged 18 to 35 years. The control group is individuals aged betwee 36 and 54 years. College is a surrogate measure for education. It identifies individuals who had a least two-years of college education while unemployed identified those who were unemployed, had lost their jobs or were unable to work.

Table 2. Logistic regression- likelihood of good mental health

Covariates	B	Wald	Sig.	Exp(B)	95% C.I. EXP(B)	
					Lower	Upper
Household Structure						
Female-H	-0.44	498.54	0.000	0.64	0.62	0.67
Children	-0.02	3.97	0.046	0.98	0.96	1.00
Adults	-0.10	20.50	0.000	0.91	0.87	0.95
Demographics and SES						
Income75	0.15	30.17	0.000	1.16	1.10	1.22
Old	0.49	540.83	0.000	1.64	1.57	1.71
young	-0.15	21.76	0.000	0.86	0.81	0.92
Unemployed	-0.58	503.04	0.000	0.56	0.53	0.59
Poor	-0.03	2.09	0.148	0.97	0.93	1.01
College	-0.10	24.58	0.000	0.91	0.88	0.94
Access to Care						
Cost-Bar	-0.43	271.40	0.000	0.65	0.62	0.69
Social Support						
Satisfied	1.26	2654.43	0.000	3.52	3.35	3.69
Emotional	0.91	2272.35	0.000	2.49	2.40	2.59
Cell-Phone	-0.10	23.85	0.000	0.90	0.87	0.94
Behavioral Factors						
Ever-Smoke	-0.18	112.92	0.000	0.83	0.80	0.86
Sleep-Enough	0.95	2399.56	0.000	2.58	2.49	2.68
Current Health Conditions						
Angina	-0.16	22.97	0.000	0.85	0.80	0.91
Asthma	-0.19	64.80	0.000	0.83	0.79	0.87
Disability	-0.58	889.71	0.000	0.56	0.54	0.58
Model Fit Stats	N=84659	*Nag R²=0.321	Correct prediction 75.8%		-2Log likelihood=84893	

*Nagelkerke R².

The budget constraint is measured by the binary variables Poor and income75. The variable Poor identifies individuals who reported an annual household income less than $20,000. The variable income75 identifies individuals whose annual household income was $75,000 or more. The income reference group is individuals whose household income ranged between $20,000 and $74,000.

The availability of health resources is represented by two surrogates: cost-barrier, and social support available to the individual. Cost Barrier identifies respondents who were unable to access health care because of prohibitive costs of care, so to some degree, it also measures budgetary constraints. As indicated in Table 1 social support is measured by *emotional*, a binary variable which identifies respondents who indicated they always receive emotional and social support when needed. The control group consists of those who usually, sometimes, rarely or never receive social support. In addition, Satisfied identifies respondents who were very satisfied with their lives while the binary variable Cell-Phone identifies individuals who had cell phone available for personal use and personal communications.

Individual behaviors were measured by some binary variables including Ever-smoke Tobacco, sleep-enough or no-sleep-days. Ever-smoke identified individuals who had smoked at least 100 cigarettes in their life-time while Tobacco identified individuals who indulge in other smoke-less tobacco products such as snuff chewing tobacco and others. Sleep enough identified individuals who enjoyed enough sleep everyday in the previous 30-day period while no-sleep-days measured the number of days that an individual did not have enough sleep during the previous 30 days. Exercise identifies respondents who engage in vigorous physical activity such as running, walking, gardening and others.

Recognizing that a poor physical health status may influence the mental health of the individual, a set of binary variables that identify individuals who reported the presence of chronic condition was included in all analyses. Specifically, the binary variables Angina and Asthma identify individuals who reported a previous angina or had asthma respectively while the variable disability identifies individuals who had a disability.

RESULTS

Results of the analyses are displayed in Tables 2-5. Tables 2, 3, and 4 display results of logistic regression that estimated the likelihood of good mental health (table 2); being diagnosed with depression (table 3) and being diagnosed with anxiety disorder (table 4). The logistic regression analysis of the binary variable Good Mental Health (table 2) was based on the responses of 84,659 individuals while analyses for depression and anxiety disorders were based on responses of 15,333 and 15,323 individuals respectively (tables 3 and 4). The regression analysis of number of days of poor mental health (Table 5) was limited to the 32,222 respondents who reported experiencing at least one day of poor mental health during the previous month. For the likelihood of good mental health, logistic regression results indicate that the model correctly classified 75.8% of the respondents, while the coefficient of multiple determination derived by the regression analysis was 0 .321. For the likelihood of being diagnosed with depression, the model correctly classified 81.1% of the respondents and the coefficient of multiple determination derived was 0.263.

Table 3. Logistic regression- likelihood of Depression Diagnosis

Covariates	B	Wald	Sig.	Exp(B)	95% C.I. EXP(B)	
					Lower	Upper
Household Structure						
Female-H	0.58	119.69	0.000	1.79	1.61	1.99
Children	-0.07	5.28	0.022	0.93	0.88	0.99
Adults	-0.04	0.57	0.449	0.96	0.85	1.07
Demographics and SES						
Income75	-0.01	0.03	0.863	0.99	0.85	1.15
Old	-0.33	37.45	0.000	0.72	0.65	0.80
young	-0.28	9.09	0.003	0.76	0.63	0.91
Unemployed	0.74	151.12	0.000	2.09	1.86	2.35
Poor	-0.01	0.01	0.914	0.99	0.89	1.11
College	0.28	31.92	0.000	1.32	1.20	1.45
Access to Care						
Cost-Bar	0.14	5.09	0.024	1.15	1.02	1.30
Social Support						
Satisfied	-0.99	306.79	0.000	0.37	0.33	0.42
Emotional	-0.72	197.57	0.000	0.49	0.44	0.54
Cell-Phone	0.23	18.87	0.000	1.25	1.13	1.39
Behavioral Factors						
Ever-Smoke	0.36	63.80	0.000	1.43	1.31	1.56
Sleep-Enough	-0.56	126.66	0.000	0.57	0.52	0.63
Current Health Conditions						
Angina	0.31	15.58	0.000	1.36	1.17	1.59
Asthma	0.45	63.98	0.000	1.57	1.41	1.76
Disability	0.81	286.07	0.000	2.25	2.05	2.47
Model fit	N=15333	*Nag R^2=0.263	Correct prediction=81.1%		-2log likelihood=13263.702	

*Nagelkerke R^2.

Estimates of the likelihood of being diagnosed with anxiety disorders indicate that the model correctly classified 85.5% of the respondents and the coefficient of multiple determination derived from this regression was 0.215. As displayed in table 5, the coefficient of multiple determination derived from linear regression analysis of the number of days a respondent experienced poor mental health is 0.327. Given that the study uses cross-sectional data, the models were a pretty good fit for these data.

The results indicate that relative to residing in male-headed household, respondents residing in households headed by females with no adult males present, are associated with a significantly (p<0.0001) lower probability of experiencing good mental health, and significantly(p<0.0001) higher probability of being diagnosed with depression or anxiety disorder. Furthermore, linear regression analysis results indicate that people residing in female-headed households with no adult males present also experience a significantly (p<0.0001) greater number of days of poor mental health.

The results also indicate that, the likelihood of good mental health declined significantly (p<0.0001) as the number of adults residing in the household increased. However, the association between the number of children in the household and the likelihood of good mental health is negative but insignificant. The same is true about the association between number of adults and of children in the household with the likelihood of being diagnosed with depression or anxiety disorders.

Table 4. Logistic regression- likelihood Anxiety Disorders Diagnosis

Covariates	B	Wald	Sig.	Exp(B)	95% C.I. EXP(B)	
					Lower	Upper
Household Structure						
Female-H	0.43	54.06	0.000	1.54	1.37	1.73
Children	-0.05	2.22	0.136	0.95	0.89	1.02
Adults	-0.10	2.55	0.111	0.90	0.79	1.02
Demographics and SES						
Income75	-0.10	1.17	0.280	0.90	0.75	1.09
Poor	0.06	0.95	0.330	1.06	0.94	1.19
College	0.19	12.99	0.000	1.21	1.09	1.35
Old	-0.42	50.35	0.000	0.66	0.59	0.74
young	-0.11	1.12	0.289	0.90	0.74	1.09
Unemployed	0.68	113.39	0.000	1.98	1.74	2.24
Access to care						
Cost-Bar	0.20	9.18	0.002	1.22	1.07	1.38
Social Support						
Satisfied	-0.81	182.26	0.000	0.44	0.39	0.50
Emotional	-0.55	89.02	0.000	0.58	0.51	0.65
Cell-Phone	0.21	13.30	0.000	1.23	1.10	
Behavioral Factors						1.71
Ever-Smoke	0.44	74.89	0.000	1.55	1.40	
Sleep-Enough	-0.54	88.10	0.000	0.58	0.52	
Current Health Conditions						
Angina	0.27	10.38	0.001	1.31	1.11	1.55
Asthma	0.34	29.64	0.000	1.40	1.24	1.58
Disability	0.74	184.95	0.000	2.09	1.88	2.32
Model Fit	N=15323	*Nag R^2=0.215	Correct prediction=85.8%		-2log likelihood=11092.303	

*Nagelkerke R^2.

The results also indicate a positive and significant ($p<0.0001$) association between income and the likelihood of good mental health. However its association with the likelihood of being diagnosed with depression or anxiety disorders is statistically insignificant. Unemployed individuals have a significantly ($p<0.0001$) lower likelihood of good mental health, and higher probability of being diagnosed with depression or anxiety disorders and they also experienced poor mental health over a greater number of days. Relative to the control group (those aged 36 - 54 years) those who are young (aged 18-35) have a significantly lower likelihood of experiencing good mental health and a significantly lower likelihood of a depression diagnosis. Relative to the reference group, respondents aged 55 years or older have a higher likelihood of experiencing good mental health, a lower likelihood of depression or anxiety disorder diagnosis and experienced poor mental health for a shorter periods than the reference group. Individuals who encountered cost barriers to accessing care were significantly more likely to be diagnosed with anxiety disorders and less likely to experience good mental health. They also experienced more days of poor mental health. Respondents who received social and emotional support when needed, and those who were satisfied with their lives were significantly more likely to have good mental health and had a lower likelihood of being diagnosed with depression or anxiety disorders. They also experienced significantly shorter periods of poor mental health. The surprise finding was that individuals who had access to cell-phones for personal use were significantly (p<0.001) less likely to report good mental health, more likely to be diagnosed with depression or an anxiety disorder and they also experienced significantly more days of poor mental health. This is opposite of what was expected. Given that cell-phones provide ready communication and less isolation of individuals, it was expected that they would have effects similar to social support but these results indicate the effect to be the opposite.

Consistent with expectations, smoking significantly (p<0.0001) reduced the likelihood of good mental health, significantly (p<0.0001) increased the likelihood of diagnosis with depression and anxiety disorder and significantly increased the length of poor mental health experience. Individuals who had enough sleep had a significantly (p<0.0001) higher likelihood of experiencing good mental health, and a lower likelihood of being diagnosed with depression or anxiety disorder and significantly (p<0.0001) fewer days of poor mental health. Also as expected, individuals who participated in physical exercise had experienced significantly (p<0.0001) shorter periods of poor mental health. Finally, respondents with chronic conditions such as asthma or a disability, experienced more days of poor mental health (significant p<0.0001 for disability). They also had a significantly (p<0.0001) lower likelihood of having good mental health and a higher likelihood of being diagnosed with anxiety disorders and with depression.

Table 5. Linear Regression: Variations in Days of poor mental Health

Variable	B	Beta	t	Sig
Household Structure				
Female-Headed	920	039	8.184	000
Children	-.003	000	-.043	966
Adults	-.102	-.004	-.803	422
Demographics and Socioeconomic Status				
Poor	461	022	4.026	000
College	-.293	-.014	-2.793	005
Old	-1.424	-.065	-12.185	000
Unemployed	3.105	128	23.835	000
Access to Care				
Cost-Bar	1.117	042	8.450	000
Social Support				
Satisfied	-7.543	-.311	-59.637	000
Emotional	-1.527	-.067	-13.917	000
Behavioral factors that affect health				
Exercise	-.516	-.024	-4.942	000
No-Sleep-days	178	187	37.419	000
Ever-Smoke	765	036	7.713	000
Tobacco	645	009	1.957	050
Health conditions				
Angina	364	011	2.364	018
Asthma	307	012	2.543	011
Disability	1.741	083	16.182	000
Model Fit Statistics N = 32,222	R2=.327 Adjusted R2=.327			

QUALIFICATIONS AND IMPLICATIONS

Prior to a discussion of tentative conclusions and possible policy implications, several limitations of the study should be noted. First, the study was based on cross-sectional data and, as a consequence, causality cannot be determined. Second, self-reported mental health or days of poor mental health may suffer from faulty memories of respondents. In addition, measures based on self reported health status might not capture the clinical dimensions of an individual's mental health status with precision. Accordingly, the examination of the number of poor days of mental health might benefit from an assessment of the individual's health status, grouped by diagnostic nomenclature. Finally, a direct examination of the role played by prior use of specific components of mental health care or those services that preserve or promote mental health was not conducted because such data were not available.

Recognizing the limitations of the study, several tentative conclusions are possible. First, the adverse mental health effects of residing a single-female-headed are clearly indicated by the four equations estimated. Residing in such a household has adverse effects on the likelihood of respondents reporting good mental health, and it seems to increase the likelihood of diagnosis of depression and anxiety disorders. Furthermore, those residing in single-female-headed households experience more days of poor mental health. This finding is more convincing because the analysis controlled for other factors that affect mental health, such as other household structure variables (number of children, and adults), demographics (age) and socioeconomic status (education and employment), income, access to healthcare, social support, individual behaviors and current physical health conditions. These results convincingly indicate that single-female-headed households are not as good in producing mental health as single-male-headed households. One cannot argue that the reason for this difference is socioeconomic status, access to care, education, income, or physical health conditions because after controlling for these variables, there is still a difference. This finding suggests that there are other factors in the single-female-headed household that account for their lower ability as mental health producers. This finding also calls for studies that will delve into greater detail to document other relevant factors in single-female-headed households that could be affecting their effectiveness in producing mental health. Factors that could not be examined in this analysis could be examined through such detailed household level studies. This analysis did not include a direct examination of gender roles and their effects on health. Men's roles tend to be structured or "fixed" while women occupy the more fluid nurturing roles. Highly structured roles tend to be caUSlly related to good mental health and low rates of morbidity while the less structured nurturing roles of women are linked to poor mental health and the higher rates of morbidity (Gove, 1984).

Furthermore, this analysis did not include factors that measure the /effort/reward imbalance and how it affects health production in single-female-headed households. Women's roles tend to have high work demands with low control which affects mental health (Karasek, 1979; Söderfeldt, Ohlson, Theorell, and Jones, 2000; Wang, Lesage, Schmitz, and Drapeau,, 2008) Women who are employed outside the home might experience some power but they also experience role overloads (roles at home and at work) and greater demands. This situation might lead to lower level of personal control and to lower mental health status (Rosenfield, 1989) and probably has an adverse effect on the mental health of the other members of the household. Such questions can be answered by in-depth household level studies that would document health production factors and processes in these households.

This study could not include other factors such as gender-based stress. Gender interacts with other social determinants resulting in greater strains on women due to stressful life events and their differential sensitivity to such events. Women also have a higher risk following crises involving children, housing and reproduction, rather than those involving finances, work and their marital relationship (Nazroo, 2001). These are factors that could be examined to greater depth through studies with a greater focus on household level activities and roles.

The suggested more detailed study examining single-female-headed households could collect data on these variables (stress, effort/reward imbalance, gender-roles) and health production processes to determine what conditions/factors in single-female-headed households account for poor mental health production. Such information would be useful in directing policies in support and enhancement of mental health production by single-female-headed households. As earlier indicated, most mental health problems begin in childhood. Therefore, the household is a critical foundation unit of health production. It is also critical to the protection and maintenance of good health. Society is made up of many households. Policies that correct health production constraints at the household level will ultimately improve the health of society at large. Further household level analysis of health production will provide critical information for the formation of effective health policies that will improve health and reduce gender-based health disparities. Furthermore, these finding suggest that policies affecting mental health and access to related care should emphasize gender differences in the need for care. Such policies should ensure that women and children from single-female-headed households have access to the volume of service that is commensurate with their greater need.

Adverse effects of a restrictive budget on health resources use and the potential improvement in health status suggest several policy considerations. The negative effects of the budget constraint indicate that the adoption of policy options that improve access might improve the mental health status of the economically disadvantaged. In particular, policy analysts might consider an expansion of programs that subsidize the use of mental health care, an option that could relax the limitations imposed by the budget constraint, increase the use of health resources and improve mental health. Similarly, an increase in the number of providers who practice in disadvantaged areas might increase access to care and thereby improve mental health. It should be noted, however, that the adoption of policy options which subsidize the use of service or increase the availability of providers will likely increase the use of health services by the disadvantaged. Thus, if those in greatest need consume more mental health services, it is likely that an equitable distribution of health will be accompanied by an inequitable distribution of care.

As expected, respondents who abstained from the consumption of tobacco and engaged in vigorous physical activity were more likely to report a good mental health status and fewer days of poor mental health than their counterparts who used tobacco and reported a sedentary life style. An active life style and the abstention from using tobacco products exerted a favorable influence on mental health status. These findings support policies and practices that encourage abstention from using tobacco and active lifestyles as viable options that promote good mental health.

Finally, with the exception of the elderly, respondents reporting the presence of a chronic condition were more likely to report a poor mental health status and more days of poor mental health. Accordingly, the interaction between physical and mental health suggest that both must be considered when developing treatment regimens. Such an approach may improve both the physical and mental health status of the individual.

REFERENCES

Ahern M. M. and Hendryx M. S. (2005). Social capital and risk of chronic illnesses. *Chronic Illness*, 1(3):183-190

Ahmed, S. M., Tomson. G., Ptzold, M. and Kabir, Z. N. (2005). Socioeconomic status overrides age and gender in determining health-seeking behaviour in rural Bangladesh. *Bull World Health Organ.*, 83 (2),81-160.

Awasthi P. and Mishra R. C. (2007)Role of Coping Strategies and Social Support in Perceived Illness Consequences and Controllability among Diabetic Women. *Psychology and Developing Societies*. 19 (2): 179-197.

Barksy A. J., Peekana H. M., and Borus J. F. (2001) Somatic symptom reporting in women and men. *J. Gen. Intern. Med.*, 16(4), 266-275.

Bender, K. A. and Habermalz, S. (2006). Are There Differences in the Health– Socioeconomic Status Relationship over the Life Cycle? Evidence from Germany. *Labour*, 22 (1),107 – 125.

Bronte-Tinkew, J. and De Jong, G. (2004). Children's nutrition in Jamaica: do household structure and household economic resources matter? *Social Science and Medicine*, 58(3), 499-514.

Burt V. K., and Stein K. (2002) Epidemiology of depression throughout the female life cycle. *J. Clin. Psychiatry*. 63(Suppl 7):9-15.

Caldwell T. M., Rodgers B., Jorm A. F., et al. (2002) Patterns of association between alcohol consumption and symptoms of depression and anxiety in young adults. *Addiction*. 97(5): 583-594.

Case, A. and Paxson, C. (2001). Mothers and others: Who invests in children's health? *Journal of Health Economics*, 20 (3), 301-328.

Craft S., Asthana S., Schellenberg G., et al. (1999) Insulin metabolism in Alzheimer's disease differs according to apolipoprotein E genotype and gender. *Neuroendocrinology*. 70(2): 146-152.

Danielsson K., Flyckt L., and Edman G. (2001)Sex differences in schizophrenia as seen in the Rorschach test. *Nord. J. Psychiatry*. 55(2):137-142.

Di Carlo A., Baldereschi M., Amaducci L., et al. (2002) Incidence of Dementia, Alzheimer's Disease, and Vascular Dementia in Italy. The ILSA Study. *J. Am. Geriatr. Soc.* 50(1), 41-48.

Eaton, N. R., Keyes, K. M., Krueger, R. F., Balsis, S., Skodol, A. E., Markon, K. E., Grant, B. F.,and Hasin, D. S. (2011). An Invariant Dimensional Liability Model of Gender Differences in Mental Disorder Prevalence: Evidence From a National Sample. *Journal of Abnormal Psychology*. Advance online publication. doi: 10.1037/a0024780 *http://www.apa.org/pubs/journals/releases/abn-ofp-eaton.pdf accessed 11-11-2011.*

Gandy S., Almeida O. P., Fonte J., et al. (2001) Chemical andropause and amyloid-beta peptide. *Jama.* 285(17):2195-2196.

Glei D. A., Landau D. A., Goldman N., Chuang Y., Rogriguez G., Weinstein M. Participating in social activities helps preserve cognitive function: an analysis of a longitudinal, population-based study of the elderly. *Int. J. Epidemiol.* 2005; 34(4):864-871.

Gove, Walter R. 1984. "Gender Differences in Mental and Physical Illness: The Effects of Fixed Roles and Nurturant Roles." *Social Science and Medicine* 19:77-91.

Grossman, M. (1972) On the Concept of Health Capital and the Demand for Health. *Journal of Political Economy*, 80(2), 223-255.

Grossman, M. (2004) The demand for health, 30 years later: a very personal retrospective and prospective reflection. *Journal of Health Economics,* 23(4): 629–636.

Guyer, J. I. (1981) The Raw, the Cooked, and the Half-baked: A Note on the Division of Labor by Sex. Working Paper 4X. African Studies Center, Boston, University, Boston, Mass.

Handa, S. (1996) Expenditure behavior and children's welfare: An analysis of female headed households in Jamaica. *Journal of Development Economics*, 50(1), 165-187.

Hankin B. L,and Abramson L. Y. (1999) Development of gender differences in depression: description and possible explanations. *Ann. Med.* 31(6):372-379.

Holbrook T. L., Hoyt D. B., Stein M. B., and Sieber W. J. (2002) et al (2002)Gender Differences in Long-Term Posttraumatic Stress Disorder Outcomes after Major Trauma: Women Are At Higher Risk of Adverse Outcomes than Men. *Journal of Trauma-Injury Infection and Critical Care*, 53(5), 882-888.

Johnson, C. F. and Rogers, B. L. (1993) Children's nutritional status in female-headed households in the Dominican Republic. *Social Science and Medicine*, 37(11), 1293-1301.

Karasek, R. (1979). Job demands, job decision latitude and mental strain: Implications for job redesign. *Administrative Science Quarterly*, 24, 285-306.

Kessler R. C., Heeringa S., Lakoma M. D., Petukhova M., Rupp A. E., Schoenbaum M., Wang P. S., and Zaslavsky A. M. (2008) Individual and societal effects of mental disorders on earnings in the United States: results from the National Co morbidity Survey Replication. *Am. J. Psychiatry,* 165:703–711.

Kornstein S. G., Schatzberg A. F., Thase M. E., Yonkers K. A., McCullough J. P., Keitner G. I., Gelenberg A. J., Ryan C. E., Hess A. L., Harrison W. M., Davis S. M, Keller M. B. (2000) Gender differences in chronic major and double depression. *J. Aff. Dis.* 60:1-11.

Kroshus, E. (2008) Gender, Marital Status, and Commercially Prepared Food Expenditure. *Journal of Nutrition Education and Behavior*, 40(6), 355-360.

Kutty N. K (2008) A household production function model of the production child health and education – the role of housing-related inputs. Available at SSRN: *http://ssrn.com /abstract=1232602.*

Labelle A., Light M., Dunbar F. (2001) Risperidone treatment of outpatients with schizophrenia: no evidence of sex differences in treatment response. *Can. J. Psychiatry.*46(6):534-541.

Lapane K. L., Gambassi G., Landi F., Sgadari A., Mor V., Bernabei R. (2001) Gender differences in predictors of mortality in nursing home residents with AD. *Neurology* 56(5):650-654.

Lynch, J. W., Smith G. D., Kaplan G. A., and House J. S. (2000) Income inequality and mortality: importance to health of individual income, psychosocial environment, or material conditions. *BMJ 320*(7243) 1200-4.

Marmot, M., R. G. Wilkinson (eds.). Social Determinants of Health. New York: Oxford University Press. 1999.

Messer, E. 1983. The Household Focus in Nutritional Anthropology: An Overview. *Food Nutr. Bull.,* 5(4): 212-25.

Mayeux R., Tang M. X., Jacobs D. M., et al. (1999) Plasma amyloid beta-peptide 1-42 and incipient Alzheimer's disease. *Ann. Neurol.;*46(3): 412-416.

McDowell I. (2001) Alzheimer's disease: insights from epidemiology. *Aging* (Milano).13(3):143-162.

Melkersson K. I., Hulting A. L., Rane A. J. (2001) Dose requirement and prolactin elevation of antipsychotics in male and female patients with schizophrenia or related psychoses. *Br. J. Clin. Pharmacol.* 2001;51(4):317-324.

Messer, E. (1983). The Household Focus in Nutritional Anthropology: An Overview. *Food Nutr. Bull.,* 5(4): 212-25.

Miller G. E., Rohleder N., and Cole S. W. (2009) Chronic Interpersonal Stress Predicts Activation of Pro- and Anti-Inflammatory Signaling Pathways 6 Months Later. *Psychosom. Med.* 71:57-62.

Moscato B. S., Russell M., Zielezny M., et al. (1997) Gender differences in the relation between depressive symptoms and alcohol problems: a longitudinal perspective. *Am. J. Epidemiol.* 146(11):966-974.

Muck-Seler D., Pivac N., Jakovljevic M. (1999) Sex differences, season of birth and platelet 5-HT levels in schizophrenic patients. *J. Neural. Transm.* 106(3-4):337-347.

National Mental Health Association. (2010) Mental Health Fact sheet. *http://www.mhag.org /mental_health_facts.cfm.*

Nazroo J. Y. (2001)South Asian people and heart disease: an assessment of the importance of socioeconomic position. *Ethnicity and disease* 2001;11(3):401-11.

Netuveli G., Wiggins R. D., Montgomery S. M., Hildon Z., and Blane D. (2008) Mental health and resilience at older ages: bouncing back after adversity in the British Household Panel Survey. *J. Epidemiol. Commun. H.* 62:987-991.

Ngom, P., Wawire, S., Gandaho, T., Klissou, P., Adjimon, T. et al (2000) intra-household decision-making on health and resource allocation in Borgou, Bénin. Acessed 7/2011 at *http://www.popcouncil.org/pdfs/frontiers/FR_FinalReports/Benin_Decision_Making.pdf.*

Nishizawa S., Benkelfat C., Young S. N., et al. (1997) Differences between males and females in rates of serotonin synthesis in human brain. *Proc. Natl. Acad. Sci. US.* 94(10):5308-5313.

Ochoa S., USll J., Haro J. M., et al. (2001) Comparative study of the needs of patients with schizophrenia by gender. *Actas. Esp. Psiquiatr.* 29(3): 165-171.

Onyango, A. Tucker, K. and Eisemon, T. (1994) Household headship and child nutrition: A case study in Western Kenya. *Social Science and Medicine*, 39, (12), 1633-1639.

Owens, P., Myers, M., Elixhauser, A., and Brach, C. (2007) *Care of Adults With Mental Health and Substance Abuse Disorders in US Community Hospitals,* 2004—HCUP Fact Book No. 10.

Pai M. and Barrett A. E. Long-Term Payoffs of Work? Women's Past Involvement in Paid Work and Mental Health in Widowhood. *Res. Aging.* 2007; 29(5): 436-456.

Petersson, B. (1998) Gender differences and mental health. *European Psychiatry*, 13(4) 137s-138s.

Petrila, J., Andel, R., Constantine, R. and Robst, J. (2010) Public Expenditures Related to the Criminal Justice System and to Services for Arrestees With a Serious Mental Illness. *Psychiatr. Serv.* 61:516-519.

Robbins, M. S. Briones, E. Schwartz, J. S., Dillon, F. R. Mitrani, V.B. (2006) Differences in Family Functioning in Grandparent and Parent-Headed Households in a Clinical Sample of Drug-Using African American Adolescents. *Cultural Diversity and Ethnic Minority Psychology*, 12, (1), 84-100.

Rosenfield, Sarah. 1989. "The Effects of Women's Employment: Personal Control and Sex Differences in Mental Health," *Journal of Health and Social Behavior* 30:77-91.

Salehi A., Gonzalez Martinez V., Swaab D. F. A sex difference and no effect of ApoE type on the amount of cytoskeletal alterations in the nucleus basalis of Meynert in Alzheimer's disease. *Neurobiol Aging.* 1998;19(6):505-510.

Schmeer, K. (2009) Father absence due to migration and child illness in rural Mexico. *Social Science and Medicine*, Volume 69, Issue 8, October 2009, Pages 1281-1286.

Söderfeldt, B., Ohlson, C. G., Theorell, T., Jones, I. (2000). The impact of sense of coherence and high-demand/low-control job environment on self-reported health, burnout and psychophysiological stress indicators. *Work and Stress* 14 (1),1-15.

Silverstein B. (2002) Gender differences in the prevalence of somatic versus pure depression: a replication. *Am. J. Psychiatry.* 2002;159(6):1051-1052.

Spearing M. K. Schizophrenia. Bethesda, M. D.: National Institutes of Mental Health, *National Institutes of Health*; June 1, 1999. NIH Publication No. 99-3517.

Thornton J. (2002) Estimating a Health Production Function for the US: Some New Evidence. *Applied Economics*, 34(1);59-62.

USll J., Araya S., Ochoa S., Busquets E., Gost A., and Marquez M. (2001). Gender differences in a sample of schizophrenic outpatients. *Compr. Psychiatry.* 42(4):301-305.

Wang J., and Patten S. B. (2002). Prospective study of frequent heavy alcohol use and the risk of major depression in the Canadian general population. *Depress Anxiety.* 15(1):42-45.

Wang, J. L. Lesage, A., Schmitz, N. and Drapeau, A. (2008). The relationship between work stress and mental disorders in men and women: findings from a population-based study. *J. Epidemiol. Community Health,* 62, 42-47.

Wilkinson R. G. Health inequalities: relative or absolute material standards? *British Medical Journal* 1997; 314:591-5.

Wilkinson R. G. and Marmot M. (Eds) 2003. Social Determinants of Health: the Solid Facts. Second Edition. World Health Organization, Copenhagen Denmark 2003.

Wilkinson R. G. Class mortality differentials, income distribution and trends in poverty 1921-1981. *Journal of Social Policy 1989*; 18 (3): 307-35.

Wilkinson R. G. National mortality rates: the impact of inequality? *American Journal of Public Health* 1992; 82: 1082-4.

World Health Organization (WHO) (2006) Gender disparities in mental health. Available at: *www.who.int/mental_health/media/en/242.pdf. Accessed 11-11-2011.*

WHO (2002) Gender and Mental Health accessed 11/11/2011 from *http://whqlibdoc.who.int /gender/2002/a85573.pdf.*

WHO (2010) mental health: strengthening our response. Fact sheet N°220, September 2010. Accessed 11-16-2011 at *http://www.who.int/mediacentre/factsheets/fs220/en/index.html.*

WHO (2010) Ten Facts about mental health. Accessed 11-16-2011 from *http://www.who.int/features/factfiles/mental_health/mental_health_facts/en/index.html.*

Xu H., Gouras G. K., Greenfield J. P., et al. (1998) Estrogen reduces neuronal generation of Alzheimer beta-amyloid peptides. *Nat. Med.* 4(4):447-451.

Yee J. R., Cavigelli S. A., Delgado B., and McClintock M. K.. Reciprocal Affiliation Among Adolescent Rats During a Mild Group Stressor Predicts Mammary Tumors and Lifespan. *Psychosom Med.* 2008; 70:1050-1059.

Yonkers et al., (2003) Chronicity, relapse, and illness—course of panic disorder, social phobia, and generalized anxiety disorder: Findings in men and women from 8 years of follow-up *Depress Anxiety* ,17(3):173-9.

Yoo, J. and Lim, L. (2009) The trend in the income status of children in female-headed families: A replication and update. *Children and Youth Services Review*, 31,(4),482-488.

In: Psychology of Gender Differences
Editor: Sarah P. McGeown

ISBN 978-1-62081-391-1
© 2012 Nova Science Publishers, Inc.

Chapter 15

QUALITATIVE SEX DIFFERENCES IN SPATIAL LEARNING

V. D. Chamizo and C. A. Rodríguez[*]
Universitat de Barcelona, Spain

ABSTRACT

A sex or gender difference in spatial learning is a controversial topic with uncertain results. A selection of studies [25, 26, 37, 41] in the standard rat and also in humans is reviewed. These studies show different strategies used by the two sexes to solve navigation tasks, as well as a marked distinction between what the participants learn and what they prefer (i.e., learning vs. performance), which reveals new insights in this literature. The measure used being a critical factor. Both the origins of these differences and some possible implications are discussed.

INTRODUCTION

There is evidence that male and female rats can use different types of spatial cues when navigating. Female rats tend to focus on landmarks (which are often near to a goal objects), while males prefer geometry, as a source of information. The same claim is consistent in the human literature (for reviews see [1, 2, 3]). These results are consistent with the predictions of the range size hypothesis described in several species of mammals. The crucial idea is that sex differences in task performance have arisen from a process of natural selection: a difference in range expansion between males and females is associated with a difference in spatial cognition [4]. In people that difference arises largely because men hunted and women gathered; in other animals it arises from the fact of polygyny (see Section 7 for more details).

---

[*] E-mail addresses: *victoria.diez.chamizo@ub.edu, claraarodriguez@ub.edu*. Chapter supported by a grant from the Spanish 'Ministerio de Ciencia e Innovación' (PSI2010-20424) to VDC.

A Background Story: The Proposal by Cheng (1986)

Cheng [5] (see also Gallistel [6]) was the first author to present evidence that rats can use geometric information to locate a hidden goal. He trained male rats in a rectangular arena, where the two short walls of the box and one of the long walls were black, while the other long wall was white. In addition, distinctive visual patterns were placed in each of the box's corners (as well as other non-geometric cues). Food was buried in one corner of the box, and the rats had to search for it. Although rats learned to search in the correct location for the food, they made frequent rotational errors searching in the corner diagonally across from the one where the food was hidden.

The only characteristic that the target corner and the corner diagonal from it shared in common was having one long wall to the left and one short wall to the right, which implies that the information provided by the non-geometric sources of information to find the food location did not seem to be important. Cheng concluded that the rats used the geometric framework of the box itself. Similar results have been found not only with rats but also with other species (for reviews, see [7, 8]).

According to Cheng and Gallistel, learning about geometric information (i.e., like the metric relations of distances and angles between a target place and the shape of an apparatus) occurs in a specialized module, which is impenetrable to non-geometric information (although see [9]). Features such as landmarks are considered to be related to this featureless metric frame by means of address labels [5]. If this is the case, an important question to answer is: Does shape or geometry learning consist of the conditioning of approach responses to a goal that is defined in terms of the spatial relationship that it maintains regarding a particular geometry, like the shape of an apparatus (i.e., an associative point of view) or alternatively, is this a kind of learning different and independent of the traditional ways of learning (like classical and instrumental conditioning), as Cheng claims? In other words, is knowledge about shape or geometry location acquired in the same way as knowledge about other relations between events? (for a related question see [10]).

Two main predictions should be considered in this controversial topic. If geometry and landmark learning represent quite independent modes of solution [5, 6], one might not expect to see any interaction or competition between them. Consequently, no evidence of cue competition effects (like blocking and overshadowing) should be found between geometric and non-geometric information. However, Miller and Shettleworth [11] have claimed that changes in the associative properties of the geometric cues are governed by the same principles that apply to more traditional stimuli. Consequently, one might expect to see interactions or competition between geometric and non-geometric information. Although the evidence is not yet clear, the more common outcome is that landmark learning does not interfere with, overshadow, or block the learning of geometry (in favor of this result with rats see [12, 13, 14, 15,]; with humans [16]. For the opposite result with rats see [17, 18, 19]; with humans [20, 21]. But neither Cheng nor any of the studies mentioned in this paragraph examined sex differences when using rats. What would have happened if they had also considered female rats?

Shape and Landmark Cues: Differential Preference or Salience for Males and Females

When solving maze tasks, it has been suggested [22, 23] that male rodents tend to use geometric information, such as the shape and dimension of the experimental room, while females rely more on landmarks, such as specific objects near the maze. In the study by Williams, Barnett, and Meck [22], with rats and a radial-maze, after acquisition, two manipulations were conducted. The two manipulations were alteration of the geometry of the testing room and rearrangement of the landmark cues. The results revealed that alteration of the geometry of the testing room clearly affected normal males (as well as females treated with estradiol benzoate), but these changes did not affect normal females (or neonatal castrated males). Normal male rat performance was not impaired when landmark cues were rearranged, while normal female performance was impaired (for a similar result in a circular pool, see [24]).

One problem with the study by Williams et al. [22] is the lack of description of the experimental room. Theoretically, the room's geometry determined the males' superior performance when learning the geometric relations between food caches and the overall shape of the environment (i.e., global shape learning). However, a salient and distant landmark (like a bright light or a window) could have been present in the room, guiding the males' performance so that geometry would not be implicated. The aim of the study by Rodríguez, Torres, Mackintosh, and Chamizo [25], with rats and a pool, was to evaluate whether there are qualitative sex differences in the acquisition of a spatial task when two sources of information (i.e., the geometry of the apparatus and one landmark) simultaneously indicate the goal's position (i.e., a hidden platform) by means of a simple but highly controlled situation. In the two experiments of the study, circular black curtains surrounded the pool, half of which could be triangular. Moreover, five pretraining trials were conducted in the circular pool without the landmark but with the platform present. During the training phase, rats were given eight trials per day over five days (a total of 40 trials). In Experiment 1, at the point of the triangular part of the pool, one salient landmark, a beach ball hanging from a false black ceiling, was presented so that the two sources of information (i.e., the landmark and the shape) indicated the position of the hidden platform. The rats could learn that the hidden platform was at a certain distance from both the landmark and the point of the triangle with a straight wall both to the right and to the left. No other room cues could provide additional information to find the platform. The shape of the pool and the landmark were rotated from trial to trial, and the position of the platform also changed for each trial, thus preserving a constant relation between the platform, the shape, and the landmark. All rats improved their performance as the experiment progressed, and spatial learning took place equally in males and in females. Then, on a test trial without the platform, the two sources of information (i.e., the landmark and the shape) were put into conflict by presenting them 180° apart. The amount of time that the rats searched in two different areas (one in front of the landmark, although at the incorrect shape, and the other in front of the triangular shape, although without the landmark) was recorded. Following Williams et al. [22] and Roof and Stein [24], the test trial prediction was that males would spend more time searching for the platform in the shape area than in the landmark area, while the reverse was predicted for the females. The results revealed a clear preference in females for the landmark area over the shape area, while males' performance did not show any clear preference between the two areas. In addition, males spent more time searching for the platform in the shape area than females, while males and females did not differ in the landmark area. In Experiment 1, it was also examined the possibility that the estrous cycle of females could have had an influence on their performance; it did not.

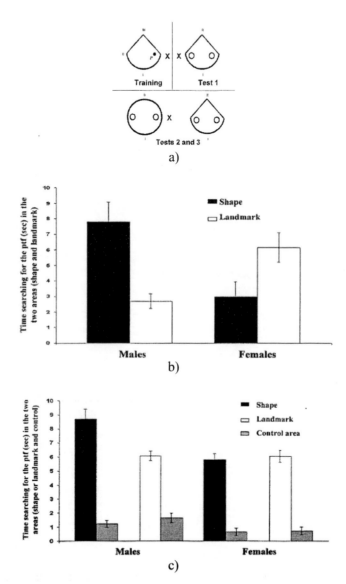

Figure 1. Experiment 2 [25]: A schematic representation of the pool and the position of the landmark, X, as well as the hidden platform (P) A (Top): Left panel, for acquisition; right panel, for test 1. (Bottom): for tests 2 and 3. B: Mean time spent in the two recording areas (shape and landmark) by the subjects during test trial 1. C: Mean time spent in the two recording areas (shape or landmark and control) by the subjects during test trials 2 and 3 (shape and landmark, respectively). Error bars denote standard error of means.

Would the males have shown a significant preference for the shape with a new set of "stimuli" (i.e., shape and landmark)?

The aim of Experiment 2 [25] was to test such a possibility (see Figure 1). The landmark used was a small ninepin instead of the big beach ball as in Experiment 1. The solution based on the shape of the pool was such that now the target point had a straight wall to the left and a circular wall to the right instead of two straight walls on both sides as in Experiment 1. Therefore, the rats could learn that the hidden platform was at a certain distance from both the new landmark and the new shape. All rats improved their performance as the experiment progressed, and spatial learning took place equally in males and in females. After training, in a test trial without the platform, the two sources of information (i.e., the landmark and the shape) were put into conflict by presenting them 180° apart. A second purpose of this experiment was to measure what males and females had learned about the two sources of information independently of their preferences. For this purpose, two additional test trials (tests 2 and 3) were also conducted and counterbalanced. In one trial, the landmark was present in the circular pool (i.e., in the absence of the triangular shape), and in the other trial, the triangular shape was present in the absence of the landmark. According to Williams et al. [22], male rats are predisposed to attend to a single aspect of the environment (global shape), while female rats use multiple environmental cues (global shape and landmarks). The results of the preference test (i.e., test trial 1) revealed that while female rats spent more time in the landmark area than in the shape area, the reverse was true for males. These results, as well as Experiment 1, clearly agreed with the claim that males and females can use different types of spatial information when solving maze tasks [22, 24]. In addition, males spent more time searching for the platform in the shape area than females, while females spent more time searching for the platform in the landmark area than males.

Experiment 2 [25] (i.e., tests 2 and 3) also revealed that males and females had learned to find the platform using the two sources of information. When the landmark and the shape were tested one by one, the results showed that males had learned about the landmark (i.e., the less preferred source of information) and females had learned about the shape of the pool (i.e., the less preferred source of information). These last results seem to contradict the claim of Williams et al. [22], suggesting that while male rats are predisposed to attend to a single aspect of the environment (global shape), female rats use multiple environmental cues (global shape and landmarks). According to these authors, when multiple sources of information are presented together, male rats learn the geometric relations between food caches and the overall shape of the environment such that those sources of information overshadow all others and prevent them from becoming associated with the food caches. In contrast, female rats appear to process and use both geometric and non-geometric sources of information when they are presented together.

The results of tests 2 and 3 of Experiment 2 [25] show that males and females process and use both geometric and non-geometric sources of information when they are presented together. It is true that the different measures of the three test trials gave quite different results, showing a clear distinction between learning and performance. On test trial 1, female rats did not seem to know much about shape, while males did not seem to know much about the landmark. Then, test trials 2 and 3 clearly revealed that such was not the case. Using a variety of tests was crucial to know what the rats had learned. The present experiments also show a clear male advantage on geometry or shape learning.

Overshadowing and Blocking between Shape and Landmark Learning: The Importance of Sex Differences

If male and female rats rely on landmark and geometry cues to different degrees, then a natural progression of the Rodríguez et al. study [25] was to see whether this would affect the extent to which competition could be seen between these cues. That was the aim of the study by Rodríguez, Chamizo, and Mackintosh [26]. Experiment 1 was designed to check for overshadowing. The term overshadowing refers to the finding that the presence of a second relevant cue will cause animals to learn less about a first than they would have done if trained on the first cue in isolation (Pavlov [27]). Because overshadowing depends on the relative salience of both overshadowing and overshadowed stimuli (Mackintosh [28]), one might reasonably expect that if overshadowing is observed, it would be asymmetrical, with shape learning overshadowing landmark learning more than landmark learning overshadowing shape learning in males (as McGregor, Horne, Esber, and Pearce [13] have already shown), and precisely the opposite effect in females, where landmark learning should overshadow shape learning to a greater degree than shape learning should overshadow landmark learning. Experiment 1 [26], with four groups of rats, had a classical overshadowing design (see Table 1) in which two experimental groups (Compound cue groups) were trained in a compound cue learning task (i.e., learning was with the single landmark and one corner of the pool both predicting the platform's position), while two corresponding control groups (Single cue groups) were trained with a single cue. For one control group the position of the hidden platform was predicted by a single landmark presented in a circular pool, while for the other control group it was predicted by one corner of the triangular-shaped pool in the absence of the landmark. A subsequent test trial was conducted, without the platform, in the presence of a single cue. For both one experimental group and the control group trained with the single landmark, the tested cue was the single landmark; and the other experimental group and the control group trained in the triangular-shaped pool, were tested in the triangular-shaped pool with no landmark. Would the experimental groups perform worse than the control groups and would there be any sex difference in any such overshadowing effect? Although all rats improved their performance as training progressed, on day 1 the rats learning with the two cues, the compound groups (Compound-S and Compound-L), were faster than the rats learning with a single cue (Landmark and Shape); moreover, males were faster than females. The results of the test trial revealed an overshadowing effect between geometry and landmark learning. Evidence of overshadowing was provided by the superior performance of single groups by comparison with compound groups. More importantly, overshadowing was asymmetrical, both in males and in females. Specifically, in males, shape learning overshadowed landmark learning, but not vice-versa; while in females, landmark learning overshadowed shape learning, but not vice-versa. These effects were not influenced by the females' estrus cycle.

Experiment 2 of the study by Rodríguez et al. [26] (2a and 2b) examined whether prior training with either geometry or landmark cues would block learning about the other cue when, in a second phase of the experiment, both sources of information simultaneously signalled the location of the platform (see Table 2). Traditionally, blocking is observed when prior establishment of one element of a compound cue as a signal for reinforcement reduces or blocks the amount learned about the other cue (Kamin, [29]). Experiment 2a had a classical blocking design in which two experimental groups were trained in phase 1 with a single cue.

For one group the position of the hidden platform was predicted by a single landmark presented in a circular pool, while for the other group it was predicted by one corner of a triangular-shaped pool in the absence of the landmark. In the second phase of the experiment, the two experimental groups and two new groups, control groups, were trained in a compound cue learning task.

Table 1. Design of Experiment 1 [26]. Overshadowing

Group	Phase 1	Test
Compound-L	landmark + shape	landmark
Landmark	landmark	landmark
Compound-S	landmark + shape	shape
Shape	shape	shape

Table 2. Design of Experiment 2a [26]. Blocking

Group	Phase 1	Phase 2	Test
Experimental-L	shape	landmark + shape	landmark
Control-L	---	landmark + shape	landmark
Experimental-S	landmark	landmark + shape	shape
Control-S	---	landmark + shape	shape

For all animals both sources of information (i.e., one corner of the pool and the single landmark) simultaneously indicated the platform's position. Subsequent test trials were conducted, without the platform, with only one cue present: the single landmark in the circular pool for the experimental group trained in the phase 1 with the triangular-shaped pool and for one control group; and the triangular-shaped pool for the experimental group trained in the phase 1 with the landmark in the circular pool and for the second control group. Would the experimental groups perform worse than the control groups (i.e. show blocking)? And would there be any difference between males and females in the nature or magnitude of any such blocking effect? In phase 1, all rats improved their performance as training progressed. Then, in phase 2, the two control groups obviously learned to find the platform more slowly than the two experimental groups, although more rapidly than these latter groups had made on days 1-3 in phase 1. The results of the test trial revealed a blocking effect between geometry and landmark learning. Evidence of blocking was provided by the superior performance of control groups by comparison with the pretrained groups. Most importantly, it was also found that the variable sex played a significant role in this effect because blocking was asymmetrical. Specifically, in males, shape learning blocked landmark learning, but not vice-versa; while a reciprocal blocking effect was obtained in females (shape learning blocked landmark learning and landmark learning blocked shape learning). These effects were not influenced by the females' estrus cycle.

Then, in Experiment 2b, only with male rats, it was attempted to increase the chance that landmark learning could block shape learning by giving extended initial training with the landmark. (i.e., 80 trials instead of 40 trials, as in Experiment 2a). The experiment was conducted with two groups of rats only. For one group the position of the hidden platform was initially predicted by the single landmark presented in the circular pool. In the second phase of the experiment, the single cue group and one new group were both trained in a compound cue learning task; for all animals both sources of information (i.e., the single landmark and one corner of the triangular-shaped pool) simultaneously indicated the platform's position. Subsequent test trials were conducted, without the platform, with only the triangular-shaped pool present (i.e., in the absence of the landmark). After such an extended single training with the landmark, on the test trial single cue rats showed a worse performance than the rats without the single training (i.e., landmark learning could block shape learning).

The results of the study by Rodríguez et al. [26] are inconsistent with the suggestion that learning about the shape of an environment takes place in a special module that is impenetrable to non-geometric information [5, 6]. Two main conclusions can be drawn from this study [26]. The first is that cue competition effects such as overshadowing and blocking can be found between shape learning and landmark learning; the second is that the competition between shape learning and landmark learning is influenced by the sex of the subjects, implying that the outcome of such experiments depends on the relative salience of landmark and shape information. The clear general implication of the overshadowing and blocking experiments that we have just reviewed is that the mechanism responsible for shape or geometry learning seems to be clearly associative, since it interacts with landmark learning in the same way as the conditioning of a light interacts with the conditioning of a tone [29]. A second straightforward implication of this study (see also Rodríguez et al. [25]) is that the model proposed by Miller and Shettleworth [11] should incorporate a flexible term to explain sex differences.

Does the Estrus Cycle Influence Hippocampal-Dependent Navigation Tasks in Rats?

Many studies have shown a profound impairment on a variety of spatial tasks after lesions in the hippocampus [30, 31, 32]. The study by Morris, Garrud, Rawlins, and O'Keefe [30] revealed that hippocampal lesion rats showed a profound impairment in a place navigation task (i.e., with a circular pool and a hidden platform); and this effect disappeared when a visible platform was used. Both control rats (i.e., sham operated) and rats with a different lesion (i.e., a superficial cortical lesion) learned to escape rapidly from the water in the two kinds of tasks (i.e., with the hidden platform and with the visible platform). Morris et al. [30] concluded that the performance of the task in which the rats had to learn about the location of a hidden platform in relation to distal cues is hippocampal-dependent but not the other kind of task in which the platform is visible, thus supporting the idea that the ability of navigation, which is essential for the survival of animals, depends critically on the integrity of this limbic structure.

Spatial tasks have been considered hormonally dependent (for a demonstration in the radial maze, see Williams el al. [22]). The hormonal and reproductive cycle of female rats, called estrus cycle, lasts about four-five days and consists of four distinct phases: proestrus, estrus, metaestrus and diestrus. These different phases of the estrus cycle correlate with different levels of the sex hormone estradiol circulating. According to Woolley and McEwen [33], during the phase of the estrus cycle in which occurs the peak level of estradiol (i.e., the proestrus phase), the hippocampus shows an increase in synaptic density in the apical cells of the pyramidal cells of the CA1 area of up to 30%. These changes have been suggested to affect spatial performance. But the literature is inconsistent in the direction of these changes (for three different results see [34, 35, 36]). For example, Warren and Juraska [34] trained two groups of female rats (one with high hormonal levels and the other with low hormonal levels) in a similar place navigation task like the one used by Morris et al. [30]. The results of a test trial, without the platform, at the end of acquisition showed that female rats with low hormonal levels outperformed females with high hormonal levels. However, Healy, Braham, and Braithwaite [36], who trained and tested two groups of female rats (one with high hormonal levels and the other with low hormonal levels) but in a different way to Warren and Juraska [34], also found differences in the performance of the two groups, but exactly in the opposite direction: unexpectedly, females with high hormonal levels performed the task significantly better than females with low hormonal levels. Finally, Berry, McMahan, and Gallagher [35] did not find any effect when they trained and tested two groups of female rats also differing in their hormonal levels, neither in the acquisition nor in a final test trial. How could this be? Of particular note, these studies have used different procedures and measures.

The main aim of the next study reviewed (Rodríguez, Aguilar, and Chamizo [37]) was to conduct experiments in a highly controlled situation, using the Morris pool, to specifically see whether landmark learning is affected by the female's estrus cycle. Circular black curtains surrounded the pool, with two external three-dimensional landmarks inside this enclosure, so that no other room cues (like the shape of the room) could provide additional information to find the platform. The landmarks were hung from a false ceiling and rotated from trial to trial with the platform, thus preserving a constant relation between the platform and the landmarks (i.e., eliminating olfactory and auditory cues outside the curtains). Four starting points were used. During acquisition, the rats were required to escape from the pool by swimming to an invisible platform that was located in the same place relative to one configuration formed by the two landmarks which were placed relatively far and equidistant from the hidden platform (D and A in Figure 2). After training the rats were tested, without the platform, in the presence of the landmarks, with the pool surface spatially divided into four quadrants: where the platform should have been, right to it, left to it and opposite to it. The time the rats spent in all the quadrants was measured.

The test trials revealed a preference for searching in the correct quadrant of the pool. In Experiment 1 such a test performance was identical in two groups of females, one tested with high hormonal levels (i.e., in the proestrus phase) and the second one tested with low hormonal levels (i.e., either in the estrus, metaestrus or diestrus phase); in addition, these two groups differed from a third group of male rats (i.e., males had a better performance than females). Experiment 2 replicated the females' previous results with a better procedure. The experiment compared the performance of two groups of female rats which were both trained and tested always in the same estrus phase (i.e., every four days only), one group in the proestrus phase, and the second group in the estrus phase. The implication of these results is that the estrus cycle seems to have little impact on the performance of female rats when landmark learning in a navigation task. The previous sex difference found in Experiment 1 disappears (unpublished results) if the two landmarks are trained and tested relatively near from the hidden platform position (B and C in Figure 2).

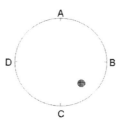

Figure 2. A schematic representation of a pool and the position of four landmarks (A, B, C, and D), as well as the hidden platform (*black circle inside the pool*).

Relatively Near vs. Relatively Far Landmarks: Human Participants

A model of hippocampal function proposed by Jacobs and Schenk [38] predicts a dissociation between proximal and distal cues between males and females. Some authors (i.e., Chai and Jacobs [39], Barkley and Gabriel [40] have claimed that their work provide support for this model. Following Jacobs and Schenk [38] sex differences arise from preferences for cues that provide either direction (i.e., far cues, most preferred by males) or position (i.e., near cues, most preferred by females). Directional cues are distant objects that appear to remain stationary with respect to each other as an organism wanders about a specific terrain or virtual arena (e.g., stars and mountains). This kind of information is difficult to use to pinpoint a location. In contrast, positional cues are close or local objects that are often used to pinpoint a location.

Chai and Jacobs [39] used virtual navigation to explore two types of landscapes. Their participants were trained to collect a visible target (e.g., a blue spike-like crystal) that was located either in a landscape containing only directional (i.e., graded, gradient) cues or positional (i.e., pinpoint) cues (Experiments 1 and 2, respectively). After training, the participants underwent test trials without the crystal. In these trials, they were told to go back to the crystal's location from the previous phase and stay there until the end of the trial. At the conclusion of the trial, the researchers calculated the distance between the participant's position and the target position. The test results showed that the men got closer to the target position under both conditions but that the men's advantage was larger when the directional cues were available. The participants' self-reported information corroborated these results. Chai and Jacobs suggested that an often reported male advantage in the presence of distant objects and geometric cues is derived from these objects' functions as directional cues, as males rely more heavily on directional cues than females.

If the results reported by Chai and Jacobs [39], represent a more general manifestation of the response patterns from men and women to proximal- and distal-space visual objects, then similar results should also be found with respect to other tasks. The purpose of the study by Chamizo, Artigas, Sansa and Banterla [41] was to determine whether sex differences in a virtual navigation task can be observed in the absence of directional cues. Specifically, four pinpoint landmarks (i.e., proximal cues) were used. If the aforementioned differences exist, then other factors in addition to directional cues may underlie the sex differences that often accompany spatial learning tasks. The aim of Experiment 1 was to study sex differences that occur when the participants use virtual navigation while learning with pinpoint landmarks: two relatively near and two relatively distant landmarks in relation to a hidden platform. To that end, there were four landmarks present at each training trial (i.e., A, B, C, and D in Figure 2), arranged symmetrically around the circumference of the pool, and two groups of participants (i.e., men and women). At the end of the training (24 trials in total), one test trial was administered in the presence of either one or two of the distant landmarks, without the platform. The amount of time that the students had spent in the platform quadrant was recorded. All participants improved their performance as the trials progressed, and spatial learning took place equally in men and in women. When the two landmarks located relatively distant from the platform during training were tested both men and women showed a preference for the platform quadrant, indicating that these landmarks were sufficient for determining the location of the platform. Thus, the landmarks relatively near the platform did not prevent learning about the landmarks relatively distant away from it. However, when only a single distant landmark was present, neither group showed a preference for the platform quadrant in the test. A relatively distant landmark could not unambiguously define the location of the platform. This pattern of results clearly indicates configural learning. Most importantly, Experiment 1 found a clear gender difference when the two distant landmarks were simultaneously present in the test. In this case, the men outperformed the women when searching for the platform.

Experiment 2 (Chamizo et al. [41]) replicated the previous results by showing that the men outperformed the women at the test trial when both of the distant landmarks were present. However, when the distant landmarks were presented individually instead of together, this difference disappeared, and the performance clearly declined to chance level. Experiment 2 also revealed that no sex differences existed when the landmarks near the platform were present. In the near conditions, the participants' performances in the platform quadrant were the best and always above the level of chance. Thus, proximity to the goal was the main determinant of landmark control for all the participants. This pattern of data favors elemental learning, a type of learning which is based on individual landmarks instead of multiple landmarks (i.e., configural learning).

Overall, the results of the study by Chamizo et al. [41] confirm, if only partially, the male advantage shown in previous studies on virtual navigation [42, 39, 43, 44, 45, 46]. Moreover, Chai and Jacobs's [39] study showed with pinpoint cues that the men outperform the women. This result was replicated only with the relatively distant landmarks, not the relatively near landmarks in which men and women did not differ. Of particular note, the two studies have used different procedures and measures. The experiments by Chamizo et al. [41] do show a clear male advantage when searching is based on relatively distant landmarks in the absence of directional cues, which clearly suggests that other factors, in addition to making use of directional cues, can underlie the sex differences in spatial learning processes.

Sex Differences in Spatial Cognition: One Biological Explanation

As Mackintosh suggests [2 □see also 47], there can be little doubt that males and females do differ in particular cognitive skills and that the precise nature of these differences is still an open question; for example, a test battery that emphasizes spatial and mathematical items will favor males, but one that emphasizes some aspects of language, perceptual speed, and memory will favor females. An important question to answer is can these differences be changed with experience? Recent research shows that this is the case [48].

Previous authors have claimed (Coluccia and Louse [3]) that sex differences tend to appear only when the task is difficult. In other words, spatial tasks high in cognitive demands are accompanied by sex differences, whereas spatial tasks low in cognitive demands are not. The results by Chamizo et al. [41] support this suggestion. The tests with the near landmarks would count as easy tasks, but the test with the two distant landmarks would be considered difficult, as the test with only one distant landmark is the most difficult overall. Both the human and the rat data are consistent with the hypothesis that a sex difference in spatial cognition arises only when there is a difference between the sexes in range size [4,2]. When males occupy a larger home range than females, they also show evidence of superior spatial ability. In most monogamous species, males and females share the same territory. That is not the case in polygynous or promiscuous species (polygynous males mate with more than one female in a single breeding season, and therefore have larger ranges). In ancient times, men hunted while women gathered [49]. Ancient hunting, like persistence hunting, implies exhausting the pray over a long distance and then killing it as the animal collapses. Later ways of hunting, using missile weapons, also implied hunters covering long distances. But both, humans and rodents, have the same consequence –a difference in range size, which is the more proximal cause of the difference in spatial cognition (although see [50] for a different account).

In rodents, the data that support the range size hypothesis tend to be consistent with the fertility and parental care hypothesis, which states that female reproductive success, is enhanced by reduced mobility during reproductive periods [for a review see 4].

IN CONCLUSION: IMPORTANT IMPLICATIONS

When scholars have made the effort to analyse the variable sex or gender from a qualitative point of view, sometimes important and unexpected results have been found. For example, Nardi, Newcombe, and Shipley [51] have shown that terrain slope can be used as a cue to find a goal. When that is the case, women rely less than men on slope cues, preferring to solve the task using other strategies, even if they are less effective. The causes of this sex difference are still unknown.

For many years in our western culture it has been assumed that men and women do not differ in cognitive skills or abilities. To question this assumption was considered 'politically incorrect'. But such an idea is an error that could have important practical consequences. For example, the perceptual strategies which are responsible for visuospatial disorientation in several mental illnesses could be different in the two genders. Consequently, an implication would be to consider alternative treatment strategies and behavioral therapies for men than for women when dealing with disorientation problems in old age and in several mental illnesses. In line with these arguments, it has been claimed (Beinhoff, Tumani, Brettschneider, Bittner, and Riepe [52]) that gender-specificity of neuropsychological performance needs to be accounted for in clinical diagnosis of Alzheimer's disease. According to Beinhoff et al. [52], gender is a factor explaining variance in the pattern of cognitive decline where, in relation to visuospatial memory, men seem to show an advantage. In conclusion, basic research is certainly needed to clarify all these challenging issues.

REFERENCES

[1] D. Kimura, *Sex and Cognition*. The MIT Press, Cambridge, MA (1999).

[2] N. J. Mackintosh, *IQ and Human Intelligence* (2nd ed.). Oxford University Press, Oxford (2011).

[3] E. Coluccia and G. Louse, Gender differences in spatial orientation: a review. *Journal of Environmental Psychology, 24*, pp.329-340 (2004).

[4] C. M. Jones, V. A. Braithwaite, and S. D. Healy, The evolution of sex differences in spatial ability. *Behav. Neurosci.*, 117, pp.403-411 (2003).

[5] K. Cheng, A purely geometric module in the rat's spatial representation. *Cognition*, 23, pp.149-178 (1986).

[6] C. R. Gallistel, *The organization of learning*. MIT Press, Cambridge, MA (1990).

[7] K. Cheng and N. S. Newcombe, Is there a geometric module for spatial orientation? Squaring theory and evidence. *Psychonomic Bulletin and Review, 12*, pp.1-23 (2005).

[8] J. M. Pearce, The 36th Sir Frederick Bartlett lecture: An associative analysis of spatial learning. *Quarterly Journal of Experimental Psychology, 62*, pp.1665-1684 (2009).

[9] K. Cheng, Whither geometry? Troubles of the geometric module. *TRENDS in Cognitive Sciences*, 12, pp.355-361 (2008).

[10] V.D. Chamizo, Acquisition of knowledge about spatial location: Assessing the generality of the mechanism of learning. *The Quarterly Journal of Experimental Psychology B, 56*, pp.107-119 (2003).

[11] N. Miller and S. Shettleworth, Learning about environmental geometry: an associative model. *Journal of Experimental Psychology: Animal Behavior Processes, 33*, pp.191-212 (2007).

[12] A. Hayward, A. McGregor, M. A. Good, and J. M. Pearce, Absence of overshadowing and blocking between landmarks and the geometric cues provided by the shape of a test arena. *The Quarterly Journal of Experimental Psychology B, 56*, pp.114-26 (2003).

[13] A. McGregor, M. R. Horne, G. R. Esber, and J. M. Pearce, Absence of overshadowing between a landmark and geometric cues in a distinctively shaped environment: a test of Miller and Shettleworth (2007). *Journal of Experimental Psychology: Animal Behavior Processes, 35*, pp.357-370 (2009).

[14] J.M. Pearce, J. Ward-Robinson, M. Good, C. Fussell, and A. Aydin, Influence of a beacon on spatial learning based on the shape of the test environment. *Journal of Experimental Psychology: Animal Behavior Processes, 27*, pp329-344 (2001).

[15] P. L. Wall, L. C. P. Botly, C. K. Black, and S. J. Shettleworth, The geometric module in the rat: Independence of shape and feature learning in a food finding task. *Learning and Behavior, 32*, pp.289-298 (2004).

[16] C. F. Doeller, C. and N. Burgess, Distinct error-correcting and incidental learning of location relative to landmarks and boundaries. *Proceedings of The National Academy of Sciences of the United States of America, 105*, pp.5909-5914 (2008).

[17] M. Graham, M. Good, A. McGregor, and J. M. Pearce, Spatial learning based on the shape of the environment is influenced by properties of the objects forming the shape. *Journal of Experimental Psychology: Animal Behavior Processes, 32*, pp.44-59 (2006).

[18] M. R. Horne and J. M. Pearce, Potentiation and overshadowing between landmarks and environmental geometric cues. *Learning and Behavior*, 39, pp.371-382 (2011).

[19] J. M. Pearce, M. Graham, M. Good, P. M. Jones, and A. McGregor, Potentiation, overshadowing, and blocking of spatial learning based on the shape of the environment. *Journal of Experimental Psychology: Animal Behavior Processes,* 32, pp.201-214 (2006).

[20] P. N. Wilson and T. Alexander, Blocking of spatial learning between enclosure geometry and a local landmark, *Journal of Experimental Psychology: Learning, Memory, and Cognition,* 34, pp.1369–1376 (2008).

[21] P. N. Wilson and T. Alexander, Enclosure shape influences cue competition effects and goal location learning, *Quarterly Journal of Experimental Psychology,* 63, pp.1552–1567 (2008).

[22] C. L. Williams, A. M. Barnett, and W. H. Meck, Organizational effects of early gonadal secretions on sexual differentiation in spatial memory. *Behavioral Neuroscience,* 104, pp.84-97 (1990).

[23] C. L. Williams and W. H. Meck, The organizational effects of gonadal steroids on sexually dimorphic spatial ability. *Psychoneuroendocrinology,* 16, pp.155-176 (1991).

[24] R. L. Roof and D. G. Stein, Gender differences in Morris water maze performance depend on task parameters. *Physiology and Behavior,* 68, pp.81-86 (1999).

[25] C. A. Rodríguez, A. A. Torres, N. J. Mackintosh, and V. D. Chamizo, Sex differences in preferential strategies to solve a navigation task. *Journal of Experimental Psychology: Animal Behavior Processes,* 36, pp.395–401 (2010).

[26] C. A. Rodríguez, V. D. Chamizo, and N. J. Mackintosh, Overshadowing and Blocking between Landmark Learning and Shape Learning: the Importance of Sex Differences. *Learning and Behavior,* 39, pp.324-335 (2011).

[27] I. P. Pavlov, *Conditioned reflexes.* Oxford University Press, Oxford (1927).

[28] N. J. Mackintosh, Overshadowing and stimulus intensity. *Animal Learning and Behaviour,* 4, pp.186-192 (1976).

[29] L. J. Kamin, Predictability, surprise, attention and conditioning. In B. A. Campbell and R. M. Church (Eds.), *Punishment and aversive behavior.* Appleton-Century-Crofts, New York, pp.279-296 (1969).

[30] R. G. M. Morris, P. Garrud, J. N. P. Rawlins, and J. O'Keefe, Place-navigation impaired in rats with hippocampal lesions. *Nature,* 297, pp.681-683 (1982).

[31] J. M. Pearce, A. D. L. Roberts, and M. A. Good, Hippocampal lesions disrupt navigation based on cognitive maps but not heading vectors. *Nature,* 396, pp.75-77 (1998).

[32] R. J. Sutherland, Q. Whishaw, and B. Kolb, A behavioral analysis of spatial localization following electrolytic, kamate- or colchicine-induced damage to the hippocampal formation in the rat. *Behavioral Brain Research,* 7, pp.133-153 (1983).

[33] C. S. Woolley, and B. S. McEwen, Roles of estradiol and progesterone in regulation of the hippocampal dendritic spine density during the estrus cycle in rat. *Journal of Comparative Neurology,* 336, pp.293-306 (1992).

[34] S. G. Warren, and J. M. Juraska, Spatial learning across the rat estrus cycle. *Behavioral Neuroscience,* 111, pp.255-266 (1997).

[35] B. Berry, R. McMahan, and M. Gallagher, Spatial learning and memory at defined points of the estrus cycle: effects on performance of a hippocampal-dependent task. *Behavioural Neuroscience,* 111, pp.267-274 (1997).

[36] S. D. Healy, S. R. Braham, and V. A. Braithwaite, Spatial working memory in rats: no differences between the sexes. *Proceedings of the Royal Society B,* 266, pp.2303-2308 (1999).

[37] C. A. Rodríguez, R. Aguilar, and V.D. Chamizo, Landmark learning in a navigation task is not affected by the female rats' estrus cycle. *Psicológica,* 32, pp.279-299 (2011).

[38] L. F. Jacobs and F. Schenk, Unpacking the cognitive map: The parallel map model of hippocampal function. *Psychological Review,* 110, pp.285–315 (2003).

[39] X. J. Chai and L. F. Jacobs, Sex differences in directional cue use in a virtual landscape. *Behavioral Neuroscience,* 123, pp.276–283 (2009).

[40] C. L. Barkley and K. I. Gabriel, Sex differences in cue perception in a visual scene: Investigation of cue type. *Behavioral Neuroscience,* 121, pp.291–300 (2007).

[41] V. D. Chamizo, A. A. Artigas, J. Sansa, and F. Banterla, Gender differences in landmark learning for virtual navigation: The role of distance to a goal. *Behavioural Processes,* 88, pp.20-26 (2011).

[42] R. S. Astur, M. L. Ortiz, and R. J. Sutherland, A characterization of performance by men and women in a virtual Morris water task: A large and reliable sex difference. *Behavioural Brain Research,* 93, pp.185–190 (1998).

[43] J. M. Jr Dabbs, E. L. Chang, R. A. Strong, and R. Milun, Spatial ability, navigation strategy, and geographic knowledge among men and women. *Evolution and Human Behavior,* 19, pp.89–98 (1998).

[44] L. A. M. Galea, and D. Kimura, Sex differences in route learning. *Personality and Individual Differences,* 14, pp.53-65 (1993).

[45] N. J. Sandstrom, J. Kaufman, and S. A. Huettel, Men and women use different distal cues in a virtual environment navigation task. *Cognitive Brain Research,* 6, pp.351–360 (1998).

[46] D. M. Saucier, S. M. Green, J. Leason, A. MacFadden, S. Bell, and L. J. Elias, Are sex differences in navigation caused by sexually dimorphic strategies or by differences in the ability to use the strategies? *Behavioral Neuroscience,* 116, pp.403–410 (2002).

[47] D. F. Halpern, *Sex differences in cognitive abilities* (3rd ed.). Lawrence Erlbaum, NJ (2000).

[48] Z. Estes and S. Felker, Confidence mediates the sex difference in mental rotation performance. *Archives of Sexual Behavior* in press.

[49] I. Silverman, J. Choi, and M. Peaters. The Hunter-Gatherer Theory of Sex Differences in Spatial Abilities: Data from 40 Countries. *Archives of Sexual Behavior,* 36, pp.261-268 (2007).

[50] D. Voyer, A. Postma, B. Brake, and J. Imperato-McGinley, Gender differences in object location memory: A meta-analysis. *Psychonomic Bulletin and Review,* 14, pp.23-38 (2007).

[51] D. Nardi, N. S. Newcombe, and T. F. Shipley, The world is not flat: can people reorient using slope?, *Journal of Experimental Psychology: Learning, Memory, and Cognition,* 37, pp.354-367 (2011).

[52] U. Beinhoff, H. Tumani, J. Brettschneider, D. Bittner, and M. W. Riepe, Gender-specificities in Alzheimer's disease and mild cognitive impairment. *Journal of Neurology,* 255, pp.117-122 (2008).

INDEX

D

Q

R

S

Y